The Lotus Notes Cram Sheet

This Cram Sheet contains the key facts about the IBM Certified Professional exams. Review this information last thing before entering the test room, paying special attention to those areas where you feel you need the most review. You can transfer any of the facts from your memory onto a blank piece of paper before beginning the exam.

Exam cram information has been broken down between the eight sections covering the three exams covered in this book, namely:

- 610—Notes/Domino 6 Application Development Foundation Skills
- 611—Notes/Domino 6 Application Development Intermediate Skills
- 612—Notes/Domino 6 Developing Web Applications

APPLICATION DESIGN

1. When customizing twisties, each image should be no wider than 6 pixels in order for your icons to be visible in a view. The font size of the column text determines how high your image should be. For a column with text that has a font size of 10, each image should be no higher than 12 pixels.

2. You can include HTML on a page, form, or subform in a number of ways. If you have existing HTML or you prefer to use HTML instead of the formatting tools Designer offers, you have the following options:

    - Convert a page, form, or subform to HTML and use the HTML editor to change the HTML.
    - Import HTML. Designer renders the imported HTML on the page, form, or subform already translated from HTML.
    - Paste HTML directly on a page, form, or subform. The HTML stays in HTML format.
    - Enter HTML directly on a page, form, or subform. The HTML stays in HTML format.

APPLICATION AUTOMATION

3. You can now set up basic security for an agent by using the Security tab of the new Agent Properties dialog box.

4. You can customize the Tools menu in Designer to include menu items that launch other applications or your own custom formulas.

5. Data Connection Resources use the Domino Enterprise Connector Services (DECS) to enable you to define a connection to an external data resource (non-Domino database).

DESIGN ELEMENTS

6. Embedded elements are objects and controls that can be embedded on a page, form, subform, or document. Elements that can be embedded include Views, Folders, Outlines, Navigators, and Date Pickers.

7. You can create and stack multiple layers beneath and above one another. Transparent layers reveal layers underneath; opaque layers conceal layers underneath. After you create a layer, you can change the position, HTML properties, and background color and image of the layer.

8. A JavaScript library is a place for storing and sharing common JavaScript programs and code. You can insert an existing JavaScript library into a page, form, or subform, either inline or into the JS Header.

9. To display a custom icon, create the icon as an image resource, then enter the name of the image resource as the default value for the column (for example, logo.bmp). An image resource can be a GIF, BMP, or JPEG graphic. The recommended size for a column icon is .2 inches wide and .18 inches high.

NEW FUNCTIONS

10. The following enhancements have been made to formula language programming:

    - Assignment statements can be nested

23. WebQueryOpen and WebQuerySave are the two form events that can use the @Command formula to trigger an agent from the Web. The two @Commands you can use are:

- @Command({ToolsRunMacro}) is launched last in a formula.
- @Command([RunAgent]) launches wherever it appears in a formula.

MANAGE AND MAINTAIN

24. DIIOP, a task related to Web browsing, enables Java applets/applications created with Notes Java classes to access Domino data.

25. *Global Web Setting* documents enable you to apply *Web Site Rules* documents to all the servers within a domain or a specific server.

26. Web Site Rules are applied to Web Site documents and appear as their response documents in the Internet Sites view.

27. Web Site Rule documents help maintain Web sites by providing a consistent navigation scheme and allowing relocation or reorganization without losing existing links.

28. Each Web Site Rule document has three constant fields: Description, Type of rule, and Incoming URL pattern. All other fields are based on the type of rule selected: Substitution, Redirection, Directory, and HTTP Response Header.

SECURITY

29. Notes uses what is called Validation and Authentication, which is two security procedures that interact with the users Notes ID.

30. Web users don't need or have a Notes ID. They use Basic Authentication which authenticates against the Name and Internet password fields in a Person document.

31. Field encryption is controlled through an Encryption Key that is created and stored in a Notes ID. Web users don't have a Notes ID, so aren't able to encrypt or decrypt a field.

32. Anonymous access doesn't validate, authenticate, or record database activity. You don't know who is accessing the system.

33. Maximum Internet access limits access to databases from Web clients.

PROGRAMMING

34. JavaScript is client-side processing and does not require a trip to the server, which improves performance.

35. Common JavaScript is JavaScript code that is applied to both clients in seven events—onFocus, onBlur, onChange, onLoad, onUnLoad, onSubmit, and onHelp.

36. HTML can render in Notes if the Render pass through HTML in Notes parameter is selected in the form or page properties. Otherwise it is static text.

37. Domino URL commands provide navigational elements by adding them as HTML on forms or buttons as:

```
http://Host/Database/
DominoObject?Action&Arguments
```

38. URL actions are—?OpenElement, ?OpenDatabase, ?OpenView, $defaultview?OpenView, $About?OpenAbout, $help?OpenHelp, $icon?OpenIcon, ?OpenFrameset, ?OpenAgent, ?OpenForm, $defaultform?OpenForm, ?OpenNavigator, $defaultNav?OpenNavigator, ?CreateDocument, ?OpenDocument, ?EditDocuemtn, ?SaveDocument, ?DeleteDocument, ?OpenImageResource, ?OpenFileResource, and $Preferences.nsf?OpenPreferences.

39. The following are some of the @Functions that work on the Web:

- @ClientType retrieves client information.
- @BrowserInfo retrieves information about the browser.
- @URLOpen retrieves Web site specified in the URL.
- @Success and @Failure are input validation formulas.
- @Command ([*parameter*]) expands or collapses categories in a view.

40. To change the default column and row settings HTML code can be added to the column header and the programmers pane. Treat view contents as HTML has to be checked on the View properties.

41. Java Applets are client-side programs and can be included in forms, documents, and pages. Designers can import an applet, link to an applet, or store the applet in the shared resource section of the database.

42. CGI variables are used to collect information about the user.

`EditProfileDocument`—Duplicates `EditProfile`

`ExitNotes`—Duplicates `FileExit`

`FolderDocuments`—Duplicates `Folder`

`NavNext`—Duplicates `NavigateNext`

`NavNextMain`—Duplicates `NavigateNextMain`

`NavNextSelected`—Duplicates `NavigateNextSelected`

`NavNextUnread`—Duplicates `NavigateNextUnread`

`NavPrev`—Duplicates `NavigatePrev`

`NavPrevMain`—Duplicates `NavigatePrevMain`

`NavPrevSelected`—Duplicates `NavigatePrevSelected`

`NavPrevUnread`—Duplicates `NavigatePrevUnread`

`RefreshWindow`—Duplicates `ReloadWindow`

`RunAgent`—Duplicates `ToolsRunMacro`

`RunScheduledAgents`—Duplicates `ToolsRunBackground Macros`

`SwitchForm`—Duplicates `ViewSwitchForm`

`SwitchView`—Duplicates `ViewChange`

`ComposeWithReference`—Creates a response document containing a reference to the main document.

`EditQuoteSelection`—Makes selected text look like an Internet-style reply.

`EditRestoreDocument`—Restores a soft-deleted document to the view or folder from which it was deleted.

`RefreshFrame`—Refreshes a specified frame in a frameset.

NEW AND ENHANCED URL COMMANDS

14. URL commands that have been added or modified in Lotus Notes and Domino 6:

    `OpenImageResources`—Opens a graphic resource in an application.

    `OpenFileResources`—Opens a file resource in an application

    `ReadViewEntries`—Accesses view data in XML form without appearance attributes such as fonts, list separators, date formats, HTML settings, view templates, and frame redirections.

WEB DESIGN ELEMENTS

15. GIF, BMP, and JPG type graphics can be used to create images on the Web.

16. Java applets are self-contained programs that don't require a roundtrip back to the server from the Web. Applet file types are .class, .java, .jar, .zip, .cab, .jpg, .jpeg, .gif, and .au.

17. Layers give the flexibility of positioning, placement and layering on forms, subforms, or pages.

18. Three libraries; Java, JavaScript, and LotusScript where code can be maintained and shared.

19. Two HTML events are available to Forms and Pages. HTML Head Content passes information to the <Head> tag. HTML Body Attributes passes information to the <Body> tag.

20. Formulas and LotusScript that can be used to manipulate profile documents:

    • @GetProfileField—Retrieves value from profile document.

    • @SetProfileField—Sets value in a profile document.

    • @Command([EditProfile])—Opens a profile document or if one doesn't exist, creates a new profile document.

    • @Command([EditProfileDocument])—Same as above only this will execute where it is coded.

    • GetProfileDocument method of NotesDatabase—Opens a profile document or if one doesn't exist, creates a new profile document.

    • GetItemValue method of the NotesDocument class—Retrieves value from profile document.

21. $ fieldnames used by Domino with predefined functionality:

    $PublicAccess—Designates a form as available to public access.

    $$Return—Used to create custom message after a Web user submits a document.

    $$HTMLHead—Passes information to the <html> tag.

    $$ViewTemplateDefault—Creates a template that all views will use. View templates can standardize the format and layout of views when they are rendered on the Web.

    HTML—Any HTML code in this field is passed directly to the browser and all other fields are ignored.

22. Events that work on both the Notes and Web clients:

    • JSHeader—Used on forms, pages and subforms. JavaScript can be applied to both clients.

    • onFocus, onBlur, and onChange—Are used on fields. LotusScript can be used on the Notes client and JavaScript, Common JavaScript can be used on both clients.

    • onLoad, onUnload, onSubmit, and onHelp—Are used on forms and pages. Formulas and LotusScript can be used on the Notes client and JavaScript, and Common JavaScript can be used on both clients.

    • onClick—Used on buttons and actions. Formulas, Simple actions and LotusScript can be used on the Notes client and JavaScript, and Common JavaScript can be used on both clients.

- Braces ({}) can be used to delimit text constants, enabling you to specify a text constant by enclosing characters, including spaces, numbers, and special characters, in quotation marks ("") or braces.
- Quotation marks or braces delimit the text of the remark. For example: REM {comments};
- Lists can be subscripted so the list subscript operator ([]) returns one element of a list.
- Temporary variables can be reassigned.

11. New formula language functions that are likely to be on the exams:

    @CheckFormulaSyntax—Checks commented-out formula code for errors.

    @Compare—Compares two lists pair-wise.

    @Count—Returns the number of elements in a list. Unlike @Elements, which returns a zero if the value it is evaluating is a null string or not a list, @Count returns a 1, which can prevent errors from being generated in complex formulas.

    @DocLock—Locks, unlocks, or returns the locked status of the current document.

    @DoWhile—Executes one or more statements iteratively while a condition remains true. Checks the condition after executing the statements.

    @Eval—Compiles and runs each element in a text expression as a formula at run-time.

    @FileDir—Returns the directory portion of a pathname.

    @For—Executes one or more statements iteratively while a condition remains true. Checks the condition after executing the statements.

    @GetField—Returns the value of a specified field. @GetField, @ThisName, and @ThisValue provide a means to write portable code. Instead of specifying field names in formulas, use these @Functions to write code that can be copied as is from one formula to another.

    @GetHTTPHeader—Returns the value of an HTTP request-header field.

    @HashPassword—Encodes a string.

    @IfError—Returns a null string ("") or the value of an alternative statement if a statement returns an error.

    @IsNull—Tests for a null value.

    @ReplicaID—Returns the replica ID of the current database.

    @ServerAccess—Tests the access level that a specified user has to a server.

    @SetHTTPHeader—Sets the value of an HTTP response-header field.

    @Sort—Sorts a list.

    @StatusBar—Writes a message or messages to the status bar.

    @ThisName—Returns the name of the current field.

    @ThisValue—Returns the value of the current field.

    @ToNumber—Converts a value with a data type of text or number to a number value.

    @ToTime—Converts a value with a data type of text or time to a date-time value.

    @URLDecode—Decodes a URL string into regular text.

    @URLEncode—Encodes a string in a URL-safe format.

    @UrlQueryString—Returns the current URL command and parameters, or the value of one of the parameters.

    @VerifyPassword—Compares two passwords, enabling you to determine whether a password has a hash or standard password format.

    @WebDbName—Returns the database name in URL format. You no longer have to parse and replace substrings in @DbName.

    @While—Executes one or more statements iteratively while a condition remains true. Checks the condition before executing the statements.

ENHANCED FUNCTIONS

12. Formula language functions that have been modified and are likely to be on the exams:

    @DialogBox—Has a new keyword [OkCancelAtBottom].

    @DbColumn—(Domino data source or ODBC data source) Allows "ReCache" in the first parameter to refresh the cache where "" (cache) is specified in a previous lookup to the same data source.

    @DbCommand—(Domino data source or ODBC data source) Enables you to list folders and display next or previous groups of documents in a view. This only works in Web applications.

    @DbLookup—(Domino data source) Allows the keywords [FailSilent], [PartialMatch], and [ReturnDocumentUniqueID] as a new parameter.

    @SetDocField—Can now be used to set the value of a field in the current document.

    @Text—Converts rich text.

    @UserAccess—Accepts keyword parameters that can return the user's database access level or test for specific user privileges for a database.

NEW @COMMANDS

13. New @Commands that are likely to be on the exams:

    Clear—Duplicates EditClear

    CloseWindow—Duplicates FileCloseWindow

    DatabaseDelete—Duplicates FileDatabaseDelete

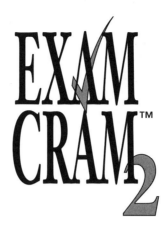

Lotus Notes® and Domino® 6 Application Development

Tim Bankes

David Hatter

CERTIFICATION

Lotus Notes® and Domino® 6 Application Development Exam Cram 2 (Exams 610, 611, 612)

International Standard Book Number: 0-7897-2917-2

Library of Congress Catalog Card Number: 2003109247

Printed in the United States of America

First Printing: December 2003

06   05   04   03   4   3   2   1

Trademarks

All terms mentioned in this book that are known to be trademarks or service marks have been appropriately capitalized. Que Publishing cannot attest to the accuracy of this information. Use of a term in this book should not be regarded as affecting the validity of any trademark or service mark.

Warning and Disclaimer

Every effort has been made to make this book as complete and as accurate as possible, but no warranty or fitness is implied. The information provided is on an "as is" basis. The authors and the publisher shall have neither liability nor responsibility to any person or entity with respect to any loss or damages arising from the information contained in this book or from the use of the CD or programs accompanying it.

Bulk Sales

Que Publishing offers excellent discounts on this book when ordered in quantity for bulk purchases or special sales. For more information, please contact

U.S. Corporate and Government Sales

1-800-382-3419

corpsales@pearsontechgroup.com

For sales outside of the U.S., please contact

International Sales

1-317-428-3341

international@pearsontechgroup.com

Publisher
Paul Boger

Executive Editor
Jeff Riley

Acquisitions Editor
Carol Ackerman

Development Editor
Lorna Gentry

Managing Editor
Charlotte Clapp

Project Editor
Tricia Liebig

Production Editor
Margo Catts

Indexer
Larry Sweazy

Proofreader
Leslie Joseph

Technical Editors
Deborah Brown
Deborah Miller
Amrit Singh

Team Coordinator
Pamalee Nelson

Multimedia Developer
Dan Scherf

Interior Designer
Gary Adair

Cover Designer
Anne Jones

Page Layout
Bronkella Publishing

CERTIFICATION

Que Certification • 800 East 96th Street • Indianapolis, Indiana 46240

A Note from Series Editor Ed Tittel

You know better than to trust your certification preparation to just anybody. That's why you, and more than two million others, have purchased an Exam Cram book. As Series Editor for the new and improved Exam Cram 2 series, I have worked with the staff at Que Certification to ensure you won't be disappointed. That's why we've taken the world's best-selling certification product—a finalist for "Best Study Guide" in a CertCities reader poll in 2002—and made it even better.

Best Study Guides

As a "Favorite Study Guide Author" finalist in a 2002 poll of CertCities readers, I know the value of good books. You'll be impressed with Que Certification's stringent review process, which ensures the books are high-quality, relevant, and technically accurate. Rest assured that at least a dozen industry experts—including the panel of certification experts at CramSession—have reviewed this material, helping us deliver an excellent solution to your exam preparation needs.

We've also added a preview edition of PrepLogic's powerful, full-featured test engine, which is trusted by certification students throughout the world.

As a 20-year-plus veteran of the computing industry and the original creator and editor of the Exam Cram series, I've brought my IT experience to bear on these books. During my tenure at Novell from 1989 to 1994, I worked with and around its excellent education and certification department. This experience helped push my writing and teaching activities heavily in the certification direction. Since then, I've worked on more than 70 certification-related books, and I write about certification topics for numerous Web sites and for *Certification* magazine.

In 1996, while studying for various MCP exams, I became frustrated with the huge, unwieldy study guides that were the only preparation tools available. As an experienced IT professional and former instructor, I wanted "nothing but the facts" necessary to prepare for the exams. From this impetus, Exam Cram emerged in 1997. It quickly became the best-selling computer book series since "...*For Dummies*," and the best-selling certification book series ever. By maintaining an intense focus on subject matter, tracking errata and updates quickly, and following the certification market closely, Exam Cram was able to establish the dominant position in cert prep books.

You will not be disappointed in your decision to purchase this book. If you are, please contact me at etittel@jump.net. All suggestions, ideas, input, or constructive criticism are welcome!

Ed Tittel

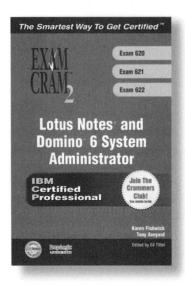

From Tim Bankes:

This book is dedicated to my family. This book, as with many of my successes in life, are a result of my parents and all they have done for me throughout my life. I can never thank them enough. To my sisters for their endless advice, friendship, and love. To my nephew and nieces for making family events even more special than they already were.

It is difficult, if not impossible, to give enough credit to Carol Ackerman, Tricia Liebig, and Lorna Gentry (as well as the rest of the Que team) for their relentless efforts and encouragement throughout the writing of this book. I am sure that Dave and I haven't made their jobs any easier but they managed to pull us through. Carol, thank you in sempiternity.

I would also like to thank my co-workers at Libertas Technologies, LLC. I am sure that countless late nights working on this book couldn't have helped my disposition at the office. It has been an honor and privilege to work with such a talented and wonderful group of professionals and friends. To my co-author, Dave Hatter. A good partner and a great friend. What do you think…shall we write one more?

Finally, I would like to thank God—not only for giving me the patience, fortitude, and ability to complete this book, but for everything positive in my life, today and tomorrow.

From Dave Hatter:

This book is dedicated first and foremost to the world's greatest wife and mother, Leslee Hatter, without whose indefatigable patience and support I would never have finished it. I love you very much! Also to the world's greatest children: Samuel, Wyatt, and Emma Rose Hatter. Their love is the best thing that ever happened to me and without a doubt, they are proof that children are a gift from God and should be treasured as such. I love you guys more than words can say and I appreciate your patience with me while I was putting in long hours on this book!

I want to thank several other people who have been instrumental in my life: my father, Jack Hatter, who instilled in me a strong work ethic and took care of me for nine long years as a widower; my grandfather, George "Newt" Young, a Marine Corps combat veteran of WWII, who was my hero and is sorely missed; my "second mom," Rose Welzel, who was always there for me when I needed something and will be missed but never forgotten. And to the many other family members and friends too numerous to mention: I love you all very much and owe all that I am to you!

The team at QUE, namely Carol Ackerman, Tricia Liebig, and Lorna Gentry, deserve tremendous thanks for putting up with us during this long process. It was their hard work and perseverance that brought this book to fruition. Carol especially deserves our thanks as she had the unfortunate task of trying to keep us on track.

And I would be remiss not to thank my co-author Tim Bankes. Tim is a long-time friend and business partner and this book would not exist without his knowledge, insight, and effort. Looks like no more 3 a.m. phone calls for a while! To our military personnel, police officers and fire fighters, I appreciate all you do every day to keep us safe and free. May God bless you, your families, and our great country, the United States!

Finally, I thank God for giving me the knowledge, ability, and stamina to do this book. When you consider that I'm really just a country boy from Kentucky, it is proof that with God, all things are possible!

ࢠ

About the Authors

Tim Bankes is CEO of Libertas Technologies, LLC, a technology solutions provider focused on Web-based software development and consulting. Tim assists companies in integrating Internet technologies into their core business by implementing real business strategies for Internet, intranet, and extranet e-business and e-commerce solutions. Tim has nearly 10 years of programming and management experience with various technologies, including Lotus Notes/Domino, IBM Websphere, Microsoft IIS/ASP, and others. Tim has been working with Lotus Notes/Domino for nearly nine years and is a Principal Certified Lotus Professional: Application Developer (R4, R5) and System Administrator (R4).

Tim has authored books for the Pearson (formerly Macmillan Computer Publishing) imprints QUE and New Riders, including *Lotus Notes/Domino R5 Essential Reference* (New Riders Publishing), *CLP Fast Track: Lotus Notes/Domino 5 Application Development* (New Riders Publishing) and has contributed as a co-author to *Domino R5 System Administration* (New Riders Publishing) and *Special Edition Using Lotus Notes and Domino 4.6* (Que Publishing). Tim is currently completing another new title with Dave Hatter, namely *Domino R6 Programmer's Reference*. In addition, Tim has been a featured speaker for searchDomino.com, covering topics such as Lotus Notes/Domino application development and Lotus Notes/Domino application development certifications. Tim was also a featured speaker at The View Admin2003 conference held in Las Vegas, April 30–May 2, 2003.

Prior to joining Libertas, Tim was an independent consultant. Using extensive, real-world experience, Tim assisted organizations in building "best-of-breed" Internet, intranet, and extranet solutions. Remaining technically agnostic, Tim worked with companies to make them more efficient, effective, and accountable to deliver a high return-on-investment by focusing on business solutions using the most appropriate and cost-effective technologies.

Prior to working independently, Tim was the Director of Application Development for Eviciti Corp., a professional services partner that worked with companies to integrate the Internet into their core business. Within one year, Tim grew the Application Development team from 12 people to approximately 25 people. His responsibilities included managing practice leaders, application developers, the IT technology team, and coordinating resources among various offices. In this role, Tim was responsible for building quality custom applications, providing direction, as well as establishing policies and processes to ensure the successful planning, development, execution, and deployment of solutions. Prior to Eviciti, Tim was a partner and Principal Information Systems Consultant with Definiti, Inc., where he specialized in the design, development, and deployment of comprehensive, enterprise groupware/workflow solutions.

He holds a B.B.A. in Information Systems, a B.B.A. in Management, as well as a certificate in International Business from the University of Cincinnati.

Dave Hatter is president of Libertas Technologies, LLC, a technology solutions provider focused on Web-based software development and consulting. Dave has nearly 11 years of programming experience with a number of tools and environments including IBM Websphere and Microsoft IIS/ASP, and has been working with Lotus Notes/Domino for nearly 9 years. He has the following industry certifications: Principal Certified Lotus Professional: Application Developer (R4, R5, 6) and System Administrator (R4), Microsoft Certified Professional (Windows NT), CompTIA i-Net+, Network+, e-Biz+ and Master CIW Designer. Additionally, Dave has a B.S in Information Systems from Northern Kentucky University.

Dave is a graduate of Leadership Kentucky (2000) and Leadership Northern Kentucky (2000). He was named the NKU Young Alumnus in 1997 and U.S. senator Jim Bunning's Republican Man of the Year in 1998. His former company, Definiti, was named a Beacon Award Finalist, 2000, for "Best e-Business Solution—Supplier Relationship Management" for the KAM application that he designed, developed, and managed for the Cognis Corporation (formerly Henkel).

Dave has authored/co-authored 11 books for the Pearson (formerly Macmillan Computer Publishing) imprints Que, Sams, and New Riders, including *Lotus Notes and Domino R6 Application Development Training Guide* (forthcoming), *Lotus Notes and Domino R6 Development Unleashed, Fast Track: CLP Application Development, Domino System Administration, Lotus Notes and Domino Essential Reference, Windows NT Server Security Server Handbook, Lotus Notes and Domino Server 4.6 Unleashed, Special Edition Using Lotus Notes and Domino 4.6, Special Edition Using Lotus Notes and Domino 4.5, Using Lotus Notes 4.5,* and *Special Edition Using Lotus Notes 4.0*. Additionally, he has served as the technical editor for five Pearson titles: *Domino System Administration, Teach Yourself Lotus Notes in 14 Days, Lotus Notes and Domino 4.5 Developer's Guide, Lotus Notes and Domino Server 4.6 Unleashed,* and *Teach Yourself Lotus Notes 4.6 in 24 Hours.*

Dave feels strongly about community service and stays active in the local community in a number of ways. He serves as councilmember and Webmaster for the City of Fort Wright, Kentucky; KY Geographic Information Advisory Council (state board), Water Cooler Talk Chair (2001-2002 and 2002-2003), and New Economy Transition Team (N.E.T.T): e-Government Chair (2001-2002 and 2002-2003) for the Northern Kentucky Chamber of Commerce; member of the NKU Alumni Council, Technology Instructor in the NKU Community Education program; Webmaster and member of the Kenton County Republican Party Executive Committee; Cub Scout Den Leader, Pack 831, Fort Wright, Kentucky; and Lector at Saint Agnes Church.

Dave writes a technology column for Better Living Magazine and can be seen as a regular monthly guest on WXIX's (Channel 19, serving the Greater Cincinnati area) *19 in the Morning* and on Insight Communication's (Channel 6, serving Northern Kentucky) *Northern Kentucky Magazine*. For scheduling information, visit www.libertastechnologies.com. Dave can be reached at dhatter@libertastechnologies.com or 859-426-1046.

About the Contributing Author

Deborah Brown is a Certified Instructor at a Lotus Authorized Education Center in Southfield, Michigan. Deborah has worked in the computer industry for more than 15 years developing and programming applications. She has worked with numerous technologies such as COBOL, dBase, Microsoft technologies, DB2, and for the last 7 years as a Lotus Notes/Domino instructor. Deborah has obtained the following certifications: Principal CLP (Certified Lotus Professional) and CLI (Certified Lotus Instructor); Application Development and System Administration R4, R5, and ND6; IBM Certified Application Developer and System Administrator – Lotus Collaborative Solutions certificates; and she is an IBM Certified Specialist – DB2.

Deborah has authored and co-authored Lotus Certified courseware. She has also worked with AdvancedCLP as a beta tester and technical editor for their Lotus Notes/Domino practice tests. In addition, Deborah has won the Lotus Certified Instructor award twice, which is presented yearly during CLI Day at Lotussphere.

Prior to becoming a CLI, Deborah worked at Ameritech Telephone Company. She was originally a mainframe analyst working on the billing systems and yellow pages. Deborah spent the rest of her career at Ameritech in the Education department. She started as a trainer of PC software-Word, Excel, 1-2-3, Access, and other desktop applications. She won an Excellence award for creating and implementing the Fast-Track training program that consisted of combining multiple applications into one training course. Deborah designed and wrote the courseware, and setup a portable classroom that was used to deliver the training throughout the region.

Deborah is also very active in her community on the local and state level. She has worked on numerous campaigns for City Council and State Representatives. Deborah is always ready to lend a hand for environmental clean-up projects and working with various community activities.

About the Technical Reviewers

Deborah Miller began as a developer in Lotus Notes 3 and has been working with Notes for over seven years, creating and maintaining Notes and Domino applications simple to complex for corporations and government agencies, with a client base varying from the departmental to the international user.

Ms. Miller has degrees in Computer Information Systems and Literary Criticism, and is an IBM Certified Application Developer - Lotus Notes and Domino 6.

Amrit Pal Singh is working as a systems engineer with Polaris Software Lab Limited, a CMMI Level 5 company. He has a bachelor of engineering (Honors), Computer Sciences, from a top-notch college of India. His core area of expertise includes Web-based Notes development and Domino.Doc. He has worked on many Lotus projects for clients such as General Electric, Gillette, and Snecma Moteurs.

Contents at a Glance

Table of Contents

Acknowledgments

Tim and Dave would like to thank all of the team members at Libertas Technologies (Carl Allison in particular) for having the patience to work with us while we were writing this book and for sharing our vision for building a client-focused company we can all be proud to work at (who is John Galt?).

Tim and Dave would also like to thank Jerry Harden and the fine folks at Riverwatch Group, Inc. (www.riverwatch.com) for application hosting and support. Riverwatch is a full service Notes/Domino ASP. Riverwatch was one of the first ISP/ASP companies to recognize the need for fully managed Notes and Domino services and has been providing world-class Notes/Domino hosting since 1997. If you need managed Notes/Domino hosting, we heartily recommend Riverwatch.

Dave Hatter would like to thank the greatest songwriter of our time, Ronnie Van Zant, and his band, Lynyrd Skynyrd, for helping him get through many a long night working on this book. Fly on Free Bird!

Tim Bankes would also like to thank Lynyrd Skynyrd for keeping Dave occupied while he is writing. As long as he is listening to music, he is not talking. And as long as he is not talking, then I am getting my work done.

We Want to Hear from You!

As the reader of this book, *you* are our most important critic and commentator. We value your opinion and want to know what we're doing right, what we could do better, what areas you'd like to see us publish in, and any other words of wisdom you're willing to pass our way.

As executive editor for Que Publishing, I welcome your comments. You can email or write me directly to let me know what you did or didn't like about this book—as well as what we can do to make our books better.

Please note that I cannot help you with technical problems related to the topic of this book. We do have a User Services group, however, where I will forward specific technical questions related to the book.

When you write, please be sure to include this book's title and author as well as your name, email address, and phone number. I will carefully review your comments and share them with the author and editors who worked on the book.

Email: feedback@quepublishing.com

Mail: Jeff Riley
Executive Editor
Que Publishing
800 East 96th Street
Indianapolis, IN 46240 USA

For more information about this book or another Que title, visit our Web site at www.examcram2.com. Type the ISBN (excluding hyphens) or the title of a book in the Search field to find the page you're looking for.

Introduction

The *Lotus Notes/Domino 6 Application Development Exam Cram 2* is specifically designed to help you understand, take, and pass the three exams required to obtain a certification as an IBM Certified Application Developer—Lotus Notes and Domino 6. This book serves as a concise and focused study aid for people preparing for the three exams required to achieve this designation, rather than as a compendium of knowledge about Lotus Notes/Domino. The series reinforces and clarifies information with which the student should already be familiar, and is designed to help the student review and test on information that is likely to be on the exams. Although the series attempts to be a comprehensive testing resource, it is not designed to be a single source for student preparation. Instead, it works hand-in-hand with real-world experience, hands-on practice, and other study guides.

Notes/Domino 6 Certification Path for New and Upgrading Professionals

This book is designed to help you make the most of your study time by presenting concise summaries of information that you need to understand to succeed on the exams.

The exams required for certification as an IBM Certified Application Developer Lotus Notes and Domino 6 are as follows:

➤ *610*—Notes/Domino 6 Application Development Foundation Skills

➤ *611*—Notes/Domino 6 Application Development Intermediate Skills

➤ *612*—Notes/Domino 6 Developing Web Applications

Exam 610 covers Notes/Domino 6 Application Development Foundation Skills. This exam is covered in the following chapters:

➤ Chapter 2—Exam 610—Database Management

➤ Chapter 3—Exam 610—Application Architecture

➤ Chapter 4—Exam 610—Design Elements

➤ Chapter 5—Exam 610—Security

➤ Chapter 6—Exam 610—Programming

The following statistics describe Exam 610:

Passing Score	75%
Minutes Allowed	60
Total Exam Questions	45 (40 scored, 5 unscored)
Single Answer Questions	45
Multiple Answer Questions	0
Choices of A-D (4 options)	45
Choices of A-E (5 options)	0
Scenario-Based Questions	Yes
Questions Requiring "Hands On" Development	No

Exam 611 covers Notes/Domino 6 Application Development Intermediate Skills. This exam is covered in the following chapters:

➤ Chapter 7—Exam 611—Database Management

➤ Chapter 8—Exam 611—Application Architecture

➤ Chapter 9—Exam 611—Design Elements

➤ Chapter 10—Exam 611—Security

➤Chapter 11—Exam 611—Workflow

➤ Chapter 12—Exam 611—Programming

The following statistics describe Exam 611:

Passing Score	75%
Minutes Allowed	60
Total Exam Questions	45 (40 scored, 5 unscored)
Single Answer Questions	45
Multiple Answer Questions	0
Choices of A-D (4 options)	45
Choices of A-E (5 options)	0
Scenario-Based Questions	Yes
Questions Requiring "Hands On" Development	No

Exam 612 covers Notes/Domino 6 Developing Web Applications. This exam is covered in the following chapters:

➤ Chapter 13—Exam 612—Application Architecture

➤ Chapter 14—Exam 612—Design Elements

➤ Chapter 15—Exam 612—Manage and Maintain

➤Chapter 16—Exam 612—Programming

➤ Chapter 17—Exam 612—Security

The following statistics describe Exam 612:

Passing Score	75%
Minutes Allowed	60
Total Exam Questions	45 (40 scored, 5 unscored)
Single Answer Questions	45
Multiple Answer Questions	0
Choices of A-D (4 options)	45
Choices of A-E (5 options)	0
Scenario-Based Questions	Yes
Questions Requiring "Hands On" Development	No

Taking a Certification Exam

To schedule and take any of the exams outlined within this book, you must register with an approved testing vendor. The available vendors are:

➤ *CATGlobal*—Offers online registration at `http://www.catglobal.com/CATGlobal8/`

➤ *IBM Learning Centers*—Offers online registration at `www.lotus.com/certification`

➤ *Pearson VUE (using IBM Learning Centers)*—Offers online registration at `http://www.pearsonvue.com/ibm/`

➤ *Prometric Learning Centers*—Offers online registration at `http://www.2test.com`

Arriving at the Exam Site

Be sure to arrive at the exam site 15 minutes early. No matter what your scheduled time to take the exam may be, the clock does not begin until you initiate the start of the exam. You need a photo ID to present prior to entering the exam room. You are not permitted to bring anything into the exam room, although scratch paper and a pencil are provided.

Be sure to review the Cram Sheet prior to entering the exam room as well. That will reinforce key topics that you are likely to see on the exam. The Cram Sheet contains distilled, key facts about the IBM Certified Application Developer—Lotus Notes and Domino 6 exams. Review this information last thing before entering the test room, paying special attention to those areas where you feel you need the most review.

In the Exam Room

Most likely, there will be other terminals in the same room as you and you may have other test takers testing simultaneously (most likely another certification). Try to ignore their presence and focus on your exam. When entering the room, you are likely to have a choice of which terminal to use. Try to give yourself as much room as possible from other test takers. If you are fortunate enough to take the exam when no one else is in the room, you should take the opportunity to speak out loud when reading the questions. You may find it easier to concentrate and understand the questions if you recite the questions as you read them.

Most importantly, you need to relax, stay calm, and simply answer the questions as best you can. You will have plenty of time to complete the exam, so there is no reason to become anxious about how much time remains. If you don't know the answer to a question, reread the question. If the question is still unclear, simply mark the question and return to it later. The easiest and most difficult questions are mixed randomly throughout the exam. Often, reading later questions may help you answer a previous question. Regardless, you will want to use whatever time you can to complete the entire exam. Missing one or two of the more difficult questions is common and won't cause you to fail the exam.

After you have completed the exam, your score is computed immediately and displayed on the screen. One copy is printed automatically and will be waiting for you outside the exam room. You can have multiple copies printed (and stamped for authenticity) upon request.

If you do happen to fail (or stated in a more politically correct way, your score does not reach the minimum required score), there is no required grace period before you can take the test again. As soon as you can schedule the next exam, you can try again (as early as the next day!). Of course, taking the exams is expensive and takes time. Using this book will help ensure that you pass the tests the first time. Regardless of whether you pass or fail, you can schedule and take the exams in any order. Ideally, because the exams are structured to build upon the previous exams, it may prove to be beneficial to take the exams in the order that was intended.

How to Prepare for an Exam

Begin by studying the material that relates to the test for which you are preparing. It also helps tremendously for you to get as much hands-on experience with the concepts as possible. When you feel that you have grasped the concepts, take the practice tests in this book. After you have mastered this material, you should schedule the exam you have been preparing for and use the book as a final review to ensure that you have retained the information.

Nothing is more useful than hands-on experience. You should have already been working with the Notes Designer Client for some time prior to picking up this book. As you work through the sections of this book, try the commands and follow along with the screen shots included in this book. That will help you better understand the topics being discussed and reinforce the material as you review it.

Classroom training and computer training are extremely helpful in preparing for these exams. Classroom training can be expensive, but if you can participate, it is certainly worth the time and expense. Nevertheless, you can easily pass the exams outlined in this book without taking classroom training or computer training.

Naturally, you can find a wealth of information about the topics tested on these exams on the Internet and in other publications. Many of the available resources are located at the end of each chapter in the "Need to Know More?" section.

About This Book

Each Exam Cram chapter follows the same basic outline and structure. Each section is created with the focus on getting you relevant exam information in a clear, concise manner. Each chapter contains the following sections and elements:

➤ Terms You'll Need to Understand

This is a list of important terms the reader needs to look out for and understand after completing each chapter.

➤ Concepts and Techniques You'll Need to Answer

Concepts and/or actions you need to master by the end of the chapter.

➤ Specific topical concepts

Details on actual competencies required to pass each CLP exam.

➤ Notes

A Note is an aside piece of information that is related to the regular content flow.

➤ Exam Alerts

The Exam Alert is an important element for a certification title.

➤ Tips

The Tip element is a shortcut or more efficient way to accomplish a task.

➤ Exam Prep Questions

A series of mock test questions with an explanation of the correct answers.

➤ Need to Know More?

Pointers to other resources, Web sites, and other printed material that can further reinforce topics covered in each title.

How This Book Helps You

This book is written by experienced IBM Certified Application Developer—Lotus Notes and Domino 6 application developers and is tightly coupled with the Lotus exam objectives for Exams 610, 611, and 612 so that you can make the most of your study time and increase your likelihood of passing the exams the first time.

This book is specifically intended to help students prepare for Lotus's Application Development track, comprising Exam 610: Notes/Domino 6 Application Development Foundation Skills, Exam 611: Notes/Domino 6 Application Development Intermediate Skills, and Exam 612: Notes/Domino 6 Developing Web Applications. Upon the successful completion of Exam 610: Notes/Domino 6 Application Development Foundation Skills, you will receive the IBM Certified Associate Developer—Lotus Notes and Domino 6 designation. Successful completion of all three exams earns you the IBM Certified Application Developer—Lotus Notes and Domino 6 designation. To earn the much sought-after IBM Certified Advanced Application Developer—Lotus Notes and Domino 6 designation, you may then take one elective exam from the following list: Exam 273: LotusScript in Notes for Advanced Developers, Exam 513: Using JavaScript in Domino Applications, and Exam 516: Using Java in Domino Applications. For more information on the IBM Certified Professional for Lotus Software program, please visit `http://www.lotus.com/certification`.

Self-Assessment

You should be able to quickly assess your readiness for the exam by taking the practice exams available in this book or a practice exam provided by a third-party provider. (Links to these companies are provided later in this chapter.) At the end of each chapter are some sample questions that will help you rate yourself on your knowledge of the subject matter presented in the prior chapter. However, only a few questions are presented at the end of each chapter and they do not cover the breadth or depth of material that you will be required to know to pass the exams. Therefore, the sample exams are provided on CD to give you a more accurate assessment of your knowledge and likelihood of passing the exams. Nevertheless, these are only *practice exams*, and although you may see *similar* questions on the exams, they will be markedly different. Consequently, the questions provided should be used as guides to delineate areas where you need to focus more of your study time. For example, if you have trouble answering a few of the questions that cover new functions and commands available with Lotus Notes/Domino 6, be sure to study *all* the new functions and commands, not just the functions or commands that deal with the questions you had trouble with. By focusing on areas where you are the weakest, you can make the best use of your time and better position yourself to pass the exam(s) the first time, with flying colors!

If you are an experienced developer and have been working with Lotus Notes and Domino for several months or years, you probably have a good grasp of the basic and more challenging aspects of Lotus Notes and Domino (for example, the security model or replication). Therefore, you can focus more of your time on the new capabilities made available with the latest release. You may find that many of the questions appear very simple (because they cover more basic material than you have been working with for some time), whereas others seem more difficult (because they cover new material or material that you seldom use). Studying the material in this book and taking the practice exams will help you understand which areas are troublesome and, more importantly, help you learn what you need to learn to pass the certification exams and prove your expertise!

Notes/Domino 6 Certification in the Real World

According to statistics posted on Lotus's Web site, the IBM Certified Application Developer—Lotus Notes and Domino 6 (previously titled the CLP) certification has grown to over 75,000 certified global professionals since its inception in 1992.

The Certified Lotus Professional program has integrated its certification titles Certified Lotus Specialist (CLS), Certified Lotus Professional (CLP), Principal Certified Lotus Professional (PCLP), and Certified Lotus Instructor (CLEI, CLI and PCLI) over to the new IBM Software Group Certification titles. Consequently, Lotus Notes/Domino has joined Websphere, Tivoli, and DB2 in forming a single, unified IBM Certified Professional program. According to Lotus, the new combined program will "simplify certification skill levels across all four brands while taking advantage of the combined marketing power of IBM plus each of the individual software brands." To all certified Lotus/Domino Application Developers, this is a great thing!

The IBM Certified Professional program is divided into three categories:

➤ IBM Certified Associate (entry level)

➤ IBM Certified Professional (intermediate level)

➤ IBM Certified Advanced Professional (advanced level)

In addition, IBM uses six job roles to further categorize certifications. They are:

➤ Administrator (Database and System)

➤ Developer (Application and Solution)

➤ Designer

➤ Implementer/Integrator (Deployment Professional)

➤ Instructor

➤ Advisor (Sales)

The existing Lotus/Domino certifications will be mapped to new IBM certifications as displayed in Table 1.1 below:

Table 1.1 Updated Certification Titles

Old Lotus Certification	New IBM Branded Certification
CLS—Notes Domino 6 Application Development Foundations Skills	IBM Certified Associate Developer—Lotus Notes and Domino 6
CLP IBM Lotus Domino 6 Application Developer	IBM Certified Application Developer—Lotus Notes and Domino 6
Principal CLP IBM Lotus Domino 6 Application Developer	IBM Certified Advanced Application Developer—Lotus Notes and Domino 6
Principal CLP Collaborative Solutions Application Developer	IBM Certified Advanced Application Developer—Lotus Collaborative Solutions
CLS—Notes Domino 6 System Administration Operating Fundamentals	IBM Certified Associate System Administrator—Lotus Notes and Domino 6
CLP IBM Lotus Domino 6 System Administrator	IBM Certified System Administrator—Lotus Notes and Domino 6
Principal CLP IBM Lotus Domino 6 System Administrator	IBM Certified Advanced System Administrator—Lotus Notes and Domino 6
Principal CLP Collaborative Solutions System Administrator	IBM Certified Advanced System Administrator—Lotus Collaborative Solutions

For a complete list of the new certifications under the IBM Certified Professional Program, go to `http://www.lotus.com/services/education.nsf/35ed29d961be6ad0852566da004c5cbb/af0260977a3cdc8185256d05004da486?OpenDocument`.

Confused? Don't be. There is more information available online. Visit `http://www.lotus.com/certification` for more information.

The Ideal Notes/Domino 6 Certification Candidate

Why get certified? In today's job market, you hardly have a choice. Although no certification guarantees technical knowledge or capability, it is a common, global benchmark between you and your fellow developers. There is no question that certifications help identify your technical expertise, job-related skill, and your skill level. The new IBM Certified Professional program helps developers strengthen their skills and income potential.

Put Yourself to the Test

The following items are points to consider before pursuing the IBM Certified Professional certification.

Education Background

➤ Have you taken any classes or computer-based training on Lotus Notes/Domino 6?

If yes, then you are well ahead of the curve. Classroom training and computer-based training puts you in great shape to begin your path toward certification. Classroom materials and computer-based training cover exam material with remarkable similarity, so any learning in those environments is especially applicable.

Currently, IBM Software Services for Lotus Education and NETg (part of the Thompson Company) are offering a jointly developed Lotus Notes and Domino 6 upgrade curriculum in computer-based training. They offer training specifically designed for administrators, designers, and both.

The current offerings for the IBM Lotus Domino Designer 6: New Features Curriculum (which has a suggested retail price of $299, order part number: AH0HYNA) are

➤ IBM Lotus Domino Designer 6 for Release 5 Developers, Part 1: New Features

➤ IBM Lotus Domino Designer 6 for Release 5 Developers, Part 2: Enhancements

➤ IBM Lotus Domino Designer 6 for Release 5 Developers, Part 3: Tools

Another offering from IBM is the IBM Lotus Domino Administrative & Development Bundle (which has a suggested retail price of $399, order part number: AH0HWNA). This program consists of the three titles listed previously as well as the following titles:

➤ IBM Lotus Domino 6: Preparing Domino Release 4 Administrators

➤ IBM Lotus Domino 6: Preparing Domino Release 4 Developers

For the administrators, IBM is offering the IBM Lotus Domino 6: New Features Curriculum (which has a suggested retail price of $199, order part number: AH0HXNA). This program consists of the following titles:

> ➤ IBM Lotus Domino 6 for Release 5 Administrators, Parts 1: Preparing

> ➤ IBM Lotus Domino 6 for Release 5 Administrators, Parts 2: New Features

For more information, visit IBM's Education site at `https://education.lotus.com/rw/lewwschd.nsf/87FACC133CAA9B23852565C80048B8E1/D204002BFC21811085256B6000500BAD?OpenDocument`

➤ Have you used any self-test software on Lotus Notes/Domino 6?

If there was one tip that I could give to prepare you for taking the Lotus Notes/Domino 6 certification exams, it's to take practice exams as often as possible (after reading this book, of course).

Lotus Education provides the following authorized courseware (go to the URL listed earlier for more information regarding these programs):

> ➤ Electronic End User Courseware Licensing Program

> ➤ Lotus End User courseware

Some of the other companies that offer practice exams are

> ➤ Self Test Software from KaplanIT—`http://www.selftestsoftware.com`

> ➤ Advanced CLP—`http://www.advancedclp.com`

> ➤ CertFX—`http://www.certfx.com`

> ➤ Thomas Consulting—`http://www.thomas-consulting.com`

➤ Are you currently certified in Lotus Notes/Domino R5?

If yes, you can become re-certified by taking Exam 601: Notes Domino 6 Application Development Update. This exam covers only new features made available in Notes/Domino 6 and is a much easier path to take to update your certification (one exam is much easier than three).

➤ Were you certified prior to R5?

Although being certified in a release prior to 6 is helpful, you will find that a lot of new material has been added since R4 (and prior). A general knowledge of Notes is helpful and certainly shortens the learning curve, but you will have the disadvantage of having to learn the features made available in R5 as well as Notes/Domino 6.

➤ Are you certified as a Domino System Administrator?

Having a certification as a Domino System Administrator is not a requirement to get certified as an Application Developer. In fact, for the most part, the competencies are quite distinct. Nevertheless, because certain aspects of Notes and Domino 6 are tightly integrated into system administrative capabilities (such as database access control and server document settings), additional knowledge in system administration is helpful.

Hands-On Experience

As previously mentioned, there is no substitute for experience. Ideally, the more experience you can accumulate prior to taking the exam, the better you will perform. If your experience in Notes/Domino 6 is limited but you have significant experience using previous releases, focus on the release notes and the "What's New" section of the Designer Help database.

Testing Your Exam Readiness

I cannot over-state the importance of taking practice exams until you can consistently score 90% or higher. Ideally, take the practice exams included in this book and on CD as well as any other practice exams that you can acquire (some links to companies that offer practice exams are listed previously in this chapter) until you score 100%. This thorough understanding of the exam question format and content will give you a solid chance at passing the real exam. Taking exams is not inexpensive. So do everything you can to pass the first time. Employers, customers, and peers won't know how many times you took an exam prior to passing, but the cost of exams can add up—not to mention the cost to taking time out of your day and adding more stress to your life.

Assessing Your Readiness for the Exams

After completing this book and taking the practice exams provided in Chapters 18–23, you are well on your way to becoming certified (or at the very least, certifiable). Take the practice exams and re-study material on which you are still unclear. Follow that up with third-party self-test software, if you can, and spend plenty of time using the Designer 6 client. That's what you should be doing anyhow! Good luck!

Typical Notes/Domino 6 Certification Exams

The goal of *Notes/Domino 6 Application Development Exam Cram 2* is to serve as a concise and focused study aid for people preparing for the IBM Certified Application Developer-Lotus Notes and Domino certification, rather than as a comprehensive compendium of knowledge about Lotus Notes/Domino. In fact, the sole purpose of this book is to help you prepare for and pass the three exams required to obtain a certification as an IBM Certified Application Developer—Lotus Notes and Domino. Although we have worked hard to make this book a comprehensive preparation resource, it is important for you to realize that this book should be used in conjunction with real-world experience, hands-on practice, and other study guides.

Assess Exam Readiness

The best way to assess your readiness to take the live certification exams is to take the practice exams included in this book. Additionally, you should strongly consider other practice exams, such as those available from Self Test Software (www.selftestsoftware.com). You can then use the results of the tests to help you determine which parts of this book to focus in on first. After you have completed a chapter, take the sample questions at the end and continue to study the material you have problems with. After you can consistently score 90% or higher on the sample tests, you should be ready. Good luck!

The Exam Situation

Register for a certification test by contacting CATGlobal (www.catglobal.com/ CATGlobal8), Pearson VUE (http://www.vue.com/), or Prometric Testing Centers (www.2test.com, or call 1-800-74-LOTUS). You can choose a location and a time to fit your schedule.

After you arrive at the testing center, you will be required to show two forms of photo identification and sign a log in sheet.

You will not be allowed to bring in any external materials and most likely will be asked to turn of any cell phones or pagers. In fact, you may be required to leave your phone and/or pager outside the testing area.

Keep in mind you will be watched during the exam, by the exam proctor, by video cameras, or by both. IBM wants to ensure that you pass the exam on your own merits.

Typically the proctor takes you to a PC and helps you log in with your ID number. At that point you have the option to read the online instructions or begin the test. If you have any lingering questions, I suggest that you read the instructions before you begin.

Some form of scratch paper will be provided; often it will be a small dry erase board or small note pad. Don't hesitate to use it if you think it will help, but remember that you won't be allowed to take any notes you make with you after the exam.

Finally, I would suggest that you take your cram sheet with you and give it a once-over immediately before you enter the testing center—just be sure to leave it in the car.

Exam Layout and Design

After you log in, the program will provide instructions concerning the test. After you officially start, the timer begins. You will have 1 hour to answer 45 multiple-choice questions, only 40 of which will be scored. You must achieve a score of 75% to pass the exam.

You can track your progress throughout the exam. When the test ends, the program immediately grades the exam and provides you with your score, informing you of whether or not you passed. Afterward, the testing center will provide a printout displaying your score and graphs showing how many correct answers you had in various categories. Unfortunately, the printout doesn't specify which questions you answered correctly or incorrectly. The test center then provides the results to Lotus.

Testing Formats

All three of the IBM Certified Application Developer-Lotus Notes and Domino exams use a multiple-choice format and may ask situation-based questions. For more information about the format, please see the Introduction.

Exam Taking Basics

First and foremost, you need to relax, stay calm, and focus on success. Don't allow yourself to get nervous and lose your focus if you run into a batch of difficult questions at the start of the exam. You will have plenty of time to complete the exam, so there is no reason to become anxious about how much time remains, and missing one or two of the more difficult questions because of lack of time won't cause you to fail the exam. Be sure to arrive early and it's always a good idea to make a restroom stop before the test. Try to clear your mind and relax, and think about how good it will feel to earn your IBM Certified Application Developer—Lotus Notes and Domino certification!

Question Handling Strategies

The following bulleted list outlines some basic question handling strategies that we have found to be helpful:

➤ Read each question slowly and carefully.

➤ Based on the number of questions on the tests and the 1 hour allotted to each test, you have about 1.34 minutes per question. Don't rush, but don't dilly-dally, either.

➤ Read each question twice before choosing an answer.

➤ If you are uncertain of the answer, pick the choice you think is the best answer and mark the question for review. Often, you first instinct is correct.

➤ Try to keep track of questions that you are uncertain about and look for other questions on the test that might help you determine the answer.

➤ Don't spend too much time on any one question. If you don't know the answer, mark it and come back to it during the exam review.

➤ Use the scratch paper or white board to work through questions if you need to.

➤ Always, I repeat *always*, review your marked items and make sure you have selected the best answer.

➤ If necessary, quietly recite the questions as you read them, which may help you focus on the question.

➤ If you have time, go through the entire test a second time and ensure that you haven't made any mistakes.

Master the Inner Game

The Lotus Application Development exams are not extremely difficult, but they do require comprehensive knowledge about Domino application development and proper preparation. Although this book should be a fundamental part of your exam preparation, we recommend that you couple it with practice test software, which will mimic the testing environment and help you gauge your progress and your speed.

Additionally, there is no substitute for hands-on experience. If you aren't currently building real-world applications with Domino 6, you might consider creating a database that you can use to create and test design elements and experiment with different options.

Finally, it's always helpful to do an intense review as close to the actual test as possible. Take your cram sheet with you and review it right up to the last minute, before you enter the testing room.

Need to Know More?

The following resources may be helpful in your exam preparation and if you are interested in acquiring a more well-rounded knowledge of Domino.

 Steve Kern and Deborah Lynd. *Lotus Notes and Domino 6 Development, Second Edition*. Indianapolis: Sams, 2003. ISBN: 0672325020.

 Jeff Gunther and Randall Tamura. *Special Edition Using Lotus Notes and Domino 6, Second Edition*. Indianapolis: Que, 2003. ISBN: 0789728486.

 Tommi Tulisalo, Rune Carlsen, Pekka Hartkainen, Grant McCarthy, Gustavo Pecly. *Domino Designer 6: A Developer's Handbook, First Edition*. IBM, 2002. ISBN: 073842658X.

 SearchDomino.com, www.searchdomino.com.

 Lotus Certification and Education Web site, www.lotus.com/services/education.nsf/wdocs/certificationhomepage.

 Self Test Software, www.selftestsoftware.com.

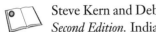 CertFX, www.certfx.com.

PART 1

Notes Domino 6 Application Development Foundation Skills: Exam 610

Database Management

Terms you'll need to understand:

✓ Integrated Development Environment (IDE)
✓ Design template
✓ Inheritance
✓ Document locking
✓ Database Access Control List (ACL)
✓ Design synopsis

Techniques you'll need to master:

✓ Defining what constitutes a Notes database
✓ Controlling what gets replicated
✓ Copying a database
✓ Creating a blank database
✓ Creating a design template
✓ Creating database help documents
✓ Creating database icons
✓ Monitoring/maintaining replication
✓ Preventing design inheritance
✓ Printing from the designer
✓ Setting database properties
✓ Setting up design inheritance
✓ Setting up document locking
✓ Troubleshooting database access
✓ Using design synopsis to analyze application elements
✓ Using design templates to refresh an application design

This chapter briefly describes the various IBM Lotus Notes and Domino 6 clients available (as well as how each client is used), defines the Lotus Notes database, outlines how to create a Lotus Notes database, and describes how to set up the database for application design.

IBM/Lotus defines the Lotus Notes client as "the leading integrated email and collaborative software for the Internet."

Since Release 5.0, Lotus Notes has comprised three individual software clients, each client geared toward a specific function and user type:

➤ Lotus Notes 6 Client (for the standard user)

➤ Domino Administrator 6

➤ Domino Designer 6

The Domino Designer is an *integrated development environment* enabling Notes developers and Web designers to create, manage, and deploy secure interactive Notes client/server and Web applications.

However, in addition to the three clients offered by Lotus, you may be designing applications for other client types:

➤ *iNotes Web Access client*—A Web client that delivers Domino messaging, collaboration, and PIM (Personal Information Management) capabilities to Web browsers

➤ *iNotes for Microsoft Outlook*—A collaborative server solution that delivers the messaging, calendar, scheduling, and personal information management (PIM) services of Lotus Domino technology to Outlook 2000 and 2002 clients

➤ *Other POP/IMAP clients*—Other third-party email clients utilizing POP (Post Office Protocol) and IMAP (Internet Messaging Access Protocol)

➤ *Mobile clients*—Clients that include PDA's, Internet enabled phones, and so on

The Domino Designer 6 client enables developers to design applications for Notes clients, Web browser clients, and Mobile clients (a feature enhanced with Lotus Domino 6) with the same rapid application development (RAD) tool, which uses a consistent programming environment for all support languages. In addition, you can easily integrate third-party application development tools, and Domino 6 supports Web-based Distributed Authoring and

Versioning (WebDAV), enabling users to access and edit Domino design elements without using the Lotus Domino Designer clients (assuming that users are using a editor that supports WebDAV). This is covered in more detail in Chapter 12, "Programming."

Many (though not all) of the design elements used to design for a specific platform (for example, the native Lotus Notes client) are compatible with an alternate platform (such as a Web browser). According to Lotus documentation, about 85% of your database design is compatible with both Lotus Notes clients and Web clients. Thus, only 15% of your application would require custom development for each respective platform. These figures may be generous and may assume a level of application functionality that falls short of your application requirements. Nonetheless, many design elements are well suited for both platforms and can significantly reduce your application development investment.

Because you are preparing to become a certified Application Developer, you are probably very familiar with the Lotus Notes Client and Domino Designer client. This chapter focuses on the different considerations Domino application designers must address when designing applications for Web users, native Lotus Notes users, mobile users, or all three.

What Is a Notes Database?

The Database object is an essential element in creating Domino Web applications and/or native Lotus Notes client/server applications. A Domino database is an object store that contains data, logic, and design elements for the application.

A Domino database is not synonymous with an application. On the contrary, most sophisticated applications comprise several Domino databases. There is no inherent difference between the structural format or definition of databases for the Web, native clients/servers, or mobile applications.

A Domino application enables users to share, collect, track, and organize information. To open a Notes database for the first time from the Notes client, follow these steps:

1. Select File, Database, Open from the pull-down menu.

2. Enter the server in the server field. (Either select the server from the drop-down menu or type the name of the server if it doesn't show up.)

3. Select the database from the database list, or type the name of the database file in the filename field (be sure to include the .nsf [Notes

Storage Facility], .ntf [Notes Template Facility], or .ns5 extension [Notes database that retains the R5 on disk structure]). Alternatively, select the Browse... button to locate the database from a local drive.

 Be sure to memorize what the acronym NSF (Notes Storage Facility) and NTF (Notes Template Facility) represent.

After a database has been opened or bookmarked, you can open the database by either clicking on the bookmark or double-clicking the database icon from the workspace.

Alternatively, you can also open a database from the command line. From the command prompt (for example, MS-DOS), change to the Notes root directory. To open a database stored locally on the current machine, enter **designer Notes://*Database_Replica_ID***. To open a database stored on a server, enter **designer Notes://*Server_Name/Database_Replica_ID***. In addition, you can also open a specific document from the command line by entering **designer Notes://*Server_Name/Database_Replica_ID/Note_ID***.

 When entering the Replica ID of the database, do not include the colons.

When entering the Note ID of the document, enter the characters following the **NT** characters displayed in the beginning of the Note ID.

The ID used when the Lotus Notes client is launched must have Designer access to the database and the Domino Designer must have been opened before.

The Domino 6 Server and Notes 6 client use a different On Disk Structure (ODS) than R5 (and all previous releases). The ODS of a database does not replicate and has no effect on which client version can access a server version. The ODS only determines how the server of client writes data to the physical drive. However, some new features in Domino 6 require the latest version of the ODS (43) (for example, quote management). The Information tab of the database properties displays the ODS version. Release 3.x had an ODS of 17, Release 4.x had an ODS of 20, Release 5.x had an ODS of 41, and Notes and Domino 6 has an ODS of 43.

Be sure to understand what the ODS (On Disk Structure) is and that it does not replicate from one replica database to another.

Controlling What Gets Replicated

Replication enables Domino databases to exchange all document edits, modifications, and deletions, as well as database modifications, database access
control lists and security settings, and design elements. Of course, if the databases are located on different servers, the servers must have sufficient access
to share replication modifications with one another. Domino 6 has improved
on replication capabilities in the areas of selective, scheduled, and streaming
replication.

Domino 6 has added support for streaming replication, which improves replication
across Domino servers and Lotus Notes clients. One benefit of streaming replication is that Notes clients can begin working with replicated documents before database replication is complete.

Replication settings should not be used as security settings when designing
applications. Rather, they should be used to conserve disk space or prevent
the replication of unnecessary or irrelevant documents. Replication settings
are located from the pull-down menu you find under File, Replication,
Settings.

Be sure to understand that replication settings are not considered security features
and should be used to reduce database file size and minimize the number of documents replicated between replica databases.

You must have Manager access to set replica settings for a replica database.

You should be familiar with the various replication settings that are available
in the Replication Settings dialog box.

The Basics Tab

On the Basics tab, you can enable/disable replication, as well as change the replication schedule. The replication schedule is important for databases that may contain time-sensitive information, reside on busy servers, or be in use by mobile users.

If the Scheduled Replication Is Enabled option is selected, clicking on the Change Schedule button displays the Replication Schedule (see Figure 2.1) dialog, which allows the user the following options:

➤ Enable/Disable replication for the current location

➤ Create new replicas immediately or during the next replication (this option appears only if the Replication Is Enabled for This Location option is selected)

➤ Automatically initiate replication when Notes is started (with an option to prompt or not prompt prior to starting)

➤ Replication Interval (hours, repeat interval, and days of week)

➤ Additional Interval for high-priority databases (hours, repeat interval, and days of week)

➤ Prompt to replicate when Notes shuts down (with one option appearing if anything is waiting to be sent and another if the outbox is not empty) email

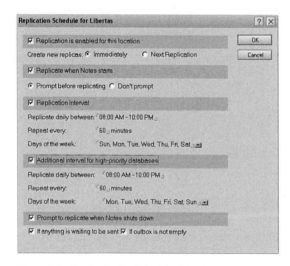

Figure 2.1 The Replication Schedule dialog box.

Another option on the Basics tab is Replicate Using Schedule for Priority Databases. For convenience, the next scheduled replication is displayed under this option.

Under the How Much Will Be Replicated section you need to understand the options to:

➤ *Send Documents to Server*—A check box that determines whether local documents (additions, modifications, or deletions) should be sent to the server during replication

➤ *Receive Documents From Server Options*—A single-select drop-down list box allows users to select

  ➤ *Full Documents*

  ➤ *Partial Documents*—(selecting this option enables the user to select two additional options: Truncate Documents Larger Than *xx* Kb, and Limit Attachment Size to *xx* Kb)

The first option reduces the document information replicated to basic information, such as author, subject, and so on, and restricts replicating rich text fields that are larger that 40KB in size. The second option truncates any attachments larger than 40KB.

When users open documents that have been shortened, the text (TRUNCATED) appears in the window title. To receive the complete document, users must select Actions, Retrieve Entire Document from the drop-down menu.

➤ *Summary Only*—Selecting this option replicates basic document information such as author and subject.

➤ *Smallest First*—Selecting this option replicates documents in order of size (smallest documents first, then summary information of larger documents, and finally rich text of large documents).

The Space Savers Tab

On the Space Savers tab, you should be familiar with the Remove Documents Not Modified In The Last *X* Days option. This option enables you to set the purge interval for this replica copy. This setting controls whether documents that have not been modified within the interval specified should be automatically deleted when the database is replicated. Documents removed as a result of this setting are also purged. Therefore, no deletion stubs are created for these documents and the deletions are not propagated to other replica databases.

Because the deletion stub is also purged, you might think that this document would then reappear because the replica would assume that this is a new document. However, by setting the Only Replicate Incoming Documents Saved or Modified After: setting, you can prevent purged documents from reappearing in the database.

In addition, this setting also determines when deletion stubs are purged from the database. Because the deletion of documents needs to replicate between replica databases, deletion stubs remain after a document has been deleted and replicate to other databases. However, deletion stubs still take up space within the database and should be removed after they have been replicated to all other replica databases.

Deletion stubs are removed if they are at least as old as the number of days specific in this setting. However, Domino does not check this value every time a database is opened. Rather, the stubs are checked to see whether they should be purged at 1/3 the number of days specified. For example, if the purge interval is 150 days, when the database replicates, Domino checks to see whether deletion stubs need to be purged if it has been 50 days since the last purge. If this is the case, any deletion stubs older than 150 days are then purged.

The **Updall** task also purges deletion stubs. This task is set to run at 2:00 a.m. by default, when Domino is installed, but can be run manually by the system administrator.

You must replicate more often than the purge interval. Otherwise, deletion stubs could be purged. Therefore, existing documents in a replica that had been deleted on another replica will be re-created. (Because the deletion stub is gone, the replica that purged the deletion stub assumes the document is a new document.)

Domino automatically removes deletion stubs regardless of whether the Remove Documents Not Modified in the Last x Days" check box has been selected.

Also on the Space Savers tab, you should know about the Receive Only A Subset Of The Documents option. This option determines what documents a replica receives by specifying that only documents in a specific folder, view, or that match a specified criteria determined in the formula language are replicated.

You cannot use **@DBLookup**, **@DbColumn**, **@Username**, **@Environment**, or **@Now** in replication formulas.

When using @IsResponseDoc in the selection formula, all response documents will be replicated. To specify that only response documents that match the criteria specified in the formula are replicated, use the @AllChildren or @AllDescendants functions. Also, if the database setting Don't Support Specialized Response Hierarchy is selected, these functions have no effect.

The Send Tab

On the Send tab, you should be familiar with the following options:

➤ *Do Not Send Deletions Made in This Replica to Other Replicas*—This option determines whether a replica can send deletions to another replica.

➤ *Do Not Send Changes in Database Title and Catalog Info to Other Replicas*— This option determines whether a replica can send changes to the database title and database catalog categories to other replicas. Therefore, database titles can be specific to each database and help identify the purpose of each specific replica.

➤ *Do Not Send Changes in Local Security Property to Other Replicas*—This option determines whether a replica can send changes made to the database encryption property to other replicas.

The Other Tab

On the Other tab, you should be familiar with the following options:

➤ *Temporarily Disable Replication for This Replica*—This option enables you to disable replication temporarily for the current replica.

 If the database is located on a cluster server, disabling replication disables scheduled replication and cluster replication.

➤ *Set Scheduled Replication Priority for This…*—This option determines the replication priority (High, Medium, Low) of this database when replicating. Connection documents can then specify times to replicate databases of each respective priority.

Priority settings have no effect on replicas located on a cluster server because they will automatically replicate whenever a change occurs.

➤ *Only Replicate Incoming Documents Saved or Modified After*—This option controls the date that a replica can receive new or modified documents since the threshold specified.

➤ *CD-ROM Publishing Date*—This option determines the publishing date for a database distributed on a CD-ROM. Therefore, users replicate only documents that were created or modified after the date specified as replicated.

The Advanced Tab

On the Advanced tab, you should be familiar with the following options:

➤ *Receive Only a Subset of Information from Other Replicas*—This option determines what documents a replica for a specific server receives by specifying that only documents in a specific folder, view, or that match a specified criteria determined in the formula language are replicated for that respective server (or all servers).

➤ *Receive These Elements from Other Replicas*—This option enables you to specify which design elements replicate between databases. The elements that can be selected are

➤ *Design Elements*—If selected, this prevents a replica from receiving any design modifications. This option is selected by default.

➤ *Agents*—If selected, this prevents a replica from receiving any agent modifications. This option is selected by default.

➤ *Replication Formula*—If selected, this ensures that replication settings do not replicate between databases. This option is not selected by default.

➤ *Access Control List*—If selected, this prevents modifications to the database's ACL from replicating. Of course, the server (or client) must have Manager access to the database to modify the database's ACL settings. This option is selected by default.

➤ *Deletions*—If selected, the replica can receive document deletions. This option is selected by default.

This setting can be overwritten by the Do Not Send Deletions Made in This Replica to Other Replicas setting, located on the Send panel of the Replication Settings dialog.

➤ *Fields*—If selected, only the specified fields are replicated. This option is not selected by default.

Creating a Blank Database

You have three options when creating a new database:

➤ Create a new database from scratch.

➤ Create a new database based on an existing template.

➤ Copy an existing database and modify its design.

The following section discusses how to create a new database from scratch or from a template. A final subsection explains how to copy a database.

Creating a New Database from Scratch or a Template

Domino ships with several functional database templates. *Design Templates* are databases that contain the structure for the databases (design elements such as pages, forms, and views) but do not contain documents. Although these templates are fully functional applications that can be used "out of the box" as quick solutions, they are better utilized if further modified to fit your organization's specific business needs. When modifying templates, be careful not to create additional work. Some of the design elements are complex, using LotusScript and JavaScript. Therefore, be careful not to break existing functionality. These templates are designed for

➤ Non-Web clients only

➤ Web clients only

➤ A hybrid client audience (both Web and native Lotus Notes)

The process for creating a database from a template is the same as creating a database from scratch, except that you select a template database and several template-specific options in the New Database dialog box.

Clicking the About button from the New Database dialog box displays the About document of the currently highlighted template.

When creating a new database with Domino Designer, follow these steps to create your database from scratch or when creating a database from an existing template:

1. Select the folder (bookmark) in which you want to create the database. You can create a new folder by right-clicking the bookmark bar to produce the Create Folder dialog box (see Figure 2.2). The new database is created in the currently selected folder as well as in the Recent Databases folder. You can rename the folder and change the folder icon by right-clicking the folder icon and selecting those respective options from the drop-down menu.

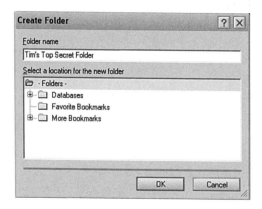

Figure 2.2 The Create Folder dialog box.

2. Select File, Database, New, or press Ctrl+N. Notes displays the New Database dialog box shown in Figure 2.3.

   In the top half you set the database's server location, title, filename, and other options. The bottom half of the dialog box contains a list of available templates.

3. In the Server list, select the server on which you want your database to reside. By default, Domino places the database in the local Notes data directory specified for the current user.

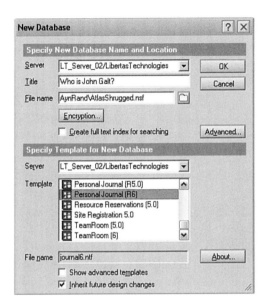

Figure 2.3 The New Database dialog box.

4. In the Title box, enter a descriptive title for the database. The length of the title cannot exceed 96 characters. Your entry will appear as the title on the application title bar when the database is opened, and as the title clients see when they browse databases to open. The text entered for the database title defaults to the filename, which is editable, of course. Domino does not require that you use unique database titles. Nevertheless, avoid using duplicate database titles. Use common sense when naming new databases. For example, multiple databases used within an application should share a common naming scheme. The title must be limited to 96 characters. However, logic dictates that the title be kept to a minimal length (32–36 characters) that still meaningfully describes the database.

5. In the File Name box, enter the name of the database file. The name should have an .nsf extension (unless you are creating a database template that has an .ntf extension), such as Contacts.nsf. Domino automatically adds the .nsf extension if you leave it out. Because Domino supports multiple platforms, it is generally good practice to limit filenames to eight characters. Similarly, consider the implications of using mixed case filenames because platforms such as Unix are case sensitive. It is generally a good practice to establish a standard naming convention for the filenames and directories.

With Domino 6, agents contained in Domino databases with an .ntf extension no longer execute. Therefore, agents can be enabled on the template database (with the .ntf extension) so that they inherit to other databases but they do not actually execute on the template database.

 You should not use network drives when selecting the path for Domino databases. Doing so gives people an opportunity to access the database without going through a Notes server, which makes it easier for your database to become corrupted.

When you enter a filename, the database is put into the default data directory for the selected server. For example, if the data directory is c:\lotus\notes\data, the full path and filename is c:\lotus\notes\data\ filename.nsf. You can enter a directory and filename such as docs\ filename.nsf. The database is then put into c:\lotus\notes\data\ database\filename.nsf, if c:\lotus\notes\data is the data directory. If you selected Local as your server, you can enter a full path and filename for your database, such as d:\lotus\notes\docs\filename.nsf. When installing the Domino server and Notes clients, the default data path for the server is c:\lotus\domino\data\. The default data path for the client is c:\lotus\notes\data\.

If the database being created is intended to serve as a template for other Domino databases, and you want it to display in the list of available templates, you must give the filename an .ntf extension and place the database in the root Notes data directory (c:\lotus\domino\data\ filename.ntf for the server and c:\lotus\notes\data\filename.ntf for the client when you are creating local databases). The lotus\notes\data directory specified here is also the default directory displayed when creating new databases or opening existing databases. Giving the database an .ntf extension causes the database not to appear in the File, Open Database dialog box, but does cause it to appear in the list of available templates you see when you create new databases.

6. If you are creating a local database, you have the option to encrypt it. Database encryption utilizes dual-key RSA cryptosystem to encrypt the data contained within the database. To encrypt a local database, choose Encryption, select Locally Encrypt This Database Using, and then choose an encryption type. Three levels of encryption are available:

➤ Simple Encryption

➤ Medium Encryption (the default encryption level when encryption is enabled)

➤ Strong Encryption

The stronger the encryption that is being enforced on the Domino database, the slower the performance. Also, if the database is encrypted with either Medium or Strong Encryption, it cannot be compressed by third-party disk compression programs.

If you encrypt a local database, anyone who uses your computer must use your ID file and enter your password to access the encrypted database. You do not have to encrypt the database during its creation. Therefore, you can decide to encrypt the database later if you do not know whether encryption is currently required. In addition, you can enable/disable the encryption at any time after originally establishing these settings.

If you have set the encryption settings to a particular level and want to modify these settings (for example, the current encryption level is set to Simple Encryption but you want to increase the encryption level to Medium Encryption), you must first select Do Not Locally Encrypt This Database and completely close the database (including the Database Properties dialog box, if it is open). Then click on Encryption Settings, located within the Database Properties dialog box, and select the new encryption level.

7. To create a full text index for the database, select Create Full Text Index for Searching. This option can also be selected or modified after the database has been created from the Database Properties dialog box, on the Full Text tab. Creating a full text index for a database increases the performance of user-initiated searches as well as functions and commands that perform searches and document lookups. However, when a database is full-text indexed, additional drive space is required for the full-text database.

8. To optimize the database performance and design, click the Advanced tab to open the Advanced Database Options dialog box (see Figure 2.4). Table 2.1 describes the new settings available within the Advanced Database Options dialog box.

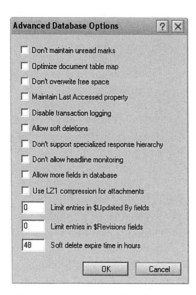

Figure 2.4 The Advanced Database Options dialog box.

Table 2.1 Advanced Database Options	
Dialog Box Selection	**Description**
Don't Maintain Unread Marks	Determines whether the count of unread documents within the database will be tracked. Some databases may not need to track unread documents. Therefore, disabling this feature increases performance. You can also disable views from displaying unread marks, but this does not measurably improve performance. When modifying this selection, you must compact the database for this setting to take affect.
Optimize Document Table Map	This option uses only the forms referenced by the documents contained within each view, and associates only the tables using the document forms to update each respective view, thus increasing performance. With the Document Table Bitmap Optimization setting, Domino internally maintains tables containing information about documents contained within each view. Domino uses these tables when it updates or rebuilds the view indexes. If the views contain selection formulas that specify which forms to use, enabling this setting optimizes performance by using only the tables that use the forms specified in the view selection formula.

Table 2.1 Advanced Database Options *(continued)*	
Dialog Box Selection	**Description**
Don't Overwrite Free Space	As a security feature, Domino automatically overwrites deleted data with new data, ensuring that deleted data cannot be recovered. This causes additional I/O operations to the disk. Marking this selection increases performance but you should consider alternative security options if you choose to do so. Because enabling the Don't Overwrite Free Space option creates potential security risks, this option should be considered only if the information stored within the database is not sensitive information, if it is constantly being reused by new data in a database with a lot of activity, or if the database is located only on a secure server (is encrypted, and so on).
Maintain Last Accessed Property	When enabled, Domino tracks who last read the document. Disabling this option causes Domino to track only who last modified each document, which increases performance because this decreases the disk I/O.
Disable Transaction Logging	After transaction logging has been set up, all Domino database transactions are logged. Disabling this feature increases performance but is generally discouraged because it makes it more difficult to recover from system failures. Transactions are logged in batch mode, when scheduled or when system resources are available.
Allow Soft Deletions	Enabling/disabling this option determines whether users with sufficient Delete access have the capability to flag documents for soft deletions.
Don't Support Specialized Response Hierarchy	By default, all documents contain information that enables them to reference parents, siblings, and response documents. This information is used by only two specialized functions: **@AllChildren** and **@AllDescendants**). Disabling this option does not affect the capability to show response documents and their respective hierarchy in views. When modifying this selection, you must compact the database for this setting to take affect.

Table 2.1 **Advanced Database Options** *(continued)*	
Dialog Box Selection	**Description**
Don't Allow Headline Monitoring	This feature controls whether users can set up headline monitoring for this database. However, except for databases that contain highly secure information, you typically want to allow for headline monitoring. Working in conjunction with subscription lists, users can use headline monitoring in order to be notified when a document of interest is saved in the database.
Allow more fields in database	This feature enables you to create additional fields in the database. By default, all the field names in a database cannot exceed 64 kilobytes. Typically, this would limit the database to approximately 3,000 fields. However, selecting this option enables the database to contain up to 23,000 fields!
Use LZ1 compression for attachments	New with Domino 6 is the capability to use the LZ1 algorithm (rather than the Huffman algorithm) to compress attachments. The LZ1 algorithm is much quicker and more efficient than the Huffman algorithm. When working with databases in a mixed environment of R5 and R6 clients, attachments are automatically compressed with the Huffman algorithm.
Limit Entries in **$UpdatedBy** Fields	Enables you to limit the number of entries in the **$UpdatedBy** field. This field contains the canonical name of each person who edited the Notes document. If each document has a lot of activity and many modifications, reducing the number of revisions tracked per document can increase performance. When the limit is reached, the oldest entry is removed.
Limit Entries in **$Revisions** Fields	Enables you to limit the number of entries in the **$Revisions** field. This field contains the date and time each Notes Document was edited. If each document has a lot of activity and many modifications, reducing the number of revisions tracked per document can increase performance. When the limit is reached, the oldest entry is removed. By default, this field contains up to 500 entries. Because each entry requires 8 bytes of disk space, the larger this field becomes, the slower the database performance. Domino uses the values contained within the **$Revisions** field to resolve replication conflicts. Therefore, it is important that the history contained

Table 2.1 Advanced Database Options *(continued)*	
Dialog Box Selection	**Description**
	within this field span enough time to properly resolve any conflicts that may occur. Lotus suggests that this value should not be less than 10 to avoid additional replication/save conflicts.
Soft delete expire time in hours	If the Allow Soft Deletions option is selected (also in the Advanced Database Options dialog), this setting determines how long (in hours) the documents are held prior to being deleted.

9. From the template list, you have the option to select a template you want to use to create your database. Templates are Domino databases that are installed by default for the Domino server and the Notes Designer. Typically, they have an .ntf filename extension and contain no data. However, templates can also have an .nsf extension. Nevertheless, they contain design elements (outlines, framesets, pages, forms, views, agents, navigators, script, libraries, and other resources and design elements). When specifying a template, keep the following notes in mind:

➤ If you select Blank from the template list, Notes creates an empty database with no forms and one untitled view by default. Use this to create a database from scratch.

➤ The template list contains a list of templates available locally on your computer. To select a template located on a server, select Template Server and choose the server on which the template is located. The template list updates itself to list the templates available on the server you select.

➤ Templates may or may not be installed on your personal machine, depending on how the Notes installation was performed. If you do not have templates available on your machine, make sure you look for them on a Template Server.

➤ If you click Show Advanced Templates, the template list includes system templates such as the Notes Log and Mail Router Mailbox, as well as any other templates marked as advanced templates. In most cases, you do not need to create databases with these templates.

Clicking the About button from the New Database dialog box displays the About document of the currently highlighted template.

10. By default, if creating a new Domino database from a template, Domino automatically enables the Inherit Future Design Changes check box. Deselect this option if you intend to make design modifications to the new database. Keep these issues in mind:

   ➤ When this box is checked, the design of your database is automatically synchronized with the design of the template when the Design task runs on the server or the database design is manually refreshed. The Design task refreshes only those databases that are made from templates that reside on the same Domino server.

   ➤ When copying a database, the Inherit Future Design Changes check box is not available to enable/disable within the Copy Database dialog box. However, this setting is still copied over to the new database. Therefore, if the original database was set up to inherit its design from a template database, the new database is also set up to inherit its design by default. Be sure to disable this setting if you are going to make design changes to the new database.

 Private agents and personal views/folders are not refreshed when the database design is refreshed. Therefore, they must be manually copied and pasted if they are modified in the template.

11. Click the OK button to create your database. Domino then creates a new file in your Data directory, adds a database link to the currently open design bookmark, adds a database link to the Recent Databases bookmark, and opens the new database automatically to the Forms design window.

Creating a Copy of an Existing Database

Using the Domino Designer, follow these steps to create your database as a new copy of an existing Domino database:

1. Select the folder (bookmark) that contains the existing Domino database from which you want to make a new copy. You must select the

existing database bookmarked within an existing folder to make a copy. If the database bookmark has not been created, open the database by selecting Select File, Database, Open, or press Ctrl+O. The new database is created in the currently selected folder as well as in the Recent Databases folder.

2. Right-click on the database title and select Database, New Copy from the drop-down menu. This opens the Copy Database dialog box (see Figure 2.5).

In the top half of the dialog box, you can set the database's server location, title, filename, encryption, and full-text indexing as explained in the previous section. The bottom half displays a list of copy options in which you can determine which elements to copy from the original database.

Follow steps 4–11 of the previously listed instructions for creating a database from scratch or from a template. From this point forward, the process is identical.

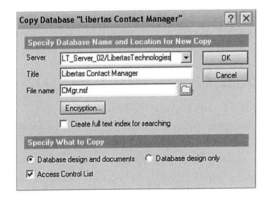

Figure 2.5   The Copy Database dialog box.

Creating a Design Template

Templates are Domino databases that are installed by default for the Domino server and the Notes Designer. Typically, they have an .ntf filename extension and contain no data. However, a template could also have an .nsf extension. Nevertheless, templates contain design elements (outlines, framesets, pages, forms, views, agents, navigators, script, libraries, and other resources and design elements).

Prior to rolling an application out to production, it is generally a best practice to make a template copy. Simply make a copy of the database (as described earlier in this chapter), giving the database name an .ntf extension. Typically, you need to copy the design only (rather than the documents as well) and you should modify the database ACL to restrict access to the database from unauthorized users. Lotus recommends the access levels described in Table 2.2:

Table 2.2 Template Access Levels	
ACL Entry	**Access Level**
Local Domain Users	Reader
Other Domain Users	No Access
Designer's Username	Manager
Database Manager (Admin)	Manager
[Anonymous]	No Access (or ACL of database)
[Default]	No Access (or ACL of database)
[LocalDomainServers]	Manager (or ACL of database)
[OtherDomainServers]	No Access (or ACL of database)

Creating Database Help Documents

The benefits of creating online help within your application are obvious. Integrating information that assists users in understanding and using your application increases its usability and value. You can use the About Database and the Using Database tools to provide online help to the users. The following sections discuss these tools in more detail, and provide information about creating or editing the About and Using databases.

The About Database

The About database describes the purpose of the database. Optionally, this document can open automatically when a user opens the database. This document is available by selecting Help, About Database from the drop-down menu. The About database should include

➤ The purpose of the database/application

➤ The intended audience

➤ The name and telephone number of the database manager

➤ The date the database was implemented

➤ Guidelines for the databases use

➤ Network requirements

The About database can be set to automatically open with the following options:

➤ When Opened in the Notes Client: Open About Database Document

➤ Launch First Attachment in About Database

➤ Launch First doclink in About Database

➤ Show About Database Document If Modified

➤ Show About Database Document when Database Is Opened for the First Time

➤ When Opened in a Browser: Open About database Document

The Using Database

The Using database describes instructions for using the database/ application. This document is available when you select Help, Using This Database from the drop-down menu. The Using Database should include

➤ An overview of the database/application

➤ The purpose of each view and its organization

➤ The purpose of each form and how to complete it

➤ The purpose of each agent, when it runs, when it is triggered, and the anticipated results

➤ The workflow process described in detail

Creating or Editing the About or Using Database

To create or edit the About database or Using database document, go to Other, Database Resources section in the Notes Designer.

You cannot add fields, subforms, or actions on the About database or Using database document. However, you can create links, buttons, hotspots, and attachments.

➤ Context-sensitive help is available from the F1 key or Help button within an application. You can associate a help document with a page, form, subform, view, or folder by writing a formula for the HelpRequest event.

 When providing help for a specific element, that setting overrides help already associated with that element.

Use @Command([OpenHelpDocument]) to specify which help documents to open or @Command([OpenPage]) to open a page. The HelpRequest event is not triggered for Web applications. However, you can still use @Command([OpenHelpDocument]) or @Command([OpenPage]) within a button located on the Web form or Web page.

Use formulas in the HelpRequest event to specify help based upon various conditions (such as if the document is new, if the document is being edited, field values, and so on).

➤ Field help provides information for each respective field. Field help is an optional property for editable fields (located on the Advanced tab) that appears at the bottom of the Notes window when a field gets focus. Fields help can contain up to 70 characters but should be kept under 55 characters for multi-lingual applications (to allow for translation). Optionally, you can also use pop-up text for a field label for each respective field.

➤ A help view can organize and display custom help documents

➤ Create a link to a separate help database, which can be opened in a separate window (similar to the Notes Client, Notes Designer, and Notes Admin help).

Creating a Database Icon

The database icon (which typically visually represents the purpose of the database) enables users to identify the database quickly on the Bookmark pane or the workspace. Database icons can be created in one of three ways:

➤ From scratch with the Notes Designer

➤ By copying an existing icon from another database

➤ By copying a graphic icon from a third-party graphics application

To add or edit the database icon, open the Notes icon editor by going to Other, Database Resources, Icon from the Designer client.

If copying an icon from another application, you cannot resize or move the icon. The size of the icon should be 32×32 pixels. If the icon is larger than 32×32 pixels, Domino is automatically truncated. To edit the icon, open the icon editor located in the Notes Designer in the Other, Database Resources section.

 You must have a mouse to create or edit the database icon.

Monitor/Maintain Replication

Replication enables replica copies of a database to exchange updates in design elements and database content. Replication can be unidirectional (one way only) or bi-directional (modifications are sent and received). The following procedures can be used to monitor replication:

➤ *Database Replication History*—Records each successful replication session.

➤ Replication Events view, displayed in the Notes Log (log.nsf) file, displays information about replication events between servers.

➤ *Replication Monitor*—Notifies recipient if a replication of a database does occur within a specified time period. (This is an administrative task.)

➤ *Database analysis tool*—Collects replication history and replication events from the log file, as well as other database-specific information, and presents the information in an analysis format. (This is an administrative task.)

Preventing Design Inheritance

Domino Designer enables you to restrict design inheritance on individual design elements or all design elements in a database. *Inheritance* is the process of distributing design changes (automatically or manually) to one or more databases that are set up to inherit some or all design elements from the template database. You can restrict design inheritance for individual design elements by selecting the option Prohibit Design Refresh or Replace to Modify. Optionally, you can also set the property Propagate This Prohibition of Design Change to propagate this setting to databases inheriting their designs. These settings can be set and modified on the design documents properties dialog (see Figure 2.6).

 A new feature with Domino 6, available on the database properties Design tab, enables the designer to set the database to Refresh Design on Admin Server Only. Therefore, databases with replicas on other servers do not attempt to refresh their designs when the Design task runs.

Users must have Designer or Manager access to replace or refresh a database design.

Some applications may have an open design, allowing designers to modify design elements to suit the application's specific requirements. If a databases design element is modified and the database is set up to inherit its design from a design template, the modifications are lost when the Design task runs (or the database design is manually refreshed). However, setting the check box to Prohibit Design Refresh or Replace to Modify protects the design refresh from overwriting the modifications.

With Domino 6, you can update multiple design element properties at one time. Select multiple design elements from the Designer client (such as views), using the CTRL or SHIFT keys. Then click the properties icon, select File, Properties from the drop-down menu, or right-click on the highlighted elements and select Design Properties... from the menu. This opens the Design Documents properties box, enabling you to set common properties for all the design elements at one time (see Figure 2.6).

Figure 2.6 Design Documents properties box.

Printing from the Designer

Using the Print Source dialog box, you can print the contents of the Programmer's pane. This includes the formula language, simple actions, HTML, LotusScript, JavaScript, and Java. From within the Domino Designer, select Print from the drop-down file menu, press CTRL-P, or right-click in the Programmer's pane and select Print from the context-sensitive menu. This displays the Print Source dialog box (see Figure 2.7).

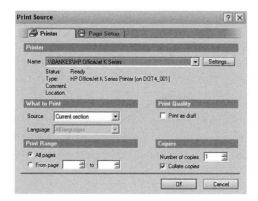

Figure 2.7   The Print Source dialog box.

From within this dialog, you can select some basic printing choices, such as Number of Copies, Print Range, and Print Quality. You also can select these options:

1. Select the name of the printer (and optionally modify the printer settings)

2. Select What to Print. The options available are:

   ➤ *Current Section*—Prints the current code being displayed in the Programmer's pane. This object is selected by default.

   ➤ *Current Object*—Prints all source code for the entire current object (for example, the current form or button).

   ➤ *All Objects*—Prints all source code for all objects available for the current design element.

   ➤ *Language*—Selects the script language to print (if more than one language is available, such as LotusScript, Java, and so on). This option is available only when the source option is Current Object or All Objects.

3. Choose OK to apply your choices and close the box.

Setting Database Properties

Many of the settings used during the creation of Domino databases can be modified after the database has been created. Many other options are not available for modification until after the database has been created. Nevertheless, these settings control the database's capabilities for Notes clients and Web clients.

The Database properties box has seven tabs on which you can specify the settings and attributes of the currently selected database. Some of these settings are global to all the documents contained within the database. Other properties control how the Domino server reacts to Web clients versus Notes clients. Some of the newer features contained on the Advanced tab can be modified to improve the database performance and take advantage of the database ODS.

All the database options are available from the Database properties box. To modify the database properties, right-click the database bookmark title and select Database, Properties from the drop-down menu to open the Database properties box shown in Figure 2.8. If the database is currently open, you can also click on the Properties Box icon from either the SmartIcon bar or click the Properties Box button located by the Preview buttons in the top-right corner of the window.

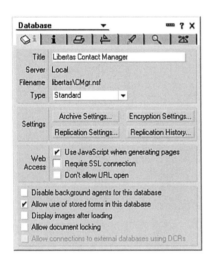

Figure 2.8   The Database properties box.

In "Creating a Blank Database," earlier in this chapter, you learned about the Advanced Tab of the Database properties box and its settings. Please refer to

Figure 2.4 and Table 2.1 to review that information. The options on each of the remaining Database properties box tabs are described in the following sections.

Database Basics Tab

The Database Basics tab is the first tab available from the Database properties box. This tab displays the settings listed in Table 2.3.

Table 2.3	Database Basic Properties	
Setting	**Setting Type**	**Description**
Title	Editable text	The database title.
Server	Display only	The server where the current database is located.
Filename	Display only	The file path and filename of the current database.
Database Type	Drop-down selection	Determines the type of design elements the database is to contain and the default functionality.
Archive Settings	Button	Opens the Archive Settings dialog box.
Encryption Settings	Button	Click the Encryption button to choose encryption settings.
		Click the Replication button to choose Replication settings.
Replication Settings	Button	Opens the Replication Settings dialog box.
Replication History	Button	Opens the Replication History dialog box.
Web Access: Use JavaScript When Generating Pages	Check box	Enables the use of additional @commands and multiple buttons on forms and converts many @commands to JavaScript.
Web Access: Require SSL Connection	Check box	Forces Web clients to log in using SSL (Secure Sockets Layer).
Web Access: Don't Allow URL open	Check box	Restricts Web users from using URL commands to open the database, forms, views, and so on.
Disable Background Agents for This Database	Check box	Determines whether background can be run on the database.
Allow Use of Stored Forms in This Database	Check box	Determines whether the setting to store form design elements in documents can be enabled.

Table 2.3 Database Basic Properties		
Setting	**Setting Type**	**Description**
Display Images After Loading	Check box	This setting controls whether images should be displayed after the entire document has been loaded.
Allow Document Locking	Check box	Allows users with Author access or higher to lock documents.
Allow Connections to External Databases Using DCRs	Check box	Allows forms using a data connection resource (DCR) to exchange data with an external database.

Info Tab

The Info tab contains general information about the Domino database (see Figure 2.9).

The information contained in the Info tab includes the disk space and document count. Click the % Used button to display the percentage of non-whitespace being used by the database. You can click the Compact button to run the Compact task on the database. The Info tab Activity display shows the date and time the database was created and last modified. User Detail indicates the User Activity, if the activity is being recorded. This tab also shows the Replica ID and the ODS version of the active database (this value is different for previous versions of Domino).

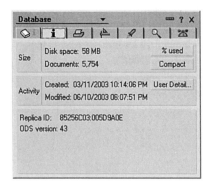

Figure 2.9   The Info tab of the Database properties box.

Printing Tab

The Printing tab (see Figure 2.10) contains information regarding settings and formatting for printed documents.

The settings on the Printing tab enable you to determine how the database documents will be printed. You can specify whether the current settings refer to the headers or footers. You can type editable text in the Header/Footer Text box, and that text will appear in the document headers and/or footers. List box settings for font, size, and style determine the text Format. Finally, you can choose whether headers and footers will appear on the first page of the document.

Design Tab

The Design tab contains design settings options for the current database.

If the database design is not hidden, the information contained in the Design tab is as described in Table 2.4. If the database design is hidden, no information is displayed on this tab, although the tab still exists. Design locking is described in more detail in "?," later in this chapter.

Table 2.4 Database Design Tab		
Setting	**Setting Type**	**Description**
Allow Design Locking	Check box	Enables developers to document locking capabilities.
List in Database Catalog	Check box	Determines whether database should be listed in database catalog.
Categories	Editable text box	If database is set to list in database catalog, determines category for database catalog.
Show in 'Open Database' Dialog	Check box	Determines whether this database should appear in the list of databases that appears when users are opening databases.
Include in Multi-Database Indexing	Check box	Determines whether the database should be included in the multidatabase search site queries.
Do Not Mark Modified Documents as Unread	Check box	Determines whether modified documents should be marked as unread documents.
Inherit Design from Master Template	Check box	Determines whether the database should inherit its design.

Table 2.4   Database Design Tab

Setting	Setting Type	Description
Template Name	Editable text	If the Inherit Design from Template check box is selected, the name of the template database is specified.
Refresh Design on Admin Server Only	Check box	If the Inherit Design from Template check box is selected and template name is specified, indicates whether the inheritance should occur on the admin server only.
Database File is a Master Template	Check box	Determines whether the database is a template for other databases.
Template Name	Editable text	If the Database is a master template, this field is used to specify the name assigned to this template.
List as Advanced Template in 'New Database' Dialog	Check box	If selected, the database appears in the template list only when the new database is created as an advanced database template.
Copy Profile Documents with Design	Check box	If selected, profile documents are copied along with design elements.
Single Copy Template	Check box	Indicates whether database is single copy template (a new feature in R6 that allows multiple databases to replace design elements with pointers or reference nodes to design elements in the single copy template).
Multilingual Database	Check box	Determines whether the database should support multiple international languages, time zones, and regions. If set, developers can build design elements and associate them with a particular language.
Default Language	Drop-down	For multilingual databases, allows developer to set default language.
Default Region	Drop-down	For multilingual databases, allows developer to set default region if default language has various regional dialects (such as in Spanish).
Default Sort Order	Drop-down	For multilingual databases, allows developer to set default sort order for multiple languages.
Unicode Standard Sorting	Check box	For multilingual databases with default sort order specified, allows developer to select/deselect Unicode sorting.

Launch Tab

The Launch tab contains information regarding launch settings for native Lotus Notes clients and Web clients.

The information contained in the Launch tab is described in Table 2.5.

Table 2.5 Database Launch Tab		
Setting	**Setting Type**	**Description**
When Opened in the Notes Client	Drop-down	Determines the default design element to open when the database is opened by a native Lotus Notes client. The default launch options for Notes clients are: ➤ Restore Last Viewed by User ➤ Open "About Database" Document ➤ Open Designated Frameset ➤ Open Designated Navigator ➤ Open Designated Navigator in Its Own Window ➤ Launch First Attachment in "About Database" ➤ Launch First Doclink in "About Database"
Name	Drop-down	The list of specific options based upon the option selected for When Opened in the Notes Client.
Restore as Last Viewed by User	Check box	Opens last design element viewed by each respective user.
Show "About Database" Document If Modified	Check box	Determines whether the About document should be displayed to Notes clients if its design has been modified since the user last accessed the database.
Show "About Database" Document When Database Is Opened for the First Time	Check box	Determines whether the About document should be displayed to Notes client when database is opened for first time.
Preview Pane Default...	Button	Determines the default Preview pane layout. This option is not available if the When Opened in the Notes Client option is set to open a Frameset.

Table 2.5 Database Launch Tab *(continued)*		
Setting	**Setting Type**	**Description**
When Opened in a Browser Drop-down		Determines the default design element to open when the database is opened by a Web client. The default launch options for Web clients are
		➤ Use Notes Launch Option.
		➤ Open "About Database" Document.
		➤ Open Designated Frameset. Selecting this option displays an additional option to select the Frameset to open.
		➤ Open Designated Page. Selecting this option displays an additional option to select the Page to open.
		➤ Open Designated Navigator in Its Own Window. Selecting this option displays an additional option to select the Navigator to open.
		➤ Launch First Doclink in "About Database".
		➤ Launch Designated Doclink. Selecting this option displays additional buttons to paste the doclink or go to the doclink.
		➤ Launch First Document in View. Selecting this option displays an additional option to select the View to use when opening the first document.

Full Text Tab

Full text indexes enable you to speed up the searching of Notes documents by creating a index of the database (which is stored in another physical database file).

You must have Designer access or higher to create a full-text index of a database.

 If a user does not have access to create, update, or delete the full-text index, these options are greyed out to the user.

The Full Text tab contains information regarding Full Text Indexing options (see Figure 2.10).

Click the Update Index button at the top of this tab to update a previously defined index. Click Create Index to open the Create Full Text Index dialog box. The Delete Index button deletes an existing index. Use the Update Frequency drop-down to specify whether updates should occur on a daily, hourly, or other scheduled basis. In the Index Settings area, you can see all the full text index settings, including Case Sensitivity, Index Breaks, Index Attachments, and Index Encrypted Fields.

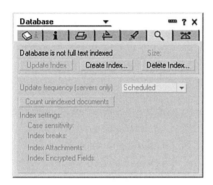

Figure 2.10   The Full Text tab of the Database properties box.

Setting Up Design Inheritance

When designing applications, you can distribute design modifications in one of three ways:

➤ Make modifications directly to the live database.

➤ Make modifications to the database template and manually replicate the design of the database.

➤ Make modifications to a master design template and manually refresh the design of the database or use the Design task to refresh the design of the database.

The third method is the most structured option for managing design modifications and the preferred method to control, track, maintain, and synchronize changes.

You typically set up design inheritance when a database is initially created or after a database has been created by modifying required parameters on the

Design tab of the Database Properties dialog. When a database is created, you can optionally specify a template on which to base the design of the new database. If an existing template is selected (from either the user's local drive or from a specified server), all the design elements from the template are copied into the new database. Optionally, you can select the check box to Inherit Future Design Changes. If this option is selected, the new database is automatically set up to inherit future design changes made to the template when the design task runs on that server or when the database design is manually refreshed by the database designed or database manager.

 Only database templates (files with an **.ntf** extension) located in the root directory of the server of the local data drive appear in the template database list when a new database is being created.

You can also set up design inheritance on an existing database by specifying the master template in the Design tab of the Database properties dialog. If the database was set up to inherit future design changes, as specified in the previous example, this will already be set up. Nevertheless, to set up a database to inherit its design from a master template, follow these steps:

1. Open the Design tab of the Database Properties dialog box.

2. Select the Inherit Design from Master Template option located in the Inheritance section of the dialog.

3. Specify the master template name in the Template Name field.

The master template will have the option specifying Database File Is a Master Template selected. The Template Name field, located under this check box, must contain the same value as the template name field specified in the database inheriting its design. These values can be any text string that meaningfully describes the database. When the design task is run on the server or the database design is manually refreshed, all the databases on that server are searched until the master template is located. Then all modified design elements are updated in the database inheriting its design. If the master database cannot be found or the value entered in the template name is incorrect, the database design is not updated.

A new check box available with Domino/Notes 6 provides the capability to specify that the database inheritance occurs only on the admin server for that database. This is enabled by selecting the Refresh Design on Admin Server Only check box (the admin server is indicated on the Advanced tab of the database Access Control List dialog box). If this option is set, the database design is refreshed only on the replica copy that exists on the server specified as the Admin server for that database. However, the master template database must still exist on the same server as the database whose design is being refreshed. (Therefore, in this case the master template must also exist on the admin server.) Additional design inheritance settings are covered in Chapter 7, "Database Management."

Setting Up Document Locking

Document locking allows users with Author access or higher to lock documents within a database. Locking a document gives exclusive rights to the person who has locked the document to modify it. Other users with the same rights cannot modify the document even if they are working on another replica on the same local area network. Therefore, document locking prevents editing of documents and replication conflicts.

To enable design element locking, specify a Master Lock Administration Server in the Advanced panel of the database Access Control dialog. Then select File, Database, Properties to open the Database properties box. On the Design tab, select the Allow Document Locking option (see Figure 2.11). Of course, document locking must be set up individually for each database.

If you are working locally and unable to connect to the administration server for the current database, attempting to lock a document causes the Master Lock Database Cannot Be Reached message to display. You are then prompted as to whether you want to proceed with locking the document. If you answer yes, there is a chance that your edits may be lost if the document is edited by another user. When this happens, you will receive an email notifying you that the changes were not saved in the document. When a document is successfully locked, the message Document successfully locked is printed to the status bar.

To unlock a document, you must use the same ID as the ID used when the document was locked. Alternatively, managers can unlock documents.

To lock a design element, simply right-click the design element and select Lock from the drop-down menu. To unlock a design element, right-click on the design element and select Unlock from the drop-down menu.

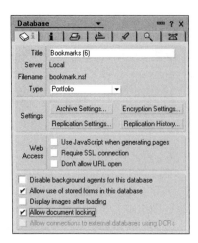

Figure 2.11   The Design tab of the Database properties box.

When one shared action is locked or unlocked, all shared actions are locked because all the shared actions are considered one design element.

Troubleshooting Database Access

The most important tool for controlling access to your application is the database's Access Control List (ACL). Within the database ACL, you define which people, groups, and/or servers have access to your database and what functions they can each perform.

Every Domino database contains an Access Control List. Users, groups, or servers with Manager access can add, modify, and remove users and groups, and they assign them specific access to the application. Whenever users attempt to access this database (from either a Notes or Web client), the ACL is used to determine their respective privileges.

ACL Fundamentals

Database security for any database on a server is handled by the database *Access Control List*. The ACL lists users, groups, and servers, and assigns them specific rights to the database. Access levels range from Manager, who has total access to the database, to No Access. The database manager creates and controls the ACL. An additional database-level security feature is local encryption, which causes local databases to be encrypted so that only the user who sets local encryption can access them.

The users, groups, and servers contained within the ACL entries are defined within the Domino Directory. The Domino Directory is actually another Domino database itself. (Prior to Domino Release 5, this database was referred to as the Public Address Book.)

Four layers of security are contained within the Domino security framework:

> Server-level security

> Database-level security

> Documents-level security

> Field-level security

Access Levels

Within the Database Access Control List are seven levels of access. Table 2.6 lists each access level and describes each level's access.

Table 2.6 Database Access Levels	
Access Control Level	**Privileges**
Manager	Can perform all functions, create and modify database ACLs, and delete the database (using the Notes client).
Designer	Can perform all the functions of an Editor (unless there are specific document-level restrictions), make modifications to the database design and design elements, and create/update a full-text index for the database. Designers cannot delete the database or modify the database ACL.
Editor	Can create, read, and edit all documents (unless there are specific document-level restrictions).
Author	An author can create, read, and edit documents he has created. However, if the Create Documents ACL setting has been disabled for this entry, users cannot create new documents. For an author to edit her own document she must have an Authors field with her name in it on the document.
Reader	Can only read documents (cannot create, edit, or delete documents).
Depositor	Can only create documents (cannot read, edit, or delete documents even if he or she created them). Users cannot see any documents, either, even those they have previously created.
No Access	No access to the database.

Theoretically, a user who has No Access to a database may still be able to view some of the database contents. If a user has been granted No Access to the database, but the Read Public Documents option has been selected, the user has access to read documents contained within a shared view/folder if the documents contain an item title (**$PublicAccess**) that has a value of **1**. This capability is used within the Notes calendaring capability.

In the Access Control List, you list users, groups, and servers who need access to your database. Users, groups, and servers are given one of the same seven access levels described in Table 2.6.

ACL Entries

ACL entries within a database can be categorized as one of the following:

➤ Username

➤ Server name

➤ Group name

➤ Database replica ID

➤ Default

➤ Anonymous

Usernames in the ACL should be entered exactly as they appear in the user's ID file. If your organization uses hierarchical names, you should enter the fully distinguished hierarchical name—for example, **Tim Bankes/ Marketing/LibertasTechnologies**. If the server on which your database resides and the person you are adding are both in the same organization, you can enter just the common name in the ACL, but the fully distinguished name is more secure, because two people cannot have the same fully distinguished name.

Server names are entered in much the same way as usernames. You should use the server's fully distinguished name—for example, **Tsunami/ Marketing/LibertasTechnologies**. But you can use the common name if the servers are in the same organization.

 Notes enables you to use the asterisk wildcard (*) to replace any component of a hierarchical name below the organization. Using wildcards, one ACL entry can grant access to everyone within a single organization or organizational unit. For example, the entry ***/LibertasTechnologies** gives access to anyone in the organization **LibertasTechnologies** (including **Tim Bankes/LibertasTechnologies** or **Dave Hatter/ Development/LibertasTechnologies**).

It is possible for users to be assigned to more than one access level by being assigned explicitly within the database ACL and by being a member of a group name in the database ACL. Table 2.7 outlines the possible scenarios in which a user might be assigned with multiple access levels.

Table 2.7 Multiple Access Levels	
Situation	**Resolution**
The user is listed individually and as a member of a group.	The access granted to the explicitly listed username takes precedence over the access granted in the group, even if the group access is higher.
The user is included in two or more groups.	The user is granted the access of the group with the highest access, even if one of the groups has been assigned No Access to the database.
The user appears in the ACL as well as in specific design element.	The specific design access refines the database access lists.

Group names in the ACL can be any group of people or servers that is defined in the Domino Directory. Using group names in your ACLs has several advantages over individual names, including the following:

➤ One group representing many users keeps the number of entries in the ACL low. This makes managing the ACL much easier.

➤ You can change the access for an entire group of people rather than changing the access of several individual users.

➤ A single group can be in the ACL in several databases. Simplify administration by centralizing changes within the Domino Directory.

➤ Using groups, you can list a descriptive name that makes up a set of people, so you don't have to worry about typing in each individual entry, just the group name.

NOTE

By default, the database Access Control List (ACL) affects only databases stored on a server. If the Enforce a Consistent Access Control List Across All Replicas of This Database property is selected, the ACL is enforced locally and across all other servers that contain database replicas of the current database. When the database replicates, all other replicas must share the same ACL list and specific settings. They can be modified on only the Administration server. After they have been modified on the Administration server, they are pushed to the other replica copies. If the database is modified on a replica copy that is not designated as the Administration server, replication is permanently disabled for that replica database.

To enable this security, choose File, Database, Access Control from the menu bar. Click the Advanced tab that appears and select the Enforce a Consistent Access Control List Across All Replicas of This Database option.

Four standard entries are created by default for every new database:

➤ *Default*—Set to No Access unless the database was created from another database or a template with the default entry set to another access level.

➤ *LocalDomainServers*—Set to Manager access.

➤ *OtherDomainServers*—Set to No Access.

➤ *Current Server*—If created on a server, this entry is set to Manager access.

➤ *The database creator*—Set to Manager access.

Beyond these standard entries in the ACL, you will add additional entries for users, servers, and groups of users or servers. These additional entries affect the bulk of the database users.

ACL entries are created with the Access Control List dialog box. You can also modify database ACL entries. Right-click the database icon for which you want to set up an ACL and select Database, Access Control (see Figure 2.12).

In the People, Servers, Groups field, you can filter the entries listed in the ACL. You can add, delete, or update entries in the list. Use the following procedure to add names to the list:

1. Click the Add button (located below the People, Servers, Groups list). Domino displays the Add User dialog box (see Figure 2.12).

2. Enter a single name in the People, Servers, Groups box. Or click the Person button to open the Names dialog box, which is used for looking up entries in the Domino Directory. The entries can be servers, server groups, people, people groups, or mixed groups.

3. When you have added all the desired ACL entries, click OK. The names now appear in the Database ACL list. The default access level of newly added entries matches the access level of the currently high-lighted entry in the ACL list.

To rename an item in the list, select the name you want to rename and click on the Rename button in the Access Control dialog box. Enter the new name or use the Domino Directory by clicking on the Person button.

To delete a name from the list, select the name you want to delete and click on the Remove button in the Access Control dialog box.

After you have entered the correct names, you can assign access levels to those names by using the following procedure:

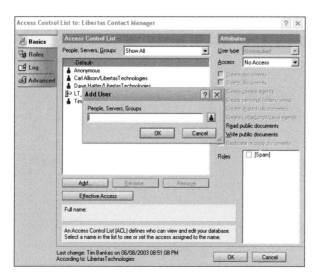

Figure 2.12   The Access Control List dialog box with the Add User dialog box open.

1. Select a name from the list in the People, Servers, Groups list box.

2. In the Attributes area of the ACL window, select the appropriate User Type.

3. Select the appropriate access from the Access pull-down list.

4. Below the Access list are eight check boxes that you should check to further refine a user's access rights. The rights available for modification depend on the access level you assigned the user. For example, the Create Documents box is unavailable for a user with Reader access because a Reader, by definition, cannot create documents. Any unavailable items are grayed out. Items that are selected and grayed out are automatically set as a result of the access level and cannot be modified. These options are covered in greater detail in Chapter 5, "Security."

5. Finally, you can select any roles assigned to this user, if any are defined, in the Roles list box.

You can add, modify, and/or remove roles by clicking on the Roles icon located on the left section of the Access Control List dialog box. Roles enable database security to assign a subset of users additional access to specific database components. Role names cannot exceed 15 characters.

You can view the change history of modifications made to the database ACL by clicking on the Log icon located on the left section of the Access Control List dialog box.

You can modify Advanced options by clicking on the Advanced icon located on the left section of the Access Control List dialog box (see Figure 2.13).

With these advanced options, you can

➤ Select the Administration Server.

➤ Determine whether the Administration Process should modify Reader and Author fields.

➤ Enforce a consistent Access Control List across all replicas of this database.

➤ Set the maximum Internet access with authenticated Web users.

➤ Look up user types for Unspecified users on the Basics tab from the Domino Directory.

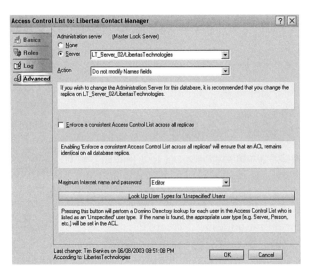

Figure 2.13   The Advanced options of the Access Control List dialog box.

Using Design Synopsis to Analyze Application Elements

The Domino *Design Synopsis* allows designers to gather a detailed report describing the design of a database. Specifically, the design synopsis report enables you to

➤ Gather information on the current database

➤ Select design elements to report on

➤ Filter contents of the report to shorten the length of the report

➤ Display the results of the report to screen or write the results to a Domino database

To create a design synopsis of the current database, perform the following steps:

1. Open the database on which you want to report.

2. Select File, Database, Design Synopsis from the pull-down menu.

3. Select the design elements on which to report from the Choose Design Elements tab by first selecting the design element type, then adding (or removing) specific design elements or all design elements.

4. On the Choose DB Info tab, select the type of information to include in the report. The options include:

   ➤ *General Information*—Includes general information such as database title, location, and categories.

   ➤ *Space Usage*—Includes file size information, number of documents, space used by the database, and so on.

   ➤ *Replication*—Includes replication information.

   ➤ *Access Lists*—Includes database ACL information, such as the database users, groups, and servers, as well as each entry's respective access level and access role.

5. On the Define Content tab, select the contents of each element type to include in the synopsis.

6. On the Format Output tab, select the separator for each element within the report (page break or blank line) and where the report output should be directed (document or database). If you select database as the output option, another dialog box enables you to select the destination database server, title, and filename.

Hide-when conditions are now supported by the design synopsis feature.

Using Design Templates to Refresh an Application Design

Using design templates when creating applications and to update existing applications enables designers to create a consistent design for multiple databases while minimizing development effort. The process of updating a database design from a design template can be manually triggered by the application designer, by an administrator running the Design task, or automatically if the Design task is scheduled to run overnight (for example, at 1:00 a.m.).

> The Design task updates all databases that are set up to inherit their design from a design template.
>
> Database designs are refreshed only by design templates that exist on the same server as the database to be refreshed.

The Designer task can be run manually from the workspace or the administrator client, or by using a console command. To run the Design tasks on a server to update all the applicable databases on that server, type **Load Design** at the console command. To refresh the design of a single database, you can optionally provide arguments to specify the database, source server, destination server, or directory to refresh.

Summary

As you would expect, Lotus Notes and Domino 6 have made significant advancements from the R5. References at the end of this chapter direct you to sources that elaborate on the specific enhancements.

The concepts of database management, specifically creating databases and managing their design, are an integral part of application development. In addition, replication and database access issues represent some of the most powerful features of Domino and Notes. Subsequently, they are covered in great detail on the certification exams. Some of the newer features, such as document locking, further expand the capabilities of Domino and Notes. You also can expect to see these items on the certification exams!

Exam Prep Questions

Question 1

Tim needs what access level to unlock documents locked by other users?

- ❑ A. Designer.
- ❑ B. Manager.
- ❑ C. Either Designer or Manager.
- ❑ D. None. Documents can only be unlocked by the user who originally locked it.

Answer B is correct. Typically documents that have been locked can be unlocked only by the user who locked the element(s) or the database manager. Although a manager cannot edit a document locked by another user, a manager can unlock the document. Answers A and C are incorrect because designers do not have sufficient rights to unlock documents if they have not originally locked them. Answer D is wrong because even though users can unlock documents they have locked, managers can unlock documents as well.

Question 2

Which is not an option for the default launch action when a database is opened in a browser?

- ❑ A. Restore As Last Viewed by User.
- ❑ B. Launch first doclink in About Document.
- ❑ C. Launch designated doclink.
- ❑ D. Open About Database document.

Answer A is correct. The option to Restore As Last Viewed by User is an option for the database launch when opened by a Notes client. Answers B, C, and D are all valid default launch options when a database is opened in a browser.

Question 3

> Where would a developer set the property in order to not send changes made to
> the database title and then catalog info to other replicas?
>
> ❑ A. In the Database properties, Basic tab.
>
> ❑ B. In the Database properties, Info tab.
>
> ❑ C. In the Replication settings, Basic tab.
>
> ❑ D. In the Replication settings, Send tab.

Answer D is correct. The Do Not Send Changes in Database Title and
Catalog Info to Other Replicas option is located on the Send tab of the
Replication Settings dialog. Answer A is incorrect because the Database
Properties, Basic tab displays the database title, but does not have a setting
to control whether changes made to the title are sent to other replicas. Be
careful, because the Database Properties, Basic tab does display a button that
opens the Replication Settings dialog (where this setting is modified).
Answer B is incorrect because the Database Properties, Info tab displays only
Size, Activity, Replica ID, and ODS information. Answer C is incorrect
because the Replication settings, Send tab contains settings for how often
replication occurs, how much is replicated, and which server to use for replication.

Question 4

> Tim wants to modify the design of eight different views in an existing database
> so that they are hidden from mobile clients. Where would Tim set this?
>
> ❑ A. Design properties.
>
> ❑ B. View properties.
>
> ❑ C. Database properties.
>
> ❑ D. This option is not available Domino/Notes 6.

Answer A is correct. With Domino/Notes 6 you can now highlight multiple
design elements (holding Shift or CTRL while clicking on each design element)
from the work pane and set common design properties by using the Design
Properties box. Answer B is incorrect because the view properties do not allow
you to modify multiple design elements at one time. Answer C is incorrect
because the database properties do not allow you to modify this setting.

Question 5

Which is not a print option when printing source code from the programmer's pane in the designer IDE?

❑ A. Simple Actions.

❑ B. Formula Language.

❑ C. Java.

❑ D. They are all print options.

Answer D is correct. All the source code options can be printed from the designer client except Imported Java (which was not listed in the question but is important to know). Answers A, B, and C are incorrect because they are all print options and selecting one answer would preclude the remaining options from being correct.

Need to Know More?

Lotus Developer Domain. "Notes 6 Technical Overview." Available in printed form or on the Web at http://www.lotus.com/ldd.

Lotus Developer Domain. "Domino 6 Technical Overview." Available in printed form or on the Web at http://www.lotus.com/ldd.

IBM International Technical Support Organization. "IBM Redbook—Upgrading to Lotus Notes and Domino 6." Available in printed form, PDF format, and HTML format from www.redbooks. ibm.com/pubs/pdfs/redbooks/sg246889.pdf.

IBM International Technical Support Organization. "Domino Designer 6: A Developer's Handbook." Available in printed form, PDF format, and HTML format from http://publib-b. boulder.ibm.com/Redbooks.nsf/RedbookAbstracts/sg246854.html?Open.

IBM International Technical Support Organization. "New Features of Lotus Domino 6.0.1: Single Copy Template." Available in printed form, PDF format, and HTML format from http://publib-b. boulder.ibm.com/Redbooks.nsf/RedbookAbstracts/redp3681.html?Open.

IBM Lotus. "Release Notes." http://www-10.lotus.com/ldd/notesua. nsf/RN?OpenView.

IBM Lotus. *Online Help Databases*: help6_admin.nsf, help6_client. nsf, help6_designer.nsf.

Application Architecture

Terms you'll need to understand:

- ✓ Bookmarks
- ✓ Embedded elements
- ✓ Outline
- ✓ Date picker
- ✓ Group scheduling control
- ✓ Editor
- ✓ Folder pane
- ✓ File upload control
- ✓ Image resource
- ✓ Style sheets
- ✓ Data Connections

Techniques you'll need to master:

- ✓ Creating, modifying, and troubleshooting for Notes clients
- ✓ Understanding Domino Application Architecture
- ✓ Executing requests from the Notes client
- ✓ Using images in applications
- ✓ Using tables to manage page layout
- ✓ Using the Designer bookmarks to organize projects
- ✓ Working with local applications

Understanding the Lotus Notes application architecture is fundamental to passing exam 610, Notes Domino 6 Application Development Foundation Skills. This understanding is also fundamental to application development in general! This chapter covers the Domino Designer development environment and the technologies supported by the Domino Designer. Specifically, the application architecture, Notes design elements, and how to utilize the design elements in developing for Notes clients are covered.

The most important element with any Domino application is Notes documents. Lotus Notes documents contain application data and design data. In addition, design elements are special Lotus Notes documents that are a part of the database design. However, when referring to Notes documents, people are typically referring to application data documents. Likewise, references in this chapter and the remainder of this book will typically be referring to application data documents unless otherwise noted.

Creating, Modifying, Troubleshooting for Notes Clients

When the Domino Designer client is opened, the welcome page is displayed. The default welcome page displays four options to display content in the Show Me field. The four options are

➤ Quick links for common tasks (default)—These tasks include Create New Database, Open an Existing Database, Designer Help, and links to online developer resources such as the Lotus Developer Domain, Domino Enterprise Integration, Domino Global Workbench, and What's New in Domino Designer 6.

➤ *Domino Objects For LotusScript and OLE*—A graphical layout of the Front-End and Back-End classes with links to respective help documents in the Lotus Domino Designer 6 Help database.

➤ *Domino Objects for DXL Support*—A graphical layout of the DXL classes with links to respective help documents in the Lotus Domino Designer 6 Help database.

➤ *JavaScript Object Model*—A graphical layout of the DXL classes with a link to help contained in the Lotus Domino Designer 6 Help database. This help document explains how the JavaScript object model is implemented in Domino and contains links to online JavaScript help.

Languages Used to Code within the Domino Designer IDE

The Domino Designer *Integrated Development Environment* (IDE) enables developers to use the following languages to code:

➤ Notes Formula language

➤ LotusScript

➤ Java

➤ Imported Java

➤ JavaScript

The Domino Designer Client Interface

Table 3.1, Interface Functional Area, describes the functional areas contained within the Domino Designer client interface.

Although you will not be asked specifically to point out these areas for the exam, the areas of the Lotus Domino Designer interface are referenced within exam questions. And although the exam does not visually depict the development environment, you may be asked questions that refer to user interface areas (such as the Design pane), so understanding the terminology used by Lotus when referring to the development environment is important.

Table 3.1 Interface Functional Areas	
User Interface Area	**Description**
Menu bar	Context-sensitive menus of the Domino Designer commands.
Properties Box button	Opens the properties box for the active design element.
Preview buttons	Launch a Web browser or Notes client to preview the work.
Design pane	Contains the list of the design elements and resources for the database. The bookmark icon contains a list of the most recently opened databases.
Work pane	The WYSIWYG ("what you see is what you get") environment for creating and modifying forms, pages, views, and other design elements specific to an application or database. Lists all the specific design items in the current database for the selected design element. The Design action buttons, which are listed across the top of the Work pane, change depending on the current design element being modified. These buttons then perform actions respective to the currently displayed items in the Work pane.

Table 3.1 Interface Functional Areas *(continued)*	
User Interface Area	**Description**
Window tabs	Each item that you are currently working on has its window tab. When each tab is clicked, the window the tab represents is opened.
Design Action buttons	Used to trigger common tasks associated with the current design element being used.
Bookmark bar	Displays *bookmarks*, which are graphical links to help you quickly access and organize your databases.
Objects tab	Lists all the objects (specific parts of the design element such as forms, fields, or buttons when working within a form design element) and events (object-related actions to which you can attach scripts to perform activities in an application—when the event occurs, the script attached to the event executes) for the currently selected design element to which logic (code) can be added. When clicking on the various items, the script area changes to reflect the language type and logic that can be added for the current object. Logic is then added into the script area.
Info list	Scrollable window that displays the objects and coding reference information for the design element currently displayed in the work area.
Title bar	Displays the title of the current design element, object, or event.
Reference tab	Lists the fields and functions available for the currently selected object. Code can be pasted from the list to the script area or pop-up help. Reference tab is language sensitive and lists help available for the currently selected event. If a formula event is selected, the reference lists all the Database fields, @Functions, and @Commands available. When you select a JavaScript event the Document Object Model is listed. Likewise, when LotusScript is selected, the Reference tab displays the Domino classes. Code can be pasted from the list or Designer help can be opened.
Script area	Area where script (LotusScript or JavaScript), command language, and formula language are written for the current object selected. When you select a JavaScript event you are given the choice to code for the Web client or the Notes client. Certain events can be coded to both clients, and you can do this by choosing Common Javascript.
Errors box	Displays errors generated during the compile when working with LotusScript.

Figure 3.1 displays the Lotus Domino Designer and the various design elements contained within it.

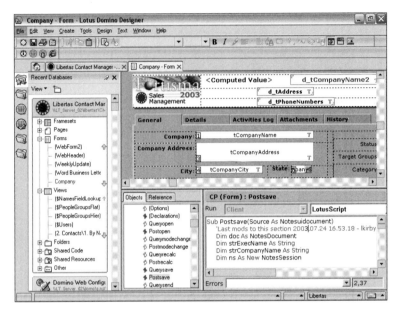

Figure 3.1   Domino Designer R6 interface.

Forms and Documents

Typically, users use Notes forms to create, open, and modify documents. (Documents can exist, however, without forms to display them.) The *form* is the physical template providing the structure and formatting of the document to be displayed to the user. For example, the form might contain the document layout, field layout, text, images, background color, and so forth. Regardless of whether the user is a Web client or Notes client, Domino uses the Access Control List (ACL) to determine whether the user has rights to create, read, modify, or delete documents.

Four types of data can be stored in documents:

➤ Text

➤ Numbers

➤ Dates/times

➤ Rich text (graphics, tables, sections, objects, and so forth)

Troubleshooting Database Access

If users are having problems accessing the Domino database(s), consider investigating the following potential causes of failure:

➤ The target server is down, and no clustered servers are available to serve as failover servers. Consider setting up Advanced server options such as clustering and failover.

➤ Users have insufficient access to perform the requested operation. Investigate the database Access Control List to ensure that users have been set up with sufficient database access.

➤ The Database file is being used through the operating system, possibly by a third-party backup system, so that access is locked. Ensure that the database file is not currently being backed up, or that the previous backup has not failed and the backup process has locked the file from being used. Also ensure that the operating system user rights have not been modified to restrict access to the file or file directory.

➤ The full-text index frequency is set to immediate, and the server is continually updating the database full-text index. Consider modifying the full-text index update to update less frequently.

➤ Users are assigned to more than one access level. Table 3.2 refers to some common user access conflicts that occur when users are assigned to more than one access level and their respective resolutions.

Table 3.2 User Access Conflicts	
Conflict	**Explanation**
The user is listed individually and as a member of a group.	The access granted to the explicitly listed username takes precedence over the access granted in the group, even if the group access is higher.
The user is included in two or more groups.	The user is granted access of the group with the highest access.
The user appears in the ACL as well as in specific design element access lists.	The specific design access refines the database access.

Understanding Domino Application Architecture

Domino databases are containers for the applications. The database design elements and actual data are both stored within the Domino databases.

The Domino database is an object store, containing various types of Notes documents. These Notes documents comprise design elements, design logic contained in designer code, Access Control List information, as well as the actual data entered and used by the application users. Table 3.3 describes the major components of a Domino database.

Each database is an actual file with an .nsf extension. The .nsf represents Notes Storage Facility.

Table 3.3 Components of a Domino Database	
Component	**Function**
Access Control List (ACL)	Defines the users of the database and their respective rights within each database.
Design elements	The building blocks of an application, such as frames, forms, views, images, cascading style sheet, and so on.
Logic design	Logic is added through the use of elements to calculate, modify, and access values as well as automate tasks and functions.
Data	The information within the application. Users use design elements to read, create, modify, and delete data.

The types of Domino applications that can be created enable users to share, collect, track, and organize information.

The differential for defining Web applications versus Notes client/server applications lies within the database. The specific database properties, which specify how design elements are used and how they are presented to the user, are dependant on the client type and how the Domino server treats the contents of the database. Specifically, if the database client making a request to the server is doing so with a Lotus Notes client, the server uses the native, proprietary .nsf format (using the Domino Remote Procedure Call [RPC]) to serve the information. However, if the client is making the request with a Web client (HTTP), the Domino server (running the HTTP server task) converts the information to HTML and serves the contents to the Web client. Specifically, Lotus Notes and Domino attempts to convert the Notes Document Object Model (DOM) and the Domino Remote Procedure Call (RPC) to the stateless Web environment by using Sun Microsystems Java and JavaScrip to translate native Lotus Domino design elements to browser (HTTP) design elements.

When creating applications that are to be accessed by Web (HTTP) clients as well as native Notes clients, various features need to be addressed—not only in the design elements used within the application, but in the server settings, database properties, form properties, view properties, and other settings for individual design elements.

Typically, applications residing on the Domino server are accessed by Notes clients, Web clients, or both. The Domino server performs the following tasks:

➤ Interprets client requests

➤ Executes requests within the Domino application (based on the access rights of the user making the requests)

➤ Serves HTML results from HTTP user requests

The Notes client was designed specifically for Domino applications. Therefore, when using Notes clients, users can

➤ Use menu options and shortcuts

➤ Run applications locally and work offline

Web browsers access the Domino applications on Domino servers (HTTP Web servers) that are running the HTTP task. When the HTTP task is loaded, the Domino server provides the HTML interface to the Domino applications for Web clients.

Prior to adding text to a page or form, or after text has been added to a page or form, you can modify the properties through the Text properties box. Because the text directly affects the appearance of the application, it is important to understand the properties that can be modified, which are the following:

➤ Text appearance (font type, text size, text, and color)

➤ Paragraph alignment, spacing, and list types

➤ Margins, tabs, tab stops, and pagination

➤ Paragraph borders (styles, effects, and thickness)

➤ Hide-when settings (for client type or document state, or based on formula)

➤ Styles

When a design element is selected in the Design list, all the existing design elements specific to the selected design element are displayed in the Work pane. To open a specific design element, double-click on the element or highlight the design element (single-click on the design element) and press Enter.

Because Domino Designer is its own executable application, you can start it directly without first opening the Notes client (by launching `designer.exe`). However, you can still launch the Domino Designer from within the Notes client by either clicking on the Designer icon or by selecting View, Design from the drop-down menu to open a database in the Designer.

The Domino Designer provides an interface to enable you to create and modify design elements contained within the Domino database. Design elements are the building blocks for applications and are used to create applications. Creating, modifying, and troubleshooting design elements is covered in more detail in Chapter 4, "Design Elements." The functions used within Domino and the design elements used in their implementation are listed in Table 3.4.

Table 3.4 Design Element Functionality	
Design Element	**Application Task/Functionality**
Framesets	Collections of frames in which you can add structure to your application. A frame is a section, or pane, contained within a frameset window, which is independently scrollable.
Pages	Display and organize information. Contain text, images, applets, and other objects. Information cannot be entered in pages.
Forms	Contain fields where users enter values. These values are stored in Notes Documents.
Views	Contain index and display lists of the documents contained within the database.
Folders	Containers that store documents. Using the same design as views, folders remain empty until users or programs add documents to the folder.
Agents	Programs that perform a series of automated tasks based upon a schedule, event, or a user's request.
Outlines	A skeleton of an application containing outline entries representing individual elements within the application.

Table 3.4 Design Element Functionality *(continued)*	
Design Element	**Application Task/Functionality**
Subforms	A collection of fields, graphics, buttons, and actions you plan to use in more than one form.
Fields	The part of an application that collects data. Shared fields can be defined for use on one or more forms.
Actions	Perform tasks when triggered, allowing automation of tasks found in the Notes menu, defined by formulas, or defined by a LotusScript program.
Script Libraries	A place for storing code that can be shared in the current application through the use of LotusScript, JavaScript, and Java. Code can also be stored for other applications through the use of JavaScript and Java.
Images	Image resources that can be used throughout the application.
Files	Allows sharing of non-NSF files within the current database and across different databases.
Applets	Stores applet resources of related java files.
Style Sheets	Cascading Style Sheets that provide the capability to control page layout, headers, links, text, fonts, styles, color, margins, etc.
Data Connections	Design elements that enable you to establish a data exchange between a Domino application and an external data source.
Database Resources	The database icon, the Using Database document, the About Database document, and database scripts.
Navigators	Graphical road maps (similar to image maps) that direct users to specific parts of an application or database, or allow users to take actions without having to open a view.

For the exam, be sure to know all the design elements available in Domino 6 and the definition of each element.

You can insert certain design elements into the design of either forms or pages. These elements are referred to as *embedded elements*. Table 3.5 outlines the design elements that can be embedded into forms or pages, provides a brief description of the design elements, and indicates which client type can use this embedded design element (either the native Notes client or Web clients).

Table 3.5   Embedded Elements

Element Type	Description	Client Type
Outline	Displays navigation control linking to other design elements (pages, forms, views, and so on.)	Notes/Web
View	Displays view objects.	Notes/Web
Navigator	Displays navigator objects.	Notes/Web
Date Picker	Displays calendar view of the months.	Notes
Scheduler	Displays the Group Scheduling Control, which schedules multiple people at the same time.	Notes
Editor	Enables you to embed one or more forms into an existing form or embed an editor to link to an embedded view.	Notes/Web
Folder Pane	Displays folder objects.	Notes/Web
File Upload Control	Displays the file upload to enable users to insert attachments.	Web

With Domino R6, you can now embed elements from databases other than the current database. Cross-database referencing enables you to select an alternate database (using the database name) from a list of local databases. This does not apply to Date Picker, Scheduler, Folder Pane, or the File Upload Control.

With Domino R6, you can now embed multiple views on a page, form, or subform for either Web clients or Notes clients. Other features now available when using embedded views with Domino R6 are

➤ The capability of deleting marked documents in an embedded view

➤ Capability to show the action bar

➤ Feature to use a transparent background on the design element so that any image or color defined behind the embedded view will be displayed (for example, the form background image or color)

Other design features supported by both Web clients and Notes clients are

➤ Horizontal rules

➤ Computed text

➤ Buttons

➤ Action Bar buttons

➤ Hot spots

When using buttons on forms intended for Web clients, keep in mind that the user's browser must support JavaScript. To display multiple buttons, the Web Access: Use JavaScript When Generating Pages database property must be enabled. If this setting has not been enabled, Domino does one of two things:

1. Domino recognizes only the first button on the document and automatically converts it into a Submit button.

2. If there is not a button on the form, Domino automatically creates a Submit button.

Often, neither provides the desired result because this button will be displayed on the page enabling users to save the document. Consequently, it is important to enable this setting. Of course, remember to create your own Submit button if it is required. Also keep in mind when creating buttons that not all commands and formula actions are supported on the Web. Similarly, some commands and formula actions are supported only on the Web.

After the hotspot has been created, you can modify its properties to

➤ Specify the target frame for the hotspot link

➤ Specify the image map tab order for the hotspot

➤ Enter alternate text for the hotspot

Executing Requests from the Notes Client

There are several advantages/disadvantages to accessing the Domino server with a Notes client rather than using a Web (HTTP) client. When using a native Notes client, some of the advantages are that you have access to menu options and shortcuts specific to the Domino application. In addition, you can run the application locally (offline) without being connected to a Domino server.

Another useful feature available to Notes clients that is not available to Web clients is the use of layout regions. Layout regions can be inserted into forms and are typically used within custom dialog boxes. They are composed of a 32-bit image that can contain fields, images, buttons, and text, which you can position anywhere within the layout region by using absolute positioning. However, they cannot contain rich text, file attachments, Java applets, and a select group of other objects.

Using Notes-Enabled Features to Troubleshoot Applications

To troubleshoot your application that is to be used by Notes clients, preview the design changes directly when editing the application design by following these steps:

1. Open the design element you want to preview from the Notes Designer.

2. Using the pull-down menu, select Design, Preview in Notes, or click on the Notes preview button.

3. Choose File, Close to close the preview window.

Using Images in Applications

An *image resource* is a shared graphics file that can now be stored in its native image type (JPEG or GIF).

Inserting Images into Forms or Pages

To insert an image resource into a form or page, follow these steps:

1. Open the form or page in the Notes Designer.

2. Position the cursor in the desired location on the image.

3. Select Create, Image Resource from the pull-down menu.

4. Select the image type to display (GIF Images, JPEG Images, or All Images).

5. Select the database that contains the image resource by selecting a database name from the drop-down menu or by clicking the folder icon to select a database from an alternate server.

6. Select the image name to insert.

7. Click OK.

Alternatively, you can also add, delete, and rename image resources from the Insert Image Resource dialog by clicking on the New, Delete, or Rename buttons located below the Image Resource Selection fields.

Importing Graphics and Supported Image Types

Graphics can be incorporated by any of the following means:

➤ Copy and paste a graphic from the Clipboard.

➤ Use the pull-down menu to create a picture.

➤ Use the pull-down menu to import a graphic file.

➤ Use the pull-down menu to create an image resource.

➤ Use the pull-down menu to insert a shared image from the shared resources.

When importing images into a page or form, the image types supported are

➤ BMP

➤ CMG

➤ GIF

➤ JPEG

➤ Lotus PIC

➤ PCX Image

➤ TIFF 5.0 Image

When designing applications for the Web, use GIFs or JPEGs because they are supported on the Web. Otherwise, other image types are converted on the fly by the Domino server.

Modifying Picture Properties

After an image resource has been inserted, the picture properties can be modified for each resource on a series of tabs, described as follows:

➤ Basic picture information, such as image source name, text wrap settings, scaling, alternate text, caption, and hotspot settings (see Figure 3.2)

➤ Border settings

➤ Alignment, indentation, list, and spacing settings

➤ Margins, tab stops, and pagination settings

➤ Hide-when attributes

➤ Paragraph styles

➤ HTML properties, such as HTML item name and HTML tag settings

Figure 3.2   The Information tab of the Picture properties.

Creating Pictures

To create a picture, follow these steps:

1. Open the page or form in which you want to insert the picture.

2. Place the cursor in the location where you want to place the picture.

3. Select Create, Picture from the drop-down menu.

4. Select the file type to display from the options in the dialog box.

5. Select the file or type the filename you want to insert.

6. Click Import.

Working with Image Maps

An *image map* is a graphic on which designers can place programmable hot spots.

NOTE   A hot spot is a programmed area, either text or a picture, where users can click to execute a programmed action, run a formula, execute LotusScript, execute JavaScript, or open a link.

To create an image map, you can either paste a previously copied image onto the operating system Clipboard or import an existing image file. The image map can be any file format other than .PIC and will be stored and displayed in its native file format.

To create an image map, follow these steps:

1. Create a page or form (or open an existing page or form).

2. Add a graphical image to the page by selecting Create, Image Resource from the pull-down menu.

3. Select the image to be used as the image map.

4. Add selectable hot spots by selecting Picture, Add Hot spot Rectangle from the pull-down menu. You can alternatively select to add a hot spot circle, polygon, or default hot spot (which selects the entire graphic image).

Using Tables to Manage Page Layout

Tables allow for summarization of information, to simplify display and modification of data using a consistent table format. In addition, with tables you can align text and graphics in rows and columns and position elements on pages or forms. To create a new table, select Create, Table from the pull-down menu. Then select the number of rows and columns, the table width, and table type.

The types of tables that can be created are displayed in Table 3.6.

Table 3.6 Table Types	
Table Type	**Description**
Basic	Displays a basic table displaying the number of rows and columns specified.
Tabbed	Allows for separate types of information on separate tabs. Each tab corresponds to a row in a typical tab layout. This feature is available to both Notes clients and Web clients.
Animated	Cycles separate lines of text and/or graphics to display in sequence, using the timing interval and transition effect specified. Each line of text can display a different format. This feature is not supported on the Web.
Caption	Displays each row as a clickable caption.

Table 3.6 Table Types *(continued)*	
Table Type	Description
Programmed	Displays a different row based upon a field value located within the form named after the table. For example, if the name of the table is TableProfile, then the name of the field would be **$TableProfile**. This feature is available to both Notes clients and Web clients. When being used on the Web, the **$TableProfile** field property must be set to Refresh Choices on Keyword Change. The database property to Use JavaScript when Generating Pages must also be selected.

Modifying Table Properties

After it is created, you can further modify the table properties by selecting Table, Table Properties from the pull-down menu.

A table can have a combination of fixed-size and auto-sized columns. (Auto-sized columns adjust to the width specified by the fixed-width columns.) The space between row and column borders can be increased and decreased from the Table Layout tab of the table properties. Any changes made to the row and column spacing applies to all the rows and columns in a table. The minimum height field also applies to an entire table.

Tables can also be recursive (or nested)—that is, a table can be nested within an existing table. The nesting limit is eight tables deep. This feature is available to both Notes clients and Web clients.

After a table has been added to the page or form, the Table Properties box allows for considerably more customization than in previous versions on Notes. Some of the features available with tables include the following:

➤ You can auto-size a column based on the content of the column.

➤ Tabs can be positioned on all sides of the table (top, bottom, right, or left).

➤ You can set equal sizes for each of the tabs.

➤ Tables with collapsible sections can use row captions (which look like the Maximize and Minimize buttons for Windows) by selecting the Users Pick Row via Caption option in the Table properties box.

Text can be set to wrap across cells horizontally—that is, after the vertical size of the cell is filled, the text begins filling the cell located horizontally next to the original cell. To wrap text across cells, open the Table Margins properties box. In the Table Wrap section, select Inside Table Wrap Text Between Cells. Then adjust the At Height field to specify how much the cell should be filled in before the text wraps to the next cell. After the cells are filled, the remaining text is collected in the last cell.

Modifying Tables for Use in Both Notes and Web Clients

Tables are a very useful feature when you are developing applications, and their functionality has been dramatically improved. Tables can include fields, graphics, subforms, hot spots, objects, sections, file attachments, Java applets, embedded design elements, and nested tables.

When you are using tables on the Web, cells that contain no information are suppressed (hidden) when they are displayed to Web clients. To avoid this, you can insert blank, transparent GIFs into the empty table cells so that they are not suppressed. A more efficient way to prevent table suppression is to place a blank space within the table cell (using   as HTML).

The following list includes some other considerations to keep in mind when you have tables intended for both Web and Notes clients:

➤ For Notes clients, you can specify border attributes for each cell. For Web clients, all the table cells are either visible or hidden. The attributes of the top left cell determine the border attributes for the entire table.

➤ Gradient cell background colors are not supported on the Web.

➤ Table drop shadows are not supported on the Web.

➤ Margin settings are not supported on the Web.

➤ Some collapsible features are not supported on the Web, such as animated tables using the Switch Row Every _ Millisecond feature.

Using the Designer Bookmarks to Organize Projects

Bookmarks enable designers to create links to Notes elements, Internet sites, programs, or files on the user's file system. In addition, you can use bookmarks to create folders and organize projects. To create a bookmark, you can drag-and-drop a document link, window tab, file, or folder to the bookmark bar.

To create a design element folder, follow these steps:

1. Click a folder on the bookmark bar to open the folder. Click the Create Folder button.

2. Type in the folder name in the Folder Name field.

3. Select the location for the new folder.

By default, the folder is placed at the end of the database design element list.

A new feature available with Notes 6 is the addition of a Startup folder and a History folder. Items contained in the Startup folder start automatically when the Notes client is launched. The History folder shows you all the documents, views, databases, or Web pages that have been opened in the client.

Working with Local Applications

Each major release of Domino has included significant modifications to the Notes and Domino architecture and database structure. The Domino 6 Server and Notes 6 client use a different *On Disk Structure* (ODS) than R5 (and all previous releases). The current ODS of Notes and Domino 6 is version 43.

The ODS of a database does not replicate and has no effect on which client version can access a server version. The ODS only determines how the server or client writes data to the physical drive. Therefore, even if the Notes clients are using releases prior to Notes 6 and Domino 6, they can still access the databases on the Domino 6 server (which is using an updated ODS). The user can safely replicate the local database to the database on the server. Even though design elements do replicate, the ODS does not. However, new design elements are still not supported on the older client.

 To upgrade the ODS of the local database, simply compact the database.

To revert an upgraded copy back to an earlier design (for example, to revert a Notes 6 database back to a Notes 5 database), you can make a copy of the database, using an .ns5 extension, use the compact tool on the administrator client, and select the feature to Keep or Revert Database Back to R5 Format, or use the server console command `load compact path/database -r`.

 Simply changing the extension of the Domino database to **.ns5** does not modify the ODS of the database. You must use one of the methods previously described, such as compacting the database or making a new copy.

Summary

When designing applications for Notes clients, the designer's ability to troubleshoot performance problems, access problems, or other application design problems is often tested. Applications may perform adequately and efficiently when first deployed, but suffer from problems as they grow in size and usage. Understanding common database application architecture is a necessary skill for any Domino developer. More to the point, understanding how to create, modify, and troubleshoot for Notes clients is essential for passing the exam. Furthermore, when you understand the Domino application architecture, you are well positioned to understand the remainder of the information required to pass the exam. You can expect to see questions covering some of the specific design capabilities detailed in this chapter, such as the use of images, tables, and bookmarks.

Exam Prep Practice Questions

Question 1

Which folder contains a historical list of databases recently used by the designer?

❏ A. Bookmarks

❏ B. Favorites

❏ C. Recent

❏ D. History

Answer D is correct. A new feature with Notes/Domino 6 is the History folder. This folder shows you all the documents, views, databases, or Web pages that have been opened in the Notes Client. Answer A is incorrect because although bookmarks provide easy access to applications and databases, they are not historically listed. Answer B is incorrect because the favorites folder is not historically listed, either. Answer C is incorrect because there is no Recent folder.

Question 2

"Contains the list of the design elements and resources for the database. The bookmark icon contains a list of the most recently opened databases" is the definition of what?

❏ A. Design pane

❏ B. Info list

❏ C. Work pane

❏ D. Reference tab

Answer A is correct. Answer B is incorrect because the Info list is a scrollable window that displays the objects and coding reference information for the design element currently displayed in the work area. Answer C is incorrect because the Work pane is a WYSIWYG ("what you see is what you get") environment for creating and modifying forms, pages, views, and other design elements specific to an application or database. Answer D is incorrect because the Reference tab lists the fields and functions available for the currently selected object.

Question 3

Which of the design elements cannot be embedded into forms or pages?

- ❏ A. View
- ❏ B. Navigator
- ❏ C. Folder page
- ❏ D. Page

Answer D is correct. A page element cannot be embedded on a form. Answers A, B, and C are incorrect because a view, navigator, and folder pane can all be embedded within a form.

Question 4

What version of the ODS does Notes 6 and Domino 6 use?

- ❏ A. 17
- ❏ B. 20
- ❏ C. 41
- ❏ D. 43

Answer D is correct. Notes 6 and Domino 6 use ODS version 43. Answers A, B, and C are incorrect because Notes R3.x uses ODS 17, Notes/Domino R4.x uses ODS 20, and Notes/Domino R5.x uses ODS 41.

Question 5

Which of the following is not a table type you can use when creating a new table?

- ❏ A. Basic
- ❏ B. Animated
- ❏ C. Caption
- ❏ D. Programmed
- ❏ E. None of the above

Answer E is correct. All the options listed (A, B, C, and D) are available when you create a new table. In addition, a fifth available option is to use the Tabbed table type option.

Question 6

Which design feature is supported by both Web clients and Notes clients?

- ❏ A. Horizontal rules
- ❏ B. Computed text
- ❏ C. Action Bar buttons
- ❏ D. Hot spots
- ❏ E. None of the above

Answer E is correct because all the design features listed in questions A, B, C, and D can be used for both Web clients and Notes clients.

Question 7

Which of the following methods is not an acceptable way to revert a Notes 6 database back to a Notes 5 database?

- ❏ A. Make a copy of the database, using an .ns5 extension on the new database
- ❏ B. Use the Compact tool on the administrator client, and select the feature to Keep or Revert Database Back to R5 Format
- ❏ C. Change the extension of the database to **.ns5** from the file level (for example, using Windows Explorer)
- ❏ D. Use the server console command **load compact path/database –r**

Answer C is correct. You cannot simply modify the extension of the filename from the operating system. Answers A, B, and D are all incorrect because they all successfully revert the ODS of the Domino 6 database (ODS 43) to the R5 format (ODS 41).

Need to Know More?

IBM International Technical Support Organization. *Domino Designer 6: A Developer's Handbook*. Available in printed form, PDF format, and HTML format from `publib-b.boulder.ibm.com/Redbooks.nsf/RedbookAbstracts/sg246854.html?Open`.

IBM Lotus, "Release Notes."

IBM Lotus, Online Help Databases: `help6_admin.nsf`, `help6_client.nsf`, `help6_designer.nsf`

Design Elements

Terms you'll need to understand:

✓ Actions
✓ Agents
✓ Columns
✓ Fields
✓ Folders
✓ Forms
✓ Hotspots
✓ Layers
✓ Links

✓ Navigators
✓ Pages
✓ Sections
✓ Views
✓ View icons
✓ Document hierarchy
✓ Data Types
✓ Shared Resources

Techniques you'll need to master:

✓ Recognizing design elements as the fundamental building blocks of Domino applications.
✓ Using Layers as a design tool in Domino 6.
✓ Understanding enhancements to design
  elements such as forms, views, subforms,
  folders, and navigators.
✓ Differences in form versus page functions
  (forms collect and/or display data; pages
  only display data).

✓ What the new design elements are and
  how they each work.
✓ What views do and how you can use them
  to display documents.
✓ Distinctions between the different types of
  links.

Domino design elements are the basic building blocks used to develop Domino applications. These powerful, flexible tools enable you to create sophisticated, robust applications with speed and ease.

This chapter covers all the major design elements, such as forms, subforms, views, and agents, and what you'll need to know if asked about them on the test. This is a lengthy chapter and there is a lot to learn, but after you have mastered this material, you should be well on your way to passing the test.

The Domino Designer Integrated Development Environment (IDE)

In Notes 6, applications are built with the Domino Designer, a full-featured Integrated Development Environment (IDE) with excellent functionality. There are numerous ways to open a Notes database in the Designer; the following list outlines the quickest and easiest technique:

1. Select the database to open.

2. Right-click the database icon, which presents a pop-up menu.

3. Select Open in Designer, which launches the Designer IDE. Figure 4.1 shows an open database in the Domino Designer.

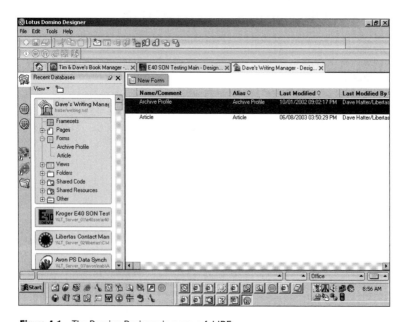

Figure 4.1 The Domino Designer is a powerful IDE.

Each of the elements specified in Figure 4.1 is briefly explained as follows:

➤ The Design pane is always open in the Designer and presents you with a list of all the design elements available in a Notes database. Simply click any design element and a list of any/all of those types of design elements is displayed in the Work pane.

➤ The Work pane is used to display the list of design elements of a particular type. When one element is opened (double-click on it), the Work pane becomes the work area in which you create and modify design elements.

When a design element is created, or opened for modification, the Programmer's pane is displayed in a new window beneath the Work pane. The Programmer's pane is used to add programming logic to design elements and is broken down into three distinct areas: the Script area, the Object tab, and the Reference tab. In the Script area you can write code in any of the supported languages (LotusScript, Java, JavaScript, or the formula language). For example, you can use the formula language to enter a view selection formula or write an agent in LotusScript. The Objects tab lists the objects and events that can be scripted in the current design element. The Reference tab is a handy resource that serves as a context-sensitive resource for coding options

Domino 6 Design Elements

After you have opened a database in the Designer, you can begin to work with the design elements it contains. Table 4.1 summarizes the design elements available in Domino 6.

Table 4.1 Common Design Elements and Their Uses	
Elements	**Typical use**
Agents, actions, applets, script libraries	Automate tasks and manipulate information.
Pages, forms, applets, subforms, shared fields, views, and folders	Collect, organize, manipulate, and display data.
Framesets, applets, navigators, outlines, image maps, hotspots, and buttons	Provide application navigation.
Images, navigators, image maps	Enhance aesthetics.
Files, style sheets, data connections	Extend applications.

Remaining sections of this chapter discuss how to create, use, and troubleshoot these elements.

Creating, Modifying, and Troubleshooting Actions

An *action* is a programmable button that can be used to automate tasks. Actions normally appear in the Action bar, which can be displayed in forms, subforms, pages, folders, and views. Additionally, actions may be displayed in the Actions menu in the Notes client. Actions can be shared, enabling you to use an action in multiple forms, pages, views, and so on. Actions are most often used in the following situations:

> ➤ When you want to automate a function, but don't want the code stored with each individual design element.

> ➤ When Web clients need substitutes for Notes client menu choices (through the Action bar).

> ➤ When users need to see all the possible choices in a nonscrolling row at the top of a form or page or view. When buttons are placed in a form or page, they scroll with the form.

> ➤ When the function the action performs isn't limited to a particular section of a form or page.

> ➤ When you want to share an automated function between several design elements, making the maintenance of the application easier.

There are two basic types of actions: single use and shared. A single use action can be used only in the form, view, folder, or page where it is created. A shared action is stored as a database resource and can be used across multiple forms, subforms, views, folders and pages. Shared actions are covered in Chapter 9, "Design Elements."

Action Coding Choices

When you create an Action, you have several coding choices, depending upon which environment (Web or Notes client) the Action will be used. Additionally, you may elect to use one of the predefined System actions Lotus has included.

You can use any of the following choices to program actions that will be used in Notes client applications:

➤ Simple actions

➤ Formulas

➤ JavaScript

➤ Common JavaScript (shared library).

NOTE

Common JavaScript is new to Domino 6 and can be used to write JavaScript code that can be used in certain limited events for both Notes client and Web applications.

➤ LotusScript

You can use JavaScript or Common Javascript (shared library) to program actions that will be used in Web client applications.

System Actions

Domino provides a set of predefined actions, known as *system actions*, that automate some of the most basic and common Notes features. The system actions are included in the following list:

➤ *Categorize*—Add values to the Categories field in the current document.

➤ *Edit Document*—Edit the current document.

➤ *Forward*—Copy the current document to a new email memo.

➤ *Move to Folder*—Move the current document to a specified folder.

➤ *Remove from Folder*—Remove the current document from a specified folder.

➤ *Send Document*—Send the current document via email.

NOTE

System actions that use system commands do not work on the Web. Instead, create custom actions to replicate their functionality.

Single-Use Actions

Follow these steps to create a single-use action that can only be used in the design element that hosts it:

1. In the Notes Designer client, open the form or view.

2. Choose Create, Action, Action, which launches the Action properties box and displays the Info tab, shown in Figure 4.2.

3. Enter a name for the action.

4. Optionally, enter a label. This is a new feature in Domino 6; it enables you to enter a formula that will compute a value to display for the Action's label. If a label is not supplied, the name will be used for the label.

5. If you plan to display the action within a specific frame, select the target frame.

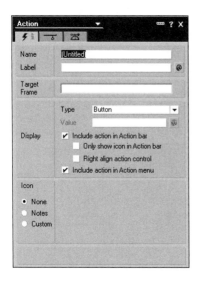

Figure 4.2   The Action properties box enables you to define how your action will display.

6. Select the display parameters of the action, which are defined in the following list:

   ➤ Select the position in which the action should appear in the Action bar or the Actions menu.

   ➤ If you want the action to appear in the Action bar, click Include Action in the Action Bar check box. You then have two additional options. Only Show Icon in Action Bar determines whether the text caption (label) appears with the icon;Right Align Action control determines whether the action appears right-aligned or not.

➤ Determine whether the action should appear in the Actions menu.

7. If you are displaying the action as a button on the Action bar, you can select a graphic icon to display in the button. If you want to use an image resource, determine whether it is to be Notes, which uses the palette of available icons that come with Notes, or Custom, which enables you to select any image that you supply.

8. Optionally, Click the Action Hide When tab (it looks like a window shade) if you want to hide the action under certain conditions.

9. Select the appropriate choices, which are fairly self-explanatory. If the action should be hidden under certain conditions, check the Hide Action if Formula Is True check box and enter a formula that evaluates to true when the hide-when conditions are met.

10. Optionally, define Publishing settings for the action in the Advanced tab.

11. Close the Action properties box.

12. In the Objects tab of the Programmer's pane, select the action you just created.

13. Expand the Run pull-down list and select the environment in which the action will run: Client or Web.

14. Choose a coding choice appropriate for the selected environment and enter code.

15. Save the design element that contains the action.

16. Test the action to ensure that it works properly.

Modifying Single-Use Actions

To modify a single-use action, follow these steps:

1. In the Notes Designer client, open the design element that contains the action.

2. Choose View, Action pane (which opens the Action pane), or select the border between the window in which the view or form is displayed and the Action pane and drag it to the desired position.

3. Double-click the action to open the Action properties box, shown previously in Figure 4.2.

4. Edit the action, following the steps listed in the section "Single-Use Actions."

Troubleshooting Single-Use Action Hide-Whens and Programming

Problems with single-use Actions usually fall into one of two categories: actions that are either hidden or visible at inappropriate times, and programming problems.

Follow these steps when troubleshooting action hide-whens:

1. In the Notes Designer client, open the design element that contains the action.

2. Choose View, Action pane (which opens the Action pane), or select the border between the window in which the view or form is displayed and the Action pane and drag it to the desired position.

3. Double-click the action to open the Action properties box, shown previously in Figure 4.2.

4. Click the Hide When tab.

5. Check the hide-when settings. If a hide-when formula has been used, ensure that the formula returns the value TRUE.

One easy way to test the formula is to create a **Computed for Display** field in a form and paste the formula into it. Then open the form and examine the value in the field. It should contain 1, the formula language value for TRUE.

6. Save the design element.

7. Test the action to ensure that it is hidden or visible at the appropriate times.

Follow these steps when troubleshooting action programming:

1. In the Notes Designer client, open the design element that contains the action.

2. Choose View, Action pane (which opens the Action pane), or select the border between the window in which the view or form is displayed and the Action pane and drag it to the desired position.

3. Click the action to display the action's contents in the Programmer's pane.

4. Begin to debug the action. The type of action determines the most appropriate method of debugging. Table 4.2 lists the best way to debug a particular action based on its code.

Table 4.2 contains some common action debugging methods.

Table 4.2 Action Debugging Methods	
Type	Method
Formula	Use the **@Prompt** function in the code to display key variables and field values and to show the progress and flow of the code.
LotusScript	Use the LotusScript debugger (File, Tools, Debug LotusScript) instead of or in conjunction with the **MsgBox** function to display key variables and field values and to show the progress and flow of the code. Additionally, users can use the **NotesLog** class to record a script's actions. This can be especially useful for debugging agents run by a Web client.
JavaScript/CommonJavaScript	Use the **alert()** function in the code to display key variables and field values and to show the progress and flow of the code.

5. Save the form or view.

6. Test the action to make sure the expected results are displayed.

7. Repeat steps 4–6 until the action works as expected.

Creating, Modifying, and Troubleshooting Agents

An *agent* is a self-contained program that can perform tasks on one or more databases. Some examples of the power and flexibility that agents provide include the following:

➤ Agents can run in any Domino environment: on a specific server, on several servers, on workstations, or when launched by Web clients accessing a Domino server.

➤ Agents can be programmed through the use of simple actions, formulas, LotusScript, or Java, enabling you to select the best language for a particular task.

➤ Agents are not tied to a specified design element, so that you can write modular, reusable code.

➤ A user can explicitly call agents from the menu, an action, a hot spot, or a URL.

➤ Agents can be scheduled to run automatically or when a specific event occurs.

➤ Agents can run other agents.

➤ Agents are easily distributed and maintained through replication.

➤ The capability to run an agent depends on several factors, including a user or server's access level in the database, the agent permissions defined in the Security tab of the server document, and whether the agent runs as the current user or the designer who signed it.

➤ Agents can be run under the authority of the user running it, or the last person or server to sign the agent, or on behalf of another user (new in Domino 6).

 The new security options for running an agent (see previous bulleted list) are likely to show up on the exam.

➤ Agents cannot make modifications to data that the user/server who signed the agent, or is running the agent (depending on how the agent has been configured), is not allowed to make.

➤ Agents can be configured to log their actions and errors to text files, agent logs, mail memos, or Notes databases, making it easy to ensure that they run properly.

Creating Agents

Table 4.3 contains the various options you can specify for the On Event trigger of an agent.

Table 4.3 On Event Trigger Options	
Option	**Description**
Action Menu Selection	Use this setting for user-activated agents or when running agents on the Web using **WebQuerySave** or **WebQueryOpen** events.

Table 4.3 On Event Trigger Options *(continued)*	
Option	**Description**
Agent List Selection	Use this setting for agents that are called by actions, buttons, URLs, or other agents, because agents with this setting do not appear in the Actions menu.
Before New Mail Arrives	Use this setting to process mail documents before they are shown in a mail database.
After New Mail Has Arrived	Use this setting for processing mail after it is shown in the mail database. The following functions (which create user interface "side-effects") cannot be used in agents of this type: ➤ **@DbColumn** ➤ **@DbCommand** ➤ **@DbLookup** ➤ **@MailSend** ➤ **@Prompt** ➤ **@Command** ➤ **@PostedCommand**
After documents have been created or modified	Use this setting for agents in which documents that are new or modified since the last run of the agent should be processed.
When documents are pasted	Use this setting for agents in which documents that have been pasted into the database should be processed. Keep in mind that **@Command** or **@PostedCommand** functions cannot be used in these agents.

The On Schedule trigger option enables you to specify the frequency with which an agent should run, as well as the schedule.

The On Schedule Trigger option offers a number of choices for scheduling the agent, as shown in Table 4.4.

Table 4.4 On Schedule Trigger Options	
More Than Once a Day	Use this setting to run the agent on a schedule several times a day. Remember that scheduling frequent runs affects your server's performance. Click the Schedule button to specify the schedule.
Daily	Use this setting to run the agent on a schedule once a day. Click the Schedule button to specify the daily schedule.
Weekly	Use this setting to run the agent on a weekly basis. Click the Schedule button to specify the weekly schedule.

Table 4.4 On Schedule Trigger Options *(continued)*	
Monthly	Use this setting to run the agent on a monthly schedule. Click the Schedule button to specify the weekly schedule.
Never	Use this setting if you want to save an agent but do not want it to run except under special circumstances, such as when it is called by another agent.

When you choose to have the agent triggered by a specific event, you also must choose a value for the *target*, which specifies the documents that it will process. Target options for an agent are defined in Table 4.5.

Table 4.5 Target Options When Trigger Is On Event	
Option	**Description**
All documents in database	The agent builds a collection of and runs against all documents in the database.
All new and modified documents	The agent builds a collection of and runs against all documents that have been created or edited since the agent was last run.
All unread documents in view	The agent builds a collection of and runs against all documents considered unread in the current view.
All documents in view	The agent builds a collection of and runs against all documents in the current view.
All Selected documents	The agent builds a collection of and runs against selected documents in the current view.
None	The agent does not attempt to process a collection of documents. @Commands may be used with Run Once agents. Run Once agents can be called from the Web using the **WebQueryOpen** and **WebQuerySave** events, as well as by direct reference in a URL if you use the **?OpenAgent** command.

When you are creating agents for use on the Web, remember that the following options are not supported:

➤ All unread documents in view

➤ All documents in view

➤ Selected documents

➤ Pasted documents

If your agent is triggered on a specific schedule, you also must choose target options. Target options for scheduled agents are described in Table 4.6.

Table 4.6 Target Options When Trigger Is On Schedule	
Option	Description
All documents in database	The agent builds a collection of and runs against all documents in the database.
All new and modified documents	The agent builds a collection of and runs against all documents that have been created and saved since the agent was last run.

To create an agent, follow these steps:

1. In the Designer, open the database in which you want to create the agent.

2. Click Agents in the Design pane.

3. Choose Create, Design, Agent, or click the New Agent button. Figure 4.3 shows an agent built with Java.

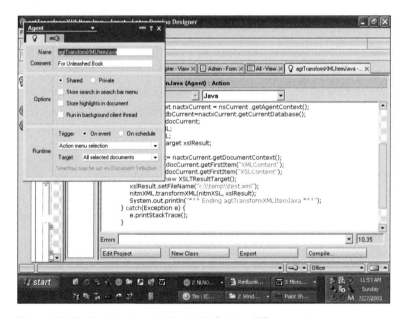

Figure 4.3   The Agent designer interface in the Designer IDE.

4. Enter a name for the agent in the Name field. Optionally enter a comment.

5. If the agent is to be used by multiple users/servers, select Shared Agent. Otherwise, the agent is saved as a personal agent that can be run only by its creator.

An improvement that developers have long clamored for has been added to Domino 6. You can now change an agent from Shared to Personal—or vice versa—after the agent has been saved.

6. Choose a trigger: On Event or On Schedule in the Runtime section. These options are explained as follows:

➤ The On Event trigger list enables you to specify to which event the agent should respond. Choose from the options shown in Table 4.3.

➤ The On Schedule trigger list enables you to specify the frequency and schedule by which an agent should run. Choose from the options shown in Table 4.4. Keep in mind that scheduled agents are not supported on the Web.

➤ For scheduled agents, set the scheduling parameters. You must also select where the agent should run from the Run On list. Remember that selecting a server or server(s) is especially important when agents modify documents in databases that are replicated among multiple servers.

7. Choose a value for Target from the options described in Tables 4.5 or 4.6, depending on the trigger type.

8. If you want to further specify the choice of documents, click Document selection in the Objects tab and add criteria to filter the documents included in the collection against which the agent will run.

9. Choose the type of agent to create from the Run pull-down list in the Programming pane. These options are

➤ *Simple Action(s)*—Select any of a number of simple actions (pre-built applets that can perform very simple tasks).

 Remember that simple actions are not customizable and are not supported in Web applications.

➤ *Formula*—Use the Notes Formula language to code an agent. @Commands may be used with Run Once agents.

➤ *LotusScript*—Use LotusScript (based on Microsoft Visual Basic) to program agents.

➤ *Java*—Code agents using Java.

➤ *Imported Java*—Import Java files into agents.

10. Save the agent.

11. Test the agent. Choose Agents, Test to conduct a test run of the agent and receive feedback from the system.

12. Modify as necessary and save.

Modifying Agents

To modify an agent, follow these steps:

1. In the Design pane, select Agents, which displays all the agents in the database in the View pane.

2. Select the agent you want to modify and double-click it.

3. If necessary, change the options that control when and how the agent is run. These options were described previously in the "Creating Agents" section.

4. Save the agent.

5. Test the agent. Choose Actions, Test to conduct a test run of the agent and receive feedback from the system.

6. Modify as necessary and save.

Troubleshooting Agents

Because agents provide such a wide array of capabilities, it is important to consider a number of things when troubleshooting agents. This section focuses on the most effective tools and techniques for debugging agents. These tools include the following:

➤ *Agent log*—You can access an Agent's Agent Log to determine key information, such as the last time and date the agent was started, how many documents were processed, the type of code run (LotusScript, for example), and the last time and date it completed. To view the Agent Log, select the agent and choose Agent, Log from the menu.

➤ *LotusScript debugger*—You can use the LotusScript debugger to debug agents written in LotusScript. The debugger enables you to track the progress of the agent as well as the value of variables and objects within the scope of the agent. To use the LotusScript debugger, choose File, Tools, Debug LotusScript from the menu and run the agent. Remember that this works only on agents launched from within Notes. Agents launched by a Web browser cannot be debugged by this method.

➤ *LotusScript Remote debugger*—You can use the LotusScript Remote debugger to debug server-side agents written in LotusScript. This is new in Domino 6.

➤ *Perform a test run of the agent*—After you have completed an agent, you can do a simulated run to see whether it performs as expected before running it on production data (with possibly disastrous results!). As part of the test run, security and schedule settings are also checked. To perform a test run, select the agent to test and choose Agents, Test from the Menu. When the agent is complete, the Agent log appears with the results.

➤ *Server console debugging*—The Domino Server console provides three commands: `Tell Amgr Schedule`, `Tell Amgr Status`, and `Tell Amgr Debug`, which display information about scheduling, agent queue status, and the status of agent debugging settings that are in effect.

➤ *NotesLog class*—The NotesLog class is a convenient and powerful option that enables you to track the progress and report errors that occur in agents written with LotusScript or Java.

➤ *Printing debug information as agent runs*—If you are using LotusScript or Java agents, you can write messages in the Notes Log database.

➤ *Using prompts at run time*—If you are using the Formula language, you can use the `@Prompt` command to report on progress and variable values. In LotusScript you can use the `MsgBox` function to achieve the same results.

Creating, Modifying, and Troubleshooting Views

Views are design elements that present a sorted and/or categorized list of documents and serve as the primary way to access data in a Notes database. Keep in mind that every database must have a minimum of one view, known as the *default view*. A view may display all documents in the database, or it may use a selection formula to select a subset of the documents. Each row in a view represents one document in the database and users can double-click that row to open the underlying document. View types are summarized in Table 4.7.

Table 4.7	View Types
Type	**Description**
Shared	Shared views can be used by any user with at least Reader access to the database, unless specifically excluded through a view access list.
Shared, contains documents not in folders	Same properties as a shared view, but displays only documents that are not also listed in a folder or folders.
Shared, contains deleted documents	Same properties as a shared view, but lists only deleted documents. This setting should be used in conjunction with Allow Soft Deletions.
Shared, private on first use	Same properties as a shared view, but becomes private the first time a user opens it.
Shared, desktop private on first use	Same properties as a Shared, Private on First Use view, but on first use is stored in the user's **Desktop6.ndk** file rather than in the database, which conserves space on the server.
Private	Private views are accessible to only those users who create them and, depending on that user's ability to create private folders and views, may be stored either in the database (if user can create private views) or in the user's **Desktop6.ndk** file.

Because views are the primary means of finding documents in a database, it is very important to build views that are both efficient and effective. When designing a new view, you should consider the following questions:

➤ Which documents should be displayed in the view?

➤ What information from the underlying documents should be displayed?

➤ Should the documents be sorted and/or categorized?

➤ Should the view use a response hierarchy to display response and response-to-response documents in a hierarchy?

➤ How should the information be formatted?

Creating Views

To create a view, follow these steps:

1. Click Views in the Design pane to see a list of all the existing views in the database.

2. Choose Create, Design, View from the menu or click the New View button, which opens the Create View dialog box (think of this box as a wizard). The Create View dialog box is shown in Figure 4.4.

3. Enter a name for the view in the View Name field.

4. Choose the view type in the View Type field (refer to Table 4.7).

Figure 4.4   The Create View dialog box works much like a wizard.

6. In the Select a Location for the New View field, select the position in the view hierarchy in which you want the new view to appear. If you want the view to appear at the top level, don't select anything here. Otherwise, select the view under which you want the new view to appear.

7. Optionally, click the Copy Style From button to select an existing view from which to base the new view (just as you would for a template). This saves time if you are creating a view that is similar to an existing view. Otherwise, select Blank to create a new view from scratch.

8. Optionally, enter a view selection formula. If you have copied the view's design from an existing view, the selection formula is copied as well and can be edited to meet your needs. If you started from scratch,

you need to enter a selection formula here. You can use the Fields and Functions button and the Formula Window button to further aid your development of the selection formula.

9. Click OK to generate the new view.

10. Double-click the new view in the Views list to open it.

11. Choose Design, View Properties to open the View properties box (shown in Figure 4.5) to the Info tab, and define the following important properties:

  ➤ Enter an alias for the view in the Alias field.

  ➤ If necessary, change the style of the view from Standard Outline (default Notes view style) to Calendar, if you want to create a calendar view.

Figure 4.5   The Info tab of the View properties box.

12. Click the Options tab, shown in Figure 4.6, to define the following important view options:

  ➤ Click the Default When Database Is First Opened check box if you want the view to always be opened first when the database is opened.

  ➤ Click Default Design for New Folders and Views if you want to use the current view as a template when creating new views.

  ➤ Click Collapse All When Database Is First Opened if you want any/all categories in the view to display collapsed.

  ➤ Click Show Response Documents In a Hierarchy if the view contains response documents, and you want to display them in a hierarchy under the documents to which they are subordinate.

  ➤ Click Show In View Menu if you want the view to be accessible from the View menu in the Notes client.

➤ Click Allow Customizations to allow users with a Notes client to change the appearance of the view. This does not work for Web applications. This feature is new in Domino 6.

➤ Click Evaluate Actions For Every Document Change to have actions associated with the view evaluated every time a document in the view changes. You should note that this feature may have a negative impact on the view performance. This feature is new in Domino 6.

➤ Click Create New Documents At The View Level if you want to allow users to create a new document from the view level. This feature is new in Domino 6.

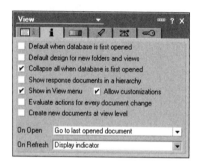

Figure 4.6   The Options tab of the View properties box.

13. Click the Style tab (third tab) to specify properties that define the appearance of the view.

14. Click the Advanced tab (fifth tab) to specify advanced settings such as the index frequency of the view and unread marks.

15. Click the Security tab (sixth tab) to define who can use the view. If you want to make the view available to users who have been granted only Public Access, be sure to click the Available to Public Access Users check box.

16. Add, edit, and delete view columns as necessary. For more information on how to create and modify view columns, please turn to the section titled "Creating, Modifying, and Troubleshooting Columns," later in this chapter.

17. Save the view.

18. Test the view to ensure that it performs as expected.

Modifying Views

To modify a view, follow these steps:

1. In the Designer, open the database that contains the view you want to modify.

2. Click Views in the Design pane to see a list of all the existing views in the database.

3. Double-click the view you want to modify.

4. Make the necessary changes.

5. Save the view.

6. Test the view to ensure that it performs as expected.

Embedded Views

Views can be embedded in forms and/or pages, which enables the developer to exert more control over how users interact with the views. For example, graphics can be used in the form or page along with the view to enhance the display.

To embed a view in a form or page, follow these steps:

1. Open the form or page in which you want to embed a view.

2. Position the cursor on the spot where the view should appear.

3. Select Create, Embedded Element, View from the menu.

4. Select the view from the list or, optionally, click Choose a View Based on a Formula to write a formula to select the view to display. The view can exist in either the current database or a different database.

5. Click OK to embed the view.

After you have embedded the view, you should keep the following things in mind:

➤ Use the Embedded View properties box to change the size of the embedded view. Right-click the embedded view and choose Properties from the menu.

➤ If you want to display the embedded view on the Web, you must decide how to display it. You have three choices: HTML, Java Applet, and based on the view's display property. To provide the most functionality for Web users, select Java Applet, which replicates most of the functionality of a native Notes view, including resizable column headings, expandable columns, dynamic column sorting, and scroll bars within the view applet window.

➤ Embedded views enable you to display only a single view category, meaning that only those documents matching the specified or computed value display. The view must have a categorized column to use this feature.

Displaying Document Hierarchy in a View

There are three basic documents types in Notes: main documents, response documents, and response-to-response documents. Response and response-to-response documents maintain a parent-child relationship to other documents and often it is necessary and desirable to display this relationship when displaying these documents in a view. The parent-child relationship between documents is known as the *document hierarchy*.

For example, in a discussion database, comments are traditionally displayed in a hierarchical fashion. In Domino, this is also known as *indenting response documents*.

It's easy to display the hierarchy of documents in a view, but there are several considerations you must remember.

➤ The database must have response or response-to-response documents in it.

➤ The view must have the Show Response Documents in a Hierarchy option enabled.

➤ The view must have a selection formula that explicitly includes response documents or must select all documents.

➤ The view must have a responses-only column.

Assuming that these criteria are met, creating a view that displays a document hierarchy is easy; just follow these steps:

1. Open an existing view, or create a new view in a database that contains response and/or response-to-response documents.

2. Add a selection formula the selects all documents or explicitly selects response documents.

3. Immediately to the left of the column under which the responses should be indented, add a column to the view and on the Column Info tab of the Column properties box, enable the Show Responses Only option.

4. Enter a column formula that will display information from the response documents.

5. Save and test the view.

 A view should have only one response column.

For more information about working with columns in a view, please see the section titled "Creating, Modifying, and Troubleshooting Columns," in this chapter.

Troubleshooting Views

Table 4.8 provides a list of common view problems and their resolution.

Table 4.8 View Problems	
Problem	**Resolution**
View does not select proper documents.	Check view selection formula.
View does not display response documents.	Ensure that selection formula includes response documents; use @IsResponse.
View does not display response documents.	View set to Display Response Documents in a Hierarchy, but does not contain a Responses Only column.
Documents not properly ordered.	Columns not sorted or not sorted correctly. Check the sorting and categorization options on the Sorting tab of the View Column properties box.
View selects too many documents.	Check view selection formula.
View selects too few documents.	Check view selection formula.
Column appears in design mode but not in user mode.	Check column properties and ensure the column is not set to be hidden
Column does not display icon.	Check column properties and ensure the column is set to display icon.

Table 4.8 View Problems *(continued)*	
Problem	**Resolution**
View does not appear as Java applet in Web client.	Check view properties and ensure that the Use Applet in Browser option is enabled.
Categories appear as Not Categorized.	Underlying documents have fields being categorized that are empty. Use a formula to compute a value for these documents.
Documents appear too many times.	Document contains fields that are categories, or column properties are set to Show Multiple Values as Separate Entries.
View opens in wrong frameset.	Open view properties and check the frameset and frame properties of the view.

Creating, Modifying, and Troubleshooting Folders

Folders are design elements that, much like Views, present a sorted and/or categorized list of documents. There is one important difference, however: Folders do not use a selection formula to determine which documents to display; folders only display documents that are either manually or programmatically added. Each row in a folder represents one document in the database and users can double-click that row to open the underlying document.

Creating Folders

To create a folder, follow these steps:

1. Click Folders in the Design pane to see a list of all the existing folders in the database.

2. Choose Create, Design, Folder from the menu, or click the New Folder button, which opens the Create Folder dialog box (think of this box as a wizard). The Create Folder dialog box is shown in Figure 4.7.

3. Enter a name for the folder in the Folder Name field.

4. Choose the folder type in the Folder Type field. Each option is summarized in Table 4.9.

Table 4.9 Folder Types	
Type	Description
Shared	Shared folders can be used by any user with at least Reader access to the database, unless specifically excluded through a folders access list.
Shared, private on first use	Same properties as a shared folder, but becomes private the first time a user opens it. Folder is saved in the database if the ACL privileges allow private folders; otherwise it is saved locally.
Shared, desktop private on first use	Same properties as a Shared, Private on First Use folder, but on first use is stored in the user's **Desktop6.ndk** file rather than in the database, which conserves space on the server.
Private	Private folders are accessible to only those users who create them and, depending on that user's ability to create folders, may be stored either in the database (if user can create private folders) or in the user's **Desktop6.ndk** file.

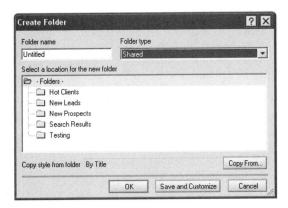

Figure 4.7   The Create Folder dialog box works much like a wizard.

5. In the Select a Location for the New Folder field, select the position in the folder hierarchy in which you want the new folder to appear. If you want the folder to appear at the top level, don't select anything here. Otherwise, select the folder under which you want the new folder to appear.

6. Optionally, click the Copy Style From button to select an existing folder from which to base the new folder (just as in using a template). This saves time if you are creating a folder that is similar to an existing folder. Otherwise, select Blank to create a new folder from scratch.

7. Click OK to generate the new folder.

8. Double-click the new folder in the Folders list to open it.

9. Choose Design, Folder Properties to open the Folder properties box (shown in Figure 4.8) to the Info tab, and define the following important properties:

➤ Optionally, enter an alias for the folder in the Alias field.

➤ Optionally, change the style of the folder from Standard Outline (default Notes folder style) to Calendar, if you want to create a calendar folder.

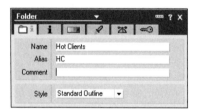

Figure 4.8 The Info tab of the Folder properties box.

10. Click the Options tab to define the following important folder options:

➤ Click the Default When Database Is First Opened check box if you want the folder to always be opened first when the database is opened.

➤ Click Default Design for New Folders and Views if you want to use the current folder as a template when creating new views.

➤ Click Collapse All When Database Is First Opened if you want any/all categories in the folder to display collapsed.

➤ Click Show Response Documents In a Hierarchy if the folder contains response documents, and you want to display them in a hierarchy under the documents to which they are subordinate.

➤ Click Show In View Menu if you want the folder to be accessible from the View menu in the Notes client.

➤ Click Allow Customizations to allow users with a Notes client to change the appearance of the folder. This does not work for Web applications. This feature is new in Domino 6.

➤ Click Evaluate Actions for Every Document Change to have actions associated with the view evaluated every time a document in the view changes. You should note that this feature may have negative impact on the view performance. This feature is new in Domino 6.

➤ Click Create New Documents at the View Level if you want to allow users to create a new document from the view level. This feature is new in Domino 6.

 Don't be surprised to see one or more questions about the many cool new view/folder features like create new documents at the view level, hide-when formulas for view columns, and custom twisties.

11. Click the Style tab (third tab) to specify properties that define the appearance of the folder.

12. Click the Advanced tab (fifth tab) to specify advanced settings such as the index frequency of the folder and unread marks.

13. Click the Security tab (sixth tab) to define who can use the folder. If you want to make the folder available to users who have been granted only Public Access, be sure to click the Available to Public Access Users check box.

14. Add, edit, and delete folder columns as necessary. For more information on how to create and modify columns, please turn to the section titled "Creating, Modifying, and Troubleshooting Columns" later in this chapter.

15. Save the folder.

16. Test the folder to ensure that it performs as expected.

Modifying Folders

To modify a folder, follow these steps:

1. In the Designer, open the database that contains the folder you want to modify.

2. Click Folders in the Design pane to see a list of all the existing folders in the database.

3. Double-click the folder you want to modify.

4. Make the necessary changes.

5. Save the folder.

6. Test the folder to ensure that it performs as expected.

Troubleshooting Folders

Table 4.10 contains a list of common folder problems and their resolution.

Table 4.10 Folder Problems	
Problem	**Resolution**
Documents not properly ordered.	Columns not sorted or not sorted correctly. Check the sorting and categorization options on the Sorting tab of the Folder Column properties box.
Column appears in design mode but not in user mode.	Check column properties and ensure the column is not set to be hidden.
Column does not display icon.	Check column properties and ensure the column is set to display icon.
Categories appear as Not Categorized.	Underlying documents have fields being categorized that are empty. Use a formula to compute a value for these documents.
Documents appear too many times.	Document contains fields that are categories, or column properties are set to Show Multiple Values as Separate Entries.
Folder opens in wrong frameset.	Open folder properties and check the frameset and frame properties of the folder.

Creating, Modifying, and Troubleshooting Columns

In Domino, a *column* is an object in a view that provides the developer a mechanism with which to display one of four possible values: the contents of an item stored in a document, a value computed using a formula, a total, or a category. A view can have a single column or as many as 289 ten-character-wide columns.

Designers also can use columns to provide order in a view, using them to sort and/or categorize documents based on the column value. Categorizing documents is a good way to group related documents. This section examines view columns in detail.

Creating a Column

To create a column in a view, follow these steps:

1. In the Designer client, open the view to which you want to add a column.

2. Choose Create, Insert New Column to place the new column in front of the currently selected column, or choose Create, Append New Column to place it after the currently selected column.

3. Double-click the column header to open the Column properties box, which is shown displaying the Column Info tab in Figure 4.9.

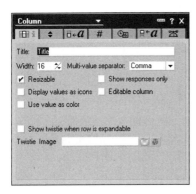

Figure 4.9 The Column Info tab of the Column properties box enables you to define the column's basic functionality.

4. Specify the column title properties in the Column Info tab (the first tab). The Column properties options for the Title tab are as follows:

   ➤ Enter a title for column. Column titles are optional and may be up to 80 characters long.

   ➤ Enter a width, which determines how many characters are to be displayed in the column for each row. If row spanning is enabled for the view, the width you enter determines how many characters are displayed before the column wraps to the next row.

   ➤ Select the multi-value separator, which should be used if the item displayed in the column contains multi-values. You have five choices: None, Space, Comma, Semicolon, or New Line.

   ➤ To allow users to dynamically resize the width of a column, click the Resizable box.

➤ If the view displays only response documents, click Show Responses Only.

➤ If you want to display an icon in the column (from one of the icons available in the Notes view column palette), click Display Values as Icons.

➤ If the column will be used to display categories or response documents, and you want to display a twistie when the column is collapsed, click Show Twistie when Row Is Expandable.

 New to Domino 6 is the capability to define custom images to display in the place of the old faithful triangle twist icon. This might just show up on the test.

5. Specify the column sorting properties in the Sorting tab (tab 2).

The options for the Sorting tab are explained in the following list:

➤ Select the sorted order of the column from the following three choices: None (column is *not* sorted), Ascending, and Descending. If the column is to be categorized, or is the first column in the view that is to be used for lookups, it must be sorted.

➤ Choose the type of column. If you don't want the column to display categories, leave it at the default setting of Standard; otherwise, select Categorized.

➤ Click Case Sensitive Sorting if the case of the items in the column should be considered when sorting. If this option is enabled, lowercase letters are sorted *before* uppercase letters.

➤ Click Accent Sensitive Sorting if the accent of the items in the column should be considered when sorting. If this option is enabled, accented characters are sorted after unaccented characters.

➤ If the sorted column displays values from a multiple-value field, select Show Multiple Values as Separate Entries if you want to show each value as a separate row. Otherwise, multiple values display as one entry and sort by the first value in the list. If you want to allow users to sort columns by clicking on the column header in a view, select Click on Column Header to Sort. You have the option to allow them to sort in Ascending order, Descending order, or both.

➤ To have the column display totals, averages, or percentages for a column containing numeric values, select one of the options in the Totals field defined in the following list. Keep in mind that Totals calculates for main documents only; response documents are not included and they create extra overhead because they must be recalculated each time a view is opened.

The choices are:

➤ None, the default, does not display any total for the column.

➤ To calculate a grand total for all main documents, select Total, which displays the total at the bottom of the column.

➤ To calculate an overall average (the main documents are totaled and that number is divided by the number of main documents) choose Average per Document.

➤ To calculate an average for each category (the documents in each category are added together and that value is divided by the number of documents), select Average per Sub-Category.

➤ To calculate a category's percentage as it relates its parents, choose Percent of Parent Category.

➤ To calculate a category's percentage as it relates to the overall view total, select Percent of All Documents.

➤ To suppress the display of subtotals for each category and subcategory, click the Hide Detail Rows check box. This makes the views cleaner and easier to read in many cases.

6. Click the Font tab (third tab) to set such attributes as the font size, face, and style. These settings are fairly self-explanatory and are not covered in detail here.

7. If the column displays numeric values, you can click the Numbers tab (fourth tab) to set the attributes controlling the numeric formatting options. These settings are fairly self-explanatory and are not covered in detail here.

8. If the column is to display date values, you can click the Date and Time Format tab (fifth tab) to set the attributes controlling the date formatting options. These settings are fairly self-explanatory and are not covered in detail here.

9. Click the Title tab (sixth tab) to set such attributes as the font size, face, and style of the column header. These settings are fairly self-explanatory and are not covered in detail here.

10. Click the Advanced tab (seventh tab) to enter a name by which the column can be referenced programmatically, and to configure the column to display as a link when published to the Web. Keep in mind that the default action of Domino is to use the leftmost column in a view as the linking column. After you change to customized linking, you cannot revert to Domino's default behavior; you must manually designate at least one column as a link column in the view.

 The Hide Column check box has been moved to the Advanced tab and you can now write a hide-when formula to conditionally hide or show a column in a view. This cool new feature is new to Domino 6 and likely to appear in a test question. Keep in mind that this is not a security feature because the value can be accessed via numerous other means.

11. In the Programmer's pane (see Figure 4.10), you can define the column value based on the following options: Simple Function, Field, or Formula, each of which is explained in Table 4.11.

Table 4.11 Column Values Options	
Option	Description
Simple Function	Functions pre-written by Lotus that enable you to add programming to generate the contents of a column (without requiring you to know a programming language).
Field	Select a field from the list of fields stored in the database.
Formula	Select this option to use the Notes formula language to generate the value displayed in the column.

12. Save the view; press F9 to view the contents of the new column.

13. Close the view.

Displaying Date/Time Values in Columns

To display a date/time value in a view column, follow these steps:

1. Open the view that should display a date/time value in a column.

2. Add a new column, or edit an existing column.

3. In the Programmer's pane, select a field that contains a date/time value, or enter a formula that computes a date/time value.

4. Double-click the column header to open the Column properties box, then click the Date and Time format tab (looks like a clock and calendar).

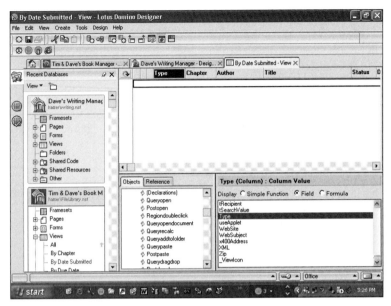

Figure 4.10   The Programmer's pane for a view column.

5. Choose how date/time values should be displayed by using User settings or Custom settings:

> ➤ *User settings*—When you choose user settings, date and time formats are based on the operating system settings.

> ➤ *Custom settings*—Custom setting give you tremendous flexibility over the way dates and times are displayed in a column. You can override the operating system display of dates as mm/dd/yyy and format dates to suit your tastes. For example, yyyymmdd.

6. Edit date/time format settings as necessary to achieve the format you want. Be sure to look at the example field to see what effect your settings have.

7. Save and test view.

Displaying Icons in Columns

A V*iew icon* is a small image that can be displayed in the column of a view. To display an icon in a view column, follow these steps:

1. Open the view that that should display an icon in a column.

2. Add a new column, or edit an existing column.

3. Double-click the column header to open the Column properties box, then click the Display Values as Icons check box on the Column info tab.

4. In the Programmer's pane, select a field or enter a formula that computes a numeric value corresponding to one of the predefined column icons (see the Domino Designer Help for the list of predefined icons), or select a field or enter a formula that will compute the name of the image resource to use.

 When using a custom icon, the image resource must be a GIF, BMP, or JPEG graphic. The recommended size for a custom column icon is a width of .2 inches and a height of .18 inches.

5. Save and test view.

Modifying a View Column

To modify a column in a view, follow these steps:

1. In the Designer client, open the view that contains the column you want to modify.

2. Double-click the column header to open the Column properties box.

3. If necessary, edit the view column as needed, following the instructions given earlier in this chapter in the section, "Creating a Column."

4. Save the view, and press F9 to view the contents of the new column.

5. Close the view.

Troubleshooting View Columns

Troubleshooting view columns generally revolves around the column properties or the column value formula. The following list attempts to cover some of the most common problems.

➤ If the column value formula generates an error or an incorrect value, double-check code and ensure that referenced field names and variables are correct.

➤ Ensure that column options such as Use Value as Color, Display Values as Icons, Show Responses Only, and Hide Column are set appropriately.

➤ Check the sorting options to ensure that the column is sorting properly. Pay careful attention to the Case Sensitive and Accent Sensitive settings.

➤ Check the column's formatting options to ensure that the data is being formatted as expected. For example, you are expecting a field value to be formatted as currency, but it appears as scientific notation.

Creating, Modifying, and Troubleshooting Fields

In Notes/Domino, *fields* are used to enter, modify, and display data stored in items. (*Item* is the technical name for a discrete data element stored in a Notes document.) Fields can be used in forms, subforms, and layout regions and layers and can be either single-use fields or shared fields. (Each is explained in the following sections.) Three key criteria must be specified when creating fields: the field name, the data type of the field, and the field type.

Naming Fields

Each field on a form must have a unique name. If you are using subforms in a form, this rule also applies. In addition to using a unique name for each field, you should keep the following points in mind:

➤ Field names cannot exceed 32 characters in length.

➤ Field names cannot contain spaces. You can use underscores (_) instead.

➤ Field names should not begin with a dollar sign ($), because this character is usually reserved for special Notes system fields.

➤ Field names cannot begin with a number (1–9).

➤ Field names cannot contain the ampersand symbol (&).

Field Data Types

The Notes database architecture supports a wide range of data types for fields. The *data type* of a field specifies the type of data that can be stored in a field. The various data types supported in Domino 6 are explained in Table 4.12.

Table 4.12	Notes Data Types
Type	**Description**
Text	Text fields store up to 15K of textual data, can be displayed in views, and have no fixed field length.
Date/Time	Date/Time fields store and display time and date information in any number of formats, the default being MM/DD/YY HH:MM:SS (internally, Domino stores times in seconds). Valid dates range from 1/1/0001 through 12/31/9999. Entering a two-digit year between 00 and 49 assumes the century starts in the year 2000. Entering two-digit years between 50 and 99 assumes the century starting in the year 1900. You can force users to enter a four-digit year in the field by selecting Require User to Enter Four Digit Years in the On Input field in the Field Properties box. If you want to display a calendar control for users, select Calendar/Time Control. The Calendar works only in Notes clients, not on the Web.
Timezone	Timezone fields display a drop-down list of all available time zones.
Number	Number fields are used to store numeric data, including numerals 0–9, the plus (+) and minus (-) signs, decimal point, and scientific notation. Number fields can be formatted in one of the four following ways: Decimal, Percent, Scientific, or Currency. Each is briefly explained in the following list: ➤ *Decimal*—Stores and displays numbers with a fixed number of decimal places specified by the developer. A number field can store up to eight non-zero decimal digits without loss of precision. ➤ *Percent*—Stores and displays numeric values as a percentage. ➤ Scientific—Stores and displays numeric values using exponential notation. ➤ Currency—Stores and displays numeric values with the currency symbol specified by the developer. The default format is the American dollar sign ($). ➤ Blank number fields are stored as an empty string (""). To make a number field always store a numeric value, use a default formula of 0.
Dialog list	Dialog list enables users to select the correct value(s) from a list of acceptable choices. The developer can determine whether the list should be mutually exclusive. The user can press Enter or click the Entry Helper button (the little arrow) to see all the choices at once, press the space bar to display choices one at a time, or type a letter to display the first choice beginning with that letter. Keep in mind that you cannot use a Dialog list in a layout region.
Check box	Check box fields enable users to select the correct value(s) from a list of acceptable choices, which are not mutually exclusive. Each choice in the list is displayed with a box users click on to select.

Table 4.12 Notes Data Types *(continued)*	
Type	**Description**
Radio button	Radio button fields enable users to select the correct value from a list of acceptable choices, which are mutually exclusive. Each choice is displayed with a button that users click to select.
List box	List box fields enable users to select the correct value(s) from a scrolling fixed-size list of acceptable choices. The developer can determine whether the list should be mutually exclusive.
Combo box	Combo box fields enable users to select the correct value from a drop-down list of mutually exclusive acceptable choices.
Rich text	Rich-text fields can be used to store large amounts of text and formatted text, and can be used for embedding or attaching objects. There is no practical size restriction (1GB) on the data placed in the field, as long as the database and disk drive can store the data. Rich text fields can be used anywhere except in a layout region, and their contents cannot be displayed in a view.
Rich text lite	Rich text lite fields are not as open-ended as a regular rich text field. They have a drop-down list that enables you to specify the type of data the user can put in the field. Any attempt to insert or paste an element not listed displays an error message. This field type is new to Domino 6.
Authors	Authors fields enable users with Author access to edit documents if they are named in the Authors field. It is important to remember that Authors fields do not override the ACL, but merely refine it.
Names	Names fields can be used to display user and/or server names in abbreviated format without the components associated with a fully qualified hierarchical name.
Readers	Readers fields can be used to limit access to specific documents by explicitly listing the users/groups who can read documents. Like Authors fields, Readers fields refine the ACL; they do not override it. If no Readers fields exist in a document, anyone with access to the database can read the document.
Password	Password fields are special type of text fields that helps to maintain privacy by displaying each character entered as an asterisk on the screen. Remember that the contents of a password field are not secure, and are visible in the Document properties box from the Notes client.
Formula	Formula fields have a special purpose: They are used to populate a subscription list, which works in conjunction with the Subscription feature in the Headlines.nsf database.
Color	Color fields display a color picker, which enables the user to select a color and return an RGB value.

Expect to see at least one question about the new Rich text lite field.

The field type is another key setting involved in adding fields to a form. The Designer supports four field types:

➤ *Computed*—Value is the result of a formula and is stored in the document. It is recomputed when the document is opened, refreshed, or saved.

➤ *Computed for Display*—Value is the result of a calculation, but the value is not stored in the document. It is recomputed when the document is created, opened, refreshed, or saved.

➤ *Computed When Composed*—Value is the result of a calculation, and the value is stored in the document.

➤ *Editable*—Value is entered by the user and is stored in the document. A default formula can be used to populate the field when a document is created, and input translations and field validation formulas can be used to manipulate data when the document is saved and to validate data when it is refreshed.

Design Considerations When Adding Fields

Before you add fields to a form, it is prudent to consider the following:

➤ The type of data to be stored in the field

➤ The method the user will use to interact with the field, such as combo box versus radio button versus text field

➤ The most logical position for the field on the form

➤ The need for security on the field

➤ The need to conditionally hide the field

➤ The presentation of the field, including font size, face, and color

Creating Single-Use Fields

A single-use field can be used only in the form or subform that hosts it. To create a single-use field, follow these steps:

1. Open the form or subform in which you want to add the field.

2. Position the cursor to the spot where you want the field to appear.

3. Choose Create, Field, which inserts a new unnamed field and opens the Field properties box to the Info tab (see Figure 4.11).

Figure 4.11   The Info tab on the Field properties box enables you to define the basic properties of a field.

4. On the Info tab, enter the following information:

   ➤ Enter a name for the field in the Name field (keep the naming conventions mentioned previously in mind).

   ➤ Select the data type of the field (defined in Table 4.12).

   ➤ Select the type of the field: Editable, Computed When Composed, Computed for Display, or Computed.

   ➤ If the field can store multiple values, select the Allow Multiple Values check box.

   ➤ If the field is computed, and you would like its value to be computed after the form's validation formula has fired, click the Compute After Validation check box.

   ➤ Choose the type of appearance the field should have, either Notes Style or Native OS Style. If you select Native OS Style, be sure to set the height and width properties.

   ➤ Set the field's tab order and, if you want the field to get the default focus (cursor is positioned in this field first), click the Give Field Initial (Default) Focus check box.

5. Select the Control tab (2nd tab) to choose the display options for the field. The choices presented on this tab vary widely, depending on the type of field you have elected to create. Be sure to check the settings for the field you are creating.

6. Select the Advanced tab (third tab) and, if necessary, enter a help description. If the field is set to display multi-values, configure the multi-values options. The font settings for a field are fairly self-explanatory and are not covered in detail. You can also set security options such as signing and encryption here.

7. Select the Fonts tab if you want to format the font of the field. The font settings for a field are pretty much self-explanatory and are not covered in detail.

8. Select the Paragraph Alignment tab to control the alignment of the field within its paragraph. The alignment settings for a field are pretty much self-explanatory and are not covered in detail.

9. Select the Hide When Options tab to control the conditions under which the field is to be visible. By default, a field is always visible. Be sure to configure the hide-when settings if the new field you are creating should not be visible at all times.

10. Select the Field Extra HTML tab to enter HTML-specific attributes for the field, such as class and style, which allows developers to use cascading style sheets.

11. Save the form or subform.

12. Test the form to ensure that the field works as expected.

Modifying Single-Use Fields

To modify a single-use field, follow these steps:

1. Open the form or subform in which you want to add the field.

2. Position the cursor to the spot where you want the field to appear.

3. Double-click the field you want to edit.

4. Follow the steps outlined in the preceding section, "Creating Single-Use Fields."

Troubleshooting Single-Use Fields

The following is a list of tips to help you in troubleshooting single-use fields:

> Check the field properties to ensure the field is set to the proper data type.

> Ensure that the type of field is set correctly. For example, if the field value should be saved as an item in the document, but is not, be sure that you have not set the field to be Computed For Display.

> If you are planning to store multiple values in a field, be sure that the field has the `multi-values` property enabled.

> If the field is of type `keywords`, but you are not getting the correct values in the list, check the formula being used to generate the list.

> If the field is computed and the computations are based on other fields in the form, be sure to check the order of the fields. Remember that in Notes, fields are computed from left to right and top to bottom.

Using Field Help and Hints

Field Help and Field Hints provide users assistance when filling out a form. Field Help creates a one-line row at the bottom of the form that displays custom messages that tell the user how to use the field. Field Hints appear as a default value in the field that goes away when the user enters the field.

 Field help text and Field hint text work only on the Notes client, not on the Web.

Creating Field Help and Field Hints

To add either Field Help or Field Hints to a field, follow these steps:

1. Open the form that contains fields to which you want to add field help and/or field hints.

2. Select a field on the form.

3. Double-click the field, which opens the field properties box.

4. Click the Advanced tab (propeller beanie).

5. Enter Field Help text in the Field Help field or enter Field Hint text in the Field Hint field.

6. Save and test the form.

Creating, Modifying, and Troubleshooting Forms

In Notes/Domino, a *Form* provides the structure for creating and displaying documents. (You can think of it as a template.) Forms contain fields, which are used to enter and save data (in items) in a Notes document. They also contain any other design elements that a designer has placed on the forms, such as text, tables, images, sections, and actions. For more information on Notes fields, please see the section, "Creating, Modifying, and Troubleshooting Fields," earlier in this chapter.

A document is loosely linked to a form through the use of the Form field, which contains the name of the form used to create a document. When a document is opened, it is usually rendered through the form named in the Form field. In some cases, a form may be stored in the document, which always causes the form to open with the stored document. It is also possible to use a form formula in a view, which causes documents to be opened with a particular form.

Forms and pages can be confusing for new developers because they seem to share many of the same capabilities. However, *pages* can only display information. If you want to collect information and save it in a Notes database, you must use a *form*.

Creating Forms

To create a form, follow these steps:

1. In the Designer client, open the database in which you want to create the form.

2. Choose Create, Design, Form, or click the New Form button.

3. Choose Design, Form Properties to define the form's properties in the Form properties box (the Info tab is displayed first), shown in Figure 4.12. Although many properties are available for a form, the following list describes the most important ones:

➤ Enter a name and alias for the form in the Name field. It is a good practice to get in the habit of always entering an alias for each form because this is the value that the system uses to reference the form.

➤ Choose the type of document the form will create in the Type field: Document, Response, or Response-to-Response.

➤ If the form is to be the default form for the database (used when a form is not specified in the Form field), click the Default Database Form check box.

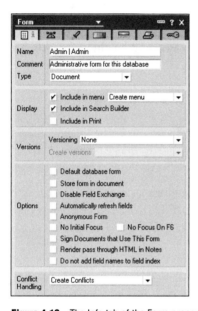

Figure 4.12   The Info tab of the Form properties box.

4. Click the Defaults tab (propeller beanie) to define the advanced properties. The most commonly used ones are described as follows:

➤ If you want the fields on the form to inherit values from the currently selected document, click the Formulas Inherit Values from Selected Document check box.

➤ If you want to have the form open in edit mode (saving the user the trouble of an additional click), click the Automatically Enable Edit Mode check box.

➤ If you have hidden fields in the form that you want to publish to the Web (these fields are generated through the use of the <INPUT> tag with the type=hidden attribute), click the Generate HTML for All Fields check box.

If the Generate HTML for All Fields option is not checked, hidden fields on the form are hidden on the Web and do not appear in the HTML source of the page.

6. Click the Launch tab to define the launch properties. Be sure to set the Frameset and Frame properties if you want the form to always open with a particular frame.

7. Click the Background tab to define the form's background color and/or graphic.

8. Click the Header tab to define a form header and height and width properties.

9. Click the Print tab to define printing properties for the form.

10. Click the Security tab to define form-level security, including who can read documents created with the form and who can create documents with the form. If the form should be available to users who have been granted only Public Access, click the Available to Public Users check box.

11. Create and format fields, text, actions, subforms, shared fields, shared actions, layout regions, tables, hotspots, and other design elements on the form.

12. Save the form.

13. Test the form to ensure that it works as expected. You can use the Preview in Notes or Preview in Web Browser features, available from the Design menu.

Modifying Forms

To modify a form, follow these steps:

1. In the Designer client, open the database that contains the form that you want to modify.

2. Click Forms in the Design Pane to see the list of existing forms in the database.

3. Double-click the form you want to edit.

4. Follow the steps outlined in the preceding section, "Creating Forms."

Troubleshooting Forms

Because of the vast functionality and complexity of forms, troubleshooting covers a lot of ground. For the sake of brevity, this chapter covers only the most basic problems. The following is a list of common form problems and their resolution.

➤ *Form displays no title or title is incorrect*—Select Window Title in the Objects tab and enter a formula to compute a window title.

➤ *Items that should be hidden are displayed in run mode*—Open the Form properties and check the hide-when formulas of the specific objects.

➤ *Items that should not be hidden are hidden in run mode*—Open the Form properties and check the hide-when formulas of the specific objects.

➤ *Forms do not open because of a formula error*—Check all computed fields and editable fields with default values.

➤ *Fields are not computed properly*—Check field formulas and remember that field formulas are computed left to right, top to bottom. Ensure that field formulas are not dependent upon fields after them.

➤ *Documents are saved without required data*—Use field validation formulas to require user input for specified fields.

➤ *Keyword fields are not dynamically repopulated when form values change*—Ensure that Refresh Choices on Document Refresh is enabled, as well as Refresh Fields on Keyword Change, which can be found on the Control tab of the Field properties box.

➤ *Fields are not inheriting values from existing document*—Open the Form properties box and ensure that Formulas Inherit Values from Selected Document is enabled.

➤ *Documents are not being saved as response documents*—Open the Form properties box and check the Type setting.

➤ *Hidden fields are not being published to Web client*—Open the Form properties box and ensure that Generate HTML for All Fields is enabled.

➤ *Form is being opened in wrong frame*—Open the Form properties box and ensure that the proper frameset and frame is set.

➤ *Form size and border are not appearing correctly*—Open the Form properties box and ensure that the size and border settings are correct.

Creating, Modifying, and Troubleshooting Pages

Pages are similar to Notes forms or static HTML pages. A *page* provides all the basic capabilities of a form with one major difference: Forms can be used to collect information and store it in Notes documents, whereas pages can only display information. Keep in mind that if you need to display and/or store information, you should use a form. Otherwise, a page can work just as well and loads more quickly and with less overhead.

Creating a Page

To create a page, follow these steps:

1. In the Designer, open the database in which you want to create the page.

2. Click Pages in the Design pane to see a list of existing pages in the database.

3. Choose Create, Design, Page or click the New Page button.

4. Choose Design, Page Properties, which opens the Page properties box (illustrated in Figure 4.13) to the Info tab and define the following important properties:

    ➤ Enter a name (and alias if desired) for the page in the Name field. To enter an alias, enter the pipe character (|) after the name and type in the alias. It is always a good idea to use an alias.

    ➤ If you are using the page on the Web, click Treat Page Contents As HTML to have everything converted to HTML.

5. If you want to change the page background, such as the color or the image, click the Background tab.

6. Click the Launch tab to change the launch options for the page. If you want the page to always open in a particular frame, be sure to choose the frameset and frame on this tab.

7. If you want the page to be available to users who have been granted only Public Access, click the Security tab and click the Available to Public Access Users check box.

8. Save the page.

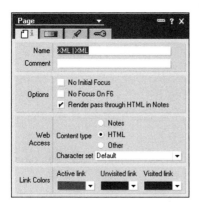

Figure 4.13 The Page properties box.

9. Test the page to ensure that it performs as expected. If the page is open, you can choose either Design Preview in Notes or Design Preview in Web Browser to view it in the proper client. If you are in the Pages view, simply click one of the preview buttons (shown in Figure 4.14) to launch the proper clients. Keep in mind that if you are building hybrid applications, you should view the page in both the Notes client and a browser.

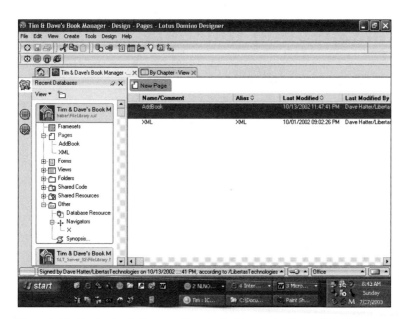

Figure 4.14 The Preview buttons provide a shortcut for viewing design elements.

Troubleshooting Pages

The following is a list of common page problems and their resolution:

➤ *Page opens in wrong frameset*—Open the Page properties box and check the Frameset and Frame Properties of the view.

➤ *Background image "tiles"*—Open the Page properties box and check the Do Not Tile Graphic option on the Color tab.

➤ *Page color is incorrect*—Open the Page properties box and check the color on the Color tab.

➤ *Page does not publish correctly on the Web*—Open the Page properties box and check the Treat Page Contents as HTML option.

➤ *Items on page are not appearing when page is opened*—Check the hide-when properties of the vanishing items.

➤ *Hidden items on the page are appearing when the page is opened*—Check the hide-when properties of the items that are appearing.

Creating, Modifying, and Troubleshooting Hotspots

Hotspots provide a simple mechanism for users to initiate an action when clicked. There are several types of hotspots:

➤ *Button*—Performs an action when clicked. Button hotspots can be coded using formulas, LotusScript, JavaScript or a simple action.

➤ *Formula pop-up*—Displays text by using a formula.

➤ *Action*—Performs an action when clicked. Action hotspots can be coded by using formulas, LotusScript, JavaScript, or a simple action.

➤ *Link*—Opens another object when clicked. Covered in more detail later in this chapter.

➤ *Text pop-up*—Displays text when clicked.

 Buttons and action hotspots vary only in appearance. Button hotspots display as buttons, whereas action hotspots appear as highlighted text.

For the sake of brevity and because the basic functionality of all hotspots is the same, only button hotspots are covered here; they are probably the most commonly used. Follow these steps to add a button hotspot:

1. Open the form, subform, or page to which you want to add a button hotspot.

2. Position the cursor where the button should appear.

3. Choose Create, Hotspot, Button.

4. Enter a caption for the button in the Label field.

5. Optionally, define other button attributes such as size, background, test styles, etc.

6. In the Programmer pane, select the environment in which the button will be used (Client or Web) in the Run pull-down list. When selecting Client, the following options are available:

   ➤ Simple actions

   ➤ Formula

   ➤ LotusScript

   ➤ JavaScript

   ➤ Common JavaScript

   When selecting Web, the following options are available:

   ➤ JavaScript

   ➤ Common JavaScript

7. Save and test form.

Modifying Hotspots

To modify a hotspot, follow these steps:

1. Open the form, subform, or page that contains the hotspot.

2. Locate and double-click the hotspot.

3. Optionally, modify the hotspot's attributes.

4. Optionally, re-program the hotspot's function.

5. Save and test the hotspot.

Troubleshooting Hotspots

The following is a list of common hotspot problems and their resolution:

➤ *Action appears/disappears when it should not*—Check and verify the hide-when formula of the formula.

➤ *Hotspot does not perform as expected*—Check and verify code.

Creating, Modifying, and Troubleshooting Links

Links provide a simple but powerful way to quickly and easily open a Web site or Notes object such as a database, view, or document. A link can either be a text link or a graphical link; Domino automatically converts the links to hytertext links that work on the Web.

There are several types of links you can create and several ways to specify how a link will work. The following is a list of the types of links you can create:

➤ *Named Element*—Named elements that can be linked include forms, framesets, folders, navigators, pages, and views.

➤ *URL Link*—Link to a hard-coded URL.

➤ *Hotspot link*—Domino objects that can be linked include anchors, documents, views, and databases.

Create a Named Element Link

To create a Named Element link, follow these steps:

1. In the Domino Designer, select the design element (see list in the preceding section) to which you want to link.

2. Choose Edit, Copy as Link, Named Element.

3. Open the Form, Subform, or Page that will contain the link.

4. Select the text or image that will be linked and choose Create, Hotspot, Link Hotspot.

5. In the Hotspot Info tab, click the Named element from the Type drop-down. Then select the appropriate design element.

6. Optionally, specify a target frame for the link.

7. Optionally, select Show Border Around Hotspot if you want to display a border around the link. This is not supported on the Web.

 Because Named Element Links rely on the name of an object, they fail if the name of an object changes. Be sure to use the alias of an object if possible to help prevent broken links.

Create a Hotspot Link

Hotspot links are powerful and easy to use. They enable you to link to a document, view, or database by using the unique ID of that object and, consequently, do not fail if the name of an object changes.

To create a link to a document, view, or database, follow these steps:

1. Open the element (Anchor, Document, View, or Database) to which you want to link.

2. Choose Edit, Copy as Link.

3. Select the appropriate link type.

4. Select the text or image to act as the link.

5. Choose Create, Hotspot, Link Hotspot.

6. Choose Link for the hotspot type on the Hotspot Info.

7. Click the paste icon.

8. Optionally, enter a target frame for the link and select Show Border Around Hotspot.

Create a URL Link

A URL link uses a Uniform Resource Locator (URL) as a link to a resource. Keep in mind that if the URL changes, the link fails. To create a URL link, follow these steps:

1. Open the form, subform, or page that contains the text or graphic to use as the URL link.

2. Select the text or graphic to link.

3. Choose Create, Hotspot, Link Hotspot.

4. Select URL as the link type on the Hotspot Info tab in the Hotspot Resource Link properties box.

5. Enter the full URL (including protocol specifier) to link to. For example: `http://www.lynyrdskynyrd.com`.

6. Optionally, select Show Border Around Hotspot if you want to display a border around the link. (This is not supported on the Web.)

Modifying Links

To modify a link, follow these steps:

1. Open the form, subform, or page that contains the link.

2. Locate and double-click the link.

3. Optionally, modify the link's attributes, including the link target.

4. Save and test the hotspot.

Troubleshooting Links

The following is a list of common link problems and their resolution:

➤ *Link appears/disappears when it should not*—Check and verify the hide-when formula of the link.

➤ *Link does not perform as expected*—Check and verify link target.

Creating, Modifying, and Troubleshooting Layers

Layers are a new tool introduced in Domino 6, enabling you to position blocks of content over each other on a form, subform, or page. There are two basic types of layers: transparent and opaque. As you might guess from the names, *transparent layers* allow content behind them to show through, whereas *opaque layers* do not.

Creating a Layer

To create a layer, follow these steps:

1. Open the form, subform, or page in which you'd like to add a layer.

2. Position the cursor where the layer should appear.

3. Choose Create, Layer.

4. Right-click the layer to open the Layer properties box, shown in Figure 4.15, and modify the layer's attributes as necessary.

5. Add content to the layer as appropriate.

 Layers in a form can contain the same elements as the form. For example, you can add text and graphics, as well as controlled-access sections, fields, and subforms. Layers in a page can contain the same elements as the page. For example, you can add text and graphics but not fields.

6. Save and test the form, subform, or page that contains the layer.

Figure 4.15 The Layers properties box.

 Layers are one of the coolest new design tools in Domino and I'd expect to see at least one question about layers on the exam.

Modifying a Layer

To modify a layer, follow these steps:

1. Open the form, subform, or page that contains the layer to modify.

2. Right-click the layer to open the Layer properties box and modify the layer's attributes as necessary.

3. Add or modify content in the layer as appropriate.

4. Save and test the form, subform, or page that contains the layer.

Troubleshooting Layers

The following is a list of common layer problems and their resolution:

➤ *Layer appears/disappears when it should not*—Check and verify the hide-when formula of the layer.

➤ *Layer does not appear in the correct level of the layer hierarchy*—Check the z-Index of the layer. The z-Index dictates the position of the layer relative to its parent. A z-Index of 0 is the top layer. You can alter the z-Index to control the stacking order of the layers.

Creating, Modifying, and Troubleshooting Navigators

Navigators enable you to build a graphical image of folders, views, and other design elements so that users can easily find information. Normally, navigators use hotspots that, when clicked, either perform some action or open a design element such as a view.

Creating a Navigator

To create a navigator, follow these steps:

1. Open the database that will contain the navigator in the Designer client.

2. Choose Create, Design, Navigator from the menu.

3. Select Design, Navigator Properties or right-click and choose Navigator properties to open the Navigator properties box, shown in Figure 4.16.

4. Enter a name for the navigator.

5. Optionally, deselect the Web Browser Compatible check box if you are not going to use the navigator on the Web.

NOTE

Be sure to select the Web Browser Compatible property if you plan to use a navigator in a Web-based application. Enabling this setting causes Domino to convert the navigator to an image map.

6. Optionally, select an initial view or folder to open along with the navigator.

7. Add items to the navigator, using either the Create menu or the SmartIcons bar. Choose to code the actions, using Simple Actions, Formulas, or LotusScript.

8. Save and test the navigator.

Figure 4.16   The Navigator properties box.

Modify a Navigator

1. Open the navigator you want to change in the Designer client.

2. Make the necessary changes to the navigator.

3. Save and test the navigator.

Troubleshooting a Navigator

The following is a list of common navigator problems and their resolution:

➤ *Navigator will not work on the Web*—Ensure that the Web Browser Compatible feature is enabled.

➤ *Navigator does not load in appropriate spot*—Ensure that Auto Adjust Panes as Runtime is enabled.

Creating, Modifying, and Troubleshooting Sections

Sections provide a collapsible area within forms and subforms. Sections can contain a variety of objects, including text, fields, and layout regions. Sections are often used to organize elements on a page or form and are handy for making a form or page with large amounts of information more useable.

There are two types of sections: standard sections and access-controlled sections. Standard sections allow any user to access the contents of the section, whereas access-controlled sections can restrict access to the contents within the section. More information about restricting access to a section can be found in Chapter 10, "Security."

Create a Section

To create a section, follow these steps:

1. Open the page or form in which you want to create a section.

2. Select the text, graphics, fields, or other elements that should be added to the section.

3. Choose Create, Section, Standard.

4. Right-click the section to open the Section properties box.

5. Optionally, modify section attributes as necessary.

6. Save and test the form or page that contains the section.

Modify a Section

To modify an existing section, follow these steps:

1. Open the page or form that contains the section you want to modify.

2. Right-click the section to open the Section properties box.

3. Modify section attributes as necessary.

4. Save and test the form or page that contains the section.

Troubleshoot a Section

The following is a list of common section problems and their resolution:

➤ *Section appears/disappears when it should not*—Check and verify the hide-when formula of the section.

➤ *Section does not auto-expand or auto-collapse when it should*—Check the auto-expand and auto-collapse options of the section.

Working with Shared Resources

Lotus has long recognized the need to make application design both modular and flexible and has made significant strides in this area through the use of shared resources and shared code.

Shared resources enable and shared code allow you to create certain types of design elements that can be reused throughout an application and maintained in a single location. Each Domino database can contain its own shared resources and shared code. In Domino 6, resources can now be shared across databases, which is a major improvement. You can create the following shared resources in Domino 6:

➤ *Style Sheets*—Cascading Style Sheets (CSS) files can be added as shared resources and then used in pages, forms, and subforms.

➤ *Files*—Any nondatabase files can be added as file resources and shared within and across databases.

➤ *Images*—Image resources are GIF, JPEG, or BMP format files that can be shared across a database in the following ways: by using graphic or icon on pages, forms, subforms, action buttons, outline entries; and by using background images on forms, documents, pages, table cells, and action buttons.

➤ *Applets—Shared Java files*—Applet files can be shared.

➤ *Data Connections*—New to Domino 6, data connections provide an intuitive, GUI interface for creating connections to backend databases such as Oracle and DB2.

You can create the following shared code items in Domino 6:

➤ *Actions*—Actions that can be used in forms, pages, folders, or views within a database.

➤ *Agents*—Stand-alone programs that can be used to automate processes in Domino.

➤ *Fields*—Fields that can be defined and used on more than one form or subform.

➤ *Outlines*—Can be used to provide hierarchical navigational in Notes applications.

➤ *Script libraries*—A place to store code to share within a database. Script libraries can contain LotusScript, JavaScript, or Java.

➤ *Subforms*—Similar to a form, can contain fields that can be shared across multiple forms within a database.

Summary

The following bullet points summarize the chapter and accentuate the key concepts you need to know for the exam.

➤ Design elements are the building blocks of Domino applications.

➤ Most design elements have been significantly enhanced, especially forms and views.

➤ Layers are a powerful new design tool added to Domino 6 to make form, page, and subform layout more flexible.

➤ Domino 6 has several new shared resources, including Style Sheets, Files, and Data Connectors.

➤ Three new field types have been added: Rich text lite, Color, and Time zone.

Exam Prep Questions

Question 1

A Named Element Link is used to link to what?

- ○ A. Anchors, documents, views, and databases.
- ○ B. A fully qualified URL.
- ○ C. Domino design elements, including forms, framsets, folders, pages, views, and navigators.
- ○ D. Files.

The correct answer is C. Named Element Links are used to link to Domino design elements, including forms, framsets, folders, pages, views, and navigators. A is incorrect because named element links do not link to anchors, documents, views, and databases. B is incorrect because named element links are not used to link to URLs. D is incorrect because named element links are not used to link to files.

Question 2

An embedded view can be used in which design elements?

- ○ A. Folders and views.
- ○ B. Layers and layout regions.
- ○ C. Agents.
- ○ D. Forms and pages.

The correct answer is D. Embedded views can be used in forms and pages.

Question 3

What are the two types of layers?

- ○ A. Transparent and opaque.
- ○ B. Top and bottom.
- ○ C. Translucent and opaque.
- ○ D. Upper and lower.

The correct answer is A. Layers can be either transparent or opaque. B, C, and D are incorrect because Layers are either transparent or opaque.

Question 4

Which new View property would Wyatt enable to allow users to create documents directly in a view?

O A. Creating documents directly is not possible.

O B. Allow Customizations.

O C. Show Response Documents in a Hierarchy.

O D. Create New Documents at View Level.

The correct answer is D. Wyatt must enable the Create New Documents at View Level property in the View properties box. A is incorrect because documents can now be created at the view level. B is incorrect because Allow Customizations is used to allow users to customize the view at runtime, which is new in Domino 6. C is incorrect because this property enables View to show response documents in a hierarchy beneath parent documents.

Question 5

Samuel wants to use an image in several forms and subforms in an application; which method would be the best choice?

O A. Paste an image in the forms and subforms.

O B. Use pass-thru HTML and the **<IMG>** tag to display the image.

O C. Use a shared image resource.

O D. Use a file resource.

The correct answer is C. Samuel should use a shared image resource because Shared resources are designed to be shared across multiple design elements. A is incorrect because you would have to paste the image into each form and subform. B is incorrect because it creates more administrative work and you must put the HTML in each form and subform. D is incorrect because a file resource is not necessarily an image and would not be rendered as a image.

Question 6

How should Emma display a customized icon in a view?

○ A. Enable the Display Values as Icons property and enter a column formula that computes to a numeric value.

○ B. Custom icons cannot be displayed in views.

○ C. Enable the Display Values as Icons property and enter a column formula that computes to the name of a file to display.

○ D. Enable the Display Values as Icons property and enter a column formula that computes to the name of a shared resource to display.

The correct answer is D. Emma must enable the Display Values as Icons property and must enter a formula that will compute to the name of a shared image resource. A is incorrect because the formula must compute the image name, not a numeric value. B is incorrect because custom icons can be displayed in a view. C is incorrect because the formula must compute to the name of a shared image resource, not a file.

Question 7

Which field types are new in Domino 6?

○ A. Rich Text Lite, Time Zone, and Color.

○ B. Rich Text Lite, Time Zone, and Password.

○ C. Rich Text, Time Zone, and Color.

○ D. Rich Text Lite, Time Zone, and Password.

The correct answer is A. B is incorrect because Password is not a new field type in Domino 6; it was new in R5. C is incorrect because Rich Text is not a new field type in Domino 6. D is incorrect because password is not a new field type in Domino 6.

Question 8

Leslee wants to use layers, which are new to Domino 6. What is one benefit of using layers?

- ○ A. There is no benefit; they work just like layout regions.
- ○ B. Layers can save space by expanding and collapsing.
- ○ C. Layers enable you to control the z-order of information, making it possible to overlap information.
- ○ D. Layers enable you to create gradient fills in a footer.

The correct answer is C. Layers enable you to create overlapping information. A is incorrect because Layers do not work like layout regions. B is incorrect because layers do not expand and collapse. D is incorrect because you wouldn't use layers to create a gradient fill in a footer.

Question 9

Which option enables you to override the OS settings for the display of date/time values in a view column?

- ○ A. User Setting.
- ○ B. Override OS Setting.
- ○ C. OS Off.
- ○ D. Custom.

The correct answer is D. The Custom setting enables you to override the OS settings for date and time display. B is incorrect because Override OS is not a valid option. C is incorrect because OS Off is not a valid option.

Question 10

Which of the following options is not valid for the schedule of an agent?

- ○ A. Never.
- ○ B. Daily.
- ○ C. Yearly.
- ○ D. Monthly.

The correct answer is C because Yearly is not a valid scheduling option. A, B, and D are incorrect because Never, Monthly, and Daily are all valid scheduling options.

Need to Know More?

 IBM. *Lotus Domino Designer 6 Help.* Help6_Designer.nsf.

 IBM. *Lotus Domino Administrator 6 Help.* Help6_Admin.nsf.

 IBM. *Domino Designer 6: A Developer's Handbook.* Redbook, 2002.

 IBM Lotus Developer Domain Web site: www.notes.net or www.lotus.com/ldd.

Security

Terms you'll need to understand:

✓ Access Control List (ACL)
✓ Server Access List
✓ Group
✓ Readers field
✓ Authors field
✓ Default access

Techniques you'll need to master:

✓ Adding security to an application
✓ Defining security levels for application users
✓ Determining Databases Group Access
✓ Securing applications: Authors fields
✓ Securing applications: Readers fields
✓ Setting database access: Default Access
✓ Setting and reading ACLs

Application security is one of the most important concepts for a developer to understand, especially in today's world of ubiquitous networking. Domino provides a multitiered security architecture that gives developers unprecedented power and flexibility, but is often confusing for new developers.

This chapter covers the information you need to be familiar with regarding the Domino security model. You should expect to see several questions regarding security on the exam, especially on Readers and Authors fields, which are two of the most misunderstood Domino security concepts.

Adding Security to an Application

Domino has long been known for providing a very robust and granular security model that can meet almost any need. Domino supports seven levels of security (shown in Table 5.1).

Table 5.1 Domino Security Model	
Level	**Description**
Network	Security provided at the network level by the network infrastructure: OS, Routers, firewalls, and so forth.
Authentication	A user is required to provide his or her credentials (username and password) to gain access to the system and to set the level of access granted.
Server Access	The Domino Server document provides numerous settings that enable administrators to control who can access the server and what actions they can perform on the server, such as creating databases or running agents.
Database Access	Each database has seven primary access levels set and controlled in the database Access Control List that can be associated with users, groups, and roles: Manager, Designer, Editor, Author, Reader, Depositor, and No Access.
Design Element Security	Forms, Views, Folders, and Agents can be secured so that only named people, groups, and roles can use them.
Document Security	Among the most powerful and flexible of the Domino security features are Author and Reader fields. See "Using Authors Fields" and "Using Readers Fields," later in this chapter.
Field Security	Domino provides the capability to secure individual fields in a document through the use of digital signatures and encryption. For more information, see Chapter 11, "Workflow."

Defining Security Levels for Application Users

The database *Access Control List* (ACL) is the frontline of Domino database security: it controls access to a database. There are seven distinct access levels in the ACL: No Access, Depositor, Reader, Author, Editor, Designer, and Manager. Table 5.2 explains each of the seven access levels from lowest to highest. Each of these access levels provides automatic privileges as well as numerous optional privileges. The automatic privileges are fairly straightforward, but the optional privileges require further explanation, which is provided in the list following Table 5.2.

Table 5.2	Database ACL		
Access Level	**Automatic Privileges**	**Optional Privileges**	**Commonly Assigned To**
No Access	None. No access is granted to the database unless one of the optional privileges are specified.	Read public documents Write public documents	The person(s), group(s), and/or role(s) that should not have access to the database (Terminated users, for example).
Depositor	Create new documents.	Read public documents Write public documents	The person(s), group(s) and/or role(s) who should be able to only add new documents but cannot read any documents.
Reader	Read documents, unless a Readers field precludes access to documents.	Create personal agents Create personal folders/views Create LotusScript/Java agents Write public documents	The person(s), group(s) and/or role(s) who should be able to read but not edit documents in the database.
Author	Read documents. Create Documents is not specified by default and must be enabled to create documents.	Create documents Delete documents Create personal agents Create personal folders/views Create LotusScript/Java agents Write public documents	The person(s), group(s) and/or role(s) who should be able to read existing documents and create new documents.

Table 5.2	Database ACL *(continued)*		
Access Level	Automatic Privileges	Optional Privileges	Commonly Assigned To
Editor	Create documents.	Delete documents Create personal agents Create personal folders/views Create LotusScript/Java agents Create shared folders/views Read public documents Write public documents	The person(s), group(s) and/or role(s) who should be able to create new documents and edit any document in the database.
Designer	All Editor rights plus the ability to modify design elements. Create documents.	Delete documents Create personal agents Create Lotus Script/Java agents Create personal folders/views Create shared folders/views Read public documents Write public documents	The person(s), group(s) and/or role(s) responsible for database design.
Manager	All designer rights plus can edit database ACL. Create documents.	Delete documents Create personal agents Create personal folders/views Create shared folders/views Create LotusScript/Java agents Read public documents Write public documents	Assign to at least one person. Good idea to add other person(s), group(s) and/or role(s) that can manage the database.

The optional ACL privileges are described as follows:

➤ *Read public documents*—Enables designated users to read documents, access views and folders, run agents, and use forms designated as Available to Public Access Users. This setting is found in the Security tab of the Forms, Views, and Folders and Agents properties boxes. This option enables users with No Access or Depositor access—not Reader access—to view specific documents, forms, views, and folders. Documents available for public access users must contain a reserved field named $PublicAccess, which should be set to the text value one ("1").

➤ *Write public documents*—Enables users without Author or Editor access to create, modify, and delete documents, using forms that have been designated as Available to Public Access Users (found on the Security tab of the Form properties box).

➤ *Create documents*—Enables users with Author access or above to add new documents to the database. Authors without this setting can read documents and edit documents they have created (if they are named in an Authors field explicitly or through a group or role), but cannot create new documents. This is an automatic privilege for Editor or higher access.

➤ *Delete documents*—Enables users to delete documents if they have at least Author access and are listed in an Author field. For access levels higher than Author, toggles the capability to delete documents off and on. For example, a user with Editor access but without Delete Documents enabled cannot delete any documents.

➤ *Create private agents*—Enables users with Reader access and above to create private agents on the server. Even if a user can create these agents, he or she may not be permitted to run them based on other security settings in the Server document in the Domino Directory.

➤ *Create personal folders/views*—Enables users to create personal folders and views on the server. Deselecting this option does not prevent users from creating personal folders and views. However, the folders or views are stored in their local workstations rather than on the server.

➤ *Create shared folders/views*—Enables users with Editor access to create folders and views that can potentially be accessed by other users. You can deselect this option to save disk space on a server and to maintain tighter control over database design.

➤ *Create LotusScript/Java agents*—Enables users to create LotusScript and Java agents that are stored in the database on a server. Although a user may create an agent, his or her ability to run it depends on access granted in the Agent Restrictions section of the Server document in the Domino Directory.

➤ *Replicate or Copy Documents*—This property is new to Domino 6 and specifies whether users with Reader access and above can replicate or copy documents.

Setting and Reading ACLs

"Best practices" dictate that you should carefully plan the ACL of a database based on the users' and server's access requirements. After this planning stage, you can add users, groups, roles, or servers to the ACL by selecting them from the Domino Directory or manually entering them.

Keep in mind that you should create roles and groups before using them in the ACL and that you must have Manager access to the database to change the ACL.

Adding Valid ACL Entries

When adding entries to an ACL, the following types are acceptable:

➤ Wildcard entries, such as `*/LibertasTechnologies`. Wildcard entries are treated as groups.

➤ Database replica IDs.

➤ User, server, and group names, such as Dave Hatter/LibertasTechnologies.

➤ Anonymous.

➤ Alternate names.

➤ LDAP name (a Light Weight Directory Access Protocol directory name).

The maximum length of an ACL entry is 255 characters. To add names to the ACL, follow these steps:

1. Select the database whose ACL you want to change.

2. Select File, Database, Access Control, or right-click the database and select Database, Access Control from the pop-up menu, which opens the database Access Control List dialog box shown in Figure 5.1.

3. Click the Add button to open the Add User prompt.

4. Enter (or select) the name of a user, server, or group, and click OK.

5. Select a user type for the new entry. This is a good idea because it provides additional security.

6. Select an access level for the new entry.

7. Optionally select the appropriate Optional Privileges for the new entry to refine the ACL.

8. Click OK to save your changes.

Add names to the ACL in hierarchical form to increase security. For example, use Dave Hatter/LibertasTechnologies rather than Dave Hatter.

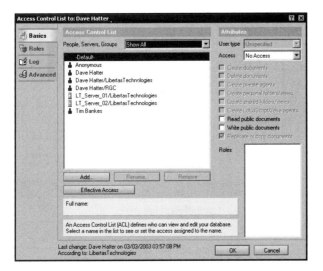

Figure 5.1   The database Access Control List dialog box.

Using Groups

Domino enables you to create *groups*, which contain a list of users, servers, and other groups that have something in common.

After a group document has been created in the Domino Directory (you may need your Administrator to do this), you can add members to the group and then use the group name in the ACL of a database to implicitly grant or deny access to all the members of the group.

 Although there is no limit to the number of names in a group, the total size of the members list cannot exceed 15KB.

After you have added a group to the ACL, you assign it permissions the same way that you would to an individual user or server.

For example, you might create a group named LiberasEditors and grant it Editor access to a database and create another group named LibertasAuthors and grant that group Author access to the database. As additional users need to access the database, you simply add them to the appropriate groups.

 It is always a best practice, whenever possible, to use groups in the ACL of a database rather than individual names to reduce administrative overhead and to reduce the size of the ACL. Remember this information for the exam.

ACL Conflicts

ACL conflicts can occur when users are named explicitly in the ACL and also in a group named in the ACL, or when users are members of more than one group in the ACL. Table 5.3 explains what happens when this situation occurs.

Table 5.3 Database ACL	
Type of Conflict	**Conflict Resolution**
A user is named both individually and as a member of a group.	The individual access level takes precedence over the access level assigned to the group.
A user is named in two or more groups.	The user receives highest level of access between the two groups.

Default ACL

When a new database is created, several entries are added to the database ACL by default:

➤ *Default*—This entry is used to grant blanket access to all users, groups, and servers not explicitly named in the ACL. For example, if you set the Default to Reader, then any user not named explicitly or in a group has Reader access to the database. Additionally, if the ACL does not contain an Anonymous entry, Anonymous (unauthenticated) users are granted access based on this entry. You cannot remove this entry from the ACL.

➤ *Anonymous*—This entry is used to grant access to unauthenticated Notes and Internet users.

➤ *Database creator user name*—The user that creates the database is automatically added to the ACL and is granted Manager access.

➤ *LocalDomainServers*—This group contains the names of the servers in the same domain as the server where the database is created. The default access for LocalDomainServers is Manager. This group should have at least Designer access so that design changes can replicate across the domain.

➤ *OtherDomainServers*—This group contains the names of the servers outside the domain of the server where the database is stored. The default access for this group is No Access.

Document Access

Since its earliest days, Notes has provided document-level security that can be enforced through the use of Authors and Readers fields, extending the database ACL and allowing you to further refine the already granular and extensive security model.

Using Readers Fields

Readers fields are a very powerful document level security feature that enable you to further refine database access by restricting the users, groups, servers, and roles that can read a particular document. A *Readers field* is a special type of text field that interacts with the database ACL, further refining it. When a Readers field is placed in a document and users, groups, servers, and roles are named in it, access to that document is restricted to the named entities. For example, if a document contains a Readers field containing Dave Hatter, Leslee Hatter, Samuel Hatter, Wyatt Hatter, Emma Rose Hatter, and Administrators, only those explicitly named entities would be able to see the document in views and open the document in forms.

Being named in a Reader field *does not* give a user access to a document if a user is already restricted at the database ACL level. For example, if a user is named either explicitly or implicitly in a Readers field, but has been granted only Depositor or No Access in the database ACL, the user cannot access the document.

However, users with Reader or higher levels of access can have their access to documents declined through the use of a Readers field. If a user has Author or higher access to a database but is not named either explicitly or implicitly in a Readers field, he cannot access that document if there are other entities in the field. Table 5.4 illustrates how a Readers field interacts with each access level.

An empty Readers field—that is, one with no entries in it—does not restrict access to the document.

Table 5.4	How Readers Fields Interact with the Database ACL
User Access Level	**User Named in Readers Field**
No Access	Users cannot open database.
Depositor	Users can only add new documents; they cannot read or edit any existing documents.
Reader	Users can read any documents that have no Readers field, an empty Readers field, or in which they are named in the Readers field. Users cannot create new documents or edit existing documents.
Author	Users can read any documents that either have no Readers field or in which they are named in the Readers field. They can also create new documents and edit any documents in which they are named in an Authors field.
Editor	Users can read any documents that either have no Readers field or in which they are named in the Readers field. They can also create new documents and edit any documents.
Designer	Users can read any documents that either have no Readers field or in which they are named in the Readers field. They can also create new documents and edit any documents, as well as change design elements.
Manager	Users can read any documents that either have no Readers field or in which they are named in the Readers field. They can also create new documents and edit any documents, as well as change design elements, manage the ACL, full-text index the database, and delete the database.

To create a Readers field in a document, follow these steps:

1. Open a database in the Designer client.

2. Select and open a form that should create a Readers field in underlying documents.

3. Place the cursor in the position where the Readers field should appear.

4. Choose Create, Field, which opens the Field properties box.

5. Name the field and set the type to Readers. If the field is expected to contain multiple names, groups, and/or roles, be sure to check Allow Multiple Values.

6. Enter a pre-defined, hard-coded list, or enter a formula that computes a list of users, groups, and/or roles. You can use the @UserName function to return the current user's name in a formula.

7. Save the form.

 In most cases it's a good idea to use more than one Readers field in a document so all users cannot be accidentally locked out of a document. You can create a secondReaders field (which is computed when composed and uses a formula to compute the names, groups, and/or roles of the application's managers and/or administrators) so that administrators have a "back door" they can use to fix the document if other Readers fields in the document are not populated correctly.

Using Authors Fields

Much like Readers fields, an *Authors field* is a special type of text field that interacts with the database ACL, further refining it. In an application, users, groups, and roles may be given Author access to a database, meaning that they can create new documents (if the optional Create Documents privilege is enabled in the ACL) and read existing documents (not secured with Readers fields). However, Author access does not grant the capability to edit documents, not even those a user has created. For a user to edit a document that she has created, she must be explicitly or implicitly named in an Authors field in the document.

Also like Readers fields, being named in an Authors field does not give a user authority to edit a document if a user is already restricted at the database ACL level. For example, if a user is named either explicitly or implicitly in an Authors field, but has been granted only No Access, Depositor, or Reader access in the database ACL, the user cannot edit the document.

However, users with Author access who are named in an Authors field in the document can edit the document. Users with access levels higher than Author (Editor, Designer, or Manager) can edit any document unless restricted by a Readers field. Table 5.5 illustrates how the Authors field interacts with each access level.

Table 5.5 How Authors Fields Interact with the Database ACL	
User Access Level	**User Named in Authors Field**
No Access	Users cannot open database.
Depositor	Users can only add new documents; they cannot read or edit any existing documents.
Reader	Users can read any documents that have no Readers field, an empty Readers field, or in which they are named in the Readers field. Users cannot create new documents or edit existing documents.
Author	Users can read any documents that have no Readers field, an empty Readers field, or in which they are named in the Readers field. They may be enabled to create documents, delete documents (if named in an Authors field), and can edit any documents in which they are named in an Authors field.
Editor	Users can read any documents that have no Readers field, an empty Readers field, or in which they are named in the Readers field. They can also create new documents, edit any documents, and delete documents (if the delete flag has been set for Editors).
Designer	Users can read any documents that have no Readers field, an empty Readers field, or in which they are named in the Readers field. They can also create new documents and edit any documents, as well as change design elements.
Manager	Users can read any documents that have no Readers field, an empty Readers field, or in which they are named in the Readers field. They can also create new documents and edit any documents, as well as change design elements, manage the ACL, full-text index the database, and delete the database.

To create an Authors field in a document, follow these steps:

1. Open a database in the Designer client.

2. Select and open a form that should create an Authors field in underlying documents.

3. Place the cursor in the position where the Authors field should appear.

4. Choose Create, Field, which opens the Field properties box.

5. Name the field and set the type to Authors. If the field contains multiple names, groups, and/or roles, be sure to check Allow Multiple Values.

6. Enter a predefined, hard-coded list, or enter a formula that computes a list of users, groups, and/or roles. You can use the @UserName function to return the current user's name in a formula.

7. Save the form.

 To enable users with Author access to edit documents that they have created, you must include them either explicitly or implicitly in one or more Authors fields. Users with Editor access or higher can edit any document that they can read. If more than one Authors field exists, entries in any Authors field will be considered valid.

Summary

The following bullet points summarize the chapter and accentuate the key concepts you need to know for the exam.

➤ Domino security is flexible, granular, and very comprehensive.

➤ Security can be set at the physical, network, database, design element, document, and field level.

➤ The seven levels (Manager, Designer, Editor, Author, Reader, Depositor, and No Access) are the core of database-level security. You should know each level and understand the differences thoroughly.

➤ A number of optional privileges can be specified in the ACL, including Create Documents, Delete Documents, Create Private Agents, Create Personal Folders/Views, Create Shared Folders/Views, Create LotusScript/Java Agents, Read Public Documents, Write Public Documents, and Replicate or Copy Documents.

➤ Document-level security can be used to refine the ACL and is accomplished through the use of Readers and Authors fields. You should understand their similarities and differences thoroughly.

Exam Prep Questions

Question 1

> What does the Anonymous entry in the database ACL do?
>
> ○ A. Nothing; Anonymous is not a valid entry.
>
> ○ B. Grants anonymous users Depositor access to a database.
>
> ○ C. Enables users to authenticate whether they know the anonymous password.
>
> ○ D. Enables a user to access a database without being authenticated.

The correct answer is D. When the Anonymous entry is added to an ACL, unauthenticated users are granted the level of access specified for the Anonymous entry. A is incorrect because Anonymous is a valid entry. B is correct because the manager of the database can specify any access level for the Anonymous entry. C is incorrect because there is no password for Anonymous users.

Question 2

> Emma has Author access to a database and is listed in the Readers fields contained within a subset of documents. However, these documents do not contain any Authors fields. What rights does she have for those documents?
>
> ○ A. Reader access.
>
> ○ B. Editor access.
>
> ○ C. Author access.
>
> ○ D. No access.

The correct answer is A. Because she is named in the Readers fields and has Author access, she can read the documents, but because she is not named in an Authors field, she is unable to edit the document. B is incorrect because she has Author access but is not named in an Authors field in the document. C and D are incorrect because she has been granted Author access.

Question 3

> What is the minimum access level required by a user to create a document in a database?
>
> ○ A. Manager.
>
> ○ B. Depositor.
>
> ○ C. Author.
>
> ○ D. Editor.

The correct answer is B. Users must have a minimum access of Depositor to create a document in a database. A, B, and C are incorrect because the minimum level of access required to create a document is Depositor.

Question 4

> Wyatt has Reader access to a database and is listed in the Authors fields on a subset of documents. What rights does he have for those documents?
>
> ○ A. Reader access.
>
> ○ B. Author access.
>
> ○ C. No access.
>
> ○ D. None of the above.

The correct answer is A. Author fields merely refine the ACL, not override it. B, C, and D are incorrect because Wyatt has been granted Reader access in the ACL.

Question 5

> Samuel is a member of a group named Libertas Document Editors, which has Editor access to a database. Samuel is also a member of a group named Libertas Document Readers, which has Reader access to the database. Samuel would be able to do which of the following?
>
> ○ A. Edit all the documents in the database.
>
> ○ B. Edit none of the documents in the database.
>
> ○ C. Edit only documents that are created by him.
>
> ○ D. He would not have access to the database.

The correct answer is A. Samuel would be granted the higher level of access groups, so as a result of his membership in the Document Editors group, he would be granted Editor access to the database. B and C are incorrect because of Samuel's membership in the Libertas Document Editors group, which grants him Editor access. D is incorrect because Samuel's membership in either group would grant him access to the database.

Question 6

Rose is a member of a group named Document Editors, which has Editor access to a database. Rose is also listed explicitly in the database ACL with Reader access to the database. With these settings in the ACL, Rose would be able to do which of the following?

- ○ A. Edit all the documents in the database.
- ○ B. Edit all the documents in the database of which she is listed as a Reader in the Readers field.
- ○ C. Edit none of the documents in the database.
- ○ D. Edit only documents that are created by him.

The correct answer is C. When a user is named explicitly in the ACL and in a group, the explicit entry takes precedence over group membership. So Rose would be granted Reader access. A, B, and C are incorrect because Rose is explicitly named in the ACL with Reader access.

Question 7

Using groups in the ACL of a database provides which benefits?

- ○ A. Eases administration.
- ○ B. Reduces the size of an ACL.
- ○ C. Faster access resolution.
- ○ D. A and B.

The correct answer is D. The use of groups in the ACL eases administration and reduces the size of the ACL. A is incorrect because the use of groups also reduces the size of the ACL. B is incorrect because the use of groups also eases the administration of the ACL. C is incorrect because the use of groups actually slows access resolution because users' membership in the groups must be confirmed.

Question 8

Which access level would be the most appropriate for a user who should be able to add documents to a database and edit documents he has created but not edit others' documents?

- ○ A. Depositor.
- ○ B. Editor.
- ○ C. Author.
- ○ D. Manager.

The correct answer is C. A user granted Author access can optionally create new documents if he has the Create Documents privilege enabled and can edit documents that he created if he is also listed in an Authors field. A is incorrect because users with Depositor access can only add documents and cannot edit any document. B is incorrect because users with Editor access can edit any document that is readable. D is incorrect because users with Manager access can edit any document that is readable.

Question 9

What are the seven levels of database access?

- ○ A. Administrator, Designer, Editor, Author, Reader, Depositor, No Access.
- ○ B. Manager, Developer, Editor, Author, Reader, Depositor, No Access.
- ○ C. Manager, Designer, Editor, Author, Reader, Depositor, No Access.
- ○ D. Administrator, Developer, Editor, Author, Reader, Depositor, No Access.

The correct answer is C. A is incorrect because Administrator is not a valid access level. B is incorrect because Developer is not a valid access level. D is incorrect because neither Administrator nor Developer are valid access levels.

Question 10

What is the minimum level of access required to change the ACL of a database?

- ○ A. Designer.
- ○ B. Editor.
- ○ C. Administrator.
- ○ D. Manager.

The correct answer is D. A user must have Manager access to change a database's ACL.

Need to Know More?

 IBM. *Lotus Domino Designer 6 Help*, (Help6_Designer.nsf).

 IBM. *Lotus Domino Administrator 6 Help*, (Help6_Admin.nsf).

 IBM. *Domino Designer 6: A Developer's Handbook*. Place: Redbook 2002.

 IBM Lotus Developer Domain Web site: www.notes.net or www.lotus. com/ldd.

Coding Formulas

Terms you'll need to understand:

✓ Formula
✓ @Function
✓ @Command
✓ Window Title
✓ Integrate Development Environment (IDE)
✓ Auto-Complete
✓ Designer Reference Panel
✓ Domino Designer
✓ Design Pane
✓ Work Pane
✓ Programmer's Pane

Concepts you'll need to master:

✓ Using field validation and translation formulas
✓ Setting default field values
✓ Creating formulas with @Commands
✓ Creating formulas with @Functions
✓ Using the Designer Reference Panel
✓ Setting programmer pane properties
✓ Setting window titles
✓ Hiding information on forms Information
✓ Making preferred tools available in the IDE

This chapter covers the Domino 6 programming topics that you'll need to know to take and pass Exam 610, including @Commands, @Functions, formulas, and the Domino Designer IDE.

Domino Programming

Like its predecessors, Domino 6 provides a powerful application development environment, in large part because a number of programming languages can be used exclusively, or in conjunction with one another, to build powerful and sophisticated applications. At the present time, Domino 6 supports the following programming languages: Notes Formulas (Formula Language), LotusScript, Java, and JavaScript. The Notes Formula language is the oldest of the four and has been around since the inception of Notes. It is a fairly easy-to-learn and easy-to-use programming language, and you can accomplish some coding tasks in Notes using only the Formula language!

According to the Lotus Designer Help database, a *formula* is "an expression that has program-like attributes." In Domino 6.x, some of the many things you can do with formulas are

➤ Create selection criteria for a view.

➤ Return a value to a field.

➤ Validate a field.

➤ Manipulate the value of a field.

➤ Create new fields in a document.

➤ Perform actions when documents are open, refreshed, or closed.

➤ Program replication formulas.

➤ Return a value in a view column.

➤ Automate buttons or hotspots

➤ Program agents.

The Domino Designer

Formula coding, like all Domino coding options, is written with Domino's user-friendly *Integrated Development Environment* (IDE), known as the *Domino Designer*. An Integrated Development Environment is an application development tool that provides a robust, complete toolset that includes debugging and online help capabilities. The Domino Designer is Domino's

IDE and it is used to build Domino applications. The Domino Designer is shown in Figure 6.1.

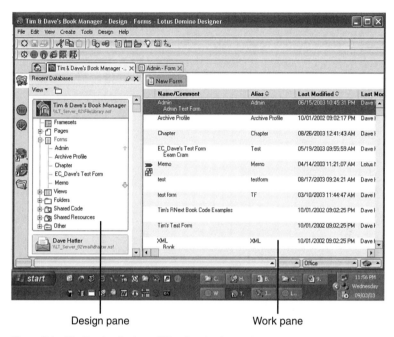

Design pane   Work pane

Figure 6.1   The Domino Designer IDE makes development a snap.

The Domino Designer Application and Design Environment

There are several ways to open the Domino Designer, but the easiest is to select a database you want to design from the Workspace and right-click it, which displays a pop-up menu. Then select Open in Designer, which opens the Domino Designer (also called the Designer for short) as shown earlier in Figure 6.1.

There are two basic "panes" within the Domino Designer window: the Design Pane and the Work Pane. The *Design Pane* maintains a list of databases that have recently been opened in the Designer, as well as the design elements they contain. The design elements are grouped by type. For example, you could select Forms to see all the forms in the database. This function is new to 6 and enables Designers to scroll and choose a specific element without listing them in the work pane. After the developer selects the type of design element to work on, the list of those elements in the database is displayed in the Work Pane.

The *Work Pane* displays a list of particular design elements of a given type, such as forms, views, or agents, within the selected database. A developer can then double-click the design element to open it, which then modifies the display of the Designer, as shown in Figure 6.2.

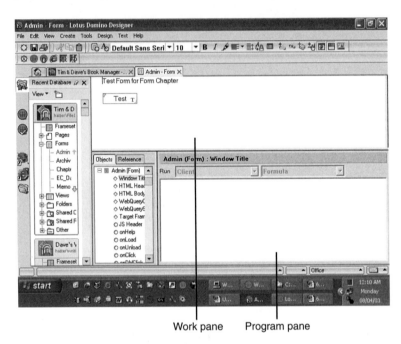

Work pane   Program pane

Figure 6.2 A form ready to be designed.

After a design element has been opened, the Designer is split into three windows. The Design Pane remains on the left side of the screen for ease of navigation between elements and databases, whereas the Work Pane is displayed at the top of the screen and is joined by the Programmer's Pane displayed at the bottom of the screen, as already illustrated by Figure 6.2. The design element opened is displayed in the Work Pane. It is within the Work Pane that developers can modify the selected element, such as by adding fields to a form or modifying the columns within a view.

The Programmer's Pane is where all the real action takes place when it comes to Domino development, as this is where programming logic is coded for Domino elements.

Setting Programmer's Pane Properties

In a much-appreciated effort to make coding as efficient and effective as possible, Lotus/IBM has made the Programmer's Pane highly configurable, and it can be customized to suit your particular tastes.

Various aspects of the Programmer's Pane can be customized, including font face, font size, font color, indention, wrapping, and other more advanced features such as Auto-Complete, which is covered shortly.

Additionally, you can make specific changes that will affect the formatting of any of the following types of code, and the exact options vary depending on the code type:

➤ Script/Java

➤ Formulas

➤ Simple Actions

To customize the Programmer's Pane, follow these steps.

1. Right-click in the Programmer's Pane, which opens a pop-up menu. Alternatively, right-click in the Programmer's Pane and click the Properties icon on the tool bar. Either of these actions opens the Programmer's Pane properties box shown in Figure 6.3.

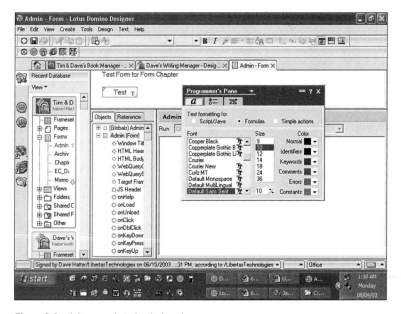

Figure 6.3   A form ready to be designed.

2. The Programmer's Pane properties box opens to the Text tab (first tab). Select the type of code to format in the Text Formatting For radio button.

3. Select the desired font face and font size. Optionally, select colors for various code elements. Colors can be selected only for LotusScript/Java and Formula code. The following list defines the code elements that can be modified:

> ➤ Normal

> ➤ Identifiers

> ➤ Keywords

> ➤ Comments

> ➤ Errors

> ➤ Constants

4. Click the Format tab (second tab) to configure the following language-specific settings:

> ➤ *Auto-Indent LotusScript*—This feature is enabled by default and is used to make LotusScript code more readable. However, you can disable it here.

> ➤ *Auto-Wrap Formulas*—This feature is enabled by default and causes long lines of Formula code to wrap. It can be disabled here.

> ➤ *Automatically add "Option Declare"*—This feature is enabled by default and is new to Domino 6. As a best practice, you should always use Option Declare in your LotusScript code to ensure that all variables must be explicitly declared.

5. Optionally, click the Auto-Complete tab (3rd tab) to configure the new Auto-Complete settings, which are covered in more detail shortly:

> ➤ *Auto List Members*—Enabled by default, this feature controls the automatic display of a context-sensitive pop-up list of available options.

> ➤ *Auto Pop-up*—Enabled by default, this feature displays a parameter list for a triggering function or method to ease coding.

> ➤ *Delay*—This option controls the amount of time (in milliseconds) between a trigger keystroke (one that matches an element name) and a second keystroke before the pop-up list displays. Another keystroke before the specified time has elapsed stops the list from popping up.

6. Close the Programmer's Pane properties box after you have made the desired changes.

Don't be surprised to see a question or two about Programmer's Pane options—in particular, the new Automatically Add "Option Declare" option on the Format tab (second tab), which is a welcome new feature, and the Auto-complete options on the third tab.

Using the Programmer's Pane Auto-complete

As stated earlier, Auto-complete is a very handy new feature of Domino 6 that uses type-ahead functionality to select and paste certain syntax elements directly into the Programmer's Pane as you are coding. If the syntax element that you have selected takes parameters, the valid parameters are displayed in the pop-up to help guide you as you code.

Auto-completion is available when coding

➤ @Commands

➤ @Functions

➤ LotusScript classes

Using Auto-complete with @Functions

To use Auto-complete when coding @Functions in the Programmer's Pane, follow these steps:

1. Enter the "at" symbol (@) and pause momentarily to launch the Auto-complete pop-up, which displays a list of all available choices, which is shown in Figure 6.4.

2. Begin typing the name of a function (type-ahead) or scroll through the list and select the appropriate function. For example:

   `@Left(`

3. After you have located the functions, press Enter to paste the function into the Programmer's Pane and close the pop-up list.

4. Optionally, for functions that take parameters, type a left parenthesis "(" to launch a pop-up containing the syntax of the first signature. The first valid parameter appears bolded. If up and down arrows display, they indicate that you can press the up and down arrow keys to display the various options.

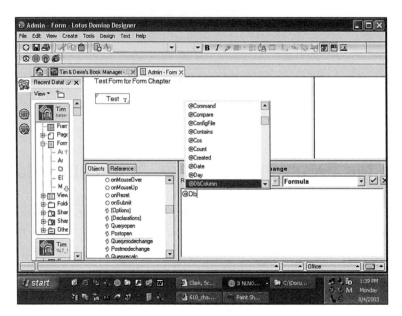

Figure 6.4 The very handy @Function auto-complete list.

5. Optionally, if the function takes multiple parameters, enter a semicolon
   (;) between each parameter, and the next parameter appears bolded.

6. Enter a right parenthesis ")" to complete the function, or simply press
   Esc to close the pop-up.

Using Auto-complete with @Commands

To use Auto-complete when coding @Commands in the Programmer's Pane,
follow these steps:

1. Enter the "at" symbol (@) and a left square bracket ([) and pause
   momentarily to launch the Auto-complete pop-up, which displays a list
   of all available choices.

2. Begin typing **Command** (type-ahead) and a left parenthesis and pause
   momentarily, or scroll through the list and select the Command, which
   then displays a list of valid commands (shown below in Figure 6.5).
   For example:

   ```
   @Command(
   ```

3. Begin typing the name of the desired command (type-ahead) or scroll
   through the list and select the appropriate command. After a command
   is selected, square brackets ([ ]) are added automatically. For example:

   ```
   @Command([AddBookmark])
   ```

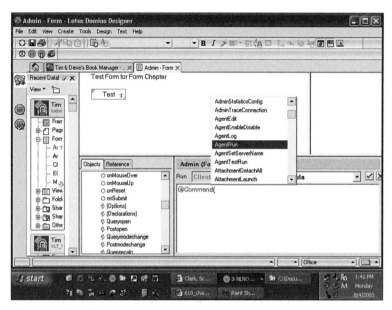

Figure 6.5 The @Command Auto-complete list.

4. Optionally, if the command takes multiple parameters, enter a semicolon (;) between each parameter, and the next parameter appears bolded.

5. Enter a right parenthesis ")" to complete the command, or simply press Esc to close the pop-up.

Using the Auto-complete with LotusScript

To use Auto-complete when coding LotusScript in the Programmer's Pane, follow these steps.

1. Declare an object and enter a space following the As keyword to open a pop-up list of available classes, which is shown in Figure 6.6.

2. Begin typing the name of a valid object, or scroll through the list and select the appropriate object.

3. Optionally, enter a period (.) after an object name, which opens a pop-up of methods and properties.

4. Optionally, from the pop-up list of methods and properties, either type ahead to select the desired element or scroll through the list and select it. Press Enter to paste the element into the Programmer's Pane.

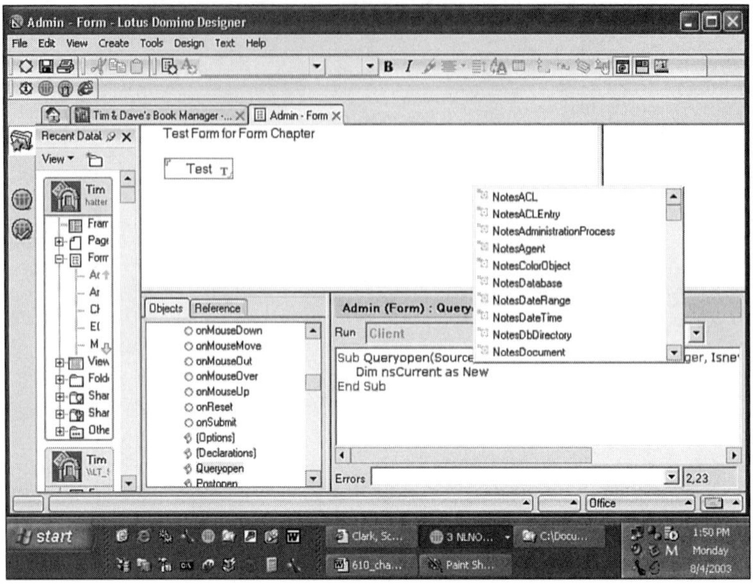

Figure 6.6 The pop-up list of available classes; where has this feature been all my life?

5. Optionally, for methods that take parameters, simply type a left paren-thesis "(" to display a pop-up box displaying the parameter list. The first parameter appears bolded.

6. Optionally, enter a comma (,) between each parameter, which makes the next parameter bold.

7. Enter a right parenthesis ")" or press Esc to close the pop-up.

Using the Designer Reference Panel

The Designer Reference Panel of the Programmer's Pane is a valuable tool that provides reference information about the current programming context, meaning that the options it displays vary depending on the programming language selected.

The Designer Reference Panel provides information for the following cod-ing choices:

➤ Formulas

➤ LotusScript

➤ JavaScript

➤ Java

The Designer Reference Panel is displayed in Figure 6.7.

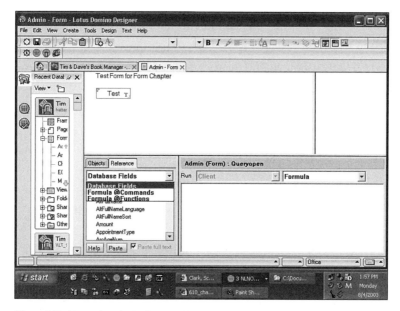

Figure 6.7   The options in the Designer Reference panel list vary based on coding language.

When coding in the Formula language you have the following reference options:

➤ *Database fields*—This option displays a list of all the fields in the current database.

➤ *Formula @Commands*—This option displays a list of all the @Commands available.

➤ *Formula @Functions*—This option displays a list of all the @Functions available.

After you have selected an item in the list, you double-click it to paste it into the Programmer's Pane to start coding, or you can click Help to get online help for the selected entry.

When coding in the LotusScript you have the following reference options:

➤ *LotusScript Language*—This option displays a list of all native LotusScript language functions.

➤ *Domino: Classes*—This option displays a list of Domino classes available in LotusScript.

➤ *Domino: Constants*—This option displays a list of all pre-defined LotusScript constants.

➤ *Domino: Subs and functions*—This option displays a list of all the fields in the current database.

➤ *Domino: Variables*—This option displays a list of all the LotusScript variables.

➤ *OLE Classes*—This option displays a list of all the OLE Classes installed on the machine.

When coding in Java you have the following reference options:

➤ *Core Java*—This option displays a list of all Java classes.

➤ *Notes Java*—This option displays a list of Domino classes available in Java.

➤ *Third-party Java*—This option displays a list of all third-party Java classes. At the present time this is primarily XML related and includes DOM and SAX classes.

When coding in JavaScript you have the following reference options:

➤ *Web D.O.M.*—This option displays a list of all Document Object Model (D.O.M.) methods, properties, and commands for Web clients.

➤ *Notes D.O.M.*—This option displays a list of all Document Object Model (D.O.M.) methods, properties, and commands for Notes clients.

Using the Designer Objects Pane

The Designer Objects pane, shown in Figure 6.8, is a fundamental part of IDE and is used to select an object within the current design element to program. Similar in function to the Designer Reference Panel, it displays a context-sensitive list of objects and events and can be found in the lower left section of the Programmer's Pane.

Using the Designer Objects pane is easy. You select an object in the current design element to program, select a programming language, and begin coding—it's just that simple.

The Designer Object pane enables you to code objects and events by using any of the following choices:

➤ Formulas

➤ LotusScript

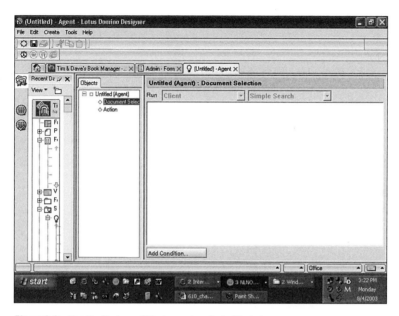

Figure 6.8   Use the Designer Object pane to select objects to program.

➤ JavaScript

➤ Java

➤ Imported Java

➤ Simple Actions

Making Preferred Tools Available via the IDE

New to Domino 6 is the really cool capability to customize and extend the Tools menu in the Designer client. You can now include menu items that launch other commonly used applications, such as a graphics editing tool or CSS editor, or you can write your own formulas to run. You can also create submenus under which you can group related tools. A customized Tools menu is shown in Figure 6.10 later in this section.

Additionally, when you add a new tool to the menu, you can define when the tool will be available so that the tool appears in the menu only when you need it. For example, you might want to keep your graphics editor available all the time, whereas the CSS editor menu option appears only when you are editing a form, page, or subform.

Be prepared to see questions about the new Tools menu options on the exam.

Adding a new tool to the Tools menu is easy; just follow these steps:

1. Select Tools, Add Tool from the menu in the Designer client, which opens the Add Tool dialog box, shown in Figure 6.9.

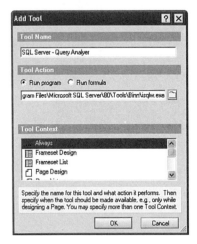

Figure 6.9 The Add Tool dialog box makes it easy to add Tools menu options.

2. Enter a descriptive name for the menu option in the Tool Name field. Make sure to use a name you'll recognize later as this is what will be displayed in the Tools menu.

3. Choose Run Program or Run Formula for the Tool Action, as follows:

   ➤ To launch an external application from the menu, choose Run Program, and then either enter the path for the executable file to launch or click the file folder icon to browse the file system to select the executable.

   ➤ To run a custom-coded formula, select Run Formula and enter a formula.

4. In the Tool Context box, choose one or more contexts in which the new menu option should be displayed. To ensure that the tool is always displayed, choose Always, otherwise, select one or more contexts in which the menu item should be displayed.

5. Click OK to save the tool and add the new option to the Tools menu.

After you have added a custom tool, it appears in the Tools menu for the contexts you defined.

To edit an existing custom tool, follow these steps:

1. Select Tools, Customize Tools from the menu, which opens the Customize Tools dialog box shown in Figure 6.10.

Figure 6.10 The Customize Tools dialog box.

2. Select the context that contains the tool to be modified and click the arrow beside it to expand the list of tools in that design context.

3. Select the tool and click the Edit button to edit the name of the tool and/or the formula that it executes.

Tools that launch an executable program actually use the **@command([Execute])** command to run the executable.

4. Click OK to save changes.

To delete a tool from the Tools menu, follow these steps:

1. Select Tools, Customize Tools from the menu, which opens the Customize Tools dialog box shown in Figure 6.10.

2. Select the context that contains the tool to be deleted and click the arrow beside it to expand the list of tools in that design context.

3. Select the tool and click Cut to remove it.

To further enhance its usability, you can use submenus to divide the Tools menu into logically grouped categories. Figure 6.11 shows my customized Tools menu.

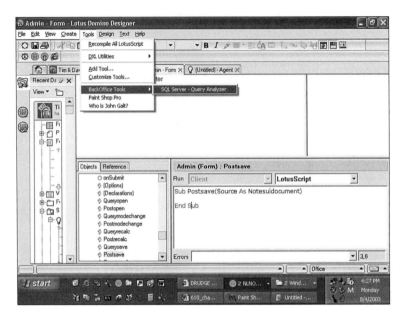

Figure 6.11 Customizing the Tools menu is a handy way to speed development.

To add a submenu to the Tools menu, follow these steps:

1. Select Tools, Customize Tools from the menu, which opens the Customize Tools dialog box shown in Figure 6.10.

2. Select the context in which the submenu should display and then click the Add Submenu button, which opens a prompt.

3. Enter a name for the submenu in the Submenu name field and click OK.

4. Position the submenu and its children within the selected context by using either drag-and-drop or the Copy and Paste buttons. Click OK.

Working with Basic Formula Language

In Domino, formulas can beused to accomplish many programming objectives, including

➤ Automating tasks

➤ Acting on a condition

➤ Comparing values

➤ Computing values

➤ Modifying values

➤ Create selection criteria: views, agents, and replication formulas

➤ Validate information

The Formula language processes back-end Notes objects, much like the back-end classes in LotusScript, whereas @Commands (a special type of @Function covered in detail in the next section) operate in the user interface. Changes made using @Commands are not reflected in the back-end (stored documents) until a document is saved, while changes made using @Functions are made real-time to the stored documents. A formula is composed of one or more @Functions, which consist of any of the elements listed in Table 6.1.

Table 6.1 Formula Elements	
Element	**Description**
@Commands	Similar to functions, @Commands execute Notes commands, most of which duplicate menu options such as File, Save.
@Functions	Prebuilt functions that perform a specific action and return a result.
Constants	Static values that do not change. Notes supports three types of constants: Text, Number, and Date. The following is an example of a text constant: "Samuel Hatter."
Variables	A named placeholder that refers to a location in memory that stores information that may change (hence the name "variable") during the execution of the program.
Keywords	Statements that perform special functions. There are five: **DEFAULT**, **ENVIRONMENT**, **FIELD**, **REM**, and **SELECT**.
Operators	Operators assign values and modify values. Domino supports a large number of operators.

Domino enables you to write one or more @Functions in a formula; functions are executed top to bottom and left to right, completing each statement before proceeding to the next with some minor exceptions. @PostedCommand and certain other @Command functions are executed in the order they appear *after* all other @Functions complete execution. The @Functions are covered in more detail in the next section.

The remainder of this section is not intended to be an exhaustive compendium of formula functions and commands; there are far too many! Rather, it is intended to provide an overview of how they are used. You can refer to the Domino Designer Help database Help6_Designer.nsf for a comprehensive list.

Creating Formulas with @Functions

@Functions have been around since the very beginning of Notes and they are the foundation of formula language development in Domino. An *@Function* is a native function that can perform a calculation or task and return a value.

All @Functions follow the same basic syntax, which consists of the "at" symbol (@), the function name, an opening parenthesis "(", a semicolon-separated list of arguments, if any, and a closing parenthesis ")." The following code snippet illustrates the basic syntax for an @Function:

```
@functionname(argument1;argumentn);
```

The following examples illustrate several @Function variations:

```
@Now;
@Count(listofvalues);
@Left(searchinstring;searchforstring);
@Prompt([style];title;prompt);
```

 Not all @Functions take parameters; for those that don't, simply omit the parentheses. For those that do take parameters, the parentheses are required.

Some functions use special arguments known as keyword arguments, which must be enclosed in square brackets ([]). The following is a list of @Functions that take keyword arguments:

➤ `@Abstract`

➤ `@Command`

➤ `@PostedCommand`

➤ `@DocMark`

➤ `@GetPortsList`

➤ `@PickList`

➤ `@MailSend`

➤ `@Name`

➤ `@Prompt`

Be sure to specify the correct data type for each argument per the @Function description.

Some functions have a "side-effect," which (according to the Domino online help) is "an action that occurs outside the immediate scope of the formula." For example, `@DbLookup` performs a database lookup and returns a value. The following is a list of @Functions that have side-effects.

➤ `@Command`

➤ `@PostedCommand`

➤ `@DbColumn`

➤ `@DbCommand`

➤ `@DbLookup`

➤ `@DDEInitiate`

➤ `@DDEExecute`

➤ `@DDEPoke`

➤ `@DDETerminate`

➤ `@MailSend`

➤ `@Prompt`

➤ `@PickList`

➤ `@DialogBox`

New and Enhanced @Functions in Domino 6

The following is a list of new @Functions in Domino 6.

➤ `@AttachmentModifiedTimes`—Returns modification date of the attached file

➤ `@BusinessDays`—Returns the number of business days in a date range

➤ `@CheckFormulaSyntax`—Checks commented formula code for errors

➤ `@Compare`—Compares two lists pair-wise

➤ `@ConfigFile`—Returns the file path to the Notes INI file

➤ `@Count`—Returns the number of elements in a list

➤ @DocLock—Locks, unlocks, or returns the lock status of the current document

➤ @DocOmittedLength—Returns the number of bytes removed from a document that has been truncated in replication

➤ @DoWhile—Executes one or more statements iteratively while a condition remains true

➤ @Eval—Compiles and runs each element in a text expression as a formula at run-time

➤ @FileDir—Returns only the directory portion of a path name

➤ @FloatEq—Compares two numbers for equality within a range

➤ @For—Executes one or more statements iteratively while a condition remains true; checks the condition after executing the statements

➤ @GetAddressBooks—Returns a list of the address books for the current user or server

➤ @GetCurrentTimeZone—Returns the OS's time zone settings in canonical time zone format

➤ @GetField—Returns the value of a specified field

➤ @GetFocusTable—Returns the row, column, and name of the table currently in focus

➤ @GetHTTPHeader—Returns the contents of an HTTP request-header field

➤ @GetViewInfo—Returns a view attribute

➤ @HashPassword—Encodes a string

➤ @IfError—Returns a null string ("") or the value of an alternative statement if a statement returns an error

➤ @IsNull—Checks for a null value

➤ @IsVirtualizedDirectory—Indicates whether virtualized directories are enabled for the current server

➤ @LDAPServer—Returns the URL and port number of the LDAP listener for the current domain

➤ @Nothing—In an @Transform formula, returns no list element

➤ @ReplicaID—Returns the replica ID of the current database

➤ @ServerAccess—Returns the access level of a specified user on the server

➤ @ServerName—Returns the name of the current server

➤ @SetHTTPHeader—Allows you to set the value of an HTTP response-header field

➤ @SetViewInfo—Filters the documents in a view according to specified criteria

➤ @Sort—Sorts a list of values

➤ @StatusBar—Writes a message to the status bar

➤ @ThisName—Returns the name of the current field

➤ @ThisValue—Returns the value of the current field

➤ @TimeMerge—Builds a single time-date value from separate time, date, and time zone values

➤ @TimeToTextInZone—Converts a time-date value to a text string, including the time zone information

➤ @TimeZoneToText—Converts a canonical time zone value to a text string

➤ @ToNumber—Converts a text string to a number

➤ @ToTime—Converts a text string to a date-time

➤ @Transform—Applies a formula to every element of a multi-value list

➤ @UpdateFormulaContext—Focuses the context of a formula to the current Notes client window

➤ @URLDecode—Decodes a URL string into text

➤ @URLEncode—Encodes a string in a URL-safe string

➤ @UrlQueryString—Returns the current URL command and parameters, or the value of a specified parameter

➤ @VerifyPassword—Compares two passwords, enabling you to determine whether a password has a hash or standard password format

➤ @WebDbName—Returns the database name as a URL format

➤ @While—Executes one or more statements iteratively while a condition remains true; checks the condition before executing the statements

The following is a list of enhanced @Functions in Domino 6.

➤ @DialogBox

➤ @DbColumn

➤ @DbCommand

➤ @DbLookup

➤ @Explode

➤ @Max

➤ @Min

➤ @Name

➤ @Now

➤ @SetDocField

➤ @Text

➤ @UserAccess

Creating Formulas with @Commands

@Commands are a special type of @Function that provide a mechanism for developers to programmatically execute a Lotus Notes/Domino command. @Commands can be loosely lumped into two groups: commands that execute options available from the menu (most of the standard menu commands can be executed by using @Command) and a number of specialized commands that perform specific tasks.

@Commands run on the UI and are primarily intended to replicate menu functionality, meaning that they are intended for use in toolbar button, hotspot, and action formulas. @Commands cannot be used in view column, view selection, hide-when, section editor, window title, field, or form formulas, or in agents that run on a server.

@Commands look much like @Functions, but with one major difference; the first argument is required and specifies the command to run. The following code snippet shows the syntax of an @Command:

```
@Command([commandname];arguments)
```

The first argument, commandname, is the name of the command to execute and it is required. Additionally, the command name must be enclosed in square brackets ([ ]). The following code snippet illustrates using the FileSave command, which is equivalent to choosing File, Save from the menu.

```
@Command([FileSave])
```

Additional optional parameters, if needed, may be specified after the commandname argument. The following code snippet illustrates using the EditDocument command, which takes two optional arguments:

```
@Command([EditDocument];mode;previewpane );
```

@Commands return the numeric value one (1) to indicate that the command completed successfully, or the numeric value zero (0) to indicate the command did not complete successfully.

Like @Functions, many commands also have side-effects. For example, using the AddDatabase command (@Command([AddDatabase])) adds a database icon to your workspace.

You must also be aware of the order of execution for @Commands, and this is especially true when writing a formula that has a number of @Functions and @Commands. In Domino 6, commands launched by @Command run in the order in which they appear in the formula, meaning that changes made by the command may affect the formula's operation. There are some exceptions to this rule; certain commands (listed in Table 6.2) are always executed after all @Functions. Additionally, in Domino 6, there are several new commands that provide equivalent functionality but are executed immediately when they are encountered in a formula.

Table 6.2 @Commands	
Evaluate After All @Functions	**Evaluate When Encountered**
EditClear	Clear
EditProfile	EditProfileDocument
FileCloseWindow	CloseWindow
FileDatabaseDelete	DatabaseDelete
FileExit	ExitNotes
Folder	FolderDocuments
NavigateNext	NavNext
NavigateNextMain	NavNextMain
NavigateNextSelected	NavNextSelected
NavigateNextUnread	NavNextUnread
NavigatePrev	NavPrev
NavigatePrevMain	NavPrevMain
NavigatePrevSelected	NavPrevSelected
NavigatePrevUnread	NavPrevUnread
ReloadWindow	RefreshWindow
ToolsRunBackgroundMacros	RunScheduledAgents
ToolsRunMacro	RunAgent
ViewChange	SwitchView
ViewSwitchForm	SwitchForm

"Evaluated when encountered" commands are new to Domino 6 and you should expect to be questioned about this handy new behavior on the exam.

As was stated earlier, most @Commands provide a way to programmatically execute menu commands, which means that they do not work over the Web. There are a number of commands that can be invoked from a Web client, but they might work somewhat differently when they are invoked from a Notes client. The Domino 6 commands that may be used on the Web are as follows:

➤ CalendarFormat

➤ CalendarGoto

➤ Clear

➤ CloseWindow

➤ Compose

➤ EditClear

➤ EditDocument

➤ EmptyTrash

➤ FileCloseWindow

➤ FileOpenDatabase

➤ FileSave

➤ Folder

➤ FolderDocuments

➤ MoveToTrash

➤ NavigateNext

➤ NavigateNextMain

➤ NavigatePrev

➤ NavigatePrevMain

➤ NavNext

➤ NavNextMain

➤ NavPrev

➤ NavPrevMain

➤ OpenDocument

➤ OpenFrameset

➤ OpenHelpDocument

➤ OpenNavigator

➤ OpenPage

➤ OpenView

➤ RefreshFrame

➤ RemoveFromFolder

➤ RunAgent

➤ SwitchView

➤ ToolsRunMacro

➤ ViewChange

➤ ViewCollapse

➤ ViewCollapseAll

➤ ViewExpand

➤ ViewExpandAll

➤ ViewRefreshFields

➤ ViewShowSearchBar

Programming Window Titles

By default, the title of a form (or page, for that matter) is "Untitled," which is not very descriptive or useful. You can use the Formula language to set the form title, which is a very good habit to get into. Just follow these steps:

1. Open the form or page.

2. Select the Window Title element on the Objects tab of the Programmer's Pane.

3. Enter a formula in the Programmer's pane.

4. Save the form or page.

5. Test the form or page.

The following example illustrates the creation of a conditional window title:

```
@If(@isNewDoc;"New Contact";"Contact:"+tLastName+ " "+ tFirstName)
```

Setting Default Field Values

You can use the Formula language to specify a default value for an editable field. To supply a default value, follow these steps:

1. Open the form in the Designer.

2. Select or create the field for which you want to add a default value.

3. Choose Default Value on the Objects tab.

4. Enter a formula in the Programmer's pane.

5. Save the form.

Create Translation Formulas

If you want to ensure that data in certain fields is formatted properly, you can use an input translation formula. When a document is saved or refreshed, the input translation formulas in the fields on the form are executed. Input translation formulas can do a number of tasks, such as

➤ Trim leading and trailing spaces off a value (@Trim).

➤ Make a value all uppercase or lowercase (@UpperCase or @LowerCase).

➤ Make a value, such as a name, a proper noun (@Propercase).

➤ Mask values such as zip codes or phone numbers by inserting characters such as hyphens, parentheses, periods, and/or commas.

To add an input translation formula to a field, follow these steps:

1. Open the form in the Designer client.

2. Select or create the field for which you want to add an input translation formula.

3. Select Input Translation on the Objects tab.

4. Enter a formula in the Programmer's pane.

5. Save the form.

The following example demonstrates a simple input translation formula that trims leading and trailing spaces off the value in a field:

```
@Trim(tLastName);
```

Create Field Validation Formulas

Input validation formulas provide a means to ensure that users enter correct and complete data by preventing users from saving a document if a field's value is invalid. Every time a document is saved or refreshed, the input validation formulas are executed to ensure that the proper values have been entered. For each field, the value is tested according to the formula, and if the value is acceptable, the formula returns true and the document can be saved. If a value is unacceptable, the formula returns false and the document cannot be saved until the proper data is entered. Additionally, the user is prompted with a message supplied by the developer to explain the problem.

When creating input validation formulas, you must use the @Failure and @Success functions. @Success returns true and allows the document to be saved. @Failure returns false and displays a prompt with a message the developer supplies as a parameter. Additionally, it causes the termination of the save.

To create an input validation formula, follow these steps:

1. Open the form in the Designer.

2. Select or create the field for which you want to add an input validation formula.

3. Select Input Validation on the Objects tab.

4. Enter a formula in the Programmer's pane.

5. Save the form.

The following example demonstrates an input validation formula that tests the tLastname field to ensure that it is not empty. If tLastname is empty, a prompt displays the message Please enter a value for last name. and the save is aborted.

```
@if(@Trim(tLastName)="";@Failure("Enter a value for last name.");@Success);
```

Using Hide-When Options to Hide Information on Forms

Many Domino design elements such as forms enable you to hide information based on the context in which it is displayed, or to use hide-when formulas to conditionally display information.

Virtually any information on a form can be hidden; just follow the steps below:

1. Open the form in the Designer.

2. Select an element on the form that should be hidden.

3. Choose Text, Text Properties from the menu, which opens the Text properties box.

4. Click the Hide tab (fifth tab), which displays the hide-when options, shown in Figure 6.12. Each of the options is explained in the following list.

Figure 6.12 Hide-when options enable you to easily hide information.

> ➤ *Notes 4.6 or later* When enabled, hides selected item from Notes client version 4.6 or higher.

> ➤ *Web browsers* When enabled, hides selected item Web browsers.

> ➤ *Mobile* When enabled, hides selected item from mobile clients.

> ➤ *Previewed for reading* When enabled, hides selected item when form is opened in the Preview pane in Read mode.

> ➤ *Previewed for editing* When enabled, hides selected item when form is opened in the Preview pane in Edit mode.

> ➤ *Opened for reading* When enabled, hides selected item when form is opened in read mode.

> ➤ *Opened for editing* When enabled, hides selected item when form is opened in Edit mode.

> ➤ *Printed* When enabled, hides selected item when form is printed.

> ➤ *Copied to the clipboard* When enabled, hides selected item when data is copied to the clipboard.

> ➤ *Embedded* When enabled, hides selected item if the embedded editor was used to embed the item.

> ➤ *Hide paragraph if formula is true* When enabled, enables the developer to specify a formula. If the formula evaluates to true, the item is hidden; otherwise it is not hidden.

   5. Select appropriate hide-when options.

   6. Save the form.

For example, you might use a hide-when formula to ensure that a certain paragraph displays only for members of the Sales group. The following brief example illustrates a hide-when formula that hides an item if the current user is not using a Web browser.

```
!@IsMember("$$WebClient";@UserRoles)
```

Summary

The following bullet points summarize the chapter and accentuate the key concepts to know for the exam:

➤ Know how default field formulas work.

➤ Know how field input translation and validation formulas work.

➤ Understand the difference between @Functions and @Commands.

➤ Know how to configure the Programmer's Pane properties.

➤ Know how the cool new Auto-complete feature can help you be a more efficient developer.

➤ Know what the Designer Reference and Designer Objects tabs do.

➤ Understand how hide-whens can help you hide information on a form.

➤ Know how to use formulas to define a window title.

➤ Know how to customize the Tools menu.

➤ Know @Commands and @Functions, especially new ones.

Exam Prep Practice Questions

Question 1

> The Object tab in the Programmer's Pane contains what type of information?
>
> ○ A. There is no Objects tab.
>
> ○ B. A listing of reference information.
>
> ○ C. A context-sensitive listing of objects that can be programmed.
>
> ○ D. A listing of embedded objects.

The correct Answer is C. A is incorrect because there is an Objects tab in the Programmer's Pane. B is incorrect because the Reference tab lists the reference information. D is incorrect because the Objects tab lists available objects for the current context.

Question 2

> The new Auto-complete feature works for which languages?
>
> ○ A. LotusScript and Formula.
>
> ○ B. Formula and Java.
>
> ○ C. JavaScript and LotusScript.
>
> ○ D. JavaScript and Formula.

The correct Answer is A. B is incorrect because Java does not have Auto-complete capability. C and D are incorrect because JavaScript does not have Auto-complete capability.

Question 3

> What is input validation used for?
>
> ○ A. Converting field values from one format to another.
>
> ○ B. Input validation is not used in Notes/Domino.
>
> ○ C. Ensuring that a field contains the proper information.
>
> ○ D. Setting the default value of a field.

The correct answer is C. Input validation is used to ensure that the proper information is entered into a field. A is incorrect because Input Translation formulas are used to format field values. B is incorrect because Input validation is used regularly in Notes. D is incorrect because default field formulas set the default value of a field.

Question 4

> @Functions are used to accomplish what?
>
> ○ A. Compute values and return results.
> ○ B. Return results.
> ○ C. Compute values.
> ○ D. Perform special LotusScript tasks.

The correct answer is A. @Functions compute and return values. B and C are incorrect because @Functions can compute values and return results. D is incorrect because @Functions are used to create formulas.

Question 5

> @Commands are typically evaluated when in a formula in Domino 6?
>
> ○ A. After all @Functions.
> ○ B. Before all @Functions.
> ○ C. As they occur in the code with some exceptions.

The correct answer is C. @Commands are normally evaluated when they occur in a formula. A and B are incorrect because in Domino 6, most commands are executed as they occur.

Question 6

> The New Customizable Tools menu enables you to do what?
>
> ○ A. Run custom formulas.
> ○ B. Run commonly used applications.
> ○ C. Both A and B.

The correct answer is C. A is incorrect because the new customizable Tools menu enables you to run commonly used applications as well. B is incorrect because the new customizable Tools menu enables you to run custom formulas as well.

Question 7

Which of the follow @Functions illustrates correct syntax?

- O A. **@Nows**
- O B. **@Now([SERVERTIME])**
- O C. **@Now(([SERVERTIME];"LT_Server_01")**
- O D. All of the above.
- O E. All of the above are incorrect.

The correct answer is E. A, B, C, and D are incorrect because each of the above forms of the @Now function is incorrect. All functions take the form @functionname(arguments);.

Question 8

"Evaluated when encountered" commands do what?

- O A. This is not a valid Domino concept.
- O B. Execute after all @Functions.
- O C. Replace the functionality of certain @Commands that evaluate after @Functions and execute immediately.
- O D. Replace @Functions.

The correct answer is C. A is incorrect because this is a new feature of Domino 6. B is incorrect because these new @Command functions evaluate immediately and can replace older commands that executed at the end of a formula. D is incorrect because @Functions are still the basis of formulas.

Question 9

> What is wrong with the @Command **@Command(AddBookmark;"www. libertastechnologies.com")**?
>
> ○ A. Nothing.
>
> ○ B. The command name, **AddBookmark**, must be enclosed in double quotes ("").
>
> ○ C. The command name, **AddBookmark**, must be enclosed in single quotes (").
>
> ○ D. The command name, **AddBookmark**, must be enclosed in brackets ([ ]).

The correct answer is D because the name of an @Command must always be enclosed in square brackets ([ ]). A, B, and C are incorrect because the command name argument must be enclosed in square brackets ([ ]).

Need to Know More?

 IBM. *Lotus Domino Designer 6 Help*, (Help6_Designer.nsf).

 IBM. *Lotus Domino Administrator 6 Help*, (Help6_Admin.nsf).

 IBM. *Domino Designer 6: A Developer's Handbook*. Redbook: 2002.

 www.lotus.com/ldd.

PART 2

Notes Domino 6 Application Development Intermediate Skills: Exam 611

Database Management

Terms you'll need to understand:

✓ Mail-in database
✓ LZ1 compression
✓ Soft delete
✓ Master Lock Administration Server
✓ Design locking
✓ Document locking
✓ View logging
✓ Design synopsis

Concepts and techniques you'll need to master:

✓ Modifying agent server document settings
✓ Creating a mail-in database
✓ Creating context sensitive database help
✓ Using Design to design an update distribution mechanism
✓ Using Replication to design an update distribution mechanism
✓ Hiding database designs
✓ Managing multiple design elements
✓ Setting database properties to improve database performance
✓ Setting database launch properties
✓ Setting up design locking
✓ Setting up document locking
✓ Setting up view logging
✓ Signing a database
✓ Troubleshooting design locking
✓ How to use design synopsis to evaluate and document the application

Domino/Notes 6 has added some significant improvements to the management, distribution, and updating of database designs. It is important to understand the topics of database management covered in this chapter. Specifically, the exam includes questions that test your knowledge of how design elements are managed and updated, how to modify database properties, and how to modify database launch properties. Also, expect to see questions on the exam that cover your knowledge of new features available with Domino/Lotus 6 in regard to design locking and document locking.

Agent Server Document Settings

The capabilities of agents and the way that agent security is handled has been significantly updated in Domino/Notes 6. Implemented in R6, agents can now

➤ *Access remote servers*—Servers who have specifically granted access to one another in the "Trusted Servers" field of the server document can have agents access information on the other server.

➤ *Save other agents*—Agents can programmatically modify, enable, disable, and save other agents located on the same server.

➤ *Allow users with editor access to run LotusScript and Java agents*—Agents can be set up to enable users with Editor access to activate agents.

➤ *Run on behalf of someone else*—Agents can be set to run with the authority of a specified user.

➤ *Set restricted/unrestricted rights for each specific agent*—If the designer (agent signer) has unrestricted agent access for the current server, he/she can set agent-specific access to not allow restricted operations, allow restricted operations, or allow restricted operations with full administration rights. By default, agents are set to not allow restricted operations.

Creating a Mail-In Database

A mail-in database enables users to send mail to a database, in much the same manner that mail would be sent to another user. Mail-in databases are useful when designing workflow applications because they provide an efficient mechanism to collect information in a central, shared database and distribute the information through email. Users can enter the name of the database in the To: field of a mail memo and the mail is then routed to the intended database. To create a Domino database that is capable of receiving mail, you need to follow these steps:

1. Create a mail-in database on a server that the required users of the application can access.

2. Create a mail-in database document in the Domino Directory on the server. This document must exist in each server that stores a replica copy of the mail-in database.

When creating the mail-in database document, the following fields are required:

➤ *Mail-in name*—The name that identifies the database. This name is used when addressing mail messages as the recipient.

➤ *Domain name*—The domain on which the database resided. This field is necessary only if your organization uses multiple domains.

➤ *Server*—The distinguished server name of the server on which the mail-in database resides.

➤ *File name*—The database directory name and filename.

Creating Context Sensitive Database Help

Context-sensitive help is available from the F1 key or Help button within an application. You can associate a help document with a page, form, subform, view, or folder by writing a formula for the HelpRequest event for views and folders, or for the OnHelp event for pages, forms, and subforms.

Use @Command([OpenHelpDocument]) to specify which help documents to open or @Command([OpenPage]) to open a page. The HelpRequest event is not triggered for Web applications. However, you can still use @Command([OpenHelpDocument]) or @Command([OpenPage]) within a button located on the Web form or Web page.

Use formulas in the **HelpRequest** event to specify help based upon various conditions (for example, if the document is new, if the document is being edited, field values, and so on).

Field help provides information for each field. Field help is an optional property for editable fields (located on the Advanced tab) that appears at the bottom of the Notes window when a field gets focus. Field help can contain up to 70 characters but should be kept under 55 characters for multi-lingual applications (to allow for translation). Optionally, you can also use pop-up text for a field label for each field.

A new feature with Domino/Notes 6 is the capability to add a field hint. Field hints enable you to enter text (instructions or hints) in editable fields that display in the editable field until the field gets focus (that is, the user clicks in the field to add text). After the field gets focus, the field hint is removed. Field Help and Field Hint are displayed in Figure 7.1.

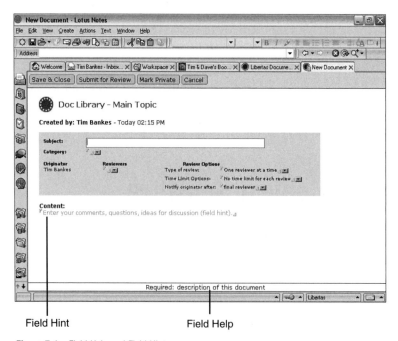

Field Hint   Field Help

Figure 7.1 Field Help and Field Hint.

Using Design to Design an Update Distribution Mechanism

When redesigning or updating an existing database, design modifications can be distributed in one of three ways:

➤ Make design changes directly to the database on the server.

➤ Make design changes in a template and replace or refresh the design to distribute the modifications to the target database.

➤ Make design changes to the master template and then refresh the design of the database (or allow the Design task to refresh the design when run).

Replacing or refreshing the design of a database is described in the following sections.

Refreshing a Database Design

When refreshing a database's design, design elements are updated by the template database. You may prohibit design refresh or replace by explicitly setting the Prohibit Design Refresh or Replace to Modify settings. This setting is located on the Design tab when viewing the Design Element properties dialog.

A database's design can be manually refreshed or refreshed automatically when the Design task runs on the server. By default, this task is set to run at 1:00 a.m. nightly, but might be modified by the Domino administrator. The design of a database might be manually refreshed in one of the following scenarios:

➤ You want the design refreshed immediately rather than waiting for the Design task to run when scheduled.

➤ The database is stored locally (the Design task doesn't update the design of the local database).

➤ You do not have Designer access to the database.

The following design elements are not updated when the design of a database is refreshed (whether the refresh is manually triggered or automatically triggered by the Design task):

➤ The database icon

➤ Database title and category

➤ Database Access Control List (however, ACL roles are updated)

➤ Database encryption settings

➤ The Using Database and About Database documents

➤ Any design element whose Prohibit Design Refresh or Replace to Modify property is enabled

➤ Any design element whose Inherit from the Design Template design property is set to Unavailable or does not exist

➤ The List as Advanced Template in the 'New Database' Dialog option located on the Design tab of the Database Properties Infobox

➤ All options on the Advanced tab of the Database Properties Infobox except the Document Table Bitmap Optimization setting and the Don't Support Specialized Response Hierarchy settings

However, the following design elements are refreshed when the design of a database is refreshed:

➤ Forms (all fields, form actions, event scripts, and so on)

➤ Views and folders (and any view actions)

➤ Agents

➤ Pages

➤ Framesets

➤ Navigators

➤ Shared fields

➤ All database Infobox settings excluding the settings described in the previous list

➤ The Document Table Bitmap Optimization setting and the Don't Support Specialized Response Hierarchy setting on the Advanced tab of the Database Properties Infobox

Using the Replace Design Command to Update a Database Design

If a database design is not set up to inherit its design from a template database, you can also update a database design by using the Replace Design command. This feature replaces the design of a database in much the same manner as the design refresh does. However, this is a manual process and is not updated when the Design task runs on the server. Only database designers and managers can manually refresh a database's design.

Follow these steps to perform this command:

1. Select the database whose design is to be refreshed.

2. Select File, Database, Replace Design from the pull-down menu. This displays the Replace Database Design dialog box (See Figure 7.2).

3. Select the template server on which the template database resides.

4. Select the template database from the list of available template databases. Only databases with an .ntf extension and that are located in the root directory of the server are displayed.

5. Optionally, you can select Show Advanced Templates to display database templates that have been set up as advanced templates.

6. Optionally, select the feature to Inherit Future design Changes. When selected, this database will automatically be set up to have the database design refreshed when the Design task is run on the server (scheduled or manually) or when the database design is refreshed by the database designer or manager.

7. Optionally, select Hide Formulas and LotusScript to hide the database design from all users. However, after a database design is hidden, it can be unhidden later.

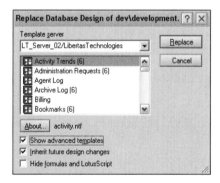

Figure 7.2   Replace Database Design dialog box.

Using Replication to Design an Update Distribution Mechanism

Replication can be used to distribute design updates in two primary ways. First, you can update a design template database, refresh the design of the production database on the same server, and then have that database replicate with databases located on other servers, thus updating their designs during replication. Alternatively, you can update the design of the template database, replicate that template to other replica templates located on the other servers, and then refresh the design of the production databases on each server.

Whether you use the Design Refresh or Design Replace options to update database designs, design changes and document updates made in one database automatically replicate to other database replicas if the servers replicating have Designer or Manager access in the database ACL. Therefore, it is important that design modifications be made on only one replica copy of the database. Then the design modifications can replicate to other database replicas during the next manual or scheduled replication.

When using a template to distribute design changes to your applications, you must place a replica of the template on each server that has a replica copy of the database set to inherit its design from the template. You need to give the servers Designer or Manager access to the database ACL (to enable the Design task to update the database design). Make design modifications to only one replica copy of the databases and make sure that the databases replicate prior to the Design task running (usually at 1:00 a.m., unless modified by the Domino administrator). Otherwise, the design of the replicas is not synchronized.

Shared code (design elements) and shared resources enable you to share design elements across databases. Therefore, you can reference a resource repeatedly within a single database or across multiple databases and store only one physical copy of the design element. Prior to this capability, a designer was required to copy and paste the design element into all the databases that required it.

 Be sure to understand the new shared design elements that can be shared across databases for the exam.

The following design elements can be shared among databases:

➤ Agents

➤ Outlines

➤ Subforms

➤ Shared fields

➤ Actions

➤ Script libraries

The following shared resources can be shared among databases:

➤ Images

➤ Files

➤ Applets

➤ Data connections

➤ Style sheets

Hiding Database Designs

You can hide the design of a database to prevent other users from viewing the database design or making changes to the database design. Hiding the database design disables all design operations and hides all formulas and scripts contained within the database. Typically, a designer would hide the design of a database that is set to inherit its design from a another database template (whose design is not hidden). Then the designer can make any required design changes on the design template and push those changes to the database whose design is hidden. When a database design is hidden, users are restricted from performing the following actions:

➤ Viewing settings for design elements (the View, Design option is no longer available from the drop-down view menu).

➤ Modifying, adding, or deleting design elements (forms, fields, pages, subforms, navigators, views, agents, simple actions, and so on).

➤ Modifying Database Open properties.

➤ Displaying the synopsis of a database.

➤ Unlocking the design of a database by making a copy or replica copy of the database. The design remains hidden even if the database is copied.

To hide the design of a database, follow these steps:

1. Create a new database based on a database template.

2. Select the new database. Then select File, Database, Replace Design from the drop-down menu. This displays the Replace Database Design dialog box (refer to Figure 7.2).

3. Select the template server on which the template database resides.

4. Select the template database from the list of available template databases. Only databases with an `.ntf` extension and that are located in the root directory of the server are displayed.

5. Select Hide Formulas and LotusScript, located at the bottom of the dialog box, to hide the database design from all users.

6. You should select the Inherit Future Design Changes check box. You cannot select or deselect this option after the design has been hidden, so this is the only way you can update the database's design after the design has been hidden.

7. Click the Replace button and click Yes to confirm.

 After you hide a database design, you cannot reverse your decision. To make the database design accessible once more, you have to delete the database and create a new copy of it.

Limiting Design Element Access to Specified Users

When designing applications, it is common that certain design elements should be accessible to only certain users (based upon the username, group, or role) or certain user types. Because Domino enables developers to build applications for multiple user types (Notes clients, Web clients, and mobile clients), you will want to hide design elements from clients (or users) that do not require access to them.

You can use outline controls to hide your application's design from users based upon their client types or user roles. For example, each outline control can be hidden based on the client type or a formula. Therefore, controls can be hidden based on the following factors:

➤ Web browsers

➤ Notes R4.6 or later clients

➤ Mobile client

➤ The evaluation of a formula

Other design elements, such as views and forms, can also be hidden from users based upon their client types. When viewing the list of design elements from the Designer client, open the Design Documents properties box and choose the Design tab to set the Hide Design Elements From settings (see Figure 7.3).

Figure 7.3   The Design tab of the Design Documents dialog box.

With Notes R6, you can now restrict forms, views, folders, agents, and navigators from being displayed in the menu by selecting the Do Not Show This Design Element in Menus of Notes R4 or Later Clients option on the Design tab of the Design Documents properties box.

You can restrict access to Notes views by utilizing the View Read Access List. The list can contain user names, groups, servers, or roles contained within the current database (see Figure 7.4). To access the View Access List, follow these steps:

1. Open the view from the Domino Designer client.

2. Click on the Security tab of the Infobox (automatically opened when the view is opened in design mode).

3. Deselect the All Readers and Above option to select individual user-names, groups, servers, or roles. The All Readers and Above option is automatically selected by default, allowing all users to access the view.

4. Select the users, groups, servers, or roles to grant access to the current view. Any users, groups, or servers not selected do not have access to the view. You can also click the Directory Lookup button (indicated by a blue person profile) to select names using a server directory or local name and address book. The users, groups, servers, and roles displayed in the list box are entries currently available in the database Access Control List.

Figure 7.4 The Security tab of the View properties Infobox.

 Denying access to views or folders does not restrict access to the documents contained within the views. Users can still access the data by using an alternate view, creating a personal view, or using the proper URL syntax to open a view.

 For the exam, remember that it is typically considered a best practice to utilize roles when restricting user access to views because they are easily modified and updated.

Access to Notes forms can also be restricted by utilizing the Form Read Access list or Create Document list. The list can contain usernames, groups, servers, or roles contained within the current database (see Figure 7.5).

Figure 7.5 The Security tab of the Form properties Infobox.

To access the Read Access list or Create Document list, follow these steps:

1. Open the form from the Domino Designer client.

2. Click on the Security tab of the Infobox.

3. To modify the default read access for documents created with this form, deselect the All Readers and Above option to select individual usernames, groups, servers, or roles. The All Readers and Above option is automatically selected by default, allowing all users to access the form.

4. Select the users, groups, servers, or roles to grant read access to documents created with this form. Any users, groups, or servers not selected will not have access to read documents with this form. You can also click the Directory lookup button (indicated by a blue person profile) to select names using a server directory or local name and address book. The users, groups, servers, and roles displayed in the list box are entries currently available in the database Access Control List.

5. To modify the default Create access for documents with this form, deselect the All Authors and Above option to select individual usernames, groups, servers, or roles. The All Authors and Above option is automatically selected by default, allowing all users to access the view.

6. Select the users, groups, servers, or roles to grant access to create documents with this form. Any users, groups, servers not selected do not have access to create documents with this form. You can also click the Directory Lookup button (indicated by a blue person profile) to select names by using a server directory or local name and address book. The users, groups, servers, and roles displayed in the list box are entries currently available in the database Access Control List.

7. Close the Infobox. Because Okay or Cancel options are available in Infoboxes, keep in mind that any changes you make take effect after the form is saved.

 For the exam, remember that setting form Read or Create access does not exclude a user from creating documents or viewing documents previously created with this form. For example, existing documents can still be copied and pasted into the database, agents can be executed to create documents, or other scripts can be executed to created documents.

In addition to restricting the Form Read Access list or Create Document list, you can also control access to forms by

➤ Excluding a form from being displayed in the Create menu and/or Create Other dialog box. This option is available on the Basics tab of the Form properties box.

➤ Creating an action button, button on a form, or link that opens a form but is hidden to users based on username, group, role, or formula.

To enable users to access forms and view documents even if the user has No Access or Depositor access to the database, create a form and make it available to Public Access users. This enables you to grant access to specific documents (or design elements) without giving the user Reader access to the entire database. To set up a form that allows public access users to use the form:

1. Open the Form Design element from the Designer client.

2. Click on the Security tab.

3. Select the Available to Public Access Users option.

For users (who have No Access or Depositor access to the database) to view public access documents, create an item in the document named $PublicAccess and assign the item a value of 1. You also need to give users access to Read Public Documents and Write Public Documents in the database Access Control List.

For No Access and Depositor access users to view documents in the database, you need to create a view and enable the Available to Public Users check box. This option is available on the Security tab of the View Infobox.

Managing Multiple Design Elements

A new feature made available with Domino/Notes 6 is the ability to modify multiple design elements sharing common design properties at the same time. Therefore, you can select multiple design elements (of the same type) from within the Work pane of the Designer client, open the Properties Infobox you saw in Figure 7.5, and modify common design properties. Properties that are common and can be modified are displayed in their editable form. Properties that are not common among the selected design elements are grayed out and cannot be edited.

Set Database Properties to Improve Database Performance

By default, newly created databases are not optimized for performance. This is especially true when you create databases designed for Web clients. Therefore, you must modify some settings to improve database performance and reduce database size. Specifically, various settings on the Advanced Options tab of the database Infobox help improve database performance.

NOTE | The database properties are described in detail in "Setting Database Properties," in Chapter 2, "Database Management."

The following sections outline settings that can be manipulated to improve performance.

Basic and Advanced Database Settings

Table 7.1 outlines database settings available on the Basics tab of the Database Infobox, and Table 7.2 outlines specific database settings, located on the Advanced tab of the Database Infobox, which help improve performance.

Table 7.1 Basic Database Options	
Dialog Box Selection	**Description**
Allow Use of Stored Forms in This Database	Enabling this option increases disk space and decreases application performance. Although storing the design of a form in a document ensures the document always displays with the specific form design, it can increase the disk space up to 20 times the original size.
Display Images After Loading	Enabling this option improves database performance. As the setting implies, when selected, all text on a form is loaded prior to the images. Therefore, users can read the text while larger, slower images are loaded. If this setting is not selected, images are loaded in conjunction with text as they appear in the document. This setting only affects Notes client users.

Table 7.2 Advanced Database Options	
Dialog Box Selection	**Description**
Unread Mark Options: Don't Maintain Unread Marks	Some databases may not need to track unread documents, and disabling this feature increases performance and reduces database size. You can also disable views from displaying unread marks, but this results in no performance improvement. The database must be compacted for this setting to take effect.
Advanced Option: Optimize Document Table Map	Using only the forms referenced by the documents contained within each view, this option associates only the tables using the document forms to update each respective view, thus increasing performance. Internally, Domino maintains tables containing information about documents contained within each view. These tables are used when the view indexes are updated or rebuilt. If the views contain selection formulas that specify which forms to use (for example **Form="Main Document"**, enabling Document Table Bitmap Optimization optimizes performance by using only the tables that use the forms specified in the view selection formula.
Don't Overwrite Free Space	As a security feature, Domino automatically overwrites deleted data with new data, ensuring that deleted data cannot be recovered. This causes additional I/O operations to the disk. Selecting this option increases performance, but alternative security options should be considered.
Maintain **LastAccessed** Property	When enabled, Domino tracks who last read the document. Disabling this option causes Domino to track only who last modified each document, thus minimizing disk I/O operations and increasing performance.
Disable Transaction Logging	After transaction logging has been set up, all database transactions are logged. Disabling this feature by making this selection increases performance but is generally discouraged because it makes it more difficult to recover from system failures. This is the better option to use on non-critical databases such as help databases or databases in which the data doesn't change very often.
Don't Support Specialized Response Hierarchy	Disabling this feature reduces the information stored to support certain @Functions used in views to display response documents (specifically, the **@AllChildren** and **@AllDescendants** functions). Therefore, this setting improves application performance and slightly reduces the database size. Views and replication formulas that do not use these two functions still display response

Table 7.2 Advanced Database Options *(continued)*	
Dialog Box Selection	**Description**
	documents as intended. The database must be compacted for this setting to take affect.
Use LZ1 Compression for Attachments	The new enhanced compression method available with Domino 6. This increases the performance when downloaded, uploaded, or opening attachments. When enabled, Domino uses LZ1 compression.
Don't Allow Headline Monitoring	When selected, prevents users from using headline monitoring for the database. Restricting the user of headline monitoring improves performance.
Soft Delete Expire Time in Hours	Soft deletions allow for deleted documents to be held in the database for the specified amount of time before being deleted. Reducing the time deleted documents are held minimizes database size and helps improve performance.
Limit Entries in **$UpdatedBy** Fields	Enables you to limit the number of entries in the **$UpdatedBy** field. This field contains the canonical name of each person or server who has edited the Notes document. If each document has a lot of activity and many modifications, reducing the number of revisions tracked per document can increase performance and reduce database size. When the limit is reached, the oldest entry is removed.
Limit Entries in **$Revisions** Fields	Enables you to limit the number of entries in the **$Revisions** field, thus increasing application performance and reducing database size. This field contains the date and time each Notes document was edited. If each document has a lot of activity and many modifications, reducing the number of revisions tracked per document can increase performance. When the limit is reached, the oldest entry is removed. By default, this field contains up to 500 entries. Because each entry requires 8 bytes of disk space, the larger this field becomes, the slower the database performance. Because this field is used to resolve replication or save conflicts, this value should never be set to less than 10.

Other Options for Optimizing Database Performance

In addition to modifying database properties, the following options can help you optimize database performance

➤ Upgrade the database to Release 6 (which uses a new, optimized On Disk Structure).

➤ Enable transaction-based logging and recovery.

➤ Compact the databases.

➤ Set database size quotas.

➤ Delete or archive inactive documents.

➤ Modify the replication formula to limit the size of the database by replicating only required documents.

➤ Modify the database purge interval to remove deletion stubs more frequently.

➤ Disable soft deletions.

➤ Disable default user activity recording.

➤ Customizing Advanced settings and file system settings that optimize disk space usage and reallocation.

Setting Database Launch Properties

The database launch properties control what users (Notes client users and Web client users) first see when they open the database.

The Launch tab (see Figure 7.6) contains information regarding launch settings for native Lotus Notes clients and Web clients. The settings for the database launch settings are located on the Launch tab of the Database properties Infobox.

Figure 7.6 The Launch tab of the Database properties box.

The information contained in the Launch tab is described in Table 7.3.

Table 7.3 Database Launch Tab		
Setting	**Setting Type**	**Description**
When Opened in the Notes Client	Drop-down	Determines the default design element to open when the database is opened by a native Lotus Notes client. The default launch options for Notes clients are ➤ Restore last viewed by user ➤ Open "About Database" document ➤ Open designated frameset ➤ Open designated Navigator ➤ Open designated Navigator in its own window ➤ Launch first attachment in "About Database" ➤ Launch first doclink in "About Database"
Name	Drop-down	The list of specific options based upon the Notes client Open options.
Restore as Last Viewed by User	Check box	Opens last design element viewed by each user.
Show "About Database" Document If Modified	Check box	Determines whether the About document should be displayed to Notes clients if its design has been modified since the user last accessed the database.
Show "About Database" Document When Database Is Opened for the First Time	Check box	Determines whether the About document should be displayed to Notes clients when database is opened for first time.
Preview Pane Default...	Button	Determines the default Preview pane layout. Select the Maximize Document Preview on Database Open to display the Preview pane automatically. This option is not available if you have the launch option set to open a frameset.

Table 7.3 Database Launch Tab *(continued)*		
Setting	**Setting Type**	**Description**
When Opened in a Browser	Drop-Down	Determines the default design element to open when the database is opened by a Web client. The default launch options for Web clients are ➤ Use Notes launch option ➤ Open "About Database" document ➤ Open designated frameset ➤ Open designated page ➤ Open designated Navigator in its own window ➤ Launch first doclink in "About Database" ➤ Launch designated doclink ➤ Launch first document in view

Setting Up Design Locking

Design element locking is a valuable tool made available with Domino/Notes 6. When enabled, design element locking ensures that designers cannot modify design elements concurrently (while other designers are modifying the same elements).

Two types of design locking are available: explicit locks and temporary locks. An *explicit* lock restricts alternate designers from opening design elements locked by other designers until they are released by the original designer (who originally locked the design element).

A *temporary* lock is the default lock placed on all design elements that are not explicitly locked by the designer modifying them. The benefit of a temporary lock is that if another designer opens the design element while it is being edited, he is warned that the design element is currently open. When the designer who has the design element open closes the element, the temporary lock is removed.

Before design elements can be locked, you must first follow these steps:

1. A Master Lock Administration server must be specified in the Advanced panel of the database Access Control dialog.

2. Design element locking must be enabled for the current database. To do so, select Allow Design Locking on the Design tab of the Database Infobox.

As soon as design locking is enabled, designers can explicitly lock design elements while they are working on them. The design elements stay locked until the designer releases them. To lock a design element, designers simply highlight the design element from the list of design elements in the Domino Designer client and select Design, Lock Design Element from the drop-down menu. Alternatively, designers can right-click on the design element and select Lock... from the drop-down menu. To unlock the design element, designers highlight the locked design element and select Design, Unlock Design Element from the drop-down menu, or right-click on the locked design element and select Unlock... from the drop-down menu.

 When a design element is locked, the lock replicates to other database replicas located on other servers.

Setting Up Document Locking

Document locking enables users with Author access or higher to lock documents within a database. Locking a document gives exclusive rights to the person who has locked the document to modify it. Other users with the same rights cannot modify the document even if they are working on another replica on the same local area network. Because of this, document locking prevents editing of documents and replication conflicts.

 Database managers cannot edit a locked document, but they can unlock previously locked documents.

To set up document locking, follow these steps:

1. Specify the administration server for the database to be used as the master lock server. The Administration Server is located in the Advanced section of the database ACL (see Figure 7.7).

2. Select Allow Document Locking, located on the Basics tab of the Database Infobox.

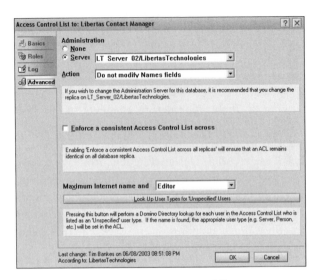

Figure 7.7   The Advanced tab of the Database ACL.

Setting Up View Logging

View logging is a new feature made available with Domino/Lotus 6 that tracks all view updates and changes in the transaction log. All logged transactions are written to disk sequentially to be committed to the database at a later time. The transaction logs can be used for backups and backup recoveries (such as if the system crashes or a hard drive fails).

Another advantage to using view logging is that many view rebuilds can be avoided. If the Domino server is restarted, this can significantly reduce the time to rebuild views. However, view logging does negatively impact server performance and should typically be avoided for most views unless they are considered vital views in an application.

View logging is enabled on the Advanced tab of the View Infobox, where you select the option Include Updates in Transaction Log.

Sign a Database

Signing a database signs all the elements in a database with the current user's signature. Prior to Domino/Notes 6, an entire database could be signed only by an Administrator (using the Notes Administrator client). With

Domino/Notes 6, a new method has been exposed to allow databases to be signed by calling the `sign` method of the Notes Database class.

The syntax for the `sign` method is:

```
Call notesdatabase.Sign([intType], [bolExistingSignaturesOnly],
➥ [strName], [strIsNoteID])
```

The `sign` method enables you to specify which design elements are signed in the `intType` property. These elements can be

➤ ACL

➤ Agents

➤ Forms

➤ About Database and Using Database documents

➤ Database icon

➤ Replication formula

➤ Shared fields

➤ All views

➤ All design elements

➤ All data documents

The `bolExistingSignaturesOnly` parameter determines whether only elements with existing signatures should be updated or whether all design elements should be updated (`True` to sign elements with existing signatures, `False` to sign all elements).

The `strName` parameter is the programmatic name or Notes ID of a single design element to be signed.

The `strIsNoteID` parameter determines whether the third parameter is a Notes ID or the programmatic name of the design element. If `True`, the third parameter is a Notes ID; if `False`, the third parameter is a programmatic name.

This method can be used only on a workstation.

Troubleshooting Design Locking

If the option to Lock a Design Element is greyed out from the drop-down menu or the Lock option is greyed out after you right-click on the design element, the design locking has not been set up for the current database. For each database to allow for design locking, the Administration server must be set on the Advanced tab of the Database Access Control List dialog box and Allow Design Locking must be enabled on the Design tab of the Database Infobox.

A design element that is not explicitly locked by the designer is always temporarily locked while it is being edited in the Notes Designer client. When the designer is finished editing the design element (and closes the open design element), the temporary locked is released.

If a designer locks a design element when working offline, or if the Master Lock Administration server is unavailable, the designer receives an error indicating that the master lock database cannot be reached. If the designer proceeds in locking the design element (a prompt appears to proceed or cancel), a provisional lock is placed on the design element. During the next replication, the database attempts to convert the provisional lock to a true element lock, and any modifications made to the design element are saved to the master database. If the conversion is unsuccessful (that is, if someone else locked the design element on the master lock database), an email is automatically sent to the designer containing the edits that could not be saved to the master lock database.

NOTE Shared actions are considered together as one design element. Therefore, when you lock a shared action you are locking all the shared actions.

Use Design Synopsis to Evaluate and Document the Application

The database design synopsis is a powerful database analysis tool that provides the capability to browse, search, and generate reports for all or some of the database design elements, code, and components. The output of reports generated by the design synopsis can be sent to a Notes database or Notes document. To access the design synopsis for a particular database, follow these steps:

1. Open the database you want to analyze.

2. Select File, Database, Design Synopsis from the drop-down menu, or select the Synopsis option located under Other in the Designer pane. This displays the Design Synopsis dialog box (see Figure 7.8).

3. Select the design elements on which to report, the database information to report, the contents of each element to report, and the output.

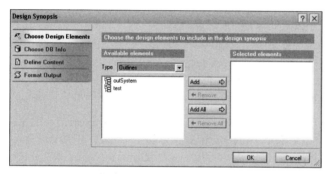

Figure 7.8   Design Synopsis dialog box.

With Domino/Notes 6, hide-when conditions are now available for reporting.

In addition to the design synopsis, you can also use the DXL Transformer to export database design and database design element information as XML and then view the XML output as HTML and, optionally, apply a style sheet to the output.

Summary

Domino/Notes 6 has vastly improved the design management capabilities and ease of use for designers. However, with these improvements comes increased complexity. Be sure to understand the new development features outlined in this chapter and how they are set up. Managing design elements, modifying database properties, modifying database launch properties, and setting up design locking and document locking are topics that you can expect to see covered on the exam.

Exam Prep Questions

Question 1

> When Cletus is attempting to modify the database launch settings, the Preview Pane Default... button is greyed out and disabled. Why can't Cletus modify this setting?
>
> ❑ A. The feature has been removed with Domino/Notes 6.
>
> ❑ B. The default launch option is set to open a designated frameset.
>
> ❑ C. The default launch option is set to open a designated Navigator.
>
> ❑ D. None of the above; this option is always available.

Answer B is correct. When the default launch option is set to open a designated Frameset, the Preview Pane options are not available. Answer A is incorrect because this option is still available with Domino/Notes 6. Option C is incorrect because the Preview Pane Default option is available if the default launch option is set to open a designated Navigator. Answer D is incorrect because, as explained, the option is not always available.

Question 2

> John Galt is designing an application for Web users. This application uses a lot of images and he is concerned about performance and wants to minimize the page load time for Web users as they open documents. Therefore, he has selected the Display Images After Loading option on the first tab of the Database properties Infobox. However, this setting does not appear to work when he previews the page by using a Web browser. Why could this be happening?
>
> ❑ A. The feature has been removed with Domino/Notes 6.
>
> ❑ B. This option does not work when previewing documents.
>
> ❑ C. The Domino Web server has not been properly configured to allow this feature.
>
> ❑ D. This feature is not available for Web clients; it affects only Notes clients.

Answer D is correct. This setting affects only Notes client users. When selected, all text on a form is loaded prior to the images. Therefore, users can read the text while larger, slower images are loaded. If this setting is not selected, images are loaded in conjunction with text as they appear in the document. Answer A is incorrect because this feature has not been removed with Domino/Notes 6. Answer B is incorrect because this feature does not work with Web clients. Answer C is incorrect because the Domino Web server does not need to be configured for this setting to work.

Question 3

Where is basic agent security set up?

- ❑ A. Agent properties.
- ❑ B. Server document.
- ❑ C. Server configuration database.
- ❑ D. Database properties.

Answer A is correct. The Security tab, located in the Agent Infobox, enables you to set some of the new agent features, such as Run as Web User, Run on Behalf of..., Allow Remote Debugging, and Allow User Activation, as well as runtime security levels, default access to view and run the agent, and public access settings. Answer B is incorrect because even though agent security settings exist in the Programmability Restrictions section, these settings are server-wide settings, not specific agent security for that agent. Answer C is incorrect because there is no specific server configuration database. Answer D is incorrect because the database properties do not affect basic agent security.

Question 4

Cletus wants to hide multiple form design elements from Web browsers simultaneously. What feature does Cletus need to use?

- ❑ A. Resource properties.
- ❑ B. Design properties.
- ❑ C. Database properties.
- ❑ D. This cannot be done.

Answer B is correct. You can modify multiple design elements sharing common design properties at the same time. Therefore, you can select multiple design elements (of the same type) from within the Work pane of the Designer client, open the Design Elements Infobox, and modify common design properties. Properties that are common and can be modified are displayed in their editable form. Properties that are not common among the selected design elements are greyed out and cannot be edited. Answers A and

C are incorrect because they do not allow you to modify multiple design elements at the same time. Answer D is incorrect because you can use the Design properties to do this.

Question 5

Design locking can be set up to allow designers to lock design elements while they are editing them so that other designers cannot modify the element while the original designers are working on it. Where is design locking set up?

❑ A. Design properties.

❑ B. Database properties.

❑ C. Resource properties.

❑ D. Server document.

Answer B is correct. Design element locking must be enabled for each database. This is done by selecting Allow Design Locking on the Design tab of the Database Infobox. After it is enabled, designers can explicitly lock design elements while they are working on them. The design elements stay locked until the designer releases the design element. Answers A, C, and D are incorrect because design element locking is only enabled from the Database properties Infobox.

Need to Know More?

IBM International Technical Support Organization. *Domino Designer 6: A Developer's Handbook*. Available in printed form, PDF format, and HTML format from `http://publib-b.boulder.ibm.com/Redbooks.nsf/RedbookAbstracts/sg246854.html?Open`.

IBM Lotus, *Release Notes*. Available at `http://www-3.ibm.com/software/lotus/support/notes/support.html`.

IBM Lotus. *Online Help Databases*: help6_admin.nsf, help6_client.nsf, help6_designer.nsf. Available at `http://www-3.ibm.com/software/lotus/support/notes/support.html`.

8

Application Architecture

. . . .

Terms you'll need to understand:

- ✓ WebDav (Web Distributed Authoring and Versioning)
- ✓ Note ID
- ✓ Universal ID
- ✓ Image resource
- ✓ Object Linking and Embedding (OLE)
- ✓ Automation controller
- ✓ Automation server
- ✓ Summary data
- ✓ Non-summary data
- ✓ Full-text index

Concepts and techniques you'll need to master:

- ✓ Accessing data in an external Domino database
- ✓ Allowing view customization
- ✓ Building a navigation structure
- ✓ Connecting to external applications
- ✓ Using form formulas to control form display in views
- ✓ Design applications based on Data Integrity issues
- ✓ Design applications based on design element IDs: UNID & NOTEID
- ✓ Design applications based on graphics elements
- ✓ Design applications based on OLE on a form
- ✓ Design applications based on Summary/Non-Summary data storage
- ✓ Design applications to optimize view performance
- ✓ Domino Application Architecture
- ✓ Set up full-text indexing

Understanding the fundamental application architecture of Domino will greatly assist you passing the certification exams. Application development has been made easier with the capability to share design elements among different databases. Although Domino is nonrelational by design, Domino still provides numerous tools and options to ensure database integrity.

To prepare for the exam, you should have a solid understanding of the Document Universal ID (UNID) and the NoteID and how they are used to quickly and easily locate documents. In addition, you should know the various design elements used in the navigation structure and how they are integrated into your application. You should understand the rich text structure and the difference between summary and nonsummary items. As Lotus Notes/Domino becomes more extensible, it is more common to use alternate third-party applications to assist with developing. Connecting to external applications is easier than ever with Domino Designer 6. Finally, full-text searching is a common feature used in many Domino applications. Consequently, you can expect to see some test questions regarding setting up and monitoring full-text searching. You can expect to see all these topics covered on the exam because they are important, not only as exam material, but when designing and developing applications!

Access Data in an External Domino Database

With Lotus Notes/Domino 6, you can share design elements, code, and shared resources among different databases. This eases database maintenance by removing the need to copy and paste identical design elements from one database to another to utilize the design elements' functionality. Each database can contain its own library of shared code and resources and access shared elements in other databases. Therefore, you can develop your application to reference design elements and resources in other databases but store (and maintain) one physical copy of the design element or resource.

The following design elements and resources can be shared among databases:

➤ *Agents*—Standalone programs that perform a specific task in one or more databases.

➤ *Outlines*—Used to quickly and easily build user-friendly navigation for your applications.

➤ *Subforms*—A collection of fields, graphics, buttons, and actions that are typically used on more than one form.

➤ *Shared fields*—Fields defined for use on more than one form.

➤ *Shared Actions*—Used in forms, pages, folders, or views to set up user-related tasks.

➤ *Script libraries*—A place for storing code that can be shared within the application that contains LotusScript, JavaScript, or Java code.

➤ *Images*—Any image file imported into the database.

➤ *Files*—Any non-NSF file imported into the database, such as an HTML file.

➤ *Applets*—Java applets imported for use in Web browsers or Notes clients.

➤ *Shared Java files*—Java applets that use multiple files can access files stored as shared resources.

➤ *Data Connection Resource (DCR)*—Design element where connections from a Domino database to a relational database are defined.

➤ *Style sheets*—Imported cascading style sheets to control the interface layout (headers, links, text, fonts, styles, color, and margins).

Allowing View Customization

A new feature made available with Lotus Notes Domino 6 is the capability to allow views to be customized by end users (who do not have Designer access to the database). This feature is enabled by the database designer (or manager), who selects the Allow Customizations check box located on the Information tab of the View properties box (see Figure 8.1).

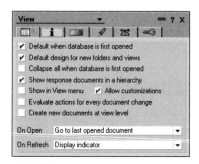

Figure 8.1   The View properties box Information tab.

When view customization has been enabled for a specific view, users can resize, reorder, and hide columns displayed in that view. These changes are maintained for users between sessions (when they close and reopen the view).

If this feature has not been enabled, the Customize View dialog box is still available to users. However, all the options are disabled, except for column sorting, which is kept for accessibility purposes.

For users to customize a view, they must first open the view, then select the drop-down menu option View, Customize This View.... This displays the Customize View dialog box (see Figure 8.2).

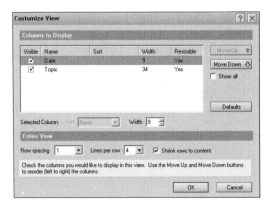

Figure 8.2   Customize View dialog box.

With this dialog box, users can reorder view columns, hide columns, change the column widths, modify the sort order, modify the row spacing and lines per row, and set the rows to shrink rows to content.

 The menu option View, Customize This View is available to Notes client users regardless of the Allow Customizations setting. This option is not available for Web clients.

Build a Navigation Structure

Outlines can be used to quickly and easily build user-friendly navigation for your applications. Much like image maps and navigators, outlines provide users with a mechanism for navigating your application. An outline creates a tree-like object that can be embedded in forms and pages. It consists of outline entries, each of which can link to a named element (page, form, view, and so forth) within or outside your application, link to a Web page, and/or perform an action (such as run an agent).

As you design and modify your application, you need to modify only the source outline. Any navigational structure that references that outline will be updated dynamically.

Outlines are covered in more detail in Chapter 9, "Design Elements," in the section titled "Embedded Elements: Outline."

Connecting to External Applications

Domino Designer 6 enables you to integrate third-party tools into the developer IDE by using *WebDav (Web Distributed Authoring and Versioning)*. In addition, when working within Domino Designer, you can launch alternate applications (for example, an image editor, and XML parser, and so on). If these third party tools support WebDav, you can save certain design elements directly back into remote Domino 6 databases.

The following design elements can be accessed by a WebDav client:

➤ File resources

➤ Images

➤ Cascading Style Sheets

By default, Domino databases are not automatically enabled for WebDav. WebDav must be enabled on the Domino server before you can use it. This is set in the Web Site document in the Domino directory (located in the Configuration, Web, Internet Sites view). On the configuration tab, Allowed Methods section, the WebDav option must be enabled (see Figure 8.3). Therefore, this must typically be enabled by the Domino Administrator. Regardless, the HTML task must be restarted for this setting to take affect.

After WebDav has been enabled for the Domino server, it must then be enabled for each Domino database within your application. Follow these steps to enable WebDav within your application:

1. Provide WebDav users with Designer access (or Manager access) in the database ACL. Also enable Create Documents and Delete Documents privileges.

2. Set the Maximum Internet Name and Password field on the Advanced tab of the database ACL to Designer or Manager access.

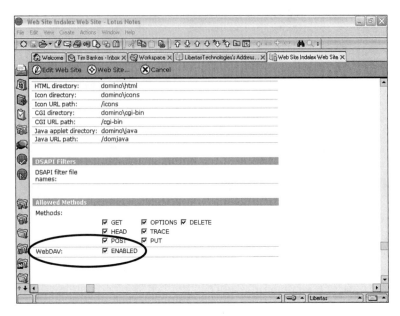

Figure 8.3 Domino Server Document, WebDav settings.

3. Enable design locking for the current database (this topic is covered in detail in Chapter 7, "Database Management").

4. If using a Web browser as the WebDav client, disable proxy server access for the browser.

5. Disable session authentication for the server. This setting is located in the Server document, Internet Protocols tab, Domino Web Engine tab, HTTP Sessions section.

6. Restart the HTTP task on the Domino server.

Currently, WebDav is supported on Windows NT, 2000, and XP. The WebDav clients that are supported are

➤ Microsoft Internet Explorer 5.0x or 6.0

➤ Windows Explorer on Windows 98, Windows NT4, Windows 2000, and Windows XP

➤ Macromedia Dreamweaver 4.01

➤ Microsoft Word 2000

After WebDav has been enabled, you need to add a Network Place in Windows mapped to the WebDav server. For the location of the Network place, specify the URL for the Domino server and database with `$files` appended to the end of the URL. For example:

```
http://domino./libertastechnologies.com/development/contacts.nsf$files
```

After you have mapped the WebDav database, you can access the WebDav elements by using the native interface of the WebDav client. Using the WebDav client, you can access, add, edit, and save the design element back to the Domino database. You can also use Windows Explorer to view the design elements that are available as a network place displayed under the My Network Places.

 File-specific attributes (such as read-only) are not supported in WebDav. Therefore, if a file is set as read-only from the file system, this property does not prevent users from editing the document.

Design element locking is supported by WebDav. Therefore, if a design element has been locked by a designer, it is not available for access by any WebDav clients.

Whether third-party applications support WebDav or not, you can customize the Tools menu in the Domino Designer client to launch other applications or execute your own custom formulas. Follow these steps to add a tool to the tools menu:

1. Select Tools, Add Tool from the drop-down menu.

2. Enter the name of tool in the Tool Name field of the Add Tool dialog box (see Figure 8.4). You can specify an accelerator character by using the underscore character ("_") prior to the letter you want to act as the accelerator character. This makes the tool accessible to users with physical disabilities and easy to access in general.

3. Select the Tool Action as either Run Program or Run Formula. If you select Run Program, enter (or select) the path to the program executable. If you select Run Formula, enter the formula to determine what tool to launch.

4. In the Tool Context section, select the context in which the tool should be available (for example, Frameset Design, Frameset List, Page Design, and so on).

5. Click OK.

Figure 8.4 Add Tool dialog box.

Now, when you are designing in one of the contexts specified in step 4 above, the tool appears as an option in the Tools menu!

After you have added tools to the Tool menu, you will most likely want to organize, delete, change the context, or add submenus for these tools. You can do this by selecting the option from the drop-down menu Tools, Customize Tools to display the Customize Tools dialog box (see Figure 8.5).

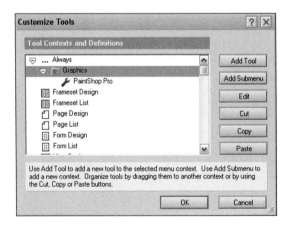

Figure 8.5 Customize Tools dialog box.

This dialog box allows you to

➤ *Add Tool*—Add new tools to the Tools menu

➤ *Add Submenu*—Add submenus to make using the tool more convenient

➤ *Edit*—Edit existing items on the Tools menu

➤ *Cut*—Remove items from the Tools menu

➤ *Copy*—Copy an existing item in the Tools menu

➤ *Paste*—Paste a previously copied item into the Tools menu

Using Form Formulas to Control Form Display in Views

The view design form formula determines which forms are used to compose, display, and/or edit documents. The form formulas give you programmatic control over which form is used, based upon a condition or formula. However, the form formula is optional. The form that is used to display a document is based upon the following conditions, which are evaluated in order of precedence (the first condition is evaluated before the second, the second condition before the third, and so on):

1. Form stored in the document

2. Form specified by the view form formula

3. Form used to create the document (stored in the Form item contained within the document)

4. Default database form

When specifying a form formula in the view/folder design, the form formula must evaluate to the name (as a string value) of a form contained within the database.

To modify the form formula in a view, open the view from the Domino Designer. Select the Form Formula object in the Objects tab. Enter the formula in the script area (see Figure 8.6).

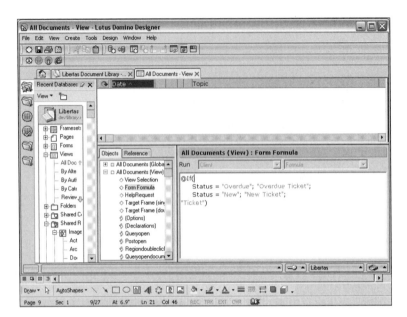

Figure 8.6 Specifying the Form Formula.

Design Applications Based on Data Integrity Issues

The Notes/Domino database architecture is not relational; rather, it is an object store. What this means is that unlike a relational database, where redundancy is minimized through normalization and linked tables, redundancy is not only common, but it is often necessary in your Notes/Domino applications. That being said, your goal should be to minimize redundancy as much as possible because it leads to wasted storage and obsolete data.

In a relational database, it is common to normalize data and store it in separate tables, which can be dynamically linked. Notes/Domino, however, doesn't provide the same level of capability in this area. For example, you build a customer relationship management application that includes company documents and contact documents. The contacts are children of the company document and need to inherit certain key pieces of information from the company if they are to display properly in the views. For example, if the contact document does not store the company name value, the document does not display properly in views based on company name. Although this value could be looked up dynamically in a form through the use of @DbLookup or the GetDocumentByKey method of NotesView in LotusScript, it must reside in the document to be displayed in views. After the value has been inherited into the child document, that value is not refreshed automatically. So if the company name changes, all the documents for that company will contain obsolete information. The only remedy to this is to create an agent that updates the company name field in the contact documents if the name is changed.

In a relational database, the company name is not likely to be stored with the contact; rather, the contact record is probably linked to the company record through a common key. If the company name changes, as in the earlier example, users automatically see the new information because of the dynamic link and the lack of redundancy. As stated earlier, in some cases, redundancy is required to make the application function correctly. However, you should plan on keeping redundancy to a bare minimum in your application.

Documents can easily be copied (or cut) and pasted into the same database or into another database, both manually (through the Notes client interface) and programmatically. For example, you could use @Command([EditCopy]) and @Command([EditPaste]) in the Formula language or the Copy and Paste methods of NotesUIDocument or the CopyToDatabase method of NotesDocument Classes.

Although copying documents is quite easy, it is important to understand the implications of doing so. When a Notes document is copied and pasted, several things happen. First and foremost, the document is assigned a new Universal ID (UNID) and a new NoteID. Second, the document's Created, Modified, Added, Modified (In This File), and Accessed dates are all changed to reflect the time and date the document was pasted. Finally, if the document is being pasted into a view, the QueryPaste and the PostPaste events of the NotesUIView object (of the currently open view) are fired, enabling you to write code to handle the pasting of documents.

After the document has been pasted into the database, the document acts like any other document in the database, including replicating from one replica copy of the database to another. The only exception to this is if the document contains Authors or Readers fields that preclude accessing and/or replicating the document. It is also worth noting here that when you copy a document and its children (responses), the original response hierarchy is maintained.

NOTE When a database is copied through the use of the File, Database, New Copy menu option, the **@Command([FileDatabaseCopy])** formula, or the **CreateCopy** method of the **NotesDatabase** class, all the documents in the database are copied and assigned new Universal IDs and new NoteIDs, as well as new time/date stamps.

Two functions especially useful when considering data integrity issues and when working with Universal IDs (UNIDs) of documents are the @GetDocField and @SetDocField functions. They are useful because they allow you to read and modify field values for documents that are not currently open. Both of these functions can only be used to modify documents that are located in the current database.

The @GetDocField function returns a value of a specified field for a specified document. The syntax of this function is:

```
@GetDocField(documentUNID; fieldname)
```

The documentUNID parameter is the universal ID of the document whose field value is to be read.

The fieldname parameter is the name of the item (fieldname) to read. This value is a string value. If the universal ID or fieldname are not valid, this function returns null.

The @SetDocField function sets a value of a specified field for a specified document. The syntax of this function is

```
@SetDocField(documentUNID; fieldname; value)
```

The documentUNID parameter is the universal ID of the document whose field value is to be modified.

The fieldname parameter is the name of the item (fieldname) to be modified. This value is a string value. If the universal ID or fieldname are not valid, this function returns null.

The value is assigned to the field. This can be a test value, text list, number, number list, time-date, or time-date range.

Design Applications Based on Design Element IDs: UNID and NOTEID

Notes/Domino documents are the fundamental storage units of a Domino database, and they are roughly analogous to records in a relational database. Like a record, a document is the container that holds logically related fields, such as contact information. Unlike records in a relational database, though, documents have a very loose structure and can be changed on the fly if you use either different forms to save the document or programs that add or delete items from the document. Although this open-ended architecture may seem like a convoluted and confusing methodology, it gives developers unparalleled flexibility.

Normally, a document is created when a user opens a form and saves his or her work. It is at this point that the document's structure is defined by the form that was used to create it. Each Editable, Computed, or Computed When Composed field on the form is saved as an item in the document. Additionally, an item with the name of "Form" is added to the document, and the name of the form that used to save the document is stored in this field. When the document is opened again, the Form item is used to determine which form should be used, and the underlying item values populate the fields on the form that has corresponding names. If a field has been deleted from the form, it still exists in the document—it just isn't displayed. If a different form is used to edit the document, new items may be added to the document.

When a new document is created in a database, it is assigned a NoteID and a Universal ID (also known as the UNID). Each of these values is used by Domino to identify the document. Additionally, you can access and use these values from your programs to identify and access documents.

A document's *NoteID* is an 8-character combination of hexadecimal values (0–9, A–F), which uniquely identifies the document within a given database. It typically looks something like 50BE. (This is what this chapter was stored in while the book was being written.) Understanding the NoteID is important because many copies of a document may exist across replica databases but each has a unique Note ID. After a Note ID has been generated, it does not change and can be used programmatically to access documents.

You can use a document's NoteID to access it by calling the GetDocumentByID method of the NotesDatabase class and passing the NoteID as a string value. The following example illustrates this process:

```
Dim ns As New notesSession
Dim ndbCurrent As notesDatabase
Dim ndocCurrent As notesDocument
Dim strNoteID as String
strNoteID="1A8E"
Set ndbCurrent=ns.CurrentDatabase
Set ndocCurrent=ndbCurrent.GetDocumentByID(strNoteID)
```

The following is a very simple program that can be added as an agent to get the NoteID of any selected document. It is displayed in an InputBox so that you can copy the NoteID and paste it if necessary.

```
Dim ns As New notesSession
Dim ndbCurrent As notesDatabase
Dim ndcUnprocessed As notesDocumentCollection
```

```
Dim ndocCurrent As notesDocument
Dim strTemp As String
Set ndbCurrent=ns.CurrentDatabase
Set ndcUnprocessed=ndbCurrent.UnprocessedDocuments
Set ndocCurrent=ndcUnprocessed.GetFirstDocument
strTemp=Inputbox( "NoteID=", "NoteID", ndocCurrent.NoteID)
```

A document's *Universal ID* is a 32-character combination of hexadecimal values (0–9, A–F) that uniquely identifies a document across all replicas of a database. For example, the Universal ID of the Notes document used to store this chapter is "0385294991E17D93852568FA00668B2F." If a database has replica copies, the same document in each replica database has a completely unique NoteID, but they will all have duplicate Universal IDs. Or in other words, if two documents have the same Universal ID, they are replicas.

 Be sure to understand the differences between the NoteID and the Universal ID, how they are stored in the document, and how they are replicated between databases.

As with NoteID, you can access documents by their Universal IDs by calling the GetDocumentByUNID method of the NotesDatabase class and passing the Universal ID as a string value. The following example illustrates this process:

```
Dim ns As New notesSession
Dim ndbCurrent As notesDatabase
Dim ndocCurrent As notesDocument
Dim strUNID as String
strUNID="6A6C0A6E10F64338852568B400661A12"
Set ndbCurrent=ns.CurrentDatabase
Set ndocCurrent=ndbCurrent.GetDocumentByID(strUNID)
```

The following code demonstrates how you can get the Universal ID of any selected document. It is displayed in an Input Box so that you can copy the UNID and paste it if necessary.

```
Dim ns As New notesSession
Dim ndbCurrent As notesDatabase
Dim ndcUnprocessed As notesDocumentCollection
Dim ndocCurrent As notesDocument
Dim strTemp As String
Set ndbCurrent=ns.CurrentDatabase
Set ndcUnprocessed=ndbCurrent.UnprocessedDocuments
Set ndocCurrent=ndcUnprocessed.GetFirstDocument
strTemp=Inputbox( "UNID=", "UNID", ndocCurrent.UniversalID)
```

Notes documents are the fundamental data storage units in a Notes database (they are roughly analogous to records in a relational database), and each document is assigned a unique identifier known as the NoteID. As mentioned earlier, the NoteID is an 8-character hexadecimal value that serves as a unique document identifier within a given database. This means that replica copies of a document in different databases have different NoteIDs. An example of a NoteID is `50BE`.

Because each document in a database has a NoteID and Notes/Domino exposes it programmatically to formulas, LotusScript, and Java, the NoteID can be used in your applications to provide a unique system-level key to access documents. One common way this is done is to use the `GetDocumentbyID` method of `NotesDatabase` to access documents without using a view.

Table 8.1 illustrates some of the most common ways you can work with the NoteID programmatically.

Table 8.1	Common Ways to Work with the NoteID	
Language	**Method/Property/Statement**	**Description**
LotusScript	**NoteID**	Property of NotesDocument; returns the NoteID of a document as a string.
LotusScript	**GetDocumentByID**	Method of NotesDatabase that when supplied a valid NoteID returns a document object for the specified document.
Java	**getNoteID**	Property of Document; returns the NoteID of a document as a string.
Java	**getDocumentByID**	Method of **Database** that when supplied a valid NoteID returns a document object for the specified document.

As you know, Notes documents are the fundamental data storage units in a Notes database. (They are roughly analogous to records in a relational database.) Each document database is assigned a universal identifier known as the document's Universal ID.

Because each document in a database has a UNID and Notes/Domino exposes the UNID programmatically to formulas, LotusScript, and Java, it can be used in your applications to provide a unique system-level key to access documents. It is fairly common for developers to create a view with a sorted column containing the UNID of all documents, which programs then use to look up documents by their UNID. Another approach is to use the GetDocumentbyUNID method of `NotesDatabase` to access documents without using a view.

Additionally, when an application uses response documents, each response document automatically inherits the UNID of the parent in a field called `$Ref`. You can access the UNID of the parent document quickly and easily access the parent document. Table 8.2 illustrates some of the most common ways you can work with the UNID programmatically.

Table 8.2	Common Ways to Work with the UNID	
Language	Method/Property/Statement	Description
Formula	@DocumentUniqueID	Returns the UNID of a document. You must use the @Text formula to convert the hexa-decimal value to a string that can be used in your formulas. Using @DocumentUniqueID in a field formula creates a link to the document.
Formula	@GetDocField	When supplied a valid UNID and the name of a field in the document, returns the value of the named field.
Formula	@SetDocField	When supplied a valid UNID, the name of a field in the document, and a new value, assigns the new value into the field.
LotusScript	UniversalID	Property of **NotesDocument**; returns the Universal ID of a document as a string.
LotusScript	ParentDocumentUNID	Property of **NotesDocument**; returns as a string the UNID of the parent document if the current document is a response. If the current document is not a response, returns "".
LotusScript	GetDocumentByUNID	Method of **NotesDatabase** that when sup-plied a valid UNID returns a document object for the specified document.
Java	getUniversalID	Property of **Document**; returns the Universal ID of a document as a string.
Java	getParentDocumentUNID	Property of **Document**; returns as a string the UNID of the parent document if the cur-rent document is a response. If the current document is not a response, returns "".
Java	getDocumentByUNID	Method of **Database** that when supplied a valid UNID returns a document object for the specified document.

Design Applications Based on Graphics Elements

An *image resource* is a graphic that can be displayed throughout an application from a central location within the database. This saves space and minimizes maintenance because any changes you make to the image are automatically reflected in each place that refers to the image resource. An image resource can be a `.gif`, `.jpeg`, or `.bmp` file, which is saved in the database. After you have created an image resource, it can be used to add graphics or icons to pages, forms, action buttons, and outline entries, or it can be used to add background images on forms, documents, pages, table cells, and action buttons.

 Image resources displayed on the Web are converted to **.gif** or **.jpeg** format.

To create an image resource, follow these steps:

1. Open the database in which you would like to add an Image Resource.

2. Expand Resources in the Design pane, and choose Images to see a list of all the image resources in the database.

3. Click the New Image Resource button, which opens the New Image dialog box.

4. Choose a file (or files) to import, and ensure that it is either a `.gif`, `.bmp`, or `.jpeg` file.

5. Click Open to add the file(s) as an image resource. Designer creates an image resource for each file.

After you have added image resources, you can follow these steps to use an image resource in your application:

1. Open a page, form, outline entry, or other design element in which you'd like to add an image.

2. Position the cursor to the place where you want the image to appear.

3. Choose Create, Image Resource from the menu.

4. Select the image type `.gif`, `.jpeg`, or All Images from the Image Type list to display the list of available Image Resources.

5. Choose the Image Resource to insert the file.

6. Click OK to add the image.

Design Applications Based on OLE on a Form

Object Linking and Embedding (OLE) enables you to extend and enhance the capabilities and functionality of your applications by integrating data from other applications, such as spreadsheets, databases, and other data sources.

The Notes client provides excellent OLE support in that it is both an OLE automation controller and server. As an *automation controller*, you can use LotusScript to access OLE objects. As an *automation server*, Notes registers itself in your Registry as an automation server so that other applications can access both front-end and back-end Notes objects.

 To access Notes objects with OLE, a Notes client must be installed on the machine where the external program will run.

Notes/Domino 6 uses COM API and OLE API, enabling other Microsoft applications to call Notes functions.

The following list outlines some of the many things OLE enables your applications to do:

➤ *Link and embed objects in forms*—This option enables you to embed an object such as a spreadsheet in a form, which then creates that object in every document created by the form. This feature is supported only in Notes client applications.

➤ *Launch objects automatically*—This option enables you to have a form automatically open an existing embedded object, or create a new one when the form is opened. In fact, the object can be opened whenever users create, edit, or read a document that uses that form. This feature does not work in Web applications.

➤ *Add custom controls to a form*—On the Windows platform, you can configure your applications to use custom controls (OCXs).

➤ *Set up forms to exchange field information with other Notes documents*—If you use applications that support NotesFX (field exchange), you can create forms that use OLE to share information with other applications in an automatic, bi-directional fashion. This option is not supported for Web applications.

➤ *Publish an action*—You can use either formulas or scripts to code actions and then add them to the Action menu of any NotesFX-enabled application. This feature works only in the Notes client environment.

➤ *Embed JavaBeans*—Much like OCXs, JavaBeans are self-contained objects written in Java that can be embedded and called from Notes forms. To use JavaBeans in this fashion, you must first install the Java Runtime Environment (JRE).

 Many OLE-based technologies available in Domino are platform-dependent, and Windows provides by far the greatest range of options.

Design Applications Based on Summary/Non-Summary Data Storage

Items can contain summary or non-summary data. *Non-summary data* is typically rich-text data that is very long text, binary data, images, and so on. *Summary data* (which is all non-rich text data) can appear in views and folders, whereas non-summary data can not.

When certain items are created, they are designated as summary fields by default. This saves time and space, and thus improves performance, when the view indexes are compiling (because only summary items are displayed in views) and/or when the databases are replicating (because users can select to replicate only summary information to local replicas).

When items are created programmatically in a document via the New method of the backend classes NotesItem (LotusScript) or Item (Java), the IsSummary property is set to FALSE by default. This means that the contents of these items will not be displayed in views, even if the field is referenced in a view column formula. For the following types of items, the IsSummary property is set to TRUE:

➤ Items created with the extended class syntax or the `AppendItemValue` of NotesDocument (LotusScript) or Document (Java)

➤ Items created with the `ReplaceItemValue` method of the NotesDocument (LotusScript) or Document (Java), or items created with LotusScript extended syntax.

When the `IsSummary` property is set to TRUE, the contents of the item can be displayed in views. Regardless of the default setting, you can explicitly modify this property to appear, or not appear, in a view by modifying the `IsSummary` property.

> For the exam, remember that rich text cannot be displayed in a view. So, the **IsSummary** property for rich text items (**NotesRichTextItem**) always defaults to FALSE and cannot be changed.

Using the formula language or simple actions to create items programmatically in a document causes the `IsSummary` property to default to TRUE, except for rich text items. Likewise, the `IsSummary` property of items created in a document through a form defaults to TRUE, with the exception of rich text items.

Design Applications to Optimize View Performance

View performance is an important topic for any Domino developer. Because of the nonrelational nature of Lotus Notes/Domino, views can pose performance challenges when designing applications, especially enterprise applications with large amounts of data and/or a large number of views. Nevertheless, there are steps you can take to maximize performance. Some of the steps you can take to maximize performance include the following:

➤ *Do not record unread marks*—Located on the Advanced tab of the Database properties box, this option causes the database to not mark documents as unread, which increases application performance and reduces disk space.

➤ *Minimize use of categorized columns that display multiple values*—If the column formula returns multiple values in a categorized column, the same document is displayed multiple times in the same view, which negatively affects application performance.

➤ *Designate more than one column for sorting in views*—Allowing users to re-sort views by different columns increases application performance and reduces application size by reducing the need to create additional views to sort the documents.

➤ *Reduce the usage of Evaluate actions for every document change with context-sensitive actions*—A new feature in Lotus Notes/Domino 6 is the capability to create context-sensitive actions. This enables you to set hide-when attributes to display/hide actions based upon a document state or formula. In addition, the view setting to Evaluate Actions for Every Document Change causes the context-sensitive actions to re-evaluate when the user clicks on documents in the view. Although this is a handy feature, using this feature slows application performance.

➤ *For Web-based applications, reduce the number of documents displayed in the view*—Taking this step reduces the amount of data being displayed in the browser and decreases page loading time.

Domino Application Architecture

Domino Notes Storage Facilities (hence, the extension `.nsf`) are object stores. Unlike relational databases, which have a very structured architecture, NSFs have a very loose structure that can be easily changed at any time, making them ideal for storing compound and loosely structured data.

Domino databases are often referred to as "object stores" because they can store any type of digital information from spreadsheets to databases, MP3s to bitmaps, and virtually anything else. In fact, Domino makes an excellent repository for any type of unstructured data because there are very few restrictions on the structure of a Domino database and Domino has a very powerful full-text search engine that makes searching this unstructured data very easy and fast.

 Be sure to memorize what the acronym NSF (Notes Storage Facility) and NTF (Notes Template Facility) represent.

Set Up Full-Text Indexing

A full-text index is a powerful search mechanism that enables users to search for documents based on a search criteria, a certain word, or certain phrases.

Creating a *full-text index* of a database speeds searches performed within a database and, optionally, allows for searching attachments and encrypted fields. Users can still search a database that has not been full-text indexed; however, it will take longer for the search to be completed and the results to be returned.

 For the exam, remember that you must have Designer access or higher to create, update, or delete a full-text index.

To view, create, update, or delete a full-text index, open the Full Text tab of the Database properties box, which contains information regarding Full Text Indexing options (see Figure 8.7).

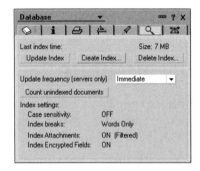

Figure 8.7   The Full Text tab of the Database properties box.

The information contained in the Full Text tab is described in Table 8.4.

Table 8.4 Database Full Text Tab		
Setting	**Setting Type**	**Description**
Update Index	Button	Updates a previously defined index.
Create Index	Button	Opens the Create Full Text Index dialog box.
Delete Index	Button	Deletes a previously created index.
Update Frequency	Dropdown	Specifies the update frequency (daily, scheduled, hourly, immediate).
Count unindexed documents	Button	Counts the number of documents not incorporated into the current full-text index.
Index Settings	Display only	Displays the full text index settings (Case Sensitivity, Index Breaks, Index Attachments, Index Encrypted Fields).

Any database can be full-text indexed, and doing so is quite simple. Just follow these steps:

1. Select the database you want to index.

2. Right-click the database icon and choose Database, Properties, which opens the Database properties box. Alternatively, you can choose File, Database, Properties.

3. Click the Full Text tab (looks like a magnifying glass), which displays the full-text search properties. This screen is shown in Figure 8.7.

4. Click the Create Index button to create a full-text index for the database, or, if an index already exists, to overwrite the old one with a new one. This opens the Create Full-Text Index dialog box shown in Figure 8.8.

5. Optionally select indexing options, each of which is explained in Table 8.5.

6. Click OK to create the index. The database will be searchable as soon as it is indexed.

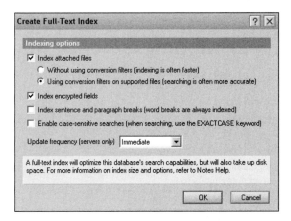

Figure 8.8 The Create Full-Text Index dialog box.

Table 8.5 Full-Text Indexing Options		
Option	**Description**	**Default Setting**
Index Attached Files	If documents in a database contain attached files, these files can be included in the index so that their contents can be searched. If this option is selected, you can choose from two indexing methods: Raw text only (faster) and Binary attachments (more accurate). The first option indexes only ASCII text in the files, which consumes less space and takes less time, whereas the second option indexes all contents, which is slower and creates larger, yet more accurate, indexes. Either way, keep in mind that text in the attached files is not highlighted if found when searching.	Off
Index Encrypted Fields	If documents in the database contain encrypted fields, they too can be indexed so that they can be searched. However, this increases the size of the index and compromises the contents of the encrypted fields.	On
Index sentence and paragraph breaks (word breaks are always indexed)	This setting can be enabled to allow proximity searches so that you can see whether a word is close to another word.	Off
Enable case-sensitive searches (when searching use **EXACTCASE** keyword)	If this setting is enabled, uppercase words and lowercase words are indexed separately. For example, "Republican" and "republican" would each be indexed, so then case-sensitive searches can be performed. Enabling this setting increases the size of an index by 5–10%.	Off
Update frequency (servers only)	For databases that reside on a Domino server, this setting enables you to dictate how often the index is rebuilt. There are four options: Immediate, Daily, Scheduled, and Hourly.	

In Domino 6, it is possible that the size of full-text indexes could increase by 10–20%, which may have an impact on disk space requirements.

Summary

Some of broad capabilities and more specific features of the Lotus Notes/Domino application architecture have been covered in this chapter. The topics you've learned about include the following:

➤ Sharing design elements among different databases, database integrity, Document Universal ID (UNID) and the Note ID, and how they are used within applications

➤ Various design elements used in the navigation structure and how they are integrated into your application

➤ The rich text structure and the difference between summary and non-summary items

➤ Connecting to external applications, and full-text searching

These topics should be familiar to experienced Domino developers. After studying this chapter, you will be prepared to answer any exam questions on these topics!

Exam Prep Questions

Question 1

> John Galt is currently working in the Domino designer. He has selected Tools, Customize Tools from the drop-down menu. Which option is not available in the Customize Tools dialog box?
>
> ❑ A. Add Tool.
> ❑ B. Add Submenu.
> ❑ C. Launch Tool.
> ❑ D. Copy Tool.

Answer C is correct. You cannot launch a tool (application) directly from within the Customize Tools dialog box. After the dialog box is closed, tools can be launched from the Tools drop-down menu. Options A, B, and D are incorrect because they are valid options. In addition, you can also Edit, Cut, and Paste tools within this dialog box.

Question 2

> Which of the following options uniquely identifies a document within a database and across multiple replicas of the database?
>
> ❑ A. Universal ID.
> ❑ B. Doc ID.
> ❑ C. Note ID.
> ❑ D. Record Replica ID.

Answer A is correct. The Universal ID is a 32-character hexadecimal value that serves as a unique identifier across all replica copies of a database. Answer B is incorrect because there is no Doc ID identifier in Domino. Answer C is incorrect because the *NoteID* of a document is an 8-character combination of hexadecimal values (0–9, A–F), which uniquely identifies the document within a given database, not across replica copies of the database. Answer D is incorrect because Record Replica ID is not an identifier in Domino.

Question 3

Which of the following is not a valid image type to use when creating image resources in Lotus Notes/Domino?

□ A. **.gif**.

□ B. **.jpeg**.

□ C. **.bmp**.

□ D. All of the above are valid image types.

Answer D is correct. An image resource can be a .gif, .jpeg, or .bmp file. Of course, answers A, B, and C are incorrect because all the image types are valid answers.

Question 4

Which of the following methods creates a Notes Item that is automatically set as non-summary data (therefore, the **IsSummary** property is set to FALSE)?

□ A. Using the **New** method of the backend classes **NotesItem** (LotusScript) or **Item** (Java).

□ B. Using the **AppendItemValue** of the NotesDocument (LotusScript) or Document (Java).

□ C. Using the **ReplaceItemValue** method of the NotesDocument (LotusScript) or Document (Java).

□ D. Using LotusScript extended syntax.

Answer A is correct. When items are created programmatically in a document via the New method of the backend classes NotesItem (LotusScript) or Item (Java), the IsSummary property is set to FALSE by default. This means that the item contains non-summary data and the contents of these items will not be displayed in views, even if the field is referenced in a view column formula. Answers B, C, and D are incorrect because for items created with the extended class syntax or the AppendItemValue of NotesDocument (LotusScript) or Document (Java), the ReplaceItemValue method of the NotesDocument (LotusScript) or Document (Java), or the extended syntax using LotusScript, the IsSummary property is set to TRUE, meaning the contents of the item contain summary data and can be displayed in views.

Question 5

Brooke is designing a new database. She is aware that performance may be an issue with this database because it is likely to store a large number of documents. Which of the following methods can she not use to help improve the performance of her view?

- ❑ A. Do not record unread marks.
- ❑ B. Optimize document table map.
- ❑ C. Minimize use of categorized columns that display multiple values.
- ❑ D. Designate more than one column for sorting in views.

Answer B is correct. This is not an option when designing views. Rather, this is an option on the Advanced tab of the Database properties box. This option, however, does improve performance for the database in general. Answer A is incorrect because this is a valid option that improves view performance. The option Do Not Record Unread Marks causes documents to no longer be marked as unread, which increases application performance and reduces disk space. Answer C is incorrect because minimizing the use of categorized columns that display multiple values can improve performance. The same document is displayed multiple times in the same view, which will negatively affect application performance. Answer D is incorrect because designating more than one column for sorting in views enables users to re-sort views by different columns. This increases application performance and reduces application size by reducing the need to create additional views to sort the documents.

Question 6

What is the minimum database ACL rights required to update a full-text index on a database that already has been full-text indexed by the database manager?

- ❑ A. Manager.
- ❑ B. Designer.
- ❑ C. Editor.
- ❑ D. Author.
- ❑ E. Anyone can update an existing full-text index.

Answer B is correct. A user can have Designer access (the minimum access displayed) or higher to create, update, or delete a full-text index. Answer A is incorrect because even though the Manager can indeed update the full-text index, that is not the minimum access required (as specified in the question). Answers C and E are incorrect because these users have insufficient access rights to update a full-text index. Answer E is incorrect because, as previously mentioned, only Designers and Managers can update the full-text index.

Need to Know More?

 Lotus Developer Domain. "Domino 6 Technical Overview." Available in printed form or on the Web at `http://www.lotus.com/ldd`.

  IBM International Technical Support Organization. *Domino Designer 6: A Developer's Handbook*. Available in printed form, PDF format, and HTML format from `http://publib-b.boulder. ibm.com/Redbooks.nsf/RedbookAbstracts/sg246854.html?Open`.

 IBM Lotus. "Release Notes." `http://www-10.lotus.com/ldd/notesua. nsf/RN?OpenView`.

 IBM Lotus. *Online Help Databases*: `help6_admin.nsf`, `help6_client. nsf`, `help6_designer.nsf`.

Design Elements

Terms you'll need to understand:

✓ Data Connection Resource (DCR)
✓ Shared actions
✓ Shared fields
✓ Subforms
✓ Framesets
✓ Outlines
✓ Profile document
✓ Embedded elements
✓ Navigators
✓ Signing
✓ Image resource

Concepts and techniques you'll need to master:

✓ Using shared actions
✓ Using shared applets
✓ Using shared fields
✓ Using profile documents
✓ Using embedded elements
✓ Using agents
✓ Using twisties
✓ Using new shared resources such as Data Connection Resources and external files

Design elements are the foundation of Domino development and there are many new and enhanced design elements in Domino 6. This chapter covers the information you need to know regarding Domino design elements for 611 exam.

In Chapter 4, "Exam 610—Design Elements," you learned about the Domino IDE and its elements. In this chapter, you also need to open a Notes database in the Domino Designer and work with the design elements. Before proceeding with this chapter, go back and review the sections of Chapter 4 titled "The Domino Designer Integrated Development Environment (IDE)" and "Domino 6 Design Elements." Follow the instructions in those sections for opening the database in the Designer and reviewing the common Domino 6 Design elements.

Working with Domino Design Elements

As you learned in Chapter 4, The Domino Designer is a powerful IDE. Figure 9.1 shows an open database in the Domino Designer.

Figure 9.1 The Domino Designer is a powerful IDE.

The following sections discuss techniques for working with the Domino design elements.

Setting and Modifying Design Element Properties

Every design element has various properties that control its appearance and functionality; for the most part, they are set using properties boxes that provide an interface for the developer to specify the settings.

To set or modify the properties of a design element, follow these steps:

1. Open a database in the Designer client.

2. Select a type of design element to modify in the Design Pane.

3. Choose an element and right-click it. This opens the Design Properties dialog box.

4. Configure settings such as Prohibit Design Refresh and Design Template Name.

Changing design properties will re-sign the design element with the electronic signature of the Notes ID in use.

Modifying Design Properties Multiple Elements

Domino 6 enables designers to configure certain design properties for multiple design elements, thus saving time and effort. To edit design properties for multiple design elements, follow these steps below:

1. Open a database in the Designer client.

2. Select a type of design element to modify in the Design Pane.

3. Choose one or more design elements and right-click. This opens the Design Properties dialog box.

4. Configure common shared settings such as Prohibit Design Refresh and Design Template Name.

Creating, Modifying, and Troubleshooting Shared Actions

An *action* is a programmable button that can be used to automate tasks. Actions normally appear in the Action bar, which can be displayed in forms, subforms, pages folders, and views. There are two types of actions: single-use actions and shared actions. A single-use action can only be used in the form, view, folder, or page where it is created. (Single-use actions are covered in Chapter 4.) Shared actions can be shared across design elements in a database, allowing you to modularize your applications and save time.

Additionally, shared actions can be used anywhere that single-use actions can be used, including in the Actions menu in the Notes client. Actions are most often used in the following situations:

➤ When you want to automate a function but don't want the code stored with each individual design element.

➤ When Web clients need substitutes for Notes client menu choices (through the Action bar).

➤ When users need to see all the possible choices in a nonscrolling row at the top of a form, page, or view. When buttons are placed in a form or page, they scroll with the form.

➤ When the function the action performs isn't limited to a particular section of a form or page.

➤ When you want to share an automated function among several design elements, making the maintenance of the application easier.

Action Coding Choices

When you create an action, you have several coding choices, depending on which environment (Web or Notes client) the action will be used in. Additionally, you may elect to use one of the predefined System actions Lotus has included.

Notes Client Coding Choices

Actions that will be used in Notes client applications can be programmed using any of the following choices:

➤ Simple actions

➤ Formulas

➤ JavaScript

➤ Common JavaScript (shared library)

➤ LotusScript

Web Coding Choices

Actions that will be used in Web client applications can be programmed using either of the following choices:

➤ JavaScript

➤ Common JavaScript (shared library)

System Actions

Domino provides a set of predefined actions, known as *System actions*, that automate some of the most basic and common Notes features. The System actions are described in the following list:

➤ **Categorize**—Used to add values to the Categories field in the current document

➤ **Edit Document**—Used to edit the current document

➤ **Forward**—Used to copy the current document to a new email memo

➤ **Move to Folder**—Used to move the current document to a specified folder

➤ **Remove from Folder**—Used to remove the current document from a specified folder

➤ **Send Document**—Used to send the current document via email

System actions that use system commands will not work on the Web. Instead, you should create custom actions to replicate their functionality.

Creating Shared Actions

Follow these steps to create a shared action that can be used in any form, page, or view.

   1. In the Notes Designer client, open the database that will contain your shared action.

2. Select Shared Code, Actions, which will display the list of existing
   shared actions.

3. Click the New Shared Action button. This opens the Shared Action
   properties box shown in Figure 9.2.

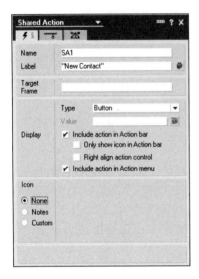

Figure 9.2 The Shared Action properties box enables you to define how your action will work.

4. Enter a name for the action.

5. (Optional) Enter a label, which is descriptive text displayed to the user.
   To enter a label, write a formula that will compute a value to display
   for the action's label. If a label is not supplied, the action's name will be
   used for the label.

6. (Optional) If you plan to display the action within a specific frame,
   select the target frame.

7. Select the location and position of the action and optionally enable the
   following options:

   ➤ Select the position in which the action should appear in the Action
   bar or the Actions menu.

   ➤ If you want the action to appear in the Action bar, click the Include
   Action in Action Bar check box. If you elect to have the action
   appear in the Action bar, you have two additional options: The first
   option, Only Show Icon in Action Bar, determines whether the text
   caption (label) appears with the icon. The second option, Right

Align Action Control, determines whether the action appears right-aligned.

➤ Determine whether the action should appear in the Actions menu.

8. If you are displaying the action as a button on the Action bar, you can select a graphic icon to display in the button. If you want to use an image, determine whether it is to be Notes (which uses the palette of available icons that comes with Notes) or Custom (which enables you to select an image resource of type GIF or JPEG).

9. (Optional) Click the Action Hide When tab (the second tab) to hide the action under certain conditions.

10. Select the appropriate choices, all of which are fairly self-explanatory. If the action should be hidden under certain conditions, check the Hide Action If Formula Is True check box and enter a formula that evaluates to TRUE when the hide-when conditions are met.

11. (Optional) Define OLE settings for the action in the Advanced tab (the third tab).

12. Close the Action properties box.

13. In the Objects tab of the Programmer's Pane, select the action you just created.

14. Expand the Run pull-down list and choose the environment in which the action will run: Client or Web.

15. Choose a coding choice appropriate for the selected environment and enter your code.

16. Save the shared action.

Using a Shared Action

Once you have created a shared action, using it is simple. Just follow these steps:

1. In the Designer client, open the database that contains the form, page, or view in which you want to use the shared action.

2. Open the form, page, or view.

3. Choose Create, Action, Insert Shared Action. This opens the Insert Shared Action dialog box.

4. Choose one or more of the shared actions displayed and click insert.

Modifying Shared Actions

To modify a shared action, follow these steps:

1. In the Designer client, open the database that contains your shared action.

2. Select Shared Code, Actions, which will display the list of existing shared actions.

3. Double-click the action to open the Action properties box, shown previously in Figure 9.2.

4. Edit the action by following the steps listed in the section "Creating Shared Actions."

Troubleshooting Shared Actions

Problems with actions usually fall into one of two categories: actions that are either hidden or visible at inappropriate times, and programming problems. Each is examined in the following sections.

Troubleshooting Action Hide-Whens

Follow these steps when troubleshooting action hide-whens:

1. In the Notes Designer client, open the database that contains your shared action.

2. Select Shared Code, Actions, which will display the list of existing shared actions.

3. Double-click the action to open the Action properties box, shown previously in Figure 9.2.

4. Click the Hide When tab.

5. Check the hide-when settings. If a hide-when formula has been used, ensure that the formula returns the value TRUE. If you are unsure, one easy way to test the formula is to create a Computed for Display field in a form and paste the formula into it. Then open the form and examine the value in the field. It should contain 1, the formula language value for TRUE.

6. Save the design element.

7. Test the action to ensure that it is hidden or visible at the appropriate times.

Troubleshooting Action Programming

Follow these steps when troubleshooting action programming:

1. In the Notes Designer client, open the database that contains your shared action.

2. Select Shared Code, Actions, which will display the list of existing shared actions.

3. Click the action to display the action's contents in the Programmer's Pane.

4. Begin to debug the action. The type of action determines the most appropriate method of debugging. Table 9.1 lists the best way to debug a particular action based on its code.

Table 9.1	Action Debugging Methods
Type	**Method**
Formula	Use the **@Prompt** function in the code to display key variables and field values and to show the progress and flow of the code.
LotusScript	Use the LotusScript debugger (File, Tools, Debug LotusScript) instead or in conjunction with the **MsgBox** function to display key variables and field values and to show the progress and flow of the code. Additionally, you can use the **NotesLog** class to record a script's actions. This can be especially useful for debugging agents run by a Web client.
JavaScript/Common JavaScript	Use the **alert()** function in the code to display key variables and field values and to show the progress and flow of the code.

5. Save the form or view.

6. Test the action to make sure the expected results are displayed.

7. Repeat steps 4–6 until the action works as expected.

Creating, Modifying, and Troubleshooting Shared Fields

In Notes/Domino, fields are used to enter, modify, and display data stored in items. (*Item* is the technical name for a discrete data element stored in a

Notes document.) Fields can be used in forms, subforms, and layout regions and can be either single-use fields or shared fields. Single-use fields can only be used in the form or subform in which they are created (these are covered in depth in Chapter 4). A *Shared field*, is a field that can be used in any form or subform in a database. Three key criteria must be specified when creating fields: the field name, the data type of the field, and the field type.

Naming Fields

Each field on a form or subform must have a unique name. In addition to using a unique name for each field, you should keep the following points in mind:

➤ Field names cannot exceed 32 characters in length.

➤ Field names cannot contain spaces. You can use underscores (_) instead.

➤ Field names should not begin with a dollar sign ($) because this character is usually reserved for special Notes system fields.

➤ Field names cannot begin with a number (1–9).

➤ Field names cannot contain the ampersand symbol (&).

Field Data Types

The Notes database architecture supports a wide range of data types for fields. They are explained in Table 9.2.

Table 9.2	Notes Data Types
Type	**Description**
Text	A field that stores up to 15KB of textual data, can be displayed in views, and has no fixed field length.
Date/Time	Date/time fields store and display time and date information in any number of formats, the default being MM/DD/YY HH:MM:SS (internally, Domino stores times in seconds). Valid dates range from 1/1/0001 through 12/31/9999. Entering a two-digit year between 00 and 49 assumes the century starts in the year 2000. Entering two-digit years between 50 and 99 assumes the century starts in the year 1900. You can force users to enter a four-digit year in the field by selecting Require User to Enter Four Digit Years in the On Input field in the Field properties box. If you want to display a calendar control for users, select Calendar/Time Control.
Timezone	Timezone fields display a drop-down list of all available time zones.

Table 9.2	Notes Data Types *(continued)*
Type	**Description**
Number	Number fields are used to store numeric data, including numerals 0 through 9, the plus (+) and minus (−) signs, decimal points, and scientific notation. Number fields can be formatted in one of four ways, as explained in the following list:
	➤ **Decimal**—Stores and displays numbers with a fixed number of decimal places specified by the developer. A number field can store up to eight nonzero decimal digits without loss of precision.
	➤ **Percent**—Stores and displays numeric values as a percentage.
	➤ **Scientific**—Stores and displays numeric values using exponential notation.
	➤ **Currency**—Stores and displays numeric values with the currency symbol specified by the developer. The default format is the American dollar sign ($).
	Blank number fields are stored as an empty string (""). To make a number field always store a numeric value, use a default formula of 0.
Dialog list	Enables users to select the correct value(s) from a list of acceptable choices. The developer can determine whether the list should be mutually exclusive. The user can press Enter or click the Entry Helper button (the little arrow) to see all the choices at once, press the spacebar to display choices one at a time, or type a letter to display the first choice beginning with that letter. Keep in mind that you cannot use a dialog list in a layout region.
Check box	Enables users to select the correct value(s) from a list of acceptable choices that are not mutually exclusive. Each choice in the list is displayed with a box users click to select.
Radio button	Enables users to select the correct value from a list of acceptable choices that are mutually exclusive. Each choice is displayed with a button that users click to select.
List box	Enables users to select the correct value(s) from a scrolling, fixed-size list of acceptable choices. The developer can determine whether the list should be mutually exclusive.
Combo box	Enables users to select the correct value from a drop-down list of mutually exclusive acceptable choices.
Rich text	Rich Text fields can be used to store large amounts of text or formatted text, and they can be used for embedding or attaching objects. There is no practical size restriction (1GB) on the data placed in the field, as long as the database and disk drive can store the data. Rich Text fields can be used anywhere except in a layout region, and their contents cannot be displayed in a view.

Table 9.2 Notes Data Types *(continued)*	
Type	**Description**
Rich text lite	Rich Text lite fields are not as open-ended as regular Rich Text fields. They have a drop-down list that allows you to specify the type of data to put in the field. Any attempt to insert or paste an element not listed displays an error message. This field type is new to Domino 6.
Authors	Authors fields enable users with Author access to edit documents if they are named in the authors field. It is important to remember that authors fields do not override the ACL but rather refine it.
Names	Names fields can be used to display user and/or server names.
Readers	Readers fields can be used to limit access to specific documents by explicitly listing the users/groups who can read documents. Like authors fields, readers fields refine the ACL; they do not override it. If no readers fields exist in a document, anyone with access to the database can read the document.
Password	A password field is a special type of text field that helps to maintain privacy by displaying each character entered as an asterisk on the screen. Remember that the contents of a password field are not secure and are visible in the Document properties box from the Notes client. This type of field is new to R6.
Formula	Formula fields have a special purpose; they are used to populate a subscription list, which works in conjunction with the Subscription feature in the **Headlines.nsf** database.
Color	Color fields display a color picker that allows the user to select a color and then returns an RGB value.

The field type is another key setting involved in adding fields to a form. The Designer supports four field types:

➤ **Computed**—The value is the result of a formula and is stored in the document. It is recomputed when the document is opened, refreshed, or saved.

➤ **Computed for Display**—The value is the result of a calculation, but the value is not stored in the document. It is recomputed when the document is created, opened, refreshed, or saved.

➤ **Computed When Composed**—The value is the result of a calculation, and the value is stored in the document. However, it is calculated only when the document is created, and it's not ever refreshed.

➤ **Editable**—The value is entered by the user and is stored in the document. A default formula can be used to populate the field when a document is created, and input translations and field-validation formulas can be used to manipulate data when the document is saved and to validate data when it is refreshed.

Creating Shared Fields

To create a shared field, follow these steps:

1. In the Notes Designer client, open the database that will contain your shared field.

2. Select Shared Code, Fields, which will display the list of existing shared field.

3. Click the New Shared Field button. This opens the Shared Field properties box shown in Figure 9.3.

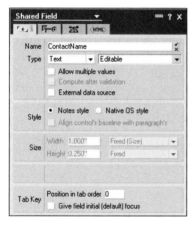

Figure 9.3   The Info tab on the Shared Field properties box enables you to define the basic properties of a field.

4. On the Info tab, enter the following information:

   ➤ Enter a name for the field in the Name field (keep the naming conventions mentioned previously in mind).

   ➤ Select the data type of the field (defined in Table 9.3).

   ➤ Select the type of the field: Editable, Computed When Composed, Computed for Display, or Computed.

   ➤ If the field can store multiple values, select the Allow Multiple Values check box.

➤ If the field is computed and you would like its value to be computed after the form's validation formula has fired, click the Compute After Validation check box.

➤ Choose the type of appearance the field should have—either Notes Style or Native OS Style. If you select Native OS Style, be sure to set the height and width properties.

➤ Set the field's tab order and, if you want the field to get the default focus (meaning the cursor is positioned in this field first), click the Give Field Initial (Default) Focus check box.

5. Select the Control tab (the second tab) to choose the display options for the field. The choices presented on this tab vary widely, depending on the type of field you have elected to create. Be sure to check the settings for the field you are creating.

6. Select the Advanced tab (the third tab) and, if necessary, enter a help description. If the field is set to display multiple values, configure the multi-values options. The Font settings for a field are fairly self-explanatory and are not covered here in detail.

7. Select the HTML tab (the fourth tab) to enter HTML-specific attributes for the field, such as class and style.

8. Enter any field-related formulas, such as a default value, input translation, or input validation formula.

9. Save the shared field.

Using a Shared Field

Once you have created a shared field, using it is simple. Just follow these steps:

1. In the Designer client, open the database that contains the form or subform in which you want to use the shared field.

2. Open the form or subform.

3. Position the cursor to the place on the form or subform where you want the shared field to appear.

4. Choose Create, Resource, Insert Shared Field. This opens the Insert Shared Field dialog box.

5. Choose one or more of the shared fields displayed and click OK.

Modifying Shared Fields

To modify a shared field, follow these steps:

1. In the Designer client, open the database that will contain your shared field.

2. Select Shared Code, Fields, which will display the list of existing shared fields.

3. Double-click the field you want to edit.

4. Follow the steps outlined in the earlier section "Creating Shared Fields."

Troubleshooting Shared Fields

The following is a list of tips to help you in troubleshooting shared fields:

➤ Check the field properties to ensure the field is set to the proper data type.

➤ Ensure that the type of field is set correctly. For example, if the field value should be saved as an item in the document, but it's not, be sure that you have not set the field to Computed for Display.

➤ If you are planning to store multiple values in a field, be sure that the field has the multi-values property enabled.

➤ If the field is of type keywords but you are not getting the correct values in the list, check the formula being used to generate the list.

➤ If the field is computed and the computations are based on other fields in the form, be sure to check the order of the fields. Remember that in Notes, fields are computed from left to right and top to bottom.

Creating, Modifying, and Troubleshooting Framesets

A frameset enables you to add structure to your applications (whether Notes or Web) by dividing the main window into subwindows (frames). Each frame in a frameset can contain a form, folder, page, document, view, navigator, Web page, or even another frameset, and it is independently scrollable. Keep in mind that you can set a frameset to launch automatically when a database, form, or page opens so that the content of a database always appears in frames.

Creating Framesets

To create a frameset, follow these steps:

1. In the Designer, open the database in which you want to create a frameset.

2. Click Framesets in the Design Pane to see the list of existing framesets.

3. Choose Create, Design, Frameset or click the New Frameset button.

4. In the Create New Frameset box that appears, as shown in Figure 9.4, select the number of frames you want to create in the Number of Frames drop-down box. (Your choices are two, three, or four frames.)

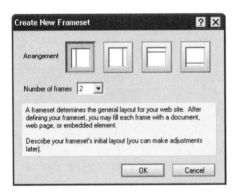

Figure 9.4   The Create New Frameset dialog box makes generating a frameset quick and easy.

5. Click the Arrangement button that represents how you want the frames laid out within the frameset.

6. Click OK, and the frameset is generated.

7. Define the frameset properties. Choose Frame, Frameset Properties from the menu to open the Frameset properties box (displayed in Figure 9.5). The Info tab is where you can define the following important frameset properties:

   ➤ Enter a name for the frameset in the Name field.

   ➤ (Optional) Enter an alias for the frameset in the Alias field.

   ➤ Enter a title for the frameset. You can enter the title as a literal, or you can click the formula button to build a formula that computes the frameset title.

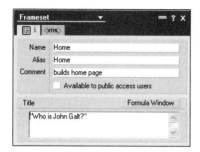

Figure 9.5   Define the frameset properties in the Frameset properties box.

> ➤ Enable the Available to Public Access Users check box if you want users who have been granted only public access to have access to the outline.

8. (Optional) Click the HTML tab and define any necessary HTML attributes.

9. Refine the frameset. You can use the Frame action buttons, the Frame menu options, or keyboard keys to tweak the appearance of your frameset, including adding new framesets within the existing frameset.

10. Specify the content of each frame. Select Frame, Frame Properties from the menu to open the Frame properties box (see Figure 9.6). In the Info tab, you can define the following important properties:

Figure 9.6   The Frame properties box.

> ➤ Enter a name for the frame in the Name field.

> ➤ Select the type of content that will populate the frame in the Type field. Your three choices are Link, Named Element, and URL.

➤ Define the content. The possible content types are described in Table 9.3.

➤ Enter the target links that are to be opened in the frame. The default is to open the link in the current frame.

Table 9.3	Possible Frame Content Types
Type	**Description**
URL	A link to another site. Be sure to enter the entire URL, including the protocol specifier.
Link	A Notes link to an anchor, database, document, or view. Click the Paste button to paste in the link.
Named Element	A Notes link to a page, form, frameset, folder, navigator, or view. If you select this option, be sure to pick the element type and then specify the actual element that should be opened. To choose the specific element, you can do one of three things: Click the Folder button to select from a list of all elements of the specified type, click the Formula button to write formulas that compute which element to open, or click the Paste button to paste in a link to the element.

11. Click the Frame Size tab (the second tab) to define the size of the frame and its scrolling attributes.

12. Click the Frame Border tab (the third tab) to define the frame's border attributes.

13. Click the Advanced tab (the fourth tab) to define the frame attributes, such as frame spacing, margin height, and margin width.

14. Click the HTML tab (the final tab) to define any HTML-specific attributes needed for the frameset.

15. Save the frameset.

Modifying Framesets

To modify a frameset, follow these steps:

1. In the Designer, open the database that contains the frameset you want to modify.

2. Click Framesets in the Design Pane to see the list of existing framesets.

3. Double-click the frameset you want to modify.

4. Make the necessary changes based on the steps outlined in the preceding section, "Creating Framesets."

Troubleshooting Framesets

The following is a list of common frameset problems and their resolutions:

➤ **The frameset displays no title or the title is incorrect.** Open the Frameset properties box and enter a formula in the Title text box.

➤ **The wrong number of frames is displayed.** Open the frameset and add or delete frames from the frameset.

➤ **The frame displays the wrong or no content.** Open the frameset and select Frame. Open the Frame properties box and ensure that the frame is set to display the desired content in the Content section of the Basics tab.

➤ **The content is not targeted to the proper frame.** Open the frameset and select Frame. Open the Frame properties box and check that the Default Target for Links in Frame setting is correct.

➤ **Frame scrolling, resizing, and size are incorrect.** Open the frameset and select Frame. Open the Frame properties box and check the settings on the Frame Size tab. Also check the Autoframe settings of the design element.

➤ **The frame borders are incorrect or are not appearing.** Open the frameset and select Frame. Open the Frame properties box and check the Frame Border settings.

Creating, Modifying, and Troubleshooting Outlines

Outlines are another useful development tool that enable you to provide user-friendly, easily maintainable, and customizable navigation for your applications. An outline consists of outline entries that can do any of the following things:

➤ Link to a named element (page, form, view, and so forth)

➤ Link to a Web page

➤ Perform an action (such as run an agent)

Using this new feature, you can create an outline that enables users to easily navigate your entire site. After you create an outline and populate it with entries that perform the necessary tasks and navigation, you embed it on a page or form so that it can be presented to users.

Keep in mind that you can create an outline in one of three ways: You can copy and modify an existing outline; you can create a new outline from scratch; or you can generate a default outline. The latter two methods are described in the following sections.

Creating Outlines from Scratch

To create an outline from scratch, you first define the outline properties and then add outline entries. To define the outline properties, follow these steps:

1. In the Designer, open the database in which you want to create the outline.

2. Click Shared Code, Outlines in the Design Pane to view the list of existing outlines.

3. Choose Create, Design, Outline from the menu, or click the New Outline button.

4. Define the outline properties. Choose Design, Outline Properties from the menu to open the Outline properties box (see Figure 9.7). In the Info tab, you can define the following important outline properties:

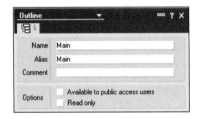

Figure 9.7 The Outline properties box is very straightforward.

➤ Enter a name for the outline in the Name field.

➤ Enter an alias for the outline in the Alias field.

➤ Click the Available to Public Access Users check box if you want users who have been granted only public access to have access to the outline.

Now, you are ready to add outline entries for each design element, action, or link you want to include in the outline. To add an outline entry, follow these steps (only the most important options are covered):

1. Click the New Entry button, which opens the Outline Entry properties box to the Info tab (see Figure 9.8).

Figure 9.8   The Outline Entry properties box.

2. Enter a name for the outline entry.

3. Enter an alias for the outline entry.

4. Select the type of outline entry you want to create in the Type field. You have four choices, as described in Table 9.4.

Table 9.4	Type of Outline Entry
Type	**Description**
None	Use this option to create a top-level category if you want to nest entries.
Action	Click the Formula button to create a formula that carries out the action.
Link	A Notes link to an anchor, database, document, or view. Click the Paste button to paste in the link.
Named Element	A Notes link to a page, form, frameset, folder, navigator, or view. If you select this option, be sure to pick the element type and then specify the actual element that should be opened. To choose the specific element, you can do one of three things:
	➤ Click the Folder button to select from a list of all elements of the specified type.
	➤ Click the Formula button to write a formula that computes which element to open.
	➤ Click the Paste button to paste in a link to the element.

5. Enter the name of the frame that should be targeted to receive content linked to it by the outline entry.

6. If you want to associate an image with the outline entry, you can click the Folder button to select the image from the file system, or you can write a formula to dynamically determine which image should be displayed. Click the Do Not Display Image check box if you don't want the specified image to be displayed.

7. If you want to have the outline entry displayed under only certain conditions, click the Hide When tab to define the hide-when criteria.

When you have finished adding outline entries, save the outline. Finally, embed the outline in a form or page and test it to ensure that it performs as expected.

Creating a Default Outline

The default outline is a handy, timesaving feature that automatically generates outline entries for all the views and folders in the database. It also creates the following entries: Other Views, Other Folders, Other Private Views, and Other Private Folders, which serve as placeholders you can replace with actual entries.

To create a default outline, follow these steps:

1. In the Designer, open the database in which you want to create the outline.

2. Click Outlines in the Design Pane to view the list of existing outlines.

3. Choose Create, Design, Outline from the menu, or click the New Outline button.

4. Define the outline properties. Choose Design, Outline Properties from the menu to open the Outline properties box (shown previously in Figure 9.7).

5. Click the Generate Default Outline button.

6. Edit existing outline entries and add new ones as needed.

7. Save the outline.

After you save the outline, embed it in a form or page and then test it to ensure that it works properly.

Modifying an Outline

To modify an outline, follow these steps:

1. In the Designer, open the database that contains the outline you want to edit.

2. Click Outlines in the Design Pane to view the list of existing outlines.

3. Double-click the outline you want to edit.

4. Modify the outline (and/or its entries), following the steps listed in the section "Creating Outlines from Scratch."

Troubleshooting Outlines

The following is a list of common outline problems and their resolution:

➤ **The outline opens in the wrong frameset.** Open the Outline properties box and check the Frame property of the outline.

➤ **The outline entries are displaying when they should be hidden, or vice versa.** Check the hide-when properties of the outline entries that are not displaying properly.

➤ **The outline entry does nothing when clicked.** Open the Outline Entry properties box and ensure that the content options are set appropriately.

➤ **The outline entry does not display an image even though you selected one.** Open the Outline Entry properties box and ensure that the Do Not Display an Image box is not checked.

➤ **The outline entry does not navigate to the proper element.** Open the Outline Entry properties box and ensure that the content options are set appropriately.

➤ **The entries do not appear in the correct position in the outline.** Check the Indent and Outdent properties of the entries.

Creating, Modifying and Troubleshooting In-View Editing

As a developer, you enable users to create documents directly from a view or folder and/or to edit existing documents through a view. To support this capability, a new event, InViewEdit, has been added to views and folders so that you can write code that specifies when a user tries to add a new document or edits an existing document from a view or folder.

In-view editing is not supported for Web users.

You should be prepared to see one or more questions about the new InViewEdit feature on the exam.

Although the InViewEdit event works in folders, new documents created from a folder are not added to the folder; instead, they must be dragged, moved, or added to the folder.

Creating Documents in a View

To allow users to create a new document from a view, simply follow these steps:

1. Open the view from which users should be able to create new documents.

2. Right-click and choose View Properties from the menu, which opens the View properties box.

3. Click the Info tab (the second tab) and enable the Create New Documents at View Level option.

4. Choose the InViewEdit event in the Objects panel of the Programmer's Pane.

5. Write the LotusScript code necessary to create a new document.

6. Save the view.

The InViewEdit events will fire for embedded views if the selection Tracks Mouse Movement is disabled on the Display tab of the Embedded View Properties box.

Modifying Documents in a View

To allow users to edit existing documents directly in a view without opening the document in a form, you must specify which columns in a view or folder contain fields that the users can edit.

The following steps outline the process required to allow users to edit documents directly in a view.

1. Open the view that will allow direct editing.

2. Select the column that will display the editable field.

3. Right-click and choose Column Properties from the menu. This opens the Column properties box.

4. Check the Editable Column option on the Info tab (the first tab) of the Column properties box.

5. Select the InViewEdit event in the View objects list in the Programmer's Pane.

6. Code the InViewEdit event with LotusScript to specify what should happened when fields are edited.

7. Save the view.

Troubleshooting in View Editing

The following is a list of common In-View editing problems and their resolution:

➤ Users are unable to edit documents in a view—Ensure that create new documents at view level option is enabled.

➤ Users are unable to edit documents in a Web based view—This feature is not supported on the Web.

➤ Users are able to edit documents in the view, but the changes are not saved—The InViewEdit event of the view must be scripted.

➤ Users are unable to edit documents in an embedded view—The Selection tracks mouse movement feature of an embedded view must be disabled.

Creating, Modifying, and Troubleshooting Subforms

A subform is much like a form; it can contain the same elements as regular forms and can be included in a form so that you can make your applications more modular. A subform can be permanently included in a form or can be included conditionally, depending on the result of a formula.

NOTE

Field names used in the subform can't be used elsewhere on the form or on another subform that will be used in the same form.

Creating a Subform

To create a new subform, follow these steps:

1. Open the database that will contain the subform in the Designer client.

2. Choose Shared Code, Subforms to see the list of existing subforms.

3. Click the New Subform button to open the subform design screen.

4. Choose Design, Subform Properties to open the Subform properties box, shown in Figure 9.9.

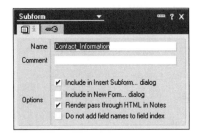

Figure 9.9 The Subform properties box.

5. On the Info tab (the first tab), enter a name for the new subform.

6. (Optional) Enter a comment to explain the subform's usage.

7. (Optional) Configure the other important subform settings, such as the following:

   ➤ **Include in Insert Subform Dialog**—Allows designers see the subform name when selecting subforms to insert in a form.

➤ **Include in New Form Dialog**—Enable this setting to make subforms appear as a choice when designers choose Create, Design Form.

➤ **Render Pass Through HTML in Notes**—Enables developers to put HTML directly into the subform.

➤ **Do Not Add Field Names to Field Index**—When enabled, this setting saves memory because field names on the subform are not saved in the field index. Checking this setting saves memory. If you do not check this setting, field names are saved to a table and then stored in memory.

Storing field names in the index enables field names to appear in places such as the Add Action dialog box.

8. Save the subform.

Inserting a Subform into a Form

To insert a subform into a form, follow these steps:

1. Open the database that contains the subform you want to insert.

2. Open a form.

3. Position the cursor on the form where you want the subform to appear.

4. Choose Create, Resource, Insert Subform. This opens the Insert Subform dialog box.

5. Select the subform to insert and click OK.

6. Save the form.

Inserting a Computed Subform into a Form

To insert a computed subform into a form, follow these steps:

1. Open the database that contains the subform you want to insert.

2. Open a form.

3. Position the cursor on the form where you want the subform to appear.

4. Choose Create, Resource, Insert Subform.

5. Choose Insert Subform Based on Formula.

6. Click OK.

7. Write a formula in the Programmer's Pane that will return the name of the subform to display.

8. Save the form.

Modifying a Subform

To modify a subform, follow these steps:

1. Open the database that contains the subform in the Designer client.

2. Choose Shared Code, Subforms to see the list of existing subforms.

3. Double-click the subform to edit.

4. Modify the subform as appropriate.

5. Save the subform.

Troubleshooting Subforms

The following is a list of common subform problems and their resolution:

➤ **Computed subform does not display.** Check and verify the formula of the computed subform.

➤ **The Computed subform displays at the wrong time.** Check and verify the formula of the computed subform.

Creating, Modifying, and Troubleshooting Layers

Layers are a new tool introduced in Domino 6 that enable you to position blocks of content over each other on a form, subform, or page. There are two basic types of layers: transparent and opaque. As you might guess from the names, *transparent* layers allow content behind them to show through, whereas *opaque* layers do not.

Creating a Layer

To create a layer, follow these steps:

1. Open the form, subform, or page in which you'd like to add a layer.

2. Position the cursor where the layer should appear.

3. Choose Create, Layer.

4. Right-click the layer to open the Layer properties box, shown in Figure 9.10, and modify the layer's attributes as necessary.

5. Add content to the layer as appropriate.

 Layers in a form can contain the same elements as the form. For example, you can add text and graphics as well as access-controlled sections, fields, and subforms. Layers in a page can contain the same elements as the page. For example, you can add text and graphics but not fields.

6. Save and test the form, subform, or page that contains the layer.

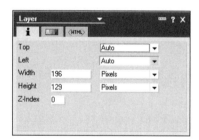

Figure 9.10   The Layer properties box.

 Layers are one of the coolest new design tools in Domino; expect to see at least one question about layers on the exam.

Modifying a Layer

To modify a layer, follow these steps:

1. Open the form, subform, or page that contains the layer to modify.

2. Right-click the layer to open the Layer properties box and then modify the layer's attributes as necessary.

3. Add or modify content in the layer as appropriate.

4. Save and test the form, subform, or page that contains the layer.

Troubleshooting Layers

The following is a list of common layer problems and their resolution:

➤ **The layer appears/disappears when it should not.** Check and verify the hide-when formula of the layer.

➤ **The layer does not appear in the correct level of the layer hierarchy.** Check the Z-index of the layer. The Z-index dictates the position of the layer relative to its parent. A Z-index of 0 is the top layer. You can alter the Z-index to control the stacking order of the layers.

Column Colors

View columns are objects that enable you to display data in a view. A new feature of Domino 6 is the ability to add colors to a column for Notes client applications. You can configure a column's background color and text color programmatically. To do so, follow these steps:

Column colors are not supported in Web applications.

1. Open a view in the Designer client.

2. Right-click the column whose color you want to configure and choose Properties from the menu. This opens the Column properties box, shown in Figure 9.11.

3. On the Info tab (the first tab), enable the Use Value as Color option.

4. Supply RGB values for the column. Specifying one value configures the column's background color, whereas specifying two values configures both the background color and the text color. The RGB values must be supplied as a colon-separated list, where each color value is a number between 0 and 255. The following example would make the background black and the text red:

255:0:0:1:1:1

Figure 9.11   The Info tab of the Column properties box.

5. Save the view that contains the column.

Specifying -1:-1:-1 will make the column revert to the column properties.

Hiding Columns

Although Domino has long supported hidden columns in a view, Domino 6 now enables developers to programmatically hide and show columns in a view. To programmatically hide a column, follow these steps:

1. Open a view in the Designer client.

2. Right-click the column you want to hide. This opens the Column properties box. Click the Advanced tab (the seventh tab), shown in Figure 9.12.

Figure 9.12   The Advanced tab of the column properties box.

3. Enable the appropriate hide-when settings:

➤ Enable Hide Column to hide the column permanently.

➤ Enable Hide Column If Formula Is True if you want to supply a formula that will make the column hidden when formula returns TRUE and will display the column when the formula returns FALSE.

➤ Enable Hide in Notes R5 or Before if you want to hide the column from Notes users using any Notes client version prior to 6.

4. Save the view that contains the column.

 Be prepared to see one or more questions on the exam about the new capabilities of columns.

Embedded Elements

Embedded elements are Domino design elements and controls that can be embedded on a page, form, subform, or document. Embedded elements often enable a developer to provide greater usability, and they also make it easier to develop a single application that has similar functionality for both Notes clients and Web browsers. Because Notes elements must be converted to HTML, many Notes elements lose some of their functionality when accessed through a Web browser. Embedded elements allow a developer to maintain much of the native Notes client functionality when developing Web applications, thus providing a rich and more user-friendly application.

The Domino elements that can be embedded include the following:

➤ Date picker

➤ Editor

➤ Folder pane

➤ Outline

➤ Scheduler

➤ Single-category views

➤ Views

Each of these elements is discussed in the following sections.

Date Picker

The embedded date picker works with open calendar views to enable a user to pick a day that is then opened in a calendar view with all the calendar entries for that day. In order to work properly, the embedded date picker must be in the same frameset as an open calendar view.

 Embedded date pickers are not supported for Web applications.

To embed a date picker, follow these steps:

1. Open the form, page, or subform that will contain the date picker. If you want to embed the date picker in a document, open the document.

2. Position the cursor where you want the date picker to appear on a page, form, subform, or in the Rich Text field of a document.

3. Choose Create, Embedded Element, Date Picker from the menu.

4. Right-click the date picker object and choose Date Picker Properties to configure the date picker's properties.

5. Save the form, page, subform, or document.

 Domino 6 enables you to specify which open calendar view should work with the date picker. By default, all open calendar views will respond to dates picked in the date picker.

Editor

Embedded editors allow you to build more user-friendly applications because you can embed one or more forms into a form, allowing a user to edit multiple documents at one time. Additionally, you can use *targeting*, in which you link an embedded editor to an embedded view, enabling users to edit documents in the view without needing to open a new window.

Although you can do nearly anything in an embedded editor that you can do in a form, the following objects should not be used in an embedded editor:

➤ Navigators

➤ Computed text

➤ Action hot spots

➤ Formula pop-up hot spots

➤ Buttons

To create an embedded editor, simply follow these steps:

1. Open a form in the Designer client.

2. Position the cursor where you want the embedded editor to appear.

3. Choose Create, Embedded Element, Editor from the menu. This opens the Insert Embedded Form dialog box.

4. Choose one of the options to determine how the editor will work:

➤ Select None to use targeting.

➤ Select an existing form from the list of forms.

➤ Enable the Insert Form Based on Formula option and write a formula that computes to the name of a form.

5. Right-click the embedded editor and choose Properties to launch the Embedded Editor properties box.

6. Enable the appropriate properties.

7. Save the form.

Outline

To use an outline in your application, you must embed it in either a form, page, or a Rich Text field in a document. To embed an outline on a form, page, or document, follow these steps:

1. Open a form, page, or document that will contain the outline.

2. Place the cursor where you want the outline to appear. If you are placing the outline in a document, you must be in a Rich Text field.

3. Choose Create, Embedded Element, Outline from the menu, which will display the Insert Embedded Outline dialog box.

4. Select the outline you wish to embed.

5. (Optional) If you want to programmatically choose which outline to display, enable the Choose an Outline Based on a Formula option and then write a formula in the Programmer's Pane that returns the name of the outline to display.

6. Right-click the outline and choose Outline Properties to configure the outline properties.

7. Save the form, page, or document that contains the outline.

Scheduler

The embedded scheduler is a very handy tool that enables you to build a form or subform that can display users' schedules, allowing users to view each other's schedules and open other users' calendar views.

There are four steps to using an embedded scheduler:

1. Embed a scheduler on a form or subform.

2. Create the fields that the scheduler needs to interact with the user.

3. Write the code needed to interface the scheduler with the fields.

4. Configure the scheduler's properties.

Each of these four steps is explained in the following sections.

Creating an Embedded Scheduler

To create an embedded scheduler on a form or subform, follow these steps:

1. Open the form or subform that will contain the embedded scheduler.

2. Position the cursor where you want the embedded scheduler to appear.

3. Choose Create, Embedded Element, Scheduler.

Multiple embedded schedulers can be embedded on a form or subform.

4. Create the fields the scheduler needs to display a schedule. The scheduler needs three pieces of information before it can display a schedule:

➤ The group or individual schedule to display

➤ The start week of the schedule

➤ The number of hours per day to display

5. Associate your fields with the embedded scheduler by selecting an object in the Objects tab of the Programmer's Pane and then enter a field name (in quotation marks) in the Script area of the Programmer's Pane. The following is a list of fields for use with the scheduler:

➤ **Required People Items**—Either provide a formula or specify the name of a field that contains the people or groups required for scheduling.

➤ **Grid Start Time**—Either provide a formula or specify the name of a field that contains the start date for the scheduler. The default time is the current date and time.

➤ **Display Hours Per Day**—Either provide a formula or specify the name of a field that contains the number of hours to display on the scheduler grid.

6. Configure the embedded scheduler's properties by right-clicking the scheduler and choosing Scheduler, Properties. Some of the more important properties are listed here:

➤ **Name**—Used to specify a name for the scheduler.

➤ **Target Frame**—Used to specify a frame where calendar views and appointment documents will display.

➤ **Initialize from Item Values**—Enable this option to make the scheduler build the initial participants list from the user-defined fields in the form.

➤ **Refresh from Item Values**—Enable this option to make the scheduler refresh data from the values of the items previously specified when a DocRecalc event fires.

➤ **Allow Sorting**—Enable this option to allow users to sort the list of attendee names.

7. Save the form that contains the embedded scheduler.

Views and Folders

Embedding a view or a folder pane in a page or form allows you much greater control over how a view looks and works on the Web. What's more, you can you combine other design elements with the view to provide additional functionality on the Web. To embed a view or a folder pane, follow these steps:

1. Open a form, subform, or page in the Designer. Alternatively, you can open a document in Edit mode to embed the view directly into a document.

2. Position the cursor to the spot where you want the view or folder pane to display.

3. Choose one of the following from the menu:

   ➤ Create, Embedded Element, Folder Pane to embed a folder.

   ➤ Create, Embedded Element, View to embed a view. Certain view-only options are described in the following list:

      ➤ Configure display options for the embedded view, which includes displaying the view as HTML, as a Java applet, or using the display properties set for the view in the view itself.

      ➤ (Optional) Enable the Choose a View Based on a Formula option to write a formula that will choose the view to open.

      ➤ (Optional) Choose a target frame on the Info tab (the first tab) of the Embedded View Properties box to specify where the document is displayed when it is opened.

4. Save the form, subform, or page that contains the embedded element.

Single-Category Views

An embedded view can be restricted to a single category in that view so that only documents that are in the chosen category will be displayed.

To make an embedded view show a single category, you must categorize the embedded view.

Follow these steps to create a single-category embedded view:

1. Open a form in the Designer client.

2. Position the cursor at the place in the form where the view should appear.

3. Choose Create, Embedded Element, View from the menu, which opens the Insert Embedded View dialog box.

4. Select the view you want and click OK.

5. In the Programmer's Pane, choose the Show Single Category event.

6. Write a formula that will return the category that should be displayed.

7. Save the form.

Customizing Twisties

The triangular images used to denote a row in a view or a section in a document that is expandable are known as *twisties*. The default triangle icons can be replaced with your own customized images.

Sections

Domino 6 allows you some control over how twisties display for collapsible sections. To customize the twisties for a collapsible section, follow these steps:

1. Using a graphics-editing program such as Photoshop or Paint Shop Pro, create a graphic with two images in it. The first image (on the left) will appear beside collapsed rows, whereas the second image (on the right) will appear beside expanded rows.

2. In the Designer client, create an image resource from the new graphic file you created.

3. Double-click the new image resource to launch the Image Resource properties box.

4. Enter 2 in the Images Across field.

5. Enable the Web Browser Compatible option if the new twistie will be displayed on the Web.

6. Open the view that will use the new twistie.

7. Double-click the column in the view that will display the twistie. This opens the Column properties box.

8. On the Column Info tab (the first tab), enable the Show Twistie When Row Is Expandable setting.

9. On the same tab, enter the name of the new image resource you created.

Views

For years, Domino developers have been forced to use the default twistie icon which was a simple (and boring) triangle. Domino 6 makes it possible to add your own customized twistie icons, and doing so is simple. Just follow these steps:

1. Repeat setps 1-5 of the previous section on customizing twisties for a collapsible section.

2. Open the view that will use the new twistie.

3. Double-click the column in the view that will display the twistie. This opens the Column properties box.

4. On the Column Info tab (the first tab), enable the Show Twistie When Row Is Expandable setting.

5. On the same tab, enter the name of the new image resource you created.

 Although customized twistie icons must not be wider than six pixels, the font size of the column text dictates the height of the twistie image.

Outlines

Domino 6 now supports customizable twistie icons for expandable items. To add customizable twistie icons to an outline, follow these steps:

1. Repeat steps 1-5 of the previous section on customizing view icon twisties.

2. Open the outline that will use the new twistie.

3. Double-click the outline entry in the outline that will display the twistie. This opens the outline entry properties box.

4. In the image section, choose an image resource.

Using Images in Applications

Notes/Domino has long supported the use of images in applications through copying and pasting images into a form and importing images into a form. In Domino R5, image resources were added to further extend the use of images in Domino applications, which greatly improves your ability to manipulate and manage images.

An image resource is a graphic that can be displayed throughout an application, from a central location within the database. This saves space and minimizes maintenance because any changes you make to the image are automatically reflected in each place that references the image resource. An image resource can be a GIF, JPEG, or BMP file and is saved in the database. After you have created an image resource, it can be used to add graphics or icons to pages, forms, action buttons, and outline entries, or it can be used to add background images on forms, documents, pages, table cells, and action buttons.

 Image resources are converted to the GIF or JPEG format.

To create an image resource, follow these steps:

1. Open the database in which you would like to add an image resource.

2. Expand Resources in the Design Pane and then choose Images to see a list of all the image resources in the database.

3. Click the New Image Resource button. This opens the New Image dialog box.

4. Choose a file (or files) to import and ensure that it is either a GIF, BMP, or JPEG file.

5. Click Open to add the file(s) as an image resource. Designer creates an image resource for each file.

After you have added some image resources, you can follow these steps to use one in your application:

1. Open a page, form, outline entry, or other design element in which you'd like to add an image.

2. Position the cursor to the place where you want the image to appear.

3. Choose Create, Image Resource from the menu.

4. Select the image type (GIF, JPEG, or All Images) from the Image Type list to display the list of available image resources.

5. Choose the image resource to insert the file.

6. Click OK to add the image.

Using External Files in Applications

Domino 6 allows you to share non-NSF files within your applications through a new design feature known as a *file resource*. To create a file resource, follow these steps:

1. Open the database that will contain the file resource in the Designer client.

2. Click Shared Resources, File to open the file's work pane.

3. Click the New File Resource button. This opens the File Open box.

4. Select the file to share as a file resource and click Open.

5. Right-click the new file resource and choose Resource Properties. This opens the File Resource properties box.

6. On the Basic tab (the first tab), name the file resource.

Using Calendar Views in Applications

Calendar views display documents in a calendar format with numerous display options, including the following:

➤ One day

➤ Two day

➤ Work-Week

➤ Week

➤ Two-Week

➤ Month

 Web users cannot create new appointments or scroll through entries within a single day.

To create a calendar view, follow these steps:

1. In the Designer, open the database in which you want to create the view.

2. Click Views in the Design Pane to see a list of all the existing views in the database.

3. Choose Create, Design, View from the menu or click the New View button. This opens the Create View dialog box (think of this box as a wizard).

4. Enter a name for the view in the View Name field.

5. Choose the view type in the View Type field. Each option is summarized in Table 9.5.

Table 9.5 View Types	
Type	**Description**
Shared	Shared views can be used by any user with at least
	Reader access to the database, unless he or she is specifically excluded through a view access list.
Shared, contains documents not in any folders	Offers the same properties as a shared view, but lists only documents. Documents not in folders that are not also listed in a folder or folders.
Shared, contains deleted documents	Offers the same properties as a shared view, but lists only deleted documents. This setting should be used in conjunction with Allow Soft Deletions.
Shared, private on first use	Offers the same properties as a shared view, but becomes private the first time a user opens it.
Shared, desktop private	Offers the same properties as a shared, private on first-use view, but on first use is stored in the user's Desktop.dsk file rather than in the database, which conserves space on the server.
	Private views are accessible to only those users who create them and, depending on that user's ability to create views, may be stored either in the database (if the user can create private views) or in the user's Desktop.dsk file.

6. In the Select a Location for the New View field, select the position in the view hierarchy in which you want the new view to appear. If you want the view to appear at the top level, don't select anything here. Otherwise, select the view under which you want the new view to appear.

7. Enter a view-selection formula. If you have copied the view's design from an existing view, the selection formula is copied as well and can be edited to meet your needs. If you started from scratch, you need to

enter a selection formula here. You can use the Fields and Functions button and the Formula Window button to further aid your development of the selection formula.

8. Click OK to generate the new view.

9. Double-click the new view in the Views list to open it.

10. Choose Design, View Properties to open the View properties box. In the Info tab, set the Style field to Calendar.

11. In the Programmer's Pane, write a formula that will evaluate to a date and time value.

12. Double-click the first column in the view to open the Column properties box. The first column in a calendar view specifies the date and time for the calendar and should be hidden. Enable the Hide Column option on the seventh tab.

13. On the Sorting tab (the second tab), enable the Sort Ascending option.

14. Add other columns as necessary.

15. Save the view.

Signing Database Design Elements

Signing is the act of associating an electronic signature with an element. Each database design element, such as a form, view, or agent, is stamped with the electronic signature of the developer who last saved it. Often times, it is necessary to re-sign design elements with a different signature.

The most simple approach to signing a database design element is to open the design element in the Designer client using the Notes ID whose signature you want to stamp on the file. Then simply save the design element; the signature of the current ID will be stamped into the design element.

Creating Shared Applet Resources

Java applets are client-side Java programs designed to run in either a Web browser or a Notes client application.

Applets can be used in any of the following Domino elements:

➤ **Form**—The applet is embedded in a form.

➤ **Page**—The applet is embedded in a page.

➤ **Document**—The applet is embedded in a Rich Text field in a document.

Applets are composed of one or more files, with one file that contains the main class, or the starting point for the applet. You can use Domino's shared applet feature to store all the files required for the applet in the database.

To create a shared applet resource, follow these steps:

1. In the Designer, open the database in which you want to create a shared applet resource.

2. Click Shared Resources, Applets in the Design Pane to see a list of all the existing applets in the database.

3. Click the New Applet Resource button. This opens the Locate Java Applet Files dialog box.

4. Select the files the applet is composed of and click OK.

Domino 6.x supports Java Virtual Machine (JVM) version 1.3.

Creating Shared Data Connection Resources (DCRs)

A Data Connection Resource (DCR) is a design element new to Domino 6 that makes it very easy to integrate Domino applications with external data sources such as Microsoft SQL server and IBM DB2.

A data source must be configured on the server before you can create a DCR. For more information on configuring a data source on the server, see the Lotus Domino Administrator Help database (**help6_admin.nsf**).

To create a DCR, follow these steps:

1. Open the database that will contain the DCR.

2. In the Design Pane, select Shared Resources, Data Connections to display the list of existing DCRs.

3. Click the New Data Connection button to open the Data Connection properties box, shown in Figure 9.13.

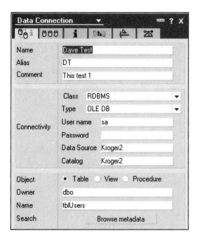

Figure 9.13   The Data Connection properties box.

4. Supply a name for the DCR.

5. Choose the class of the connection. The default is RMDBS.

6. Choose the connection type. Many databases have native drivers. When possible, use the native driver; otherwise, select a generic driver such as ODBC or OLE DB.

7. (Optional) Supply a username and password to access the database.

8. If required by the backend system, supply a database name.

9. Choose the type of database object you want to access: table, view, or procedure.

10. Supply the name of the table, view, or procedure that you wish to access. Click the Browse Metadata button to view a list of objects in the specified external database.

11. (Optional) Configure other DCR settings.

Like other design resources, you can define a DCR and then use it in many places within an application, or use it in another application.

Creating, Modifying, and Troubleshooting Profile Documents

A profile document is a special type of document that is similar in most ways to a standard document, but there are a few key differences. First, a profile document does not display in views, nor is it included in a document count of a database. Additionally, a profile document is cached in memory while the database that contains it is open, meaning that the document can be accessed very quickly, making it handy for temporary storage.

Each Domino database can have one or more profile documents that match a key used to retrieve them. The number of profile documents used in an application is completely dependent on your design requirements.

As a developer, you enable users to create and access profile documents by scripting buttons or agents with LotusScript or formulas that read and write values from the profile documents.

Users must have at least Author access in the ACL to create a profile document that is available to all users.

Creating a Profile Document

Creating a profile document is fairly simple. Just follow these steps:

Only one profile document per form can exist for each user of a database. Alternatively, only one profile document can exist for a database if that form is available to all users.

1. Open the database that will contain the profile document.

2. In the Design Pane, click Forms to see the list of existing forms.

3. Click New Form to create a new form.

4. Add fields to the form that will hold the values you wish to store.

5. From the menu, choose Design, Form Properties. This opens the Form properties box. Alternatively, right-click the form and choose Form Properties. On the Form Info tab (the first tab), deselect Include in Menu.

6. Save the form.

7. Create a button, action, or agent that uses `@Command([EditProfileDocument])` to create or access the document.

In Notes client applications, you can create or edit profile documents by using either the `@SetProfileField` function or the `@Command([EditProfileDocument])` command. For Web applications, you must use `@SetProfileField` to create profile documents because `@Command([EditProfileDocument])` does not work on the Web.

Modifying a Profile Document

Once you have created a profile document, you can use the `@GetProfileField` and `@SetProfileField` functions to access the contents of the profile document. Each function is explained in the following sections.

You cannot delete a profile document using an @Command or @Function. Use LotusScript if you must delete a profile document.

Using **@GetProfileField** to Read Values from a Profile Document

To read values stored in a profile document, you can use the `@GetProfileField` function, which will return the contents of a specified field. Its syntax is as follows:

```
@GetProfileField( profilename ; fieldname; uniqueKey )
```

The first parameter, `profilename`, is a required text value that specifies the name of the profile document you wish to read.

The second parameter, `fieldname`, is a required text value that specifies the name of the field in the document you wish to read.

The third parameter, `uniqueKey`, is an optional text value that specifies a unique key that identifies the profile document.

Although you cannot use the **@GetProfileField** function in column, hide-when, section editor, and view selection formulas, you can use it in toolbar buttons, agents, and Web-based applications.

Using **@SetProfileField** to Write Values to a Profile Document

To write values to a profile document, or to create a new profile document, use the @SetProfileField function. Its syntax is as follows:

```
@SetProfileField( profilename ; fieldname; value; uniqueKey )
```

The first parameter, profilename, is a required text value that specifies the name of the profile document you wish to update.

The second parameter, fieldname, is a required text value that specifies the name of the field in the document you wish to update.

The third parameter, value, is a required text value that will be written to the field.

The fourth parameter, uniqueKey, is an optional text value that specifies a unique key that identifies the profile document.

 Remember that if the profile document specified in the first parameter does not exist, the **@SetProfileField** function will create it.

Troubleshooting Profile Documents

The following list contains some of the most common problems encountered when using profile documents and their resolution:

➤ **A user creates a profile document, but it is not accessible to other users.** Ensure that the user creating the profile document has at least Author access in the ACL.

➤ **Users cannot access a profile document.** Ensure the proper profile name or proper key is specified.

➤ **The** @GetProfileField **function does not return the expected values.** Ensure the correct field name is specified.

Agents

Domino agents are self-contained programs that perform tasks on one or more databases. Here are some examples of the power and flexibility that agents provide:

➤ Agents can run in any Domino environment—on a specific server, on several servers, on workstations, or when launched by Web clients accessing a Domino server.

➤ Agents can be programmed using simple actions, formulas, LotusScript, or Java. This enables you to select the best language for a particular task.

➤ Agents are not tied to a specified design element, so you can write modular, reusable code.

➤ A user can explicitly call agents from the menu, an action, a hot spot, or a URL.

➤ Agents can be scheduled to run automatically or when a specific event occurs.

➤ Agents can run other agents.

➤ Agents are easily distributed and maintained through replication.

➤ The ability to run an agent depends on a user or server's access level.

➤ Agents can be run using the authority of the user running it, the last person or server to sign the agent, or on behalf of another user (new in Domino 6).

➤ Agents cannot make modifications to data that the user/server who signed the agent, or is running the agent (depending on how the agent has been configured), is not allowed to make.

➤ Agents can be configured to log their actions and errors to text files, agent logs, mail memos, or Notes databases, making it easy to ensure that they run properly.

Setting Agent Properties

To set the properties for an agent, follow these steps:

1. In the Designer, open the database that contains the agent.

2. Click Shared Code, Agents in the Design Pane to view the list of agents.

3. Double-click an agent to open the Agent properties box shown in Figure 9.14.

Figure 9.14 The Agent properties box.

4. Make the necessary changes.

5. Save the agent.

Scheduling Agents

Domino has long had the capability to schedule agents. To schedule an agent, follow these steps:

1. In the Designer, open the database that contains the agent you want to modify.

2. Click Shared Code, Agents in the Design Pane to view the list of agents.

3. Double-click an agent to open the Agent properties box.

4. Enable the On Schedule option in the Trigger section.

5. Choose Schedule from the list. The options are outlined in Table 9.6. Keep in mind that scheduled agents are not supported on the Web.

Table 9.6	On-schedule Trigger Options
Option	**Description**
More Than Once a Day	Use this setting to run the agent on a schedule several times a day. Remember that scheduling frequent runs affects your server's performance. Click the Schedule button to specify the schedule.
Daily	Use this setting to run the agent on a schedule once per day. Click the Schedule button to specify the daily schedule.
Weekly	Use this setting to run the agent on a weekly basis. Click the Schedule button to specify the weekly schedule.

Table 9.6 On-schedule Trigger Options *(continued)*	
Option	Description
Monthly	Use this setting to run the agent on a monthly schedule. Click the Schedule button to specify the monthly schedule.
Never	Use this setting if you want to save an agent but do not want it to run except under special circumstances, such as being called by another agent.

6. For scheduled agents, set the scheduling parameters by clicking the Schedule button. You must also select where the agent should run from the Run On list. Remember that selecting a server or server(s) is especially important when agents modify documents in databases that are replicated among multiple servers.

7. Choose a value for Target. The options in this list will vary depending on the trigger type. Target options are defined in Table 9.7.

Table 9.7 Target Options When Trigger Is On Schedule	
Option	Description
All documents in database	The agent builds a collection of and runs against all documents in the database.
All new and modified documents	The agent builds a collection of and runs against all documents that have been created and saved since the agent was last run.

8. Save the agent.

Hiding Agents

Sometimes the need arises to hide agents so that users cannot run them directly. To hide an agent, follow these steps:

1. In the Designer, open the database that contains the agent you want to hide.

2. Click Shared Code, Agents in the Design Pane to view the list of agents.

3. Right-click an agent and choose Design Properties to open the Design properties box.

4. Click the third tab to view the agent Hide options.

5. (Optional) Enable the Do Not Show This Design Element in Menus of Notes R4 or Later Clients option to remove the agent from recent Notes client menus.

6. (Optional) Enable the Hide Design Element from Web Browser option to hide the agent from Web clients.

7. (Optional) Enable the Hide Design Element from Notes 4.6 or Later Clients option to hide the agent from Notes clients.

Agent Activation

Domino 6 now enables developers to specify that agents can be enabled by any user with Editor access or higher in the ACL. To configure user based agent activation, follow these steps:

1. In the Designer, open the database that contains the agent.

2. Click Shared Code, Agents in the Design Pane to view the list of agents.

3. Open the agent.

4. Right-click and choose Agent Properties to open the Design properties box.

5. Click the second tab to view the agent security options.

6. (Optional) Enable the Allow User Activiation check box.

This handy new feature allows scheduled agents on a Domino server to be enabled or disabled, causing the agent to be re-signed.

Restricting Agent Operations

Domino 6 now allows developers who have unrestricted agent rights (defined in the Security tab of the Server document in the Public Directory) to specify restrictions for each agent on a case-by-case basis. The following list defines the agent restrictions that are available:

➤ **Do Not Allow Restricted Operations**—This is the default value and the most secure choice. It specifies that the agent is not allowed to perform restricted operations.

Unrestricted agents can perform low-level operations such as the following:

➤ File I/O

➤ Network I/O

➤ Calling external programs

➤ Changing the system date and time

➤ **Allow Restricted Operations**—Allows the agent to perform restricted operations.

➤ **Allow Restricted Operations with Full Administration Rights**—This is the least secure option because it allows the agent to perform restricted operations with full administration rights. Be very careful with this level of access.

 Agent restrictions have no effect on the agent for users who have restricted rights in the Public Directory.

To set agent restrictions, simply follow these steps:

1. In the Designer, open the database that contains the agent you want to modify.

2. Click Shared Code, Agents in the Design Pane to view the list of agents.

3. Double-click to open the Agent properties box.

4. Click the second tab to view the agent Security options.

5. In the Set Runtime Security field, choose one of the options explained previously.

6. Close the Agent properties box.

7. Save the agent.

 You will likely see questions about the powerful new agent features on the exam.

Setting the Effective User of an Agent

Domino allows developers to determine the authority under which an agent runs. By default, the agent will run with the authority of the developer who last saved the agent because the developer's digital signature is associated with the agent.

However, for Web-based applications, you can specify that the agent run with the authority of the Web user who invokes it. Additionally, new to Domino 6 is the capability to specify that an agent run on behalf of someone else.

To change the effective user for an agent, follow these steps:

1. In the Designer, open the database that contains the agent you want to modify.

2. Click Shared Code, Agents in the Design Pane to view the list of agents.

3. Double-click to open the Agent properties box.

4. Click the second tab to view the agent Security options.

5. (Optional) Enable the Run as Web User option to make the agent run with the authority of the Web user running it.

6. (Optional) Specify a user in the Run on Behalf Of field to make the agent run with the authority of the named user.

7. Close the Agent properties box.

8. Save the agent.

 Users specified in the Run on Behalf Of field must be named in the ACL of any databases accessed by the agent.

Exam Prep Questions

Question 1

> Profile documents provide what benefits for application development?
>
> ○ A. Profile documents are not directly viewable and editable.
>
> ○ B. Profile documents are cached.
>
> ○ C. Profile documents are automatically encrypted.
>
> ○ D. Both A and B.

Answer D is correct. Answer C is incorrect because profile documents are not automatically encrypted.

Question 2

> Which embedded element allows you to interact with a calendar view?
>
> ○ A. Date picker
>
> ○ B. Folder pane
>
> ○ C. Single-category view
>
> ○ D. Editor

Answer A is correct. Answer B is incorrect because a folder pane displays documents in a folder. Answer C is incorrect because a single-category view is used to show only documents for a particular category. Answer D is incorrect because an embedded editor is used to edit documents.

Question 3

> What are the two types of layers?
>
> ○ A. Transparent and opaque
>
> ○ B. Top and bottom
>
> ○ C. Translucent and opaque
>
> ○ D. Upper and lower

Answer A is correct. Layers can be either transparent or opaque.

Question 4

A Data Connection Resource (DCR) is used to do what?

○ A. Export data to XML.

○ B. Import data to XML.

○ C. There is no such thing as a DCR.

○ D. Connect to legacy database systems.

Answer D is correct. Answers A and B are incorrect because DCRs are used to connect to legacy systems. Answer C is incorrect because DCRs are new to Domino 6.

Question 5

By default, the effective user of an agent is _____.

○ A. the user running the agent

○ B. the username specified for the agent

○ C. the user who last signed the agent

Answer C is correct. Answer A is incorrect because the user running the agent is only the effective user when the Run as Web User option is enabled. Answer B is incorrect because usernames are not specified for an agent except when the new Run on Behalf Of feature is enabled.

Question 6

In Domino 6, agent restrictions are set where?

○ A. The Server document in the Domino Directory.

○ B. The Agent properties box.

○ C. The Design properties box.

○ D. A and B.

Answer D is correct. Answer C is incorrect because agent restrictions are controlled only in the Server document and in the Agent properties box.

Question 7

> The new files resources design element provides which capabilities?
>
> ○ A. Sharing non-NSF files in an application.
>
> ○ B. Replicating non-NSF files with other design elements.
>
> ○ C. Converting HTML to XML.
>
> ○ D. Converting text to HTML.
>
> ○ E. A and B.

Answer E is correct. Answers C and D are incorrect because file resources are not used to convert files from one type to another.

Question 8

> Which statement is true concerning the use of Data Connection Resources (DCRs)?
>
> ○ A. DCRs replace **@dblookup** and **@dbcolumn**.
>
> ○ B. You must make calls to the native database drivers.
>
> ○ C. A data source must be configured on the server before you can create a DCR.
>
> ○ D. DCRs don't replicate.

Answer C is correct. Answer A is incorrect because DCRs don't replace @Formulas. Answer B is incorrect because you don't need to make calls to native database drives. Answer D is incorrect because DCRs do replicate.

Question 9

> Which of the following options is not valid for the schedule of an agent?
>
> ○ A. Never
>
> ○ B. Daily
>
> ○ C. Yearly
>
> ○ D. Monthly

Answer C is correct. Never, Monthly, and Daily are all valid scheduling options, making answers A, B, and D incorrect.

Need to Know More?

 Lotus Domino Designer 6 Help (Help6_Designer.nsf).

 Lotus Domino Administrator 6 Help (Help6_Admin.nsf).

 IBM. *Domino Designer 6: A Developer's Handbook*. Redbook.

 www.notes.net.

 www.lotus.com/ldd.

Security

Terms you'll need to understand:

- ✓ Authentication
- ✓ Execution Control List (ECL)
- ✓ Encryption
- ✓ Role
- ✓ Form Read Access list
- ✓ Form Create list
- ✓ View Access list
- ✓ Consistent Access Control List (ACL)
- ✓ Effective access
- ✓ Extended ACL
- ✓ Administration server
- ✓ Sign fields
- ✓ Names fields
- ✓ Readers fields
- ✓ Authors fields
- ✓ Directory access

Techniques you'll need to master:

- ✓ Methods of Database encryption
- ✓ Use of Database roles
- ✓ Understanding Mail encryption
- ✓ Choosing a method of Document encryption
- ✓ Uses of Form access control
- ✓ Uses of Section access control
- ✓ Uses of View access control
- ✓ Techniques for Workstation security— Execution Control List (ECL)
- ✓ Understanding ACLs and replication

Lotus Notes/Domino has a long-standing reputation as a robust, secure platform for application development. From its inception, Notes was built upon a very flexible and comprehensive security model, which has undergone continuous enhancements during its long life. In our pervasively networked environment, building secure applications is becoming increasingly important.

This chapter covers various Domino security features that a Domino developer needs to know. Some of the topics covered in this chapter include Readers and Authors fields, Effective Access, Form Read and Create Access lists, and View Access lists, all of which you may be tested on in Exam 611.

Password Security

Passwords play a major role in the Domino security model and are used to authenticate both Notes and Web users. *Authentication* is the process of ensuring that a user or server is who it claims to be. Whether you are accessing Domino with a Notes client or a Web browser, you should always use well-crafted passwords to reduce the likelihood that someone can guess or hack your password. Use the following guidelines to help ensure that you are using a strong password:

➤ Do not use common words found in a dictionary.

➤ Use a mixture of numeric and text characters.

➤ Use mixed case characters.

➤ Intermingle punctuation characters.

➤ Use eight or more characters.

➤ Do not use easily discernable personal information.

Web Password Security

Web users who attempt to access a secured resource are required to authenticate themselves before the Domino server grants them access. For a Web user to be authenticated, he or she must supply a user name and password pair (basic authentication). The Domino server attempts to find a Person document in the Domino Directory that matches the user name supplied. If a matching Person document is not found, the user is not granted access. If a matching Person record is found, the password supplied by the user is compared to the password stored in the Internet Password field (the actual field name is HTTPPassword), which can be found on the Basics tab in the Person document.

Internet passwords are encrypted through the use of a one-way hashing algorithm. To do so, use the **@Password** function in the Input Translation event of the **HTTPPassword**.

If a match is made on the password, the user is authenticated and the Domino server then grants access based on the username supplied.

Notes Password Security

The Notes client model is somewhat different. When Notes users attempt to access a Domino server that does not allow anonymous Notes client access, the certificates stored in their Notes ID files are used to authenticate them.

Users must supply a password that matches the one stored in the Notes ID file to unlock it. Users who cannot supply the matching password are unable to use Notes.

Administration Server

ACL maintenance was greatly simplified when Lotus introduced the Administration process, better known as the Admin process or AdminP. One of the main tasks of the Admin process is to make sure that names in the ACL of a database, as well as names stored in the Names, Readers, and Authors fields, are updated when they are changed in the Domino directory.

 A key beside a server name in the ACL indicates that the server is the Administration Server.

The *Administration Server* setting is found on the Advanced tab of the ACL of each database. It is to specify which server's Admin process is used to update the ACL and to determine whether the Admin process should update Names fields in the database. Figure 10.1 shows the Administration Server options:

To set the Administration Server setting, follow these steps:

1. Open the ACL of the database whose Administration Server setting you want to modify.

2. Click the Advanced tab.

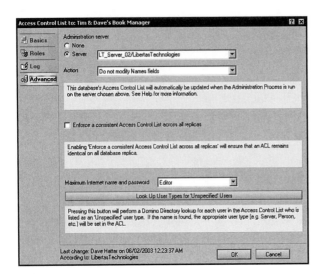

Figure 10.1 The Administration Server settings in the ACL.

3. Click the Server radio button under Administration Server and choose a server from the drop-down list.

4. Optionally, choose an Action from the following list: Do Not Modify Names Fields, Modify All Readers and Authors Fields, or Modify All Names Fields, which tells the Admin process what to do about changes to Names fields in the database.

5. Click OK to save the changes.

Consistent ACL

The *Consistent Access Control List* (ACL) feature of a database enables you to ensure that all replica copies of a database, whether on a server or workstation, maintain the same ACL.

Additionally, enforcing consistent ACLs on a database makes the Notes client enforce the ACL on local databases, meaning that users are restricted by the ACL. Users have Manager access to all local databases that do not enforce consistent ACLs.

One potential problem with enforcing the ACL locally is that Group information is stored in the Directory database on the server. To overcome the problem of not being able to confirm group membership locally, information about the group membership of the user replicating the database is stored in the database for ACL checks. If a different user attempts to access the local replica, no group information will be found for that user, so only that user's name can be used to grant/deny access.

> Be sure to enable the Enforce a Consistent Access Control List setting only on a replica whose parent server has Manager access to other replicas; otherwise, replication fails because the server has inadequate access to replicate the access control list.

Follow these steps to enforce consistent ACL:

1. Select the database to modify.

2. Choose File, Database, Access Control, or right-click and choose Database, Access Control.

3. Click the Advanced tab, as shown in Figure 10.2.

4. Click Enforce a Consistent Access Control List Across All Replicas.

5. Click OK.

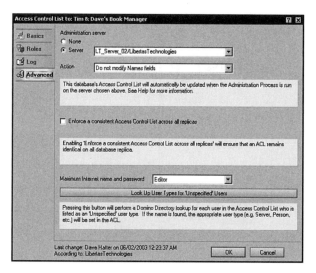

Figure 10.2 The database encryption dialog box.

> A common problem that occurs when using the Enforce Consistent Access Control List Across All Replicas option is that it can cause the database to stop replicating. This can happen if a uniform access list is not maintained and its causes include:
>
> ➤ If a user changes the ACL of a local replica copy that has Enforce Consistent ACL enabled.
>
> ➤ If Enforce Consistent ACL is enabled on a server replica that does not have Manager access.

Effective Access

In complex database applications that have many groups, it can often be difficult to determine what a user's actual access level is. In Domino 6, Lotus has made it much easier to determine what a user's actual access to a database is through the new *Effective Access* feature. A user's effective access is the actual access she has been granted to the database.

To determine a user's effective access to a database, follow these steps:

1. Select a database and choose File, Database, Access Control; alternatively, right-click and choose Database, Access Control.

2. Click the Effective Access button, which opens the dialog shown in Figure 10.3.

3. Select the name of the person or server to review and click the Calculate Access button, which reviews and reports on access for the selected user.

4. Click the Done button to close the dialog box.

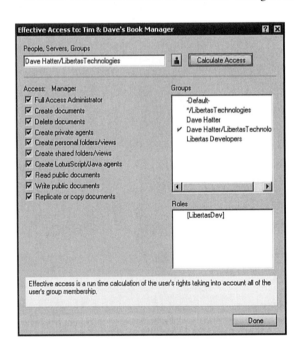

Figure 10.3   The effective access dialog box.

Directory Access

Domino provides the capability to restrict Notes client access to a Domino server's root folder or any subfolder beneath through the use of a Directory Access list.

 You must have the authority to use the Administrator client to create a Directory Access list.

You can create a Directory Access list by following these steps:

1. Open the Domino Administrator client.

2. Click the Files tab.

3. Choose the folder you want to secure. Note that any access restrictions applied to a folder apply to all subfolders as well.

4. From the Tools option on the right, select Folder, Manage ACL. Alternatively, right-click the folder and choose Manage Directory ACL, which opens the dialog shown in Figure 10.4.

5. Click the person icon to add names of users and groups who should be able to access the folder in the Who Should Be Able to Access This Directory? field.

6. Click OK to save your changes. The newly secured folder should now display a lock icon to show that it has been secured.

 By default, any Notes user who can access a Domino server can access the entire hierarchy of subfolders under the root Domino folder. You should make it a practice to restrict access to the Domino server's data directory.

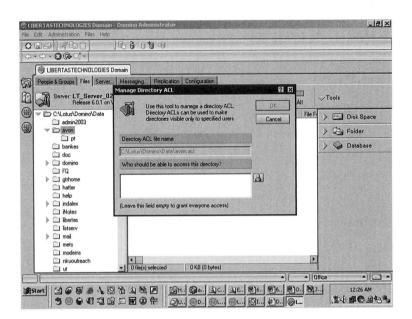

Figure 10.4 The Directory access control dialog box.

Extended ACL (xACL)

Domino 6 introduced the concept of extended access control lists (xACL). An *extended access control list* or *xACL* is an optional access control feature that can be used with a Domino Directory created from the PUBNAMES.NTF template.

Extended ACLs are part of a database and can be accessed through its Access Control list. You can use an xACL to refine the access the ACL grants a user, but you cannot use it to increase a user's access beyond that specified by the ACL. Some of the benefits of xACLs include the following:

➤ Provide access to specific parts of the Directory.

➤ Delegate administration. As an example, you can allow groups of administrators to maintain documents for a particular organizational unit.

➤ Restrict access of users who manage the Directory through any supported protocol, for example, Notes (NRPC), Web (HTTP), or LDAP.

➤ Set access to documents and fields globally rather than using multiple Readers and Authors fields.

You can implement an xACL when you need to control access to any of the following:

➤ A specific field within a specific document

➤ A specific document

➤ All documents of a specific type, such as all Person documents

➤ All documents with hierarchical names at a particular location in the directory name hierarchy, such as all documents whose names end in OU=West/O=Acme.

Extended ACLs are)configured through the Extended Access at Target dialog box, shown in Figure 10.5. The Extended Access at Target dialog box is accessed from the database Access Control List dialog box.

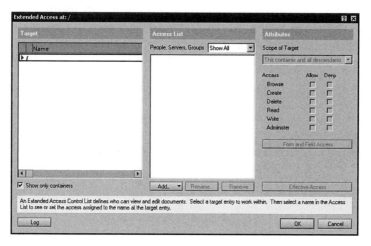

Figure 10.5   The Extended ACL dialog box.

Before you can configure an Extended Access Control list for a Directory, you must enable extended access for the database.

Enabling Extended Access to a Database

Before you enable extended access to a database, you should be aware of the following issues:

➤ If you enable extended access, you must make Directory modifications using a Domino 6 client.

➤ Extended access requires using the Enforce a Consistent Access Control List Across All Replicas option.

➤ After extended access has been enabled, Domino enforces the database ACL, extended ACL, and Readers and Authors fields for Notes clients attempting to look up names in the directory.

To enable extended)access for a Domino Directory or Extended Directory Catalog follow the steps listed here. You must have Manager access to do this.

1. Select a Directory database and open the ACL.

2. Click the Advanced tab.

3. Click the Enable Extended Access check box.

4. Answer Yes to the prompt.

5. If the Enforce a Consistent Access Control List Across All Replicas option is not enabled, click Yes when the next prompt appears to enable it. Enforce Consistent Access Control List Across All Replicas must be enabled to use xACLs.

6. Click OK in the Access Control List dialog box.

7. Click OK at the next prompt.

Configuring Extended Database Access

To configure an) extended ACL on a Directory database, follow these steps:

1. Select the Directory database that should support an extended ACL.

2. Open the database ACL.

3. On the Basics tab, click the Extended Access button, which opens the Extended Access dialog box, shown previously in Figure 10.5.

4. Expand target categories and select the target in the Target box at the left.

5. In the Access List section, choose one of the following settings for the People, Servers Groups drop-down. Choose Show Modified to display only subjects whose access is set at the target, or choose Show All to show subjects whose access is set at a higher target using the This Container and All Descendants scope setting.

6. To configure a subject for access to the selected target, click the Add button and then choose one of the following from the drop-down:

> ➤ Default to Add the Subject Default.

> ➤ Self to Add the Subject Self.

> ➤ Anonymous to Add the Subject Anonymous.

> ➤ Name, which opens a new dialog where you can type or select a name.

7. In the Attributes section, choose an entry in the Scope of Target field from the following:

> ➤ This Container and All Descendants. This is the default setting and applies the subject's access to the selected target and to all targets subcategorized below it.

> ➤ This Container Only. This setting applies the subject's access to the selected target only and not to) targets subcategorized below it.

8. Select the appropriate Allow and Deny settings in the Attributes section for the selected target.

9. Click OK to save your changes.

Database Encryption

Another important security feature of Domino is the capability to encrypt an entire database. As you may know, *encryption* is the process of using complex mathematical algorithms called keys to scramble data so that is it unintelligible to anyone who does not have the appropriate key. You can encrypt any local database to which you have Manager access by using the public key in your Notes ID.

There are three increasingly secure levels of encryption that you can apply to a local database:

➤ *Simple encryption*—Simple encryption, in the words of Lotus, "provides protection against casual snooping." It provides the fastest access to the database and enables the database to be compressed by disk compression utilities.

➤ *Medium encryption*—Medium encryption strikes a balance between performance and security. Lotus recommends this option for most users.

Databases using Medium encryption cannot be compressed by disk compression utilities.

➤ *Strong encryption*—Strong encryption should be used for the most sensitive information. Although this is the most secure level, it also exacts the most severe performance penalties. Databases encrypted with this option cannot be compressed by disk compression utilities.

 Although it may sometimes make sense to encrypt highly confidential databases when they are stored on a mobile or shared computer, there are several downsides to doing so. First, you suffer a performance penalty when using encrypted databases. Second, because the private key needed to decrypt the database is stored in your Notes ID, you are the only person who can open it. Do not lose your ID!

To encrypt a database, follow these steps:

1. Select the database you want to encrypt and choose File, Database, Properties.

2. On the Basics tab, click the Encryption Settings button, which opens the Encryption dialog shown in Figure 10.6.

3. Choose an encryption option in the Locally Encrypt This Database Using field.

4. Optionally, click the For button to change the user ID used to encrypt the database. By default the current user's ID is used. Note that if you change the user ID, only the specified user can access the database.

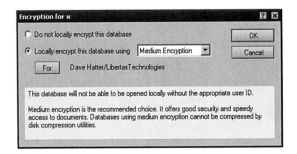

Figure 10.6 The database encryption setting dialog box.

To remove encryption, follow these steps:

1. Select the database and choose File, Database, Properties.

2. On the Basics tab, click the Encryption Settings button.

3. Click the Do Not Locally Encrypt this Database radio button.

Database encryption can be removed only by the ID that originally encrypted the database.

Database Roles

In the context of most applications, people naturally fall into groups of users that perform similar functions. Domino provides a security feature called *Roles*, which enables you to design the security of an application around required functions rather than around people.

Users, groups, and servers can be assigned roles, and after roles have been implemented, you can use them to control

➤ Access to specific views or folders

➤ Who can read documents

➤ Who can create documents

➤ Who can edit documents

➤ Who can access sections within a document

➤ Who can use actions or buttons that have been hidden with hide-when formulas

➤ Who can see text hidden with hide-when formulas

➤ Who can run an agent

Some of the many advantages of using roles include the following:

➤ Roles rarely, if ever, change, whereas users and groups often change.

➤ Roles reduce or eliminate the need to change the design of an application when users or groups change.

➤ Roles can be used in formulas such as hide-when and in Readers fields.

➤ Roles can be used to secure forms, views, documents, sections, fields, and agents.

➤ Roles are database-specific, which means there is no need have access to the Domino Directory to create them.

➤ Roles are easy to understand and implement.

➤ Roles can simplify and reduce administrative overhead.

Creating a Role in the Database ACL

Creating a Role is easy, but you must have Manager access to a database to add, update, or delete roles. Follow these steps to create a role:

1. Select the database in which you want to add a role. You must have Manager access to do this.

2. Select File, Database, Access Control from the menu. Alternatively, you can right-click the database icon and choose Database, Access Control.

3. Click Roles (at the left of the Access Control dialog box, marked by the happy and sad masks) to open the ACL Roles dialog box, shown in Figure 10.7.

4. Click the Add button, which opens the Add Roles dialog box.

5. Enter the name of the new role. Keep in mind that the maximum allowable number of characters is 15.

6. Click OK to add the role.

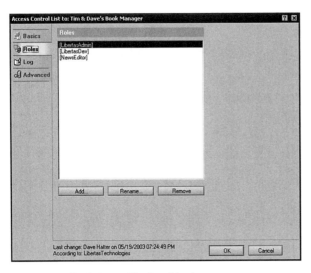

Figure 10.7   The Roles modification dialog box.

After a role has been created, you can assign it to users and groups in the ACL (if you have Manager access to the database). To do so, follow these steps:

1. Select the database in which you want to add a role.

2. Select File, Database, Access Control from the menu. Alternatively, you can right-click the database icon and choose Database, Access Control.

3. Select any entry in the ACL.

4. Select a role from the Roles dialog box. (A check appears beside each role that has been applied to an ACL entry.) The resulting settings appear in the Basics option of the ACL dialog box, as shown in Figure 10.8.

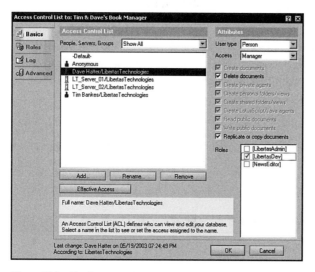

Figure 10.8   The Basics option of the database ACL dialog box with roles selected.

Be sure to remember that when a Role is created, Domino automatically encloses it in square brackets ([]). For example [Libertas Admins]. If you use a role, you must include the brackets.

After associating roles with entries in the ACL, you may begin using the roles in design elements and documents to dictate what users can do and see in each Domino database.

Using Roles to Determine User Access

Roles can be used in two basic ways to determine what a user can do. Roles can be

➤ Specified in a Form Access, View Access Folder Access, Section Access, or Agent Access list, or as the value of a Readers or Authors field.

➤ Used in a formula to determine whether a user can see a design element or use a feature such as an action.

To specify a role in a Form Access, View Access, Folder Access, Section Access, or Agent Access list, select the properties for that design element, choose the Security tab, and select the appropriate role from the list of choices.

To use roles in Readers and Authors fields, it is a simple matter of either hard-coding the appropriate role into the field formulas or using a formula to compute the proper role. (I would recommend the latter approach in most cases.)

If you want to use roles to selectively hide or show design elements within a form, you should familiarize yourself with three very important @functions that facilitate working with roles in formulas. These functions are @UserRoles, @UserNamesList, and @IsMember, each of which is defined in Table 10.1.

 Hide-when formulas do not provide true security because a user may be able to read the contents of a hidden field in other ways such as though the Document properties box, in a different form or view, or in the source code of a Web page. If absolute security is required, use one or more Readers fields in a document and/or encrypt the most sensitive fields.

Table 10.1	Functions for Working with Roles
Function	**Description**
@UserRoles	This function takes no parameters. For a database on a server, or a local database with the Enforce a Consistent Access Control List Across All Replicas option enabled, this function returns a text list of roles that have been assigned to the current user. Each role is enclosed in square brackets, as in **[LibertasDev]**. For a local database without the Enforce a Consistent Access Control List Across All Replicas option enabled, or if the user has no roles, an empty string ("") is returned. If a database is being opened by a Web client, the value **$$WebClient** is appended to the list of user roles.
@UserNamesList	This function takes no parameters. For a database on a server, or a local database with the Enforce a Consistent Access Control List Across All Replicas option enabled, this function returns a text list consisting of the current username, as well as group names and any roles for the current user. Each role is enclosed in square brackets, as in **[LibertasDev]**. For a local database without the Enforce a Consistent Access Control List Across All Replicas option enabled, or if the user has no roles, an empty string ("") is returned.

Table 10.1 Functions for Working with Roles *(continued)*	
Function	**Description**
@Ismember(string, list)	This versatile function can be used in many instances, but makes working with lists easy. It takes two parameters: a string to find within a list, and the list to search. It returns **TRUE (1)** if the string is found and **FALSE (0)** if not. You can use this function in conjunction with either **@UserRoles** or **@UserNamesList** to determine whether a user has been assigned a role.

The examples in Table 10.2 illustrate using these functions to determine a user's roles.

Table 10.2 Examples of Working with Roles in Formulas	
Example	**Result**
@IsMember("$$WebClient";@UserRoles);	-**TRUE (1)** if the client is a Web browser, otherwise **FALSE (0)**.
@IsMember("[LibertasAdmin]";@UserRoles);	-**TRUE (1)** if the user has been assigned the **[LibertasAdmin]** role, otherwise **FALSE (0)**.
@IsMember("[Readers]";@UserNamesList);	-**TRUE (1)** if the user has been assigned the **[Readers]** role, otherwise **FALSE (0)**.

To use roles in hide-when formulas to selectively show or hide a design element, use the following steps:

1. Select a design element, such as a field or action, and open its properties box.

2. Click the Hide-When tab. (It looks like a window shade.)

3. Click the Hide Paragraph If Formula Is True option.

4. Enter a formula that will ultimately evaluate to TRUE (1).

NOTE   Hide-when formulas do not provide true security because a user may be able to read the contents of a hidden field in other ways (such as through the Document properties box, in a different form or view, or in the source code of a Web page). If a field requires high security, use encryption.

Design Element Access

The Domino security model is one of the most robust and flexible available today, and its use of design element access control to restrict access to certain design elements is one reason why. This section explores the use of design element security to secure your Domino data.

Form Access

Forms are design elements that enable you to collect, manipulate, and display information stored in documents in a Domino application. It is often necessary to restrict the use of particular forms to certain people, groups, or roles. Domino accommodates this requirement through the use of Form Read Access and Form Compose Access lists.

Using Form Read Access Lists

Domino uses *Form Read Access lists* to provide control over how individuals can use forms to read the contents of documents. A Form Read Access list specifies users, groups, servers, and roles that can use a particular form to open a document.

 Remember that when you use this feature, it adds a **$Readers** field to each document.

To add a Form Read Access list to a form, follow these steps:

1. In the Designer client, open the database that contains the form.

2. Select and open the form you want to secure.

3. Choose Design, Form Properties to open the Form properties box.

4. Select the Security tab (the tab with the key on it).

5. Uncheck the All Readers and Above box in the Default Read Access for Documents Created with This Form area.

6. Select each user, group, and role that should be able to read documents composed with this form.

7. Save and close the form.

Be aware that this is not a true security feature because users may still be able to view the contents of a document by using a different form, or by viewing the document properties. Use Reader and Author fields to ensure the confidentiality of a document.

Using Form Create Access Lists

You can control who can create documents with a particular form in Domino through the use of Form Create lists. *Form Create lists* specify users, groups, servers, and roles that can use a particular form to create a new document.

Follow these steps to configure a Form Create List:

1. In the Designer client, open the database that contains the form whose use you want to limit to a specific list of users.

2. Select and open the form you want to secure.

3. Choose Design, Form Properties to open the Form properties box.

4. Select the Security tab (the tab with the key on it).

5. Uncheck the All Readers and Above box in the Who Can Create Documents with This Form area.

6. Select each user, group, server, and role that should be able to create documents composed with this form.

7. Save and close the form.

 Be aware that this is not a true security feature because users may be able to use another form in the database to create a document.

Section Access

In the Notes client, access to the contents of a section in a form can be restricted through the use of a Controlled Access section, which enables you to restrict who can edit or sign that part of a document.

After a Controlled Access section has been created, users who are not listed as Editors of that section can read, but cannot edit, the contents of the section. It is very important to note that having Editor access to a section is not the same as having Editor access to the database. A Controlled Access section further refines the ACL, and having Editor access in the ACL does not give you Editor access in a Controlled Access section. You can sign the section only if you are listed explicitly by name or implicitly through a group or role.

To add a Controlled Access section to a form, follow these steps:

1. In the Designer client, open the database containing the form to which you want to add a Controlled Access section.

2. Open the form and select the fields that should be added to the section.

3. Choose Create, Section, Controlled Access from the menu.

4. Optionally enter a title for the section.

5. Click the Formula tab of the Section properties box.

6. Choose Editable to allow the document's author to manually specify the section's editors. Choose Computed and enter a formula if you want to programmatically set the editors of the section.

7. Save the form.

If you elect to use the Controlled Access section, keep the following issues in mind:

➤ Each section in a form can have a signature attached. This is good for workflow-type applications.

➤ Controlled Access sections are not enforced locally.

➤ Users can read the fields even though they cannot edit them.

➤ Users may be able to edit the fields through a different form.

View Access

View Access lists enable you to restrict the use of views and folders to particular users, groups, servers and roles. To add a View Access list to a view, follow these steps:

1. In the Designer client, open the database that contains the view.

2. Select and open the view you want to secure.

3. Choose Design, View Properties to open the View properties box.

4. Select the Security tab (the tab with the key on it).

5. Uncheck the All Readers and Above box in the May Be Used By area.

6. Select each user, group, and role that should be enabled to use the view.

7. Save and close the view.

Be aware that this is not a true security feature because users may be able to use other views in the database to view documents.

Document Encryption

Encryption is the process of scrambling data so that only authorized users can unscramble the data. Domino supports both secret key encryption (in which one key shared among trusted users) and public key encryption (in which a public key is used to encrypt data and a private key can decode data). From early in its history, Notes has supported encryption through its capability to encrypt fields in documents, ensuring that data is secure from prying eyes.

Any field(s) in a Notes document can be encrypted, and after a field has been encrypted, only users who possess the proper key(s) can decrypt the field contents. Users without the proper key(s) see what appears to be a blank field in the document, and any attempts to use the Document Properties box to view the fields is stymied as well.

Please note that if multiple keys have been applied to encrypt a form or document, users need only one of the keys to read encrypted information.

Encrypted fields cannot be viewed through a Web browser because the keys needed to decrypt the document are stored in the Notes ID. Remember this information when preparing for the exam.

Public key encryption is used for email, whereas you can use either public or private key encryption to encrypt documents.

A document with one or more encrypted fields is considered encrypted.

Public Key Encryption

Each Notes user has a unique public key stored in his Notes ID. When public key encryption is used to encrypt a document, user names of those allowed to decrypt the document are stored in a special field called `PublicEncryptionKeys`. When the document is saved, the users named in the `PublicEncryptionKeys` field are looked up in the Domino Directory and the public keys in their Person documents are used to encrypt all the fields that are marked for encryption.

Private Key Encryption

Domino Designer supports private key encryption, also known as secret key encryption. This method of encryption requires that users create private keys and then distribute the keys to the appropriate users so that they can decrypt encrypted data. The name of each private key associated with a field is stored in a special field called `SecretEncryptionKeys`. When the document is saved, the keys named in this field are retrieved from the user's Notes ID, and used to encrypt all the fields marked for encryption.

Encrypting Documents

Domino provides numerous ways to encrypt a document; it's up to you as a developer to select the most appropriate one from the following list:

➤ *Form property*—You can use the Default Encryption Keys form property (on the Security tab of the properties box) to associate one or more encryption keys with a form, which is then used to encrypt every document created with the form.

➤ *Public keys*—You can associate one or more names in the Public Encryption keys field on the Security tab in the Document Properties box to encrypt documents by using the public keys of the named users.

➤ *Document Properties box*—If a form contains fields that can be encrypted, users can use the Document Properties box to encrypt documents using the keys stored in their ID files.

➤ *Secret encryption keys*—If a user has one or more secret encryption keys stored in her Notes ID, she can use it in conjunction with a `SecretEncryptionKeys` field to encrypt a document.

Public and private encryption keys are stored in your Notes ID, so you should always remember to back up your ID each time a key is added to avoid the risk of being permanently locked out of encrypted documents.

Encrypting Mail

Domino enables users to encrypt mail messages to ensure their confidentiality. When a user encrypts a mail message, only the body is encrypted; header fields such as the recipients and the subject are not encrypted. Domino can encrypt Notes mail and Internet mail for users who can support S/MIME.

Notes Mail

When a Notes user attempts to encrypt a mail message, Notes uses the recipient's public key, found in either the Domino Directory or the user's Personal Address Book.

Users have three basic options for encrypting Notes mail:

➤ *Encrypt sent mail*—Users can encrypt outgoing mail.

➤ *Encrypt received mail*—User can encrypt received mail.

➤ *Encrypt all documents in the mail database*—Users can encrypt all the mail in their mailbox to ensure its confidentiality.

S/MIME

Domino supports S/MIME so that Internet email can be encrypted. To use S/MIME, the sender of the email must possess the recipient's public key, which is stored as an Internet certificate in the Domino Directory, an LDAP directory, or in the sender's Personal Address Book. Additionally, the sender needs a cross-certificate so that Notes knows the public key can be trusted.

Signing Fields

Digital signatures are now an accepted means for legally transacting business in today's world. In fact, Congress recently passed a bill allowing digital signatures to be used to consummate a contract. Although this recent press has brought digital signatures into the lexicon of everyday people, they are nothing new to Notes/Domino users. Notes/Domino users have long had the ability to use digital signatures to sign fields when they save or mail sensitive data, which authenticates the identity of the sender and ensures the integrity of the data.

When a field is signed, Notes uses the private key of the author's ID and the value of the field being signed to create a unique value that serves as the digital signature. When the recipient views the document, the same hashing algorithm is used to ensure that the data has not been altered and to test the public key of the sender to verify the user's identity.

Notes makes it very easy to use digital signatures to ensure the validity of a document. Any form that contains at least one field that has the Sign If Mailed or Saved in Section attribute enabled can be signed.

 You can enable field signing only on forms that are mail-enabled or contain controlled-access sections.

Workstations (ECL)

Another component of the Notes security strategy is the *Execution Control list* (ECL) feature of the Notes client. The ECL is responsible for two basic things. The first is to determine whether the signer of the code being executed is allowed to run the code from a particular workstation. Second, if the signer can run the code, the ECL defines the level of access that the code has to various workstation functions. In particular, you can use the ECL to restrict access to database elements, the workstation's file system, and the execution of certain operations. For example, the ECL can be used to allow LotusScript programs to access the file system but to deny Java applets the same access.

When a database is opened and programming logic is executed, the signature ID last used to sign an element is checked against the ECL to determine whether that ID has been granted permission through the ECL to run. If permission has been granted either implicitly (default) or explicitly (user named in the ECL) for a particular task, the action is allowed. If not, the action is disallowed.

ECLs provide an important piece of the Notes security puzzle because they can stop rogue agents or applets from surreptitiously accessing confidential data or possibly causing irreparable harm to a user's workstation. Additionally, a workstation can be configured to enable the user to maintain the ECL, or the Domino Administrator can maintain the ECL centrally.

Configuring User-Controlled ECLs

To configure a user-controlled ECL, follow these steps:

1. Select File, Security, User Security from the main menu which will prompt you for your password.

2. Enter your password.

3. Click the What Others Do button, which opens the dialog box shown in Figure 10.9 and expand the list of ECL options.

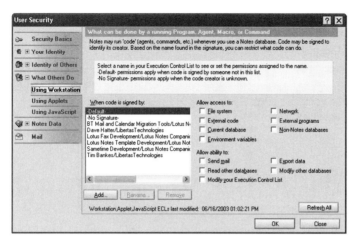

Figure 10.9   A Form Read Access list.

4. Choose the type of ECL you want to configure: Using Workstation, Using Applets, or Using JavaScript.

5. Choose an entry to configure in the When Code Is Signed By list, or click the Add button to enter a new user.

6. Set the appropriate security options for the current entry.

7. Click OK to update the ECL.

8. Click OK to close the User Security dialog box.

Summary

The following bullet points summarize the chapter and accentuate the key concepts you need to know for the exam.

➤ You can control access to Forms, Views, and Sections.

➤ Roles are an effective tool for managing user access in Domino applications.

➤ Domino provides both public and private (secret) key encryption for documents.

➤ Domino email can be both encrypted and digitally signed to protect its confidentiality and authenticity.

➤ Domino provides database encryption to secure a local database in its entirety.

➤ The Execution Control List (ECL) provides very granular workstation security.

Exam Prep Questions

Question 1

Which is not supported for Web clients?

- ○ A. Encrypted fields.
- ○ B. Names fields.
- ○ C. Readers fields.
- ○ D. Authors fields.

The correct answer is A. Web users cannot read encrypted fields. B is incorrect because Names field are supported on the Web. C is incorrect because Readers fields are supported on the Web. D is incorrect because Authors fields are supported on the Web.

Question 2

The Administration server specified for a database is responsible for what?

- ○ A. Compacting the database.
- ○ B. Monitoring database size and enforcing quotas.
- ○ C. Selecting encryption keys.
- ○ D. Keeping names in the ACL and optionally in the Names fields synchronized with the Domino Directory.

The correct answer is D, the Administration server's AdminP process is responsible for keeping names in the ACL and optionally in the Names fields synchronized with the Domino Directory. A is incorrect because the Compact task compacts databases. B is incorrect because the Administration process does not enforce quotas. C is incorrect because the Administration process has nothing to do with encryption.

Question 3

Encrypting fields on a document restricts access to what?

- ○ A. The document.
- ○ B. The contents of the encrypted fields.
- ○ C. The database.
- ○ D. You cannot encrypt fields, only documents.

The correct answer is B. Only the fields that have been encrypted require an encryption key to access them. A and C are incorrect because field-level encryption blocks access to only certain fields. D is incorrect because you can encrypt fields.

Question 4

The Execution Control List (ECL) is responsible for what?

○ A. Scheduling agents.

○ B. Controlling who can change the ACL of a database.

○ C. Controlling who can run code and what code can do on a workstation.

○ D. Controlling who can run code and what code can do on a server.

The correct answer is C. ECLs are used to control who can run code on a workstation and what that code can do. A is incorrect because the ECL has nothing to do with scheduling agents. B is incorrect because the ECL has nothing to do with changing the database ACL. D is incorrect because ECLs only affect execution on the Notes client.

Question 5

Enabling the Enforce a Consistent Access Control List property for a database does what?

○ A. Ensures that server-based databases have a consistent ACL on all replica copies.

○ B. Ensures that only an administrator can change a database's ACL.

○ C. Enforces ACLs on local databases stored on a workstation.

○ D. Ensures that local databases have a consistent ACL on all replica copies.

○ E. Both C and D.

The correct answer is E. When the Enforce a Consistent Access Control List property is enabled for a database, it ensures that all local replicas maintain a consistent ACL and that the ACL of the database is enforced locally. B is incorrect because Enforce Consistent Access Control List doesn't affect who can change the ACL. Only those with Manager access in the ACL can change the ACL. C is incorrect because Enforce Consistent Access Control List also ensures that local databases have a consistent ACL on all replica copies. D is incorrect because Enforce Consistent Access Control Lists also enforces ACLs on local databases stored on a workstation.

Question 6

Which of the following are valid design element security options?

○ A. Server access list.

○ B. Form Create list.

○ C. View Access list.

○ D. Both B and C.

The correct answer is D. Both Form Create List and View Access List are security options that can restrict access to design elements. A is incorrect because a Server access list restricts access to the server. B and C are incorrect because both Form Create lists and View Access lists are valid design element security options.

Question 7

Where is field-level encryption controlled?

○ A. Individual fields cannot be encrypted.

○ B. The Info tab of the Field properties box.

○ C. The Form Info tab of the Form properties box.

○ D. The Advanced tab of the Field properties box.

The correct answer is D. Field level encryption options are set on the Advanced tab of the Field properties box. A is incorrect because individual fields can be encrypted. B is incorrect because field-level encryption settings are controlled on the Advanced tab of the Field properties box. C is incorrect because field-level encryption settings are controlled on the Advanced tab of the Field properties box, not the Form properties box.

Question 8

Extended ACLs (xACLS) can be used in which type of database?

○ A. Databases using the log.ntf template, such as the Notes Log.

○ B. Any database.

○ C. Databases using the PUBNAMES.NTF template, such as the Domino Directory or an Extended Directory Catalog.

○ D. Databases using the PERNAMES.NTF template, such as a Personal Address Book.

The correct answer is C. Extended ACLs help delegate administration tasks in databases using the PUBNAMES.NTF template. A, B, and D are incorrect because Extended ACLs are only used with databases based on the PUBNAMES.NTF template.

Question 9

> Roles simplify database administration and can be used where to grant or deny access in a database?
>
> ❍ A. Form compose list.
>
> ❍ B. View read list.
>
> ❍ C. Readers fields.
>
> ❍ D. All of the above.

The correct answer is D. Roles can be used in any of the access control elements listed in this question. A is incorrect because Roles can also be used in View read lists and Readers fields. B is incorrect because Roles can also be used in Form compose lists and Readers fields. C is incorrect because Roles can also be used in Form compose lists and View read lists.

Question 10

> Encrypted email sent to other Domino users uses which type of key?
>
> ❍ A. Secret key.
>
> ❍ B. Public key.
>
> ❍ C. User key.
>
> ❍ D. One-way hash.

The correct answer is B. Notes mail uses public key encryption. A is incorrect because Notes mail uses public key encryption. C is incorrect because User key encryption is not a valid concept in Notes. D is invalid because one-way hashing is only used in Notes to protect user's passwords.

Need to Know More?

 IBM. *Lotus Domino Designer 6 Help.* Help6_Designer.nsf.

 IBM. *Lotus Domino Administrator 6 Help.* Help6_Admin.nsf.

 IBM. *Domino Designer 6: A Developer's Handbook.* Place: IBM, 2002.

 IBM Lotus Developer Domain Web site: www.notes.net or www.lotus. com/ldd.

Workflow

Terms you'll need to understand:

✓ Encryption
✓ Keyword fields
✓ Reserved word fields
✓ Signing
✓ Electronic signatures
✓ Access-controlled section
✓ Form formula
✓ Roles
✓ Routing
✓ Rules

Concepts and techniques you'll need to master:

✓ Creating workflow-related fields: conditional/unconditional fields
✓ Creating workflow-related fields: document encryption
✓ Creating workflow-related fields: hide-when fields
✓ Creating workflow-related fields: keyword fields
✓ Creating workflow-related fields: reserved word fields
✓ Creating workflow-related fields: signing
✓ Creating workflow-related fields: workflow-related field attributes
✓ Creating workflow-related forms: mail-enabled forms
✓ Creating workflow-related forms: setting workflow-related form attributes
✓ Creating workflow-related forms: Store Form in Document
✓ Creating workflow-related sections
✓ Creating/distributing workflow tracking databases
✓ Creating/setting up workflow roles
✓ Creating mail-in databases
✓ Creating mail-enabled forms
✓ Creating workflow applications
✓ Determining workflow control
✓ Routing documents and sending links to documents
✓ Setting field access: authors
✓ Setting field access: encryption
✓ Setting field access: groups
✓ Setting field access: readers
✓ Setting field access: signing
✓ Setting form access: groups
✓ Setting section access: groups
✓ Troubleshooting mail-enabled field problems: field attributes
✓ Troubleshooting mail-enabled form problems: workflow-related
✓ Troubleshooting workflow distribution problems: replication
✓ Troubleshooting workflow distribution problems: roles
✓ Troubleshooting workflow distribution problems: routing
✓ Troubleshooting workflow distribution problems: rules

When workflow applications are implemented, information is routed between team members. This chapter covers topics related to implementing workflow applications in Lotus Notes/Domino. For example, technical items to understand when designing workflow applications are workflow-related fields, workflow-related forms, workflow-related roles and routing rules, field access, form access, section access, and workflow distribution.

Create Workflow-Related Fields

Some standard fields commonly used within Notes applications and extensively used throughout Domino templates are well suited for workflow applications. Also, these fields are recognized by Notes mail clients if routed to a user's mail file.

Table 11.1 describes the fields in workflow applications and templates.

Table 11.1 Standard Workflow and Template Fields	
Field Name	**Description**
Body	Editable Rich Text field storing the body of the document
ComposedDate	Typically hidden and computed when composed, this is a date/time field containing the time and date the document was created. The formula for this field is typically **@Created**.
From	Computed when composed, this field contains the document author. The formula for this field is typically **@UserName**.
Subject	Editable text containing a single line of the document summary.

Conditional/Unconditional Fields

Conditional fields are fields whose values are determined based upon a formula evaluation (condition), whereas unconditional fields have a pre-determined value. When designing workflow applications, both conditional and unconditional fields are used for routing, security, tracking documents.

Workflow applications often require versioning of documents, especially if the document is being routed for mark-up and approval. Adding a reserved field $VersionOpt to a form enables users to create new versions of edited documents on a document-by-document basis. This field is a text field whose value determines which versioning action the application is to take when the document is saved.

This field must be an editable or computed text field. Computed for Display and Computed When Composed field types do not work properly.

Table 11.2 describes the options available for the $VersionOpt field.

Table 11.2 Version Tracking	
Value	**Description**
0	No version tracking.
1	New versions become responses if the user chooses File, Save As New Version.
2	New versions automatically become responses when the document is saved.
3	Prior versions become responses if the user chooses File, Save As New Version.
4	Prior versions automatically become responses when saved.
5	Prior versions become siblings if the user chooses File, Save As New Version.
6	Prior versions automatically become siblings when saved.

FoldersOptions Field

The FoldersOptions field enables users to select a folder in which new documents are to be saved without having to use the Actions, Move to Folder After Saving option. This field enables the designer to prompt the user to choose a folder or automatically save the document to the current folder.

The **FoldersOptions** field must be an editable choice list, computed number field, or computed text field. Computed for Display and Computed When Composed field types do not work properly. Do not select Allow Multi-Values or Allow Values Not in List.

The allowed values for this field are either

➤ 1—Prompts the user to choose a folder.

➤ 2—Saves the document to the current folder.

Document Encryption

Many of the features and capabilities used throughout workflow applications (discussed in this and other chapters) display and hide fields, text, and other objects based on user roles, form formulas, view selection formulas, field values, and so forth. Although these features make the application easier to use and streamline the workflow process, they do not provide true document-level security. Users can view documents and data contained within them by using alternate views or personal views, viewing field values in the document properties box, and so forth. However, documents can use encryption to ensure that data contained within fields is secure from unauthorized users.

Encryption is a type of digital lock used to protect data from unauthorized access. You can encrypt databases and/or fields. Although other Domino security features (such as database Access Control Lists, server access, and so forth) are integrated and work in conjunction with one another, encryption does not. You must have the encryption key to access the data. You cannot override or modify the security.

 When a document is encrypted, the document itself is not truly encrypted. Rather, one or more of the fields contained within the document are encrypted.

Domino uses two types of encryption for security:

➤ Public-private key encryption

➤ Secret key encryption

For more information regarding enabling encryption for specific fields and applying encryption, refer to "Encrypting Documents" in Chapter 10, "Security," for Exam 611.

Document-level encryption and signatures do not work for Web applications because both methods require keys to be stored in each user's ID. Because Web users do not use ID files, security for the Web is secured by Secure Sockets Layer (SSL). For more information regarding enabling SSL for Web applications, refer to "Set Database Access: Using SSL," in Chapter 17, "Security," for Exam 612.

Public Key/Private Key Encryption

Domino assigns a private key and a public key to each user ID. The private key is stored in the ID file. The public key is stored in the ID file and in the corresponding document where the key is publicly available (the Person document in the Domino directory). When data is encrypted, it can be decrypted only by the private key (using complex mathematical algorithms).

Public and private keys can be used to

➤ Encrypt mail

➤ Encrypt databases

➤ Sign documents, fields, and sections

If Jake wants to send encrypted mail to Leah, Jake creates a mail memo and indicates that the mail is to be encrypted. Domino gets Leah's public key from her Person document in the Domino directory and encrypts the memo. When Leah receives and opens the document, Domino uses Leah's private key to decrypt the message.

Secret Key Encryption

Secret keys can be created by any user and must be available to all the users who need to access the encrypted information. Secret encryption keys are often created and distributed by the database manager or the application designer.

Secret encryption keys can be used to

➤ Encrypt fields

➤ Provide additional security for documents

To create a secret encryption key for document encryption, follow these steps:

1. Select File, Security, User Security from the pull-down menu.

2. Expand the Notes Data section, then click Documents.

3. Click New Secret Key....

4. Enter the secret key name (see Figure 11.1). This name should be descriptive of the key purpose.

5. If the key is to be used by users who are using an international version of Notes older than release 5.0.4, select Use International Encryption.

6. Enter comments if necessary.

7. Click OK.

8. Click OK to close the User Security dialog box.

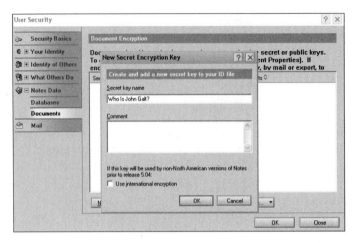

Figure 11.1 Creating a secret encryption key.

After you have created the secret encryption keys, you need to distribute the key to the authorized users. After it has been distributed, they can read the encrypted information.

To send the encryption keys via email, perform the following steps:

1. Select File, Security, User Security from the pull-down menu.

2. Expand the Notes Data section, then click Documents.

3. Select the appropriate key to distribute from the Document Encryption selection box (see Figure 11.2).

4. Click Mail Secret Key….

5. Enter the recipient information (To: and CC: fields) and modify the subject if appropriate.

6. Click Send.

7. You will be prompted to select the Allow All Recipients to Forward the Key to Others by Mail or Export? check box. Select the appropriate action.

8. Click OK.

To export a secret encryption key, perform the following steps:

1. Select File, Security, User Security from the pull-down menu.

2. Expand the Notes Data section, then click Documents.

3. Select the appropriate key to distribute from the Document Encryption selection box (see Figure 11.2).

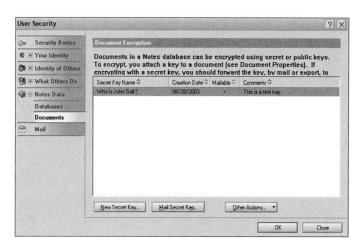

Figure 11.2   Select a secret encryption key.

4. Click Other Actions, Export Secret Key.... You also have options to Delete Secret Keys, Import Secret Keys, and view Advanced Details as well.

5. Enter the password for the export file and re-enter the password confirmation, or select No Password (see Figure 11.3).

6. Click Restrict Use to select the name of the person who is allowed to use the encryption key import file. The name is entered in the Secret Encryption Key Restrictions dialog (see Figure 11.4).

7. Click OK.

Figure 11.3   Exporting a secret encryption key.

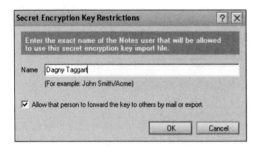

Figure 11.4 Setting encryption key restrictions.

After the secret encryption keys have been distributed, users need to merge the key with their ID files (users can use the secret encryption keys only after they have been merged with their ID files). The keys are merged from either an email message or a previously exported encryption file.

To merge an encryption key received via email, perform the following steps:

1. Open the mail message containing the attached encryption key.

2. Select Actions, Accept Encryption Key from the pull-down menu.

3. Enter the user password.

4. Click OK.

5. Enter any comments regarding the key, if required.

6. Click Accept.

To import a secret encryption key, perform the following steps:

1. Select File, Security, User Security from the pull-down menu.

2. Expand the Notes Data section, then click Documents.

3. Click Other Actions, Import Secret Key....

4. Select the encryption key file from the file system.

5. Enter the password (if required).

6. Click Accept.

Hide-When Fields

A common way to filter the information displayed to the users is to selectively hide and display fields on the form, dependant on the status of the document in the workflow process. Hide-when properties of fields (and text and other objects) can be used to control the display of information.

Keep in mind that hide-when fields are not to be used as a security feature because the item values of the document can still be accessed by the user in other forms, views, or in the field values of the document properties box.

Hide-when formulas always evaluate to either TRUE or FALSE. Hide-when attributes apply to the entire line. Therefore, if you have multiple fields on the same line, they share the same hide-when formula. To avoid this, you can place the fields on separate lines or in separate cells in a table. Therefore, each can retain its own hide-when attribute (see Figure 11.5).

Figure 11.5   Setting a hide-when formula.

Hide-when formulas can contain only formula language evaluations. If it is required that more complex expressions be used to determine the value of a hide-when formula, you can program script to populate another field on the form and then have the value of the hide-when formula evaluate to the prior field name. The formula expressions for hide-when formulas can be simple (such as @IsNewDoc) or more complex algorithms that contain multiple @If statements. Regardless, they must always evaluate to either a TRUE (1) or FALSE (0) condition. Be careful not to create an excessive number of hide-when formulas or formulas that are extremely complex. This can negatively impact application performance.

Keyword Fields

Keyword fields are computed or editable (which are more common) fields that present the user with a list of choices. The list can be predetermined by the application designer, generated by formula, or entered manually by the users of the application. The designer determines whether only one selection can be made, multiple selections can be made, or the user can add selections not currently in the list.

Table 11.3 describes the different keyword field types, how they are used, whether the option is set to allow multiple values, and whether the option to allow values not in the list is available.

Table 11.3	Keyword Field Types		
Field Type	**Description**	**Allow Multi-Values**	**Allow Values Not in List**
Dialog List	To view the dialog box, press Enter or the Entry Helper button. You can also type the first letter of a choice to jump to an entry, or press the space bar to cycle through the list of items.	Available	Available
Checkbox	Display all the items with check boxes.	Available	Not Available
Radio Button	Display all the items with radio buttons.	Not Available	Not Available
ListBox	Each choice is displayed with an expanded list box.	Available	Not Available
ComboBox	Each choice is displayed with a drop-down list box.	Not Available	Available

When creating keyword fields, the application designer must select how the available choices will be determined. These options are available on the Control tab of the Field properties box (see Figure 11.6).

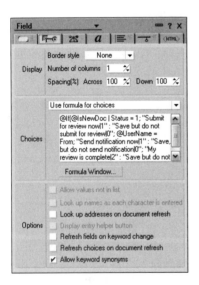

Figure 11.6 Setting keyword choices.

Table 11.4 describes the options available for determining the keyword choices.

Table 11.4	Keyword Options
Option	**Description**
Enter choices (one per line)	The Designer enters the choices in the Edit box (letters, numbers, and any punctuation, except for commas). Select Sort to sort the list in alphanumeric order.
Use Formula for choices	Enter a formula to generate the list of choices.
Use Address dialog for choices	Displays the Name dialog box to select names from the Domino directory.
Use Access Control list for choices	Displays the list of people, servers, groups, and roles in the ACL of the current database.
Use View dialog for choices	Displays a dialog box displaying entries from a column in an existing view.

Here are some benefits of using the View dialog for choices:

➤ Non-designers can maintain the choices without affecting the database design.

➤ You avoid hard-coding the keyword options.

➤ The database design can be hidden and restricted without affecting future maintenance.

➤ It is easier to upgrade the application to multi-lingual capabilities.

➤ Keyword choices are more easily modified outside the current form or database.

Reserved Word Fields

Several *reserved word fields* are intended to provide an easy mechanism for incorporating some of the more common features of Domino. Using these reserved field names enables developers to easily add functionality rather than program it from scratch. Developers need only use the reserved word names and appropriate values to create fields, and Domino automatically enables the respective functionalities.

If you try to create a field name that is a reserved word field, the Designer client generates an error message.

SendTo Reserved Field

The sendTo field is a reserved field that contains value(s) of the intended mail recipient(s) of the Notes document. This field can contain individual usernames, groups, or databases. Each is defined in the Domino directory. The value of this field can be either computed or editable. While you are designing the document and placing this field on the form, consider the placement of the field and how its value is computed. The field type can be Text, Keyword, or Names, and can contain a text string or text list. The value of the field can be

➤ Hard-coded with the recipient list.

➤ Computed with the recipient list based upon another field value located on the form (above or to the left of the current field).

➤ Computed with the recipient list based upon a formula or condition.

MailOptions Reserved Field

The MailOptions field can be used to

➤ Programmatically force a document to be routed when the user closes the document, independent of user intervention.

➤ Prompt the user to send the document when the document is closed.

The MailOptions field should be a computed text field with a value of 1 to automatically route the document, or 0 to prevent the document from routing.

For the exam, remember that if both the **MailOptions** field and the **@MailSend** function are used within the same form, the **MailOptions** field overrides the **@MailSend** function.

Form Reserved Field

The Form field is a reserved field that contains the name of the form to be used to display the document if the form design is not stored in the document. If the form design is not stored in the document opened for reading or editing, Domino uses the value contained in the "Form" item in the document. Domino automatically creates a Form item when a document is created and saved. The default Form item name is the name (or alias) of the form design element used to create the document. However, this form value can be later modified by using the formula language or script, or by opening with another form (using and alias).

 Domino automatically creates a "Form" item when a document is first saved. A designer can also include a field in the form named **Form** to override the value created by Domino. Another benefit of creating a Form field is that this value is available on new documents that have not yet been saved.

Signing

Signing a document causes Domino to combine the user's private key and the value of the signed field to create a unique electronic signature. Therefore, if the document or mail message is altered in transit, the unique signature changes. The user is then notified that the document cannot be authenticated. Creating signatures does not secure the data. It only establishes that the user who saved the document last is authentic and informs the user whether this is the case. In addition, signing works only for Notes clients and is not supported on the Web.

Electronic signatures provide the capability to verify that particular messages and documents have been modified by particular individuals. With Domino, electronic signatures ensure that the ID of the user that created or modified the specified document is genuine and that the document, and information contained within it, have not been modified since the user saved and/or mailed the document. Signing documents is important with sensitive information.

Because the signature is applied when the document is saved or mailed, the following occurs:

➤ If the document was signed, Domino checks the signature against the data to ensure that the data matches.

➤ If the signature and data match and are verified, Domino displays a message to the user identifying who signed the document.

➤ If the signature and data do not match (the data has been modified), Domino displays a message indicating that the document has been changed or corrupted since the document was last saved or mailed.

To enable documents to be signed, at least one field on the document must have the Sign If Mailed or Saved in Section property enabled in the Field properties dialog box (see Figure 11.7). In addition, the form must also be mail-enabled, containing the SendTo field or an access-controlled section.

Figure 11.7 Enabling Signatures.

If the field is located within an access-controlled section, the signature is contained within the section and generated when the document is saved.

To sign-enable an access-controlled section, one of the fields must be sign-enabled. When the document is saved, the section is signed.

 Only the section that contains the signed-enabled field is signed, not the entire document.

You can create multiple sign-enabled sections on the document by creating multiple sign-enabled fields placed in each access-controlled section.

If the field is not located within an access-controlled section, the signature is contained within the document and generated when the document is mailed.

The signing occurs when the document is mailed as a result of one of the following:

➤ The sender chooses the Sign option in the Send Mail dialog box.

➤ The form design contains a field named Sign that has a value of 1.

➤ The form has a @MailSend function that uses the [Sign] flag.

➤ The form has LotusScript code that has the SignOnSend property set to TRUE.

Workflow-Related Field Attributes

Building from the native workflow capabilities of Domino, many of the field types and attributes allow for easy implementation of workflow-specific features. Simply selecting certain field types or certain parameters on fields can enable powerful workflow and security features.

In addition to enabling signing and encryption and creating keyword fields, some other workflow-related field attributes are described in Table 11.5.

Table 11.5 Workflow-Related Field Options	
Option	**Description**
Names fields	Display and store usernames the way they appear in the user's ID.
Authors and Readers fields	Control who can read and edit documents.
Password fields	Text fields that display each character entered as an asterisk on the screen.
Field inheritance	A field can inherit its value from another document in the same database or another field in the same form. This is particularly helpful with workflow documents in which much of the information is shared among different documents.
Automatically refresh fields	The document refreshes when a different choice is selected.
Automatically refresh choices	If the options are based on a formula, they are recomputed if the document is refreshed.
Security Options	Several workflow options are available to further refine security within the document. The options available are ➤ None ➤ Sign if mailed or saved in section ➤ Enable encryption for this field ➤ Must have at least editor access to use

Create Workflow-Related Forms

In much the same manner that field attributes can be modified to enable built-in workflow capabilities, forms can also be modified to expose built-in workflow capabilities. The following sections explain how to create these workflow-related forms.

Mail-Enabled Forms

You can enable forms to easily route mail to other team members. Enabling the Present Mail Send form property causes the Send Mail dialog box to appear each time the user closes an edited document. This dialog box presents the user with the option to send the document (see Figure 11.8). The recipient of the mail is determined by the values listed in the SendTo field on the Notes document.

Figure 11.8   The Send Mail dialog box.

Some of the built-in workflow capabilities of Lotus Notes/Domino can be easily enabled or disabled if their reserved fields are set to TRUE or FALSE. This feature makes it fast and simple for designers to build powerful workflow applications.

Some of the reserved fields that can be enabled if their value is set to TRUE are

➤ MailOptions—Gives users the option to mail the document. Setting this field to FALSE disables the user's capability to mail the document to other users.

➤ SaveOptions—Controls whether the document is saved when mailed. Setting this field to FALSE disables the option to save this document to disk.

➤ Sign—Signs the document with the creator's name to verify the document is not modified by anyone other than the signer.

➤ Encrypt—Encrypts the mail document.

➤ DeliveryReport—Returns a report (mail message) when the mail has been successfully delivered to the recipient.

➤ ReturnReceipt—Returns a report (mail message) when the mail has been read by the recipient.

➤ FolderOptions—Puts the document into folders.

➤ SecretEncryptionKeys—Encrypts the document with secret encryption keys.

Setting Workflow-Related Form Attributes

The Send Document simple action is a form attribute that enables developers to easily enable mail forwarding for the current document.

The Send Document simple action sends the current document to the recipients contained in the SendTo field. This action does not work in field formulas or agents.

 When using the Send Mail Message simple action, you can mail the selected document as a document link, or you can send the entire document.

Store Form in Document

As previously explained in this chapter, when a user creates a document, the data is saved as items in the Notes document. When the user opens the document, the document uses a form to display its content; that form can be the one used to create the document or a default database form. These forms are saved in the database in which the document was created. If the document is mailed, the form that was used to create the document will not be available when the user opens the document (because the form design is not available in the user's mail database). Therefore, when documents are mailed to users in workflow applications, it may be necessary to store the form in the document.

Storing the form in the document uses more memory (as much as 20 times more disk space), but it ensures that the document can be opened even if the database where the document was created is missing, renamed, or deleted.

If a document has been created and the form is stored in the document, you can remove the form; then the document is opened with the designated form or default database form. To remove the stored form in the document, simply remove the $Title, $Info, $WindowTitle, and $Body fields.

Create Workflow-Related Sections

Workflow-related sections offer another level of displaying or restricting access to information and/or functionality within the application.

Access-controlled sections restrict who can edit or sign parts (sections) within a document. Sections are particularly useful in workflow applications because sections can be hidden or displayed as the document changes stages in the workflow process.

In addition, a section's access can be determined by an access formula (using the formula language) so workflow rules can be built into the section, therefore, determining who can access a section. Sections can also be hidden based on a formula. For more information regarding sections and security, refer to "Restrict Section Access" in Chapter 10, "Security," for Exam 611.

Create/Distribute Workflow Tracking Databases

When creating workflow-enabled applications, designers often create or include workflow-specific features contained within design elements (such as forms). These design elements may have to exist in other databases to ensure the application functions properly and consistently.

As a result of routing documents into various databases, the forms that are used to display those documents may have to be copied into the destination databases. Alternate methods that have been detailed earlier in this chapter are probably more likely to be used when the design of the destination database is unlikely to be modified. For example, documents routed to a user's mail database should store the design in the document because no one is likely to modify the design of the user's mail databases. Nevertheless, if the user has Designer access to other destination databases used for routing, it may be determined that copying the form design into those databases is the most efficient decision.

Another option for application routing is to route documents to central, shared nonmail databases (specifically, databases that are not users' mail databases) that can act as repositories. Documents are mailed to these databases in the same manner as if they were users' mail databases. To enable this, a mail-in database document is created in the Domino directory so that the mail router running on the server knows where to deliver the document.

Routing documents to nonmail databases is a useful feature for workflow business processes that are contained in multiple databases or for automatically archiving documents that have reached a threshold maturity date.

Notes views are meant to display a subset of documents to users based upon the view selection formula and how the data is to be displayed. It only makes sense, then, that they might also be used within workflow applications to help guide users through the workflow process. To determine how to build workflow-specific views, you should

➤ Consider the users for each view and what information is relevant to the various users.

➤ Use the view selection formulas to filter which documents appear in each view so that only relevant documents are displayed. You can modify the field values throughout the workflow process so that documents can be moved from one view to another for each stage of the workflow.

➤ Create column definitions that display information that is relevant to the view users.

 To prepare for the exam, become familiar with creating workflow-related views by using selection formulas, categorized columns, and so on.

Writing selection formulas does not secure data from users. Users can still access documents through other views by creating personal views and through the document's unique ID.

Complex view selection formulas can have a negative impact on performance. Put as much processing of field values within the document (as it is saved or routed) as possible, and attempt to minimize the complexity of the view selection formulas.

Create/Set Up Workflow Roles

The @UserRoles function is used when roles have been created for the current database. This function returns a text list naming the member roles of the specified user.

 Roles contain a subset of the database users, groups, or servers, and provide or restrict access to particular database design elements, functions, or document contents. Unlike groups, servers, and persons who are defined in the Domino directory, roles are defined in the database Access Control List.

The @UserNamesList function is used when roles have been created for the current database. This function returns a text list containing the specified username, any groups of which the specified user is a member, and any roles of which the specified user is a member.

With both @UserRoles and @UserNamesList, you should use the function @IsMember to create a conditional statement that determines whether the user has the rights to perform a particular function or to view particular text or fields. These fields, used in hide-when formulas, can selectively hide fields, text, or other objects based upon the roles to which the current user is assigned.

Creating Mail-in Databases

Domino databases can be designed to receive mail in the same manner that users receive mail. A mail-in database is created, typically, by the Domino administrator, and a mail-in database document is created in the Domino Directory database. Then mail can be routed directly to the mail-in database through the use of a mail address similar to a user's mail address. This feature can be very useful to application designers.

Information stored in Notes documents can be sent to a user's mail database or any other databases identified in the Domino directory within a mail-in database document. Creating a mail-in database document in the Domino directory enables the database to receive mailed documents, as if it were a user's mail database.

Mail-in Database Routing

The type of notification depends on the following:

➤ Who the notification recipients are and whether they are determined by the user or programmatically (by action buttons, agents, and form events).

➤ Whether the information to be routed is a document link, the document with the form design included, or the document content.

➤ What triggers the mail (whether it's triggered by the user or triggered programmatically, by action buttons, agents, and form events) and when is it to be sent.

When routing mail to Notes users' mail databases, the location of each user's respective database is determined within the user's Person document in the Domino directory.

The Domino mail router sends the document to a mail-in database in the same method as it would to a user's mail database.

 When mail is used to route a document, the actual document does not move from the source database to the destination database. Instead, a copy of the document is sent from the source database and the new copy in placed into the destination database.

When selecting recipients, the following methods can be used to enable mail routing:

➤ @MailSend without arguments

➤ @MailSend with arguments

➤ Form property

➤ The MailOptions field, used in conjunction with other reserved fields that control mail routing

➤ Simple action

Except for the @MailSend (with arguments), each option requires a field named SendTo on the form. You learn more about this command in "The @MailSend Command" section, later in this chapter.

Creating the Mail-In Database

The server administrator typically creates the mail-in database. Regardless, you must have at least Author access with the Create Documents privilege enabled to create mail-in documents in the Domino directory.

Users must have the Net Creator role enabled to use the Create menu to create documents. However, this does not apply to creating Person, Group, and Server documents.

Follow these steps to create a mail-in database:

1. Open the Domino Directory (otherwise known as the Public Address Book, which has a filename of names.nsf and is located in the root data directory of the server).

2. Select Create, Server, Mail-In Database. Alternatively, open the Configuration, Messaging, Mail-In Databases view and click the Add Mail-In Database button.

3. Enter the mail database name for the mail-in name that will serve as the name used in the SendTo field for mail messages being routed to the mail-in database.

4. If your organization uses multiple domains, enter the name of the domain for this mail-in database.

5. In the Server field, enter the distinguished name of the server on which the database resides.

6. Enter the database directory in which the mail-in database resides and the database filename in the File Name field. If the database resides in the default Domino directory, this field can be left blank.

7. On the Administration tab, enter the names of any additional users who change this mail-in Database document.

8. Save and close the document.

The mail-in database document must exist in the Domino Directory of every server that stores a replica of the database.

The database cannot receive mail until this document has been created.

Creating Workflow Applications

When creating workflow-enabled applications that are to be used by Notes users, designers can use reserved fields to provide some workflow capabilities.

Domino provides predefined, reserved fields that, when used, automatically add functionality that the designer would normally have to program himself/herself. Some of these reserved fields accept only a Boolean value that determines whether the specific functionality should be explicitly enabled or disabled.

Whereas some reserved fields accept only Boolean values to enable/disable their functionality, some reserved fields use user-defined values such as conditional statements and more complex formulas to determine their respective actions.

Some reserved fields that accept values to determine their action are

➤ SendTo—Routes mail to users, groups, servers, or any combination listed in this field.

➤ CopyTo—Routes a copy of mail to users, groups, servers, or any combination listed in this field.

➤ BlindCopyTo—Routes a blind carbon copy of mail to users, groups, servers, or any combination listed in this field.

➤ Categories—Automatically categorizes documents.

Whereas some reserved fields accept only Boolean values to enable their functionality, and others accept user-defined values, still others accept only predetermined constants to determine their capability.

Some reserved fields that accept only predefined constant values are

➤ DeliveryPriority—Flags mail for delivery as either High, Medium (Normal), or Low Priority. The field values accepted are L, N, or H.

➤ MailFormat—Enables cc:Mail users to view Notes mail in four formats: B—Both text and encapsulated; E—Encapsulated in a Notes database that is attached to the memo; M—Body field of document is rendered as text and pasted into the cc:Mail memo; or T—Contents of the document are rendered as text and pasted into the cc:Mail memo (cc:Mail is a former Lotus LAN email product).

➤ $VersionOpt—Controls version tracking for the document.

Determine Workflow Control

Several @Commands enable developers to execute workflow-related commands. Many of these commands are also available to users, who can manually select the appropriate action from the pull-down menu bar. However, these @Commands can also be automated as part of a workflow application (see Table 11.6).

Table 11.6 Workflow-Related @Commands	
@Command	**Description**
@Command([MailAddress])	Displays the Mail Send dialog box so that the user can select people/groups/servers to include in the address field of a mail document. The mail document must be open, in edit mode, and the cursor must be in an editable text field.
@Command([MailComposeMemo])	Creates a new blank mail memo document by using the default form in the user's mail database. This command can be used anywhere except from within a dialog box.

Table 11.6 Workflow-Related @Commands *(continued)*	
@Command	**Description**
`@Command([MailForwardAsAttachment])`	For cc:Mail, forwards a Notes/Domino document as a cc:Mail attachment.
`@Command([MailForward])`	Forwards the current document as the contents of the mail memo. The document must be open, in read or edit mode, or selected in a view or folder. You can select multiple documents and have them all copied into the body of the memo.
`@Command([MailSend])`	Displays the Send Mail dialog box. The dialog box presents the options to Encrypt, Sign, and Send the current document. The document must be open, in read or edit mode, or selected in a view or folder. In addition, the document must contain a `SendTo` field with the recipients specified.

Several functions enable developers to execute workflow-related commands. These functions can be automated as part of a workflow application.

The @MailSend Command

One of the most frequent methods used for routing mail is achieved by using `@MailSend`. `@MailSend` routes a copy of the current document to the recipient list. A document link can be included within the mail memo so that a link back to the original document is also sent to the recipients. The benefit to this method is that multiple copies of the document are not being routed throughout the organization. All users who receive the mail memo and click on the document link will link to the same original document. Of course, for the recipients to be able to open the document link, they must have access to the server where the linked document exists (recipients need physical access as well as granted permission to access the server) and have at least Reader access to the database in which the document exists.

The syntax of the `@Mailsend` document is:

```
@MailSend(sendto; copyto; blindcopyto; subject; remark; bodyFields; [flags])
```

The `bodyFields` option contains a list of the text fields to include from the original document.

The [flags] that can be included are

➤ [IncludeDocLink]—Sends the message with a doclink to the original document containing the @MailSend function.

➤ [Sign]—Attaches an electronic signature to the document.

➤ [Encrypt]—Encrypts the document. The memo's recipient must have the private key to read the document.

➤ [PriorityHigh]—Instructs the mail server to immediately route the message. Depending on the mail routing configuration, the server either places a phone call to the next server in routing topology so that the memo can be routed or immediately routes the memo to the next server in the routing topology if the servers are constantly connected. The memo is routed immediately, regardless of the replication schedule.

➤ [PriorityNormal]— Instructs the mail server to route the message by using the replication schedule. If the recipient is located in the same Notes Named Network as the sender, the message is routed immediately.

➤ [PriorityLow]—Instructs the mail server to route the message overnight, during nonpeak hours. However, if the recipient is located in the same Notes Named Network as the sender, the message is routed immediately.

➤ [ReturnReceipt]—Automatically sends a memo to the original sender of the document when the recipient reads the document.

➤ [DeliveryReportConfirmed]—Automatically sends a memo to the original sender of the document informing the sender that the attempted delivery was successful or unsuccessful. If this parameter is not used, the default action of Domino is to notify the sender only if the document cannot be delivered (causing a delivery failure).

If the @MailSend is scripted without inclusion of the recipient arguments, the document is sent to the values specified in the SendTo field within the document. This function can be used in

➤ Form and view actions

➤ Agents

➤ Fields

➤ Buttons

➤ Smart icons

@MailSend cannot be used in views (column or selection formulas), hide-when formulas, window title formulas, or form formulas.

Route Documents and Send Links to Documents

Four types of informational links can be used within Lotus Notes (not including links to URL addresses). These links must be placed within Rich Text fields. Document, view, and database links display a specific icon after they are pasted into the Rich Text field. Table 11.7 describes the four types of links that can be included.

Table 11.7	Types of Informational Links	
Link Type	**Related Icon**	**Description**
Anchor		Links information from one place within a document to another place within the same document (similar to anchor tags commonly used within HTML pages). When it is clicked, the anchor gets focus on the screen.
Document		Links to another Notes document. When it is clicked, the document is opened. This document can be stored in the same database, in another database on the same server, or in another server to which the user has access. Document links are often used to cross-reference other related Notes documents. Similarly, document links are often contained within mail messages being sent to Notes mail clients.
View		Links to a Notes view. When it is clicked, the view is opened. This view can be stored in the same database, in another database on the same server, or in another server to which the user has access.
Database		Links to another database. When it is clicked, the database is opened to the default view for that database. This database can be stored on the same server or another server to which the user has access.

Creating Document, View, or Database Links

To create links to Notes documents, views, or databases, a link first must be copied to memory (in other words, copied to the clipboard) and then pasted in an existing Rich Text field (for Notes clients) or into a form, subform, or page design element (for Notes Designers).

 NOTE To create Document Links, View Links, or Database Links, the user must have a Lotus Notes client. However, previously created links work with Web clients—that is, document links, view links, and database links that were created by a Notes client will appear for Web clients represented by the same icon as with Notes clients, and clicking on the icon opens the respective link.

To create document, view, or database links, follow these steps:

1. Perform one of the following actions, depending upon the type of link you want to copy:

   ➤ To copy the anchor link to memory, insert the cursor before the paragraph where the anchor will link to into the rich text of an existing document; select Edit, Copy As Link, Anchor Link from the pull-down menu.

   ➤ To copy the document link to memory, either highlight a document in a view or open an existing document; select Edit, Copy As Link, Document Link from the pull-down menu.

   ➤ To copy the view link to memory, open a view, then select Edit, Copy As Link, View Link from the pull-down menu.

   ➤ To copy the database link to memory, either highlight a database icon from the workspace or open an existing database; select Edit, Copy As Link, Database Link from the pull-down menu.

2. Open the document in which you want to place the link. The link can be in the body of a new email or in any Rich Text field within Notes.

3. After the cursor is within a Rich Text field, select Edit, Paste (or CTRL+V).

4. Save the document (or mail the document if it is a mail memo).

5. Click on the link icon to open the respective document, view, or database.

Forwarding Notes Documents

Another method for sharing information with team members is to forward the document contents to other users. Forwarding a Notes document creates a copy of the selected document and pastes its contents into the Rich Text body of a new mail message. To forward a document, follow these steps:

1. Select the document to forward from a view, or open an existing document and select Actions, Forward from the pull-down menu.

2. Enter the recipient mail address in the To: field.

3. Enter the subject.

4. Enter any other relevant information. The forwarded document will be contained within the Rich Text body.

5. Send the email.

Set Field Access

Notes/Domino has long provided the capability to secure data at the document level through a variety of constructs such as Readers fields and encryption. The following sections explain setting field access as a means of securing data at the document level.

Authors Field

An Authors field is a special type of text field that can be added to a document to further refine the ACL and restrict who can edit the document. A user, group, or role that has been granted Author access in a database is likely to be able to create new documents and read existing documents (not secured with Readers fields). However, they cannot edit documents (even ones that they have created), unless they are also named in the Authors field.

For example, if John Galt has been granted Author access in the ACL with the Create Documents privilege, he can create new documents. But he cannot edit any existing documents (including the ones he has authored) unless he is named explicitly or implicitly (through group membership), or has been assigned a role that has been named in an Authors field in the document.

 For the exam, remember that being named in an Authors field *does not* give a user authority to edit a document if a user is already restricted through a lower access level in the database ACL.

Encryption of Fields

Encryption is the process of scrambling data so that only authorized users can unscramble the data. Notes/Domino supports secret key encryption (public key is used to encrypt data and private key can decode data). From early in its history, Notes has supported encryption through the capability to encrypt fields in documents, ensuring that data is secure from prying eyes.

Any field(s) in a Notes document can be encrypted, and after it has been, only users who possess the proper key can decrypt and read the field contents. Users without the proper key(s) see what appears to be a blank field in the document, and any attempts to use the Document Properties box to view the fields is stymied, as well.

Using Groups to Secure Domino Elements

As was mentioned earlier in this chapter, groups can be used to grant or deny access to Domino data and can ease the administrative burden substantially. This section covers using groups to secure various Domino elements, namely fields, forms, views, and sections.

If a user is listed both explicitly and implicitly (through a group) in an ACL, the rights granted to the explicit name take precedence. For example, if Brooke has Author access to a database but is named in a group with Designer access, Brooke is granted Author access.

Similarly, if a user is listed in multiple groups (and not explicitly listed), the user is granted the highest level available within the respective groups.

As you know from previous chapters in this book, Domino provides special Readers and Authors fields that enable you to refine the database ACL and restrict access to data stored in Domino.

To use a group or groups in an Authors field to limit which users with Author access can edit a document, follow these steps:

1. In the Designer client, open the database containing the Authors field.

2. Open the form that contains the Authors field.

3. Enter a formula that returns the name of the group(s) to include, or enable the user to enter/select the group(s) in an editable field.

4. Save the form.

Any users, servers, or groups (remember that you can nest groups) named in the group(s) stored in the Authors field can edit the documents.

Readers Field

Much like an Authors field, a Readers field is a special type of text field that refines the ACL and provides additional document-level security. However, Readers fields are slightly less convoluted than some other fields and easier to understand. If a document contains a Readers field that has any users, groups, or roles specified, then only those users, groups, and roles can access the document.

 Being named in a Readers field *does not* grant access to a user who is restricted by the ACL. For example, Leah Brooke is a member of the "Readers" group, which is named in a Readers field, but she has been granted only Depositor access in the ACL, meaning that she cannot access the document.

The Readers field is a very powerful and useful security feature. Using groups in a Readers field is very similar to using them in an Authors field. Follow these steps:

1. In the Designer client, open the database containing the Readers field.

2. Open the form that contains the Readers field.

3. Enter a formula that returns the name of the group(s) to include, or enable the user to enter/select the group(s) in an editable field.

4. Save the form.

Only users, servers, or groups (remember that you can nest groups) named in the group(s) stored in the Authors field are granted permission to read the documents.

Signing

Digital signatures are rapidly becoming an accepted means for legally transacting business in today's world. In fact, Congress recently passed a bill allowing digital signatures to be used to consummate a contract. Although this recent press has brought digital signatures into the lexicon of everyday people, they are nothing new to Notes/Domino users. Notes/Domino users have long been able to use digital signatures to sign fields when they save or mail sensitive data, which authenticates the identity of the sender and ensures the integrity of the data.

When a field is signed, Notes uses the private key of the author's ID and the value of the field being signed (using a hashing algorithm) to create a unique value that serves as the digital signature. When the recipient views the document, the same hashing algorithm is used to ensure that the data has not been altered and to test the public key of the sender to verify the user's identity.

Notes makes it very easy to use digital signatures to ensure the validity of a document. Any form that contains at least one field that has the Sign If Mailed or Saved in Section attribute enabled can be signed.

Set Form Access: Groups

As was mentioned earlier in this chapter, groups can be used to grant or deny access to Domino data and can ease the administrative burden substantially. This section covers using groups to secure various Domino elements: namely fields, forms, views, and sections.

By default, any user with Author access and the Create Documents privilege can create new documents and read existing documents (barring the use of a Readers field). However, Domino forms support Form Compose and Form Read Access lists, which can refine the ACL and further secure specific forms. Form Compose and Form Read Access lists specify users, servers, roles, and groups that can create new documents with the form and that can read documents with the form. Groups and roles provide an easily maintainable mechanism for restricting access through forms. To use a group or role to restrict who can read documents with a particular form, follow these steps:

1. In the Designer client, open the database containing the form.

2. Open the form you want to secure.

3. Choose Design, Form Properties from the menu, which opens the Form properties dialog box.

4. Click the Security tab (looks like a key).

5. Deselect All Readers and Above in the Default Read Access for Documents Created with This Form.

6. Select the group(s) and/or role(s) that should be assigned Read access from the existing list (derived from the ACL) or click the Add Read Access button to select groups from the Domino Directory.

7. Close the Form properties box.

To use a group and/or role to restrict who can compose documents with a particular form, follow these steps:

1. In the Designer client, open the database containing the form.

2. Open the form you want to secure.

3. Choose Design, Form Properties from the menu, which opens the Form properties dialog box.

4. Click the Security tab (looks like a key).

5. Deselect All Authors and Above in the Who Can Create Documents with This Form section.

6. Select the group(s) and/or role(s) that should be assigned Read access from the existing list (derived from the ACL) or click the Add Create Access button to select groups from the Domino Directory.

7. Close the Form properties box.

Set Section Access: Groups

Sections are a design element that can be used in forms to make them more user-friendly and to provide additional security. When used, sections create a collapsible and expandable area inside the form that can contain fields, text, layout regions, and embedded objects. Additionally, a section can be defined as an *access-controlled section*, which restricts the ability to edit fields within the section to named users.

NOTE: Remember that the Edit Access list of a section merely refines the Database Access Control List—it does not override it. In short, a user must have Editor access or higher to edit a document.

To add an access-controlled section to a form, follow these steps:

1. In the Designer client, open the database containing the form in which you want to add an access-controlled section.

2. Open the form.

3. Position the cursor to the location on the form where the section should appear.

4. Choose Create, Section, Controlled Access.

5. Click the Access Formula tab (the third tab) on the Form Section properties box.

6. Select the type of edit access you want to create: Editable, Computed, Computed for Display, or Computed when Composed.

7. Enter a list of usernames, groups, and/or roles that should have Edit access to the section; or enter a formula that evaluates to a list of usernames, groups, and/or roles that should have Edit access to the section.

8. Save and test the form.

Troubleshoot Mail-Enabled Field Problems: Field Attributes

When using fields to enable mail routing in workflow applications, using incorrect field values, incorrect parameters, or the wrong number of parameters can cause the workflow to fail. It is important to understand the action caused by setting reserved field values and some errors commonly encountered when designing workflow-enabled applications.

When building mail-enabled forms, you often use reserved fields that have built-in functionality. Many of the reserved fields work in tandem with one another, whereas others override the functionality of one another.

For example, if the MailOptions field is set to "1" and the On Close: Present Send Mail Dialog option is enabled within the Form properties box, the MailOptions overrides the current user's choice selected in the On Close: Present Send Mail Dialog check box. Therefore, if MailOptions is set to "1," users can select Yes to save the document, No to close without saving, or Cancel to return to the document. The form will be routed regardless of the user's selection. In addition, when implementing mail routing, if the MailOptions field is set to "1" and the user triggers the document to be mailed by using a @MailSend function (possibly located within a button), the document is mailed twice.

Also, if the Sign, Encrypt, or SaveOptions fields are set to a value of "1," they will override the form property On Close: Present Send Mail Dialog. Even though they override the values in the Send Mail dialog box, they do not change what is displayed within the dialog box.

If the Sign, Encrypt, or SaveOptions fields are set to a value of "1," they override the user's setting in the Document Save dialog box.

Troubleshoot Mail-Enabled Form Problems: Workflow-Related

Some common problems encountered when using mail-enabled forms are found when setting form formulas.

A *form formula* is used within views or folders to determine which form is to be used to create or display documents opened from within the view or folder. The form formula can be used to help present different information to different users throughout the workflow process, and it thus helps users to work more efficiently. Because forms provide a structure to display the document data, different forms for different users or different stages of the process can display the information and functionality more appropriately. If documents have the design of the form stored with them (a capability that can be enabled when the document is created), the stored form design is used. Refer to Chapter 5 for more information on storing a form in a document. The order of precedence Domino uses when determining which form is to display the document is described in Table 11.8.

Table 11.8 Opening Documents with Forms in Order of Precedence	
Condition	**Result**
Form stored in document	The design elements stored within the document are used.
Form formula	If the view used to open the document has a form formula defined, the form value resulting from the formula is used.
Form item value	The form defined in the Form item field within the document is used.
Default form	If none of the preceding conditions are met, the form design element defined as the default form is used.

Form formulas must evaluate to a text value, equal to one of the forms available within the current database. It is a good development practice to always use aliases when designing forms (and other design elements). You typically want to use the form alias name in the form formula so that subsequent name changes to the displayed form name do not affect the functionality. The form formulas can be a simple text value (such as "Main") or a formula that evaluates to a text value (such as `@If(Status = "Denied"; "frmDenied"; Status = "Accepted"; "FrmAccepted"; "frmMain")`.

Follow these steps to create a form formula:

1. Open the view in the Domino Designer client.

2. Select Form Formula in the View, Objects list.

3. Enter the formula or text value for the form.

4. Save the modified view.

Troubleshoot Workflow Distribution Problems

A common problem with Domino applications is found in the area of replication. Although replication is one of the more powerful features of Domino, it can also cause confusion among users, administrators, and developers! The following sections detail some of the more common issues involved in troubleshooting workflow distribution problems.

Replication

Database replicas are special database copies of Notes databases that share the same replica ID. Database replicas enable users to use the same application in different locations (including locally while disconnected from the server), on different networks, or in different time zones. The replica ID ensures that the database replicas and the source database remain linked and can be synchronized.

Notes databases can have different filenames and still be replica copies of one another. As long as they share the same replica ID, they will replicate (either manually or on a scheduled basis). The filenames are irrelevant in regard to replication. All replicas created from the same source database share the same replica ID.

Here are some benefits of creating database replicas:

➤ Improve performance on heavily used databases.

➤ Distribute network traffic.

➤ Separate the development database from the production database.

➤ Ensure that a database is available if the production version becomes unavailable.

➤ Make the database available to users in remote locations.

➤ Create a replica containing a subset of the information that is relevant to a particular group.

➤ Allow for administration on the current server where the replica is located.

➤ Create a backup database to help restore corrupted data (corrupted documents can replicate, so this method may prove to be ineffective).

As users access different replica databases, the documents created, deleted, modified, and edited in the replicas become out of sync. The process of synchronizing the data in each database is called *replication*.

Designers can create replicas by using one of two methods:

➤ *Use the administrative process*—This method is used when you want to create replicas of multiple databases on multiple destination servers.

➤ *Manually create replica copies*—This method is used when you want to adjust replication and other database settings when creating the replica or you do not have access to use the administrative process.

After they have been created, database replicas exchange all document edits, additions, and deletions (assuming the servers have access to replicate with one another and appropriate database ACL settings).

➤ Limit the contents of a replica.

➤ Limit what a replica sends to other replicas.

➤ Assign miscellaneous replication settings, such as a replication priority.

 For the exam, remember that you must have at least Manager access to set or modify the replication settings for a database.

Successful replication is paramount in ensuring that the workflow application is successful. Users may be working on local database replicas, then replicating with the server. Similarly, there will likely be replication amongst multiple servers in a wide area network or global Domino installation. If you are experiencing replication problems, you should contact your system administrator. The administrator can evaluate the server log and other specific replication settings to help troubleshoot any issues.

If it appears that documents are not replicating between database replicas, the first corrective action is to clear the replication history of one or, if required, both the databases.

To clear the replication history of a database, follow these steps:

1. Select the database.

2. Select File, Replication, History (see Figure 11.9).

3. Click Clear.

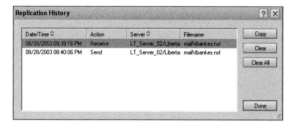

Figure 11.9 The Replication History dialog box.

Table 11.9 describes some common replication problems and probable fixes for each problem.

Table 11.9 Replication Problems and Possible Fixes	
Problem	**Possible Fix**
Replicas are different sizes.	➤ Design or document modifications have been made on one version and not yet replicated.
	➤ Replication setting causes a subset of the documents to replicate.
	➤ The documents on the source server contain reader names, which do not contain the destination server.
	➤ A view is used on one replica but not another.
	➤ One replica has personal agents, views, or folders.
	➤ One replica database has been compacted, whereas the other has not.
The source server has insufficient access.	Set the source server with higher access in the destination database ACL.
There is no destination server in an access list.	Add the destination server to the access list in the source server replica.
An intermediate server has insufficient access.	If an intermediate server lies between the source and destination server, give the intermediate server enough access to replicate all changes.

Table 11.9 Replication Problems and Possible Fixes *(continued)*	
Problem	**Possible Fix**
Replication settings are filtering documents.	Check the replication settings to ensure that documents are not being filtered.
The server is out of disk space.	Make sure the database has not exceeded the maximum database size and that the server is not out of disk drive space.
Older documents are not replicated to the new replica.	Check the Only Replicate Incoming Documents Saved or Modified After replication setting. You may have to create a new replica with an earlier date specified.
Deletions are not replicating.	➤ The source server must have Editor access or higher and have access to delete documents. ➤ The setting for Do Not Send Deletions Made in This Replica to Other Replicas is enabled on the source server. ➤ The deletions option under the setting for Replicate Incoming is not selected.
Replication cannot proceed because the databases cannot maintain uniform Access Control Lists on replicas.	The database ACL option is enabled for Enforce a Consistent Access Control List Across All Replicas of This Database.
A database replica is not receiving design changes.	The database replica on the destination server must give the source server at least Designer access, and the source server replica must give the destination server at least Reader access.
Changes to the database title do not replicate.	The replication setting for Do Not Send Changes in Database Title & Catalog Info to Other Replicas is enabled.
You receive the message **Database is not fully initialized yet**.	➤ A replica stub on a workstation hasn't been manually replicated. ➤ The server storing the replica stub doesn't have adequate access to pull information. ➤ A connection document between servers has not been created. ➤ Replication is disabled in one of the databases.
Unexpected deletions occur in a replica.	➤ A new replication formula is in place that overrides the previous formula and removes documents that do not match the formula. ➤ A replication setting is automatically removing older, unmodified documents.

Table 11.9 Replication Problems and Possible Fixes *(continued)*	
Problem	**Possible Fix**
Deleted documents reappear.	➤ A purge interval prevents replication of deletions.
	➤ A document edit writes over a document deletion.

Roles

Roles contain a subset of the database users, groups, or servers to provide or restrict access to particular database design elements, functions, or document contents. Because they are contained within the database Access Control List, they have a profound affect on the application and what permissions users are granted within the application.

A *role* in a workflow process refers to who or what initiates an action or is the recipient of an action. Roles provide a mechanism to define groups within a database. The types of work that users perform typically fall into similar functions or roles. Grouping users by function and roles creates a better design because functionality can then be built to use generic role names rather than specific usernames or group names. After roles have been established, they can be used to determine access to views, forms, documents, sections, fields, or functionality. The advantages of using roles include the following:

➤ Uses a flexible method to restrict access to a specific set of users.

➤ Can be used in formulas.

➤ Provides a method to define a group of users within a database or application.

➤ Simplifies the process of modifying any users for an application that change roles, are added, or are removed, because the application design does not need to be modified.

Roles help define and further refine control and user capabilities within the application. Using roles, you can programmatically control who can

➤ Access specific views and folders.

➤ Create documents.

➤ Read documents.

➤ Edit documents.

➤ Access sections within documents.

Defining roles makes it easier to refine the workflow process and security. Some items to consider when troubleshooting roles include the following:

➤ Identify and document the object(s) in the workflow. Keep in mind that a workflow may have multiple objects.

➤ Create a flowchart diagram of the business process. This flowchart should illustrate the relationship between workflow objects, people, and tasks.

➤ After the workflow elements have been determined and placed in a flow-chart, the process can be analyzed to determine the process of automation.

 Roles are not enforced when users are accessing a local copy of a database unless the setting to Enforce a Consistent Access Control List Across All Replicas of This Database has been enabled.

Routing

Problems with routing could be the result of invalid mail addresses, bugs in the code, or a poorly defined process.

Routing is the start, intermediate, and end points of the workflow process.

To troubleshoot routing problems in workflow distribution, first identify and document the start, end, and intermediary points of workflow. Describe and document each point in terms of the objects handled and persons within each functional area and role. The trouble encountered within the routing process determines the action plan for resolving the routing trouble.

Rules

Rules are at the heart of a workflow application. They are defined by existing or newly created business processes and procedures. Developing these rules involves nothing more than a technical implementation of rules that exist independent of the technology. Nevertheless, because the rules and their implementation within the application control the workflow, they must be correctly defined within the application.

Rules are any rules or conditions that affect the workflow object. Rules help determine various formulas that apply to workflow and security issues within an application.

To troubleshoot workflow distribution problems related to rules, identify and document the rules that control decision points. Describe the normal or default action, exception handling, and anticipated outcomes. Often, the problems associated with rules are a result of an incorrectly defined workflow and business process. That is, they may not be a result of technical issues. Nevertheless, it is important that the rules be clearly defined and understood prior to development.

Summary

Workflow, groupware, process automation, and knowledge management are major considerations in the deployment of Lotus Notes/Domino applications. The functionality of workflow makes these types of solutions attainable. Implementing workflow-enabled applications offers many benefits, including the following:

➤ Reduces overhead and production costs.

➤ Reduces errors.

➤ Makes processes more efficient and reduces their cycle time.

➤ Facilitates the capability to track the status of projects or tasks.

The topics in this chapter will not only assist you passing the certification exam, but will also assist in helping you achieve the outlined goals when designing your own Domino applications.

Exam Prep Questions

Question 1

> Public and private keys can be used to do all but what?
>
> ❑ A. Encrypt mail.
>
> ❑ B. Encrypt databases.
>
> ❑ C. Sign subforms.
>
> ❑ D. Sign sections.

Answer C is correct. Public and private keys cannot encrypt subforms. Answers A, B, and D are incorrect because Public and private keys can be used to encrypt all three of these element types.

Question 2

> Jake wants to create a secret encryption key. How would Jake go about doing this?
>
> ❑ A. Open the User Security dialog box by selecting File, User Preferences from the pull-down menu.
>
> ❑ B. Open the User Security dialog box by selecting File, Security, User Security from the pull-down menu.
>
> ❑ C. Select Create, Encryption Key from the pull-down menu.
>
> ❑ D. Users cannot create encryption keys. Jake must contact the System Administrator.

Answer B is correct. The User Security dialog box can be opened from the pull-down menu by selecting File, Security, User Security. Then clicking on Notes Data, Documents from the left navigator opens the Document Encryption screen. From there, Jake clicks on New Secret Key to open the New Secret Encryption Key dialog. Answer A is incorrect because this option has been moved since release 5. Answer C is incorrect because this is not a valid menu option. Answer D is incorrect because, as previously mentioned, the system administrator does not need to be contacted to create a New Secret Key.

Question 3

Which of the following keyword field types displays the list of people, servers, groups, and roles in the ACL of the current database?

❏ A. Use Access Control List for Choices.

❏ B. Use Address Dialog for Choices.

❏ C. Use Names Dialog for Choices.

❏ D. Use View Dialog for Choices.

Answer A is correct. The keyword field type of Use Access Control List for Choices displays the list of people, servers, groups, and roles in the ACL of the current database. Answer B is incorrect because the Use Address dialog for choices displays the Name dialog box to select names from the Domino directory. Answer C is incorrect because there is no Names dialog. Answer D is incorrect because the Use View dialog for choices displays a dialog box displaying entries from a column in an existing view.

Question 4

If a user is listed both explicitly and implicitly in the database ACL, what is true regarding the rights granted to the user?

❏ A. The lowest rights granted take precedence.

❏ B. The highest rights granted take precedence.

❏ C. The rights granted in the group take precedence.

❏ D. The rights granted to the explicit name take precedence.

Answer D is correct. Despite which access rights are higher between the explicit listing and the groups, the rights granted to the explicit name take precedence. Answer A, B, and C are wrong because which rights are highest (or lowest) are irrelevant when the user is explicitly listed.

Question 5

A document was previously created using the Store Form in document. Since then, the following items were removed from the document: **$Title**, **$Info**, **$WindowTitle**, and **$Body**. Which of the following options takes precedence in determining the form with which the document is opened?

- ❏ A. Form stored in document.
- ❏ B. Form formula.
- ❏ C. Form item value.
- ❏ D. Default form.

Answer B is correct. If the $Title, $Info, $WindowTitle, and $Body items are removed, effectively the form stored in the document is removed as well. Therefore, answer A is incorrect and B is correct because the next item to be used based upon its precedence is the Form formula (if one has been specified in the view). Answers C and D are incorrect because they have a lower precedence that B.

Question 6

Roles help define and further refine control and user capabilities within the application. Using roles, you can programmatically control who can do all of the following, except

- ❏ A. Access specific views and folders.
- ❏ B. Create documents and edit documents.
- ❏ C. Read documents.
- ❏ D. Access sections within documents.
- ❏ E. All of the above are correct.

Answer E is correct. Roles can programmatically control who can do all of the options displayed.

Need to Know More?

 Lotus Developer Domain. *Domino 6 Technical Overview*. Available on the Web at http://www.lotus.com/ldd.

 IBM International Technical Support Organization. *Domino Designer 6: A Developer's Handbook*. Available in printed form, PDF format, and HTML format from http://publib-b.boulder.ibm.com/ Redbooks.nsf/RedbookAbstracts/sg246854.html?Open.

 IBM Lotus. *Release Notes*. http://www-10.lotus.com/ldd/notesua.nsf/ RN?OpenView.

 IBM Lotus. *Online Help Databases*. help6_admin.nsf, help6_client.nsf, help6_designer.nsf.

Programming

Terms you'll need to understand:

✓ Formula
✓ @Function
✓ @Command
✓ Section
✓ Integrated Development Environment (IDE)

✓ Auto-complete
✓ Domino Designer
✓ Design Pane
✓ Work Pane

Concepts you'll need to master:

✓ Enabling Option Declare
✓ Creating formulas with @Commands
✓ Creating formulas with @Functions
✓ Using In-View editors
✓ Encrypting sections
✓ Controlling section access
✓ Signing sections
✓ Using Auto-complete
✓ Using hidden columns to sort data

✓ Using layout regions in dialog boxes
✓ Understanding the Domino Designer
✓ Working with Name values
✓ Programming columns using other column values
✓ Use applets to enhance applications
✓ Making preferred tools available in the IDE
✓ Using preferred and third-party tools in the IDE

This chapter covers the Domino 6 programming topics that you'll need to know to take and pass Exam 611, including In-View editing, @Commands, @Functions, sections, name values, and applets.

Domino Programming

Domino 6 is a powerful application development environment that enables you to rapidly build applications by using a variety of application development tools and programming languages. Domino 6 supports the following programming languages: Notes Formulas (Formula Language), LotusScript, Java, and JavaScript. The Notes Formula language is the oldest of the four and has been around since the inception of Notes. It is a fairly easy-to-learn and easy-to-use programming language, and you can accomplish some coding tasks in Notes only by using the Formula language!

Formula Basics

Lotus defines a *formula* as "an expression that has program-like attributes" (Lotus Designer Help database). Some of the many things you can do with formulas are

➤ Create selection criteria for a view.

➤ Validate a field.

➤ Return a value to a field.

➤ Manipulate the value of a field.

➤ Transform the value of a field.

➤ Create new fields in a document.

➤ Perform actions when documents are opened, refreshed, or closed.

➤ Program agents.

➤ Return a value in a view column.

➤ Automate buttons or hotspots.

➤ Program replication formulas.

Domino Integrated Development Environment (IDE) Basics

All code, including the Formula language, is written in the Domino's user-friendly *Integrated Development Environment* (IDE), known as the *Domino Designer*. An Integrated Development Environment is an application development tool that provides a robust, complete toolset that includes debugging and online help capabilities. The *Domino Designer* IDE (Designer for short) is shown in Figure 12.1.

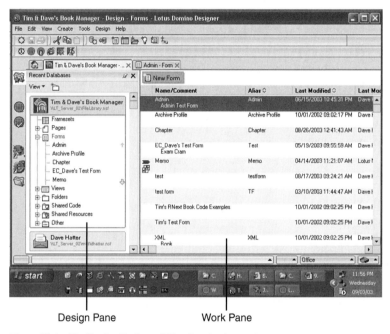

Design Pane   Work Pane

Figure 12.1 The Domino Designer IDE makes development a snap.

The Domino Designer Application and Design Environment

Although there are numerous ways to open the Domino Designer, the easiest is to select a database and right-click it, which displays a pop-up menu. Select Open in Designer, which opens the Domino Designer shown earlier in Figure 12.1.

There are two basic "panes" within the Domino Designer window: the Design Pane and the Work Pane. The *Design Pane* maintains a list of databases that have recently been opened in the Designer, as well as a list of the design elements they contain. You can click the type of design element on which you want to work, and the Designer displays a list of those elements in the Work Pane.

The *Work Pane* displays a list of design elements of a given type, such as forms, views, or agents, within the selected database. A developer can then double-click the design element to open it, which then modifies the display of the Designer, as shown in Figure 12.2.

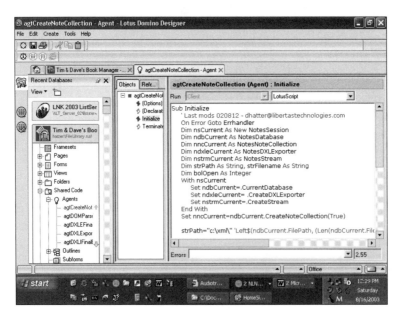

Figure 12.2 An agent ready to be coded.

Opening a design element such as an agent makes Designer split the window into three panes. The Design Pane remains on the left side of the screen, providing quick and easy navigation between elements and databases, while the Work Pane is displayed at the top of the screen and is joined by the Programmer's Pane displayed at the bottom of the screen, as shown in Figure 12.2. The design element opened is displayed in the Work Pane and developers can modify user interface elements of the selected element, such as adding fields to a form, or modifying the columns within a view.

The Programmer's Pane at the bottom is used to enter programming code and provides a plethora of handy features that will simplify and speed your development efforts.

Automatically Enable Option Declare

The bane of all experienced LotusScript programmers is the use of implicitly declared variables, which are variables that are not formally declared in the code before they are used. The LotusScript language enables developers to manually specify that all variables be formally declared before they are used (explicit declaration) through the use of the Option Declare statement in the Options section. Designer 6 now enables you to automatically insert the Option Declare statement in the Options section, ensuring that developers must explicitly declare their variables, which is a good idea because it ensures cleaner, more maintainable code.

It is a best practice to require explicit variable declaration. The Option Declare statement is a handy new feature that makes it easier to write good code. I highly recommend that you enable this feature.

To enable this option, open an element coded in LotusScript and follow these steps:

1. Right-click in the Programmer's Pane and choose Programmer's Pane Properties from the menu, which opens the Programmer's Pane Properties dialog box.

2. Click the Format tab (second tab) to access the Format options, shown in Figure 12.3.

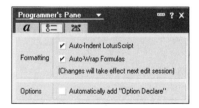

Figure 12.3   The Format tab's options.

3. Click the Automatically Add "Option Declare" check box in the Options section.

Using the Programmer's Pane Auto-complete

Auto-complete is a very handy new feature of Domino 6 that uses type-ahead functionality to select and paste certain syntax elements directly into the

Programmer's Pane as you are coding. If the syntax element that you have selected takes parameters, the valid parameters are displayed in the pop-up to help guide you as you code.

Auto-completion is available when coding the following:

➤ @Commands

➤ @Functions

➤ LotusScript classes

Using the Auto-complete with @Functions

Auto-complete is a handy new tool that can aid developers using *@Functions* to code formulas. An @Function is a native function that can perform a calculation or task and return a value. To use Auto-complete when coding @Functions in the Programmer's Pane, follow these steps.

1. Enter the "at" symbol (@) and pause momentarily to launch the Auto-complete pop-up, which displays a list of all available choices, as shown in Figure 12.4.

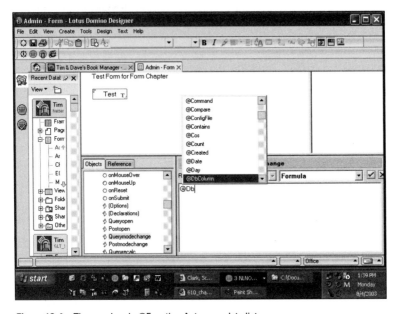

Figure 12.4   The very handy @Function Auto-complete list.

2. Begin typing the name of a function (type-ahead) or scroll through the list and select the appropriate function. For example:

```
@Left(
```

3. After you have located the functions, press Enter to paste the function into the Programmer's Pane and close the pop-up list.

4. Optionally, for functions that take parameters, type a left parenthesis "(" to launch a pop-up containing the syntax of the first signature. The first valid parameter appears bolded. If up and down arrows display, they indicate that you can press the up and down arrow keys to display the various options.

5. Optionally, if the function takes multiple parameters, enter a semicolon (;) between each parameter, and the next parameter appears bolded.

6. Enter a right parenthesis ")" to complete the function, or press Esc to close the pop-up.

Using Auto-complete with @Commands

Auto-complete can also help developers using *@Commands* to code formulas. @Commands are a special type of @Function that provide a mechanism for developers to programmatically execute a Lotus Notes/Domino command. To use Auto-complete when coding @Commands in the Programmer's Pane, follow these steps:

1. Enter the "at" symbol (@) and pause momentarily to launch the Auto-complete pop-up, which displays a list of all available choices, as shown in Figure 12.5.

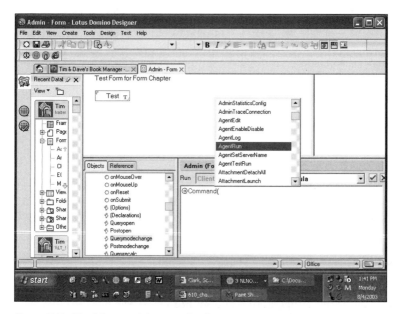

Figure 12.5 The @Command Auto-complete list.

2. Begin typing `Command` (type-ahead) or scroll through the list and select @Command, which then displays a list of valid commands. For example:

   `@Command(`

3. Begin typing the name of the desired command (type-ahead) or scroll through the list and select the appropriate command. After a command is selected, square brackets ([ ]) are added automatically. For example:

   `@Command([AddBookmark])`

4. Optionally, for commands that take parameters, type a left parenthesis "(" to launch a pop-up containing the syntax of the first signature. The first valid parameter appears bolded. If up and down arrows display, they indicate that you can press the up and down arrow keys to display the various options.

5. Optionally, if the command takes multiple parameters, enter a semicolon (;) between each parameter, and the next parameter appears bolded.

6. Enter a right parenthesis ")" to complete the command, or press Esc to close the pop-up.

Using Auto-complete with LotusScript

With LotusScript, follow these steps to use Auto-complete when coding @Commands in the Programmer's Pane:

1. Declare an object and enter a space following the As keyword to open a pop-up list of available classes, as shown in Figure 12.6.

2. Begin typing the name of a valid object, or scroll through the list and select the appropriate object.

3. Optionally, enter a period (.) after an object name, which opens a pop-up of methods and properties.

4. Optionally, from the pop-up list of methods and properties, either type ahead to select the desired element or scroll through the list and select it. Press Enter to paste the element into the Programmer's Pane.

5. Optionally, for methods that take parameters, type a left parenthesis "(" to display a pop-up box displaying the parameter list. The first parameter appears bolded.

6. Optionally, enter a comma (,) between each parameter, which makes the next parameter bolded.

7. Enter a right parenthesis ")" or press Esc to close the pop-up.

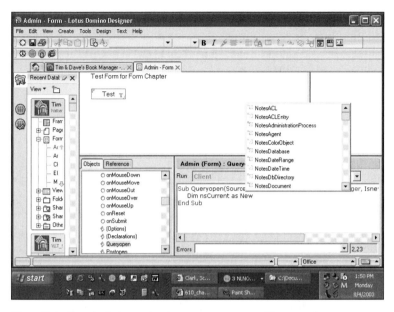

Figure 12.6 Type the **As** keyword and enter a space to open this pop-up list.

Using Find and Replace in the Programmer's Pane

Another very useful feature of the Programmer's Pane is the Find and Replace capability it provides. In a nutshell, Find and Replace works much like the Windows find and replace tools: It enables you to quickly and easily find text in your code and optionally replace it. Using Find and Replace is quite simple. In the Programmer's Pane press Ctrl+F or choose Edit, Find/Replace from the menu, either of which opens the Find and Replace dialog box, as shown in Figure 12.7.

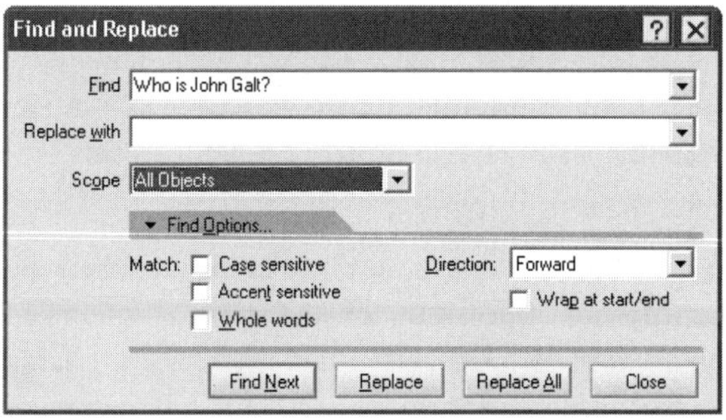

Figure 12.7 The Find and Replace dialog box is a powerful development ally.

Using Find and Replace is pretty straightforward. Enter the text string to find in the Find box, or select a previous entry in the dropdown (it conveniently remembers previous searches) and choose the scope of the search in the Scope box. You have three choices for scope:

➤ *Current Object*—search all code within the current object

➤ *Current Section Only*—search only the current section of code

➤ *All Objects*—Search all code related objects in the current element

After you have entered the text to search for and selected the scope, click the Find Next button to initiate a search. You can then continue to click the Find Next button to find all the matching text strings. If you want to replace the text for which you are searching, simply enter a new text string in the Replace box and then click the Replace button to replace the current text, or click the Replace All button to replace all matching instances.

The Find and Replace dialog also has several advanced searching features that enable you to further refine and speed your searches. These options include:

➤ Case sensitive

➤ Accent sensitive

➤ Whole words

➤ Direction

➤ Wrap at start/end

Making Preferred Tools Available via the IDE

Another cool new feature in the Domino 6 Designer is the really cool capability to customize and extend the Tools menu in the Designer client. You can now include menu items that launch other commonly used applications such as a graphics editing tool or CSS editor, or you can write your own formulas to run. You can also create submenus under which you can group related tools. A customized Tools menu is shown in Figure 12.8, later in this section.

Additionally, when you add a new tool to the menu, you can define when the tool will be available so that the tool appears in the menu only when you need it. For example, you might want to keep your graphics editor available all the time, whereas the CSS editor menu option appears only when you are editing a form, page, or subform.

Be prepared to see questions about the new Tools menu options on the exam.

Adding a New Tool to the Tools Menu

Adding a new tool to the Tools menu is easy; just follow these steps:

1. Select Tools, Add Tool from the menu in the Designer client, which opens the Add Tool dialog box, shown in Figure 12.8.

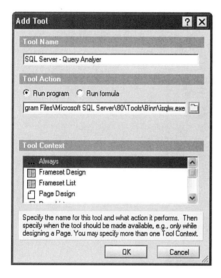

Figure 12.8   The Add Tool dialog box makes it easy to add Tools menu options.

2. Enter a descriptive name for the menu option in the Tool Name field. Make sure to use a name you'll recognize later as this is what will be displayed in the Tools menu.

3. Choose Run Program or Run Formula for the Tool Action, based on these guidelines:

   ➤ To launch an external application from the menu, choose Run Program and then either enter the path for the executable file to launch, or click the file folder icon to browse the file system to select the executable.

   ➤ To run a custom coded formula, select Run Formula and enter a formula.

4. In the Tool Context box, choose one or more contexts in which the new menu option should be displayed. To ensure that the tool is always displayed, choose Always; otherwise, select one or more contexts in which the menu item should be displayed.

5. Click OK to save the tool and add the new option to the Tools menu.

Editing a Custom Tool

After you have added a custom tool, it appears in the Tools menu for the contexts you defined.

To edit an existing custom tool, follow these steps:

1. Select Tools, Customize Tools from the menu, which opens the Customize Tools dialog box shown in Figure 12.9.

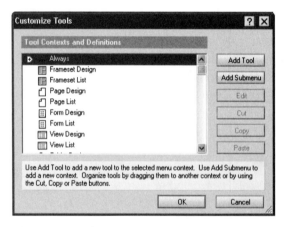

Figure 12.9 The Customize Tools dialog box.

2. Select the context that contains the tool to be modified and click the arrow beside it to expand the list of tools in that design context.

3. Select the tool and click the Edit button to edit the name of the tool and/or the formula that it executes.

Tools that launch an executable program actually use the **@command([Execute])** command to run the executable.

4. Click OK to save changes.

Deleting a Tool from the Tools Menu

To delete a tool from the Tools menu, follow these steps:

1. Select Tools, Customize Tools from the menu, which opens the Customize Tools dialog box shown earlier in Figure 12.9.

2. Select the context that contains the tool to be deleted and click the arrow beside it to expand the list of tools in that design context.

3. Select the tool and click Cut to remove it.

Customizing the Tools Menu

To further enhance its usability, you can divide the Tools menu into logical- ly grouped categories by sing submenus. Figure 12.10 shows my customized Tools menu.

Figure 12.10   Customizing the Tools menu is a handy way to speed development.

To add a submenu to the Tools menu, follow these steps:

1. Select Tools, Customize Tools from the menu, which opens the Customize Tools dialog box shown in Figure 12.10.

2. Select the context in which the submenu should display and then click the Add Submenu button, which opens a prompt.

3. Enter a name for the submenu in the Submenu name field and click OK.

4. Position the submenu and its children within the selected context by using either drag and drop or the copy and paste buttons.

Designing Applications and Choosing Appropriate Coding Options

Domino provides many coding options, making it a flexible tool for building powerful applications. Domino 6 supports the following programming options:

➤ *Simple actions*—Pre-defined functions that can be used to automate tasks with no programming. Simple actions are not customizable and are not supported on the Web.

➤ *Formulas*—Formulas are a non-procedural, interpreted language. In many cases, the Formula language is the easiest, most efficient language to use, especially when you want to do something simple, such as update a field in all the documents in a view. (This can be accomplished by building an agent that has one line of code!) Additionally, some places in Notes support only the Formula language, such as view selection formulas, view column formulas, form formulas, hide-when formulas, field default formulas, field translations formulas, and field validation formulas.

➤ *LotusScript*—LotusScript was introduced in Notes R4.0 as a more robust alternative to the Formula language, enabling developers to write structured, robust programs that take advantage of standard programming constructs such as branching, looping, iteration, and user-defined functions. It is an interpreted language, designed as a variant of Visual Basic (VB) so that developers who were already familiar with VB could quickly transition into the Notes/Domino development.

LotusScript is most often used in agents to automate complicated tasks. Although it can be used to interact with the user through the Notes User Interface (UI), it is not a good choice for Web or hybrid applications because it cannot be used directly over the Web in the same way that the Formula language can. The only way to run LotusScript over the Web is by calling an agent through the `WebQueryOpen` and the `WebQuerySave` event of a form, or by using the Domino URL syntax to call an agent, as in the following manner:

```
http://www.libertastechnologies.com/exancram.nsf/test?OpenAgent
```

➤ *JavaScript*—A client-side, industry standard scripting language that can be used in both Notes client and Web-based applications. Anytime you are building applications that are intended to serve both Notes and Web clients, it's a good idea to use JavaScript to script things such as form validations, field change events, and other client-oriented events and actions. JavaScript is the only language that is supported in both the Notes client and Web environment, making it very easy to write an application that runs in both places.

➤ *Java*—A powerful, robust, object-oriented programming language that is syntactically similar to C++. Although support for Java was first introduced in Notes 4.5, Lotus has recognized the significance of Java to the future of Web-based application development and has significantly enhanced the capability to code in Java. You can now use Java to write native Domino agents in the Designer, you can import existing Java code into agents, you can write Java applications and/or applets that use CORBA (Common Object Request Broker Architecture) to access Domino objects, or you can write Java servlets.

Choosing the right coding option is dependent upon four primary considerations: the context in which the code will be used, what the code needs to do, which coding option provides the best performance, and which coding option best leverages your skill set.

In some instances, such as view selection and column formulas, you can use only simple actions or formulas because the other coding options are not supported in this context. In other instances, such as writing agents, you can use any coding choice except JavaScript, depending on exactly what you need to accomplish. More often than not, there is no one right choice and your skills and experience will dictate the best coding option.

Coding Formulas

In Domino, formulas can be used to accomplish many programming objectives, including

➤ Automating tasks

➤ Acting on a condition

➤ Comparing values

➤ Computing values

➤ Modifying values

➤ Creating selection criteria: views, agents, and replication formulas

➤ Validating information

The Formula language processes back-end Notes objects, much like the back-end classes in LotusScript, whereas @Commands (a special type of @Function covered in detail in the next section) operate in the user interface. Changes made using @Commands are not reflected in the back-end (stored documents) until a document is saved, whereas changes made using @Functions are made in real time to the stored documents. A formula is composed of one or more @Functions, which consist of any of the elements listed in Table 12.1.

Table 12.1	Formula Elements
Element	**Description**
@Commands	Similar to functions, @Commands execute Notes commands, most of which duplicate menu options such as File, Save.
@Functions	Prebuilt functions that perform a specific action and return a result.
Constants	Static values that do not change. Notes supports three types of constants: Text, Number, and Date. The following is an example of a text constant: **Samuel Hatter**.
Variables	A named placeholder that refers to a location in memory that stores information that may change (hence the name *variable*) during the execution of the program.
Keywords	Statements that perform special functions. There are five: **DEFAULT**, **ENVIRONMENT**, **FIELD**, **REM**, and **SELECT**.
Operators	Operators assign values and modify values. Domino supports a large number of operators.

Domino enables you to write one or more @Functions in a formula; functions are executed top to bottom and left to right, completing each statement before proceeding to the next with some minor exceptions. `@PostedCommand` and certain other @Command functions are executed in the order they appear *after* all other @functions complete execution. The @Functions are covered in more detail in the next section.

The remainder of this section is not intended to be an exhaustive compendium of formula functions and commands; there are far too many! Rather, it is intended to provide an overview of how they are used. You can refer to the Domino Designer Help database (**Help6_Designer.nsf**) for a comprehensive list.

Working with @Functions

@Functions have been around since the very beginning of Notes and they are the foundation of formula language development in Domino. An *@Function* is a native function that can perform a calculation or task and return a value.

All @Functions follow the same basic syntax, which consists of the "at" symbol (@), the function name, an opening parenthesis "(", a semicolon-separated list of arguments, if any, and a closing parenthesis ")". The following code snippet illustrates the basic syntax for an @Function:

```
@functionname([argument1];[argumentn]);
```

The following examples illustrate several @Function variations:

```
@Now;
@Count(listofvalues);
@Left(searchinstring;searchforstring);
@Prompt([style];title;prompt);
```

 Not all @Functions take parameters; for those that don't, simply omit the parameters. For those that do take parameters, the parentheses are required.

Some functions use special arguments known as *keyword arguments*, which must be enclosed in square brackets ([]). The following is a list of @Functions that take keyword arguments:

➤ @Abstract

➤ @Command

➤ @PostedCommand

➤ @DocMark

➤ @GetPortsList

➤ @PickList

➤ @MailSend

➤ @Name

➤ @Prompt

 Be sure to specify the correct data type for each argument per the @function description.

Some functions have a "side-effect," which according to the Domino online help is "an action that occurs outside the immediate scope of the formula." For example, @DbLookup performs a database lookup and returns a value. The following is a list of @Functions that have side-effects.

➤ @Command

➤ @PostedCommand

➤ @DbColumn

➤ @DbCommand

➤ @DbLookup

➤ @DDEInitiate

➤ @DDEExecute

➤ @DDEPoke

➤ @DDETerminate

➤ @MailSend

➤ @Prompt

➤ @PickList

➤ @DialogBox

Working with Name Values

Domino is an excellent platform for building secure applications, and names play a key role in the Domino security model. Each user has a username that Domino uses for identification, and as a developer you need to understand names and be aware of the formulas that you can use to work with them.

Domino uses a hierarchical naming scheme for users and servers where each name may include one of the following components:

➤ *Common name (CN)*—Specifies the username or server name. A common name is required in each name.

➤ *Organizational unit (OU)*—Specifies the location of the user or server within the organization. Organizational units are optional and a valid name may contain a maximum of four.

➤ *Organization (O)*—Specifies the organization to which a user or server belongs. The organization component is required.

➤ *Country (C)*—Specifies the country in which the organization exists. Country is optional.

Domino stores names internally in canonical format, which means that the component identifiers are stored with the name. A canonical name is shown here:

```
CN=John Galt/OU=Engineering/O=20thCenturyMotors/C=US
```

Typically, a Domino displays names in an abbreviated format that does not include the component identifiers. An abbreviated name is shown here:

```
John Galt/Engineering/20thCenturyMotors/US
```

Names are the foundation of the Domino security model and are used to grant or deny access at several levels in Domino, including

➤ *Server access*—Server access list

➤ *Database access*—Database access control list

➤ *Document access*—Readers and Authors fields

➤ *Section access*—Controlled access section

➤ *Field access*—Encrypted fields

➤ *Form and View access*—Form read and compose lists and view read lists

Developers must be familiar with the components of a Domino name as well as the many functions Domino provides to programmatically manipulate names. The following list contains the most common @Functions that can be used to work with Names.

➤ @UserName—Returns the current user or server name in canonical format.

```
@UserName
```

➤ @Name—Enables you to manipulate the components of a hierarchical name. For example, you can abbreviate a canonical name, expand an abbreviated name to its canonical format, or extract particular components within the name. The following examples illustrate some common usages of this function and the values returned for a user named CN=John Galt/OU=Engineering/O=20thCenturyMotors.

```
@Name([Abbreviated];@UserName);
```
Returns John Galt/Engineering/20thCenturyMotors

```
@Name([Canonicalize];@UserName);
```
Returns CN=John Galt/OU=Engineering/O=20thCenturyMotors

```
@Name([CN];@UserName);
```
Returns John Galt

```
@Name([O];@UserName);
```
Returns 20thCenturyMotors

```
@Name([OU];@UserName);
```
Returns Engineering

```
@Name([S];@UserName);
```
Returns Galt

➤ @UserNamesList—When a database is stored on a server, or a local database has Enforce a Consistent Access Control List Across All Replicas enabled, this function returns a text list containing the following information for the current user:

➤ Common name

➤ All hierarchical names that include the username

➤ Any roles associated with the user in the ACL

➤ Optionally, if the database is on the server, all groups to which the user belongs

Using Hidden Columns to Sort View Data

View sorts are based on the setting sort properties for the columns in the view, which are based on the physical order of the columns in the view from left to right. In a view with three columns, if the first two columns have been set to sort, the documents are first sorted based on the first column and then sub-sorted on the second column.

Developers often need to sort documents in a particular order, but don't necessarily want to display the data used for the sort to the user. They can do so easily if hidden sorted columns are added in the view.

To add a hidden sorted column to a view, follow these steps:

1. Open a view.

2. Click the first column in the view and choose Create, Insert New Column from the menu.

3. In the Programmer's Pane define the value of the column from one of the following:

➤ Simple action

➤ Field

➤ Formula

4. Double-click the new column to open the Column properties box.

5. Click the second tab to set the sorting options.

6. Click the fifth tab to hide the column. To do so, enable the Hide Column check box.

Using Layout Regions in Dialog Boxes

A layout region is a fixed-length design area on a form or subform that enables you to build Notes client applications that look and behave like other Windows applications. Layout regions can contain text, graphics, buttons, images, and any field types, with the exception of rich text fields.

Layout regions are not supported for Web applications.

A common developer trick is to use a layout region in a form that will be opened in a dialog box (using the @Dialogbox function or the DialogBox method of the NotesUiWorkspace class) to prompt a user for information, or to open a form in its own window. @DialogBox opens a window that displays your form and that has OK and Cancel buttons. When the user clicks the OK button, the contents of the fields in the dialog box are transferred to fields of the same name in the underlying document. If the user clicks the Cancel button, no information is transferred.

The following code snippet shows the @DialogBox function:

```
@DialogBox( form ; [AUTOHORZFIT] : [AUTOVERTFIT] : [NOCANCEL] :
➡)[NONEWFIELDS] : [NOFIELDUPDATE] : [READONLY] : [SIZETOTABLE] :
[NOOKCANCEL] :
➡)[OKCANCELATBOTTOM] ; title )
```

To use a layout region in a dialog box, follow these steps:

Figure 12.11 demonstrates this technique.

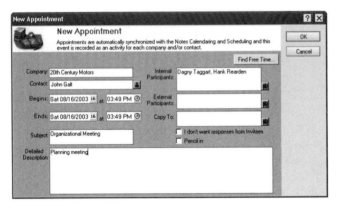

Figure 12.11   Using a dialog box to create an appointment.

1. Create a form that uses a layout region. Be sure to give the fields in the layout region the same names as the corresponding fields in the underlying form.

2. Create a button or action that uses the @Dialogbox function to open the form that contains the layout region.

Section Security

According to Lotus, a *section* "is a collapsible and expandable area defined on a form or subform." Sections can contain fields, objects, layout regions, and text, and are often used to save space on a form and to prevent unauthorized users from viewing certain information within a form or subform. Sections that restrict access are known as *access-controlled sections*, and sections can also be digitally signed and/or encrypted. The remainder of this section discusses the security options for sections.

Controlling Section Access

Access-controlled sections enable you to define users, groups, servers, and roles that can expand a section and view its contents. To create a controlled-access section, follow these steps:

1. Open the form or subform that will contain the section.

2. Select the text, fields, and other elements that you want encapsulated in the section.

3. From the menu, choose Create, Section, Controlled Access.

4. Optionally, enter the section properties, such as section title, border style, border color.

5. To specify the editors for the section, click the Formula tab (third tab).

6. In the Type drop-down, choose Editable to allow the document creator to specify the section editors, or choose one of the three computed types to write a formula that defines the section editors.

Signing Sections

Domino allows you to attach a digital signature to a section, which can be used to ensure that the contents of the section have not been tampered with. The following steps explain how to attach a signature to a section when the document is closed.

1. Open a form containing a controlled-access section.

2. Add at least one sign-enabled field in the section. To sign-enable a field, select the Sign If Mailed or Saved in Section property in the Security section of the Advanced tab (third tab) of the Field Properties box.

3. Save the form that contains the section.

Use Applets to Enhance Applications

Applets are self-contained Java programs that can be used in your Domino-based Web applications to mimic Notes client functionality and create a more Notes client-like experience for Web users. Lotus has provided four pre-built applets (defined below) that you can use in your applications. Using them is fairly simple; however, you should keep in mind that the applets require download time and may make the initial page load time seem excessive.

The predefined applets are built with Java Developer's Kit (JDK), Release 1.1.8, to support Java-enabled Web browsers.

You can use four pre-built applets in your applications:

➤ *View applet*—Enables Web users to interact with views much as they would with a Notes client. Mimics many of the traditional Domino view features, including column resizing, multiple document selection, and section collapse/expand without page regeneration.

➤ *Editor applet*—Enables Web users to change the font, color, size, and style for text in rich text fields, which would be rendered as simple a <TEXTAREA> in pure HTML.

➤ *Action bar applet*—Enables Web users to work with actions in a fixed area on the screen and to view and select subactions.

➤ *Outline applet*—Enables Web users to easily work with outlines embedded in a page or form.

Using the View Applet

The view applet can be used for views and embedded views. To display a view on the Web by using the view applet, follow these steps:

1. Open a view.

2. Choose Design, View Properties, which opens the View properties box.

3. Click the Advanced tab (fifth tab).

4. Enable the Use Applet in the Browser setting in the For Web Access section.

5. Optionally, configure other display properties.

6. Save the view.

To display an embedded view using the view applet, follow these steps:

1. Open a form or page that contains an embedded view.

2. Right-click the embedded element and choose Embedded View to open the Embedded View properties box.

3. On the info tab (first tab), in the Web Access field, choose from the following to specify how the view should be displayed:

   ➤ *Using Java Applet*—Display view using view applet regardless of the view's setting.

   ➤ *Using HTML*—The view applet is not used regardless of the view's setting.

   ➤ *Using View's Display Property*—Use the view's setting to determine whether the view applet is or is not used.

4. Optionally, configure other display properties.

5. Save the view.

Using the Editor Applet

To use the editor applet to display a rich text field, follow these steps:

1. Create or select a rich text field.

2. Right-click the field and choose Field Properties from the menu to open the Field properties box.

3. On the Field Info tab (first tab), enable Using Java Applet in the Display field of the Web Access section.

4. Optionally, configure other display properties.

5. Save the form.

Using the Action Bar Applet

To enable the action bar applet for Web users, follow these steps:

1. Open the form that contains the action bar.

2. Right-click the action bar and choose Action Bar Properties, which opens the Action Bar properties box.

3. In the Action Bar Info tab (first tab), choose Using Java Applet in the Display field of the Web Access section.

4. Optionally, configure other display properties.

5. Save the form.

To disable the applet, repeat steps 1 and 2, then select Using HTML in the Display field of the Web Access Section. Save the form.

Using the Outline Applet

To enable the outline applet for Web users, follow these steps:

1. Open a page or form containing an embedded outline.

2. Right-click the embedded outline and choose Embedded outline, which opens the Embedded Outline properties box.

3. On the Info tab (first tab), in the Web Access section, choose Using Java Applet.

4. Optionally, configure the display properties.

5. Save the page or form.

Using In-View Editors

One of the coolest new features of Domino 6 is In-View editing. You can now create documents directly from a view or folder, and you can edit existing documents through a view. A perfect example of this new feature is Domino 6 mail template, which uses this capability to enable you to enter an appointment into your calendar from the calendar view.

This In-View editing is not supported for Web users.

A new event, Inviewedit, has been added to views and folders to enable you to write code that handles what happens when a user tries to add a new document or edit an existing document from a view or folder.

You should be prepared to see one or more questions about the In-View editing feature on the exam.

Although the **Inviewedit** event works in folders, new documents created from a folder are not added to the folder; they must be dragged, moved, or added to the folder.

Creating Documents in a View

To allow users to create a new document from a view, follow these steps:

1. Open the view from which users should be able to create new documents.

2. Right-click and choose View Properties from the menu, which opens the View properties box.

3. Click the Info tab (second tab) and enable the Create New Documents at View Level option.

4. Choose the `InViewEdit` event in the Objects panel of the Programmer's Pane.

5. Write the LotusScript code necessary to create a new document.

6. Save the view.

 Inviewedit events fire for embedded views if the Selection Tracks Mouse Movement is disabled on the Display tab of the Embedded View Properties box.

Editing Documents in a View

To allow users to edit existing documents directly in a view without opening the document in a form, you must specify which columns in a view or folder contain fields that the user can edit.

The following steps outline the process required to allow users to edit documents directly in a view.

1. Open the view that is to allow direct editing.

2. Select the column that is to display the editable field.

3. Right-click and choose Column Properties from the menu, which opens the Column properties box.

4. Check Editable Column on the Info tab (first tab) of the Column properties box.

5. Select the `Inviewedit` event in the View objects list in the Programmer's Pane.

6. Code the `Inviewedit` event with LotusScript to specify what should happen when fields are edited.

7. Save the view.

Designing Applications Based on Conflict Integrity Issues

The Notes/Domino database architecture is not relational; rather, it is essentially a flat file database. What this means is that unlike a relational database, where redundancy is minimized through normalization and linked tables, redundancy is not only common, but it is often necessary in your Notes/Domino applications. That being said, your goal should be to minimize redundancy as much as possible because it leads to wasted storage and obsolete data.

Consider the example of a customer relationship management application that includes company documents and contact documents. In this example, the contacts are children of the company document and need to inherit certain key pieces of information from the company if they are to display properly in the views. If the contact document does not store the company name value, the document does not display properly in views based on the company name. Although you could look up this value dynamically in a form by using `@DbLookup` or the `GetDocumentByKey` method of `NotesView` in LotusScript, it must reside in the document to be displayed in views. After the value has been inherited into the child document, that value is not refreshed automatically. So if the company name changes, all the documents for that company will contain obsolete information. The only remedy to this is to create an agent that updates the company name field in the contact documents if the name is changed.

In a relational database, the company name is not likely to be stored with the contact; rather, the contact record is probably linked to the company record through a common key. If the company name changes, as in the earlier example, users automatically see the new information because of the dynamic link and the lack of redundancy. As stated earlier, in some cases, redundancy is required to make the application function correctly. However, you should plan on keeping redundancy to a bare minimum in your application.

Exam Prep Questions

Question 1

> To encrypt a section in Domino, you must do what?
>
> ○ A. Nothing, sections cannot be encrypted.
>
> ○ B. Choose an encryption key in the section properties.
>
> ○ C. Sign the section and it will be automatically encrypted.
>
> ○ D. Add an encrypted field to the section.

The correct answer is D. You must add an encrypted field to the section. A is incorrect because adding an encrypted field to the section encrypts it. B is incorrect because you must use an encrypted field. C is incorrect because signing a section does not automatically encrypt it.

Question 2

> What are the four types of applets Lotus provides to enhance Web applications?
>
> ○ A. Form, View, Action bar, Calendar.
>
> ○ B. Calendar, View, Action bar, Editor.
>
> ○ C. Outline, Action bar, Editor, View.
>
> ○ D. View, Editor, Outline, Form.

The correct Answer is C. The four types of applets are Outline, Action bar, Editor, and View. A is incorrect because there is no form or calendar applet. B is incorrect because there is no calendar applet. D is incorrect because there is no form applet.

Question 3

> With what types of fields can the Editor applet be used?
>
> ○ A. Text and Rich text.
>
> ○ B. Rich text only.
>
> ○ C. Text only.
>
> ○ D. The Editor applet can be used only for In-View editing.

The correct answer is B. The Editor applet works with rich text fields only. A and C are incorrect because the editor applet can be used only with rich text fields. D is incorrect because the editor applet is used to edit rich text fields on the Web.

Question 4

In-View editors provide what functionality?

○ A. Allow users to edit a document in a view without opening it.

○ B. Mimic Notes client view functionality on the Web.

○ C. Enable users to create new documents from a view.

○ D. Both A and C.

The correct answer is D. In-View editors enable you to edit a document without opening it and enable users to create new documents from a view. B is incorrect because In-View editors allow users to create and edit documents from a view. A and C are incorrect individually because an In-View editor can provide both functions.

Question 5

What does Option Declare do?

○ A. Requires explicit variable declaration in Formula.

○ B. Requires explicit variable declaration in LotusScript.

○ C. Allows implicit variable declaration in Formula.

○ D. Allows implicit variable declaration in Java.

The correct answer is B. Option Declare requires explicit variable declaration. A, C, and D are incorrect because Option Declare is used with LotusScript.

Question 6

The New Customizable Tools menu enables you to do what?

○ A. Run custom formulas.

○ B. Run commonly used applications.

○ C. Both A and B.

The correct answer is C. A is incorrect because the new customizable Tools menu enables you to run commonly used applications as well. B is incorrect because the new customizable Tools menu enables you to run custom formulas as well.

Question 7

JavaScript is generally used to write programs that execute where?

- ○ A. Domino server.
- ○ B. Notes client only.
- ○ C. Web client (browser) only.
- ○ D. Both B and C.

The correct answer is D. A is incorrect because JavaScript is normally used for client-side scripting. B is incorrect because JavaScript can be used in Web clients as well. C is incorrect because JavaScript can also be used in Notes client applications.

Question 8

The Find and Replace feature in the Designer client can be used to search for text within what scope?

- ○ A. Current Section Only, Current Object, All Objects, All Objects in Database.
- ○ B. Current selection, Current Object, All Objects, All Objects in Database.
- ○ C. Current Section Only, Current Object, All Objects.

The correct answer is C, Current Section Only, Current Object, and All Objects. A is incorrect because All Objects in Database is not a valid option for scope. B is incorrect because Current Selection is not an option for scope nor is All Objects in Database.

Question 9

The new view event **Inviewedit** enables what feature for developers?

○ A. Nothing; there is no **Inviewedit** event.

○ B. Allows developers to write code that determines what is done in views that allow In-View editing.

○ C. Allows users to conditionally hide columns.

○ D. Allows users to change the colors of a view.

The correct answer is B. **Inviewedit** enables developers to write code that determines what is done in views that allow In-View editing. A, C, and D are incorrect because the **Inviewedit** event works with the new In-View editing capability.

Question 10

The new Auto-complete feature helps developers with which coding options?

○ A. JavaScript and Java.

○ B. Java and LotusScript.

○ C. LotusScript and JavaScript.

○ D. LotusScript and Formula.

The correct answer is D. Auto-complete helps LotusScript and Formula programmers. A, B, and C are incorrect because neither Java nor JavaScript have Auto-complete.

Need to Know More?

 IBM. *Lotus Domino Designer 6 Help*, (Help6_Designer.nsf).

 IBM. *Lotus Domino Administrator 6 Help*, (Help6_Admin.nsf).

 IBM. *Domino Designer 6: A Developer's Handbook.* IBM Redbook, 2002.

 www.lotus.com/ldd.

PART 3

Notes Domino 6 Application Development Web Applications: Exam 612

Application Architecture

Terms you'll need to understand:

✓ CORBA/IIOP
✓ DECS
✓ Domino connectors
✓ Data Connection Resource
✓ Lotus Enterprise Integrator
✓ Image map

Concepts and techniques you'll need to master:

✓ Designing applications that work on Web clients
✓ Designing Web applications that read non-Domino data
✓ Planning applications that work in both Notes and Web clients
✓ Exploring page layout and navigation

This chapter covers critical information you need to understand regarding designing applications for Web clients. Chapters 14, 15, and 16 cover more detailed information on using Domino design elements, integrating HTML, and utilizing Web-specific features such as CGI variables, SSL, and so on. However, an understanding of how to design applications for the Web, how to read non-Domino data for Web applications, and how to design pages and forms for Web clients will be tested on the exams. In addition, understanding how to design applications to support both Web clients and Notes clients is also important test material.

Designing Applications That Work on Web Clients

The Domino database is the application container, an object store containing various types of Notes documents, including design elements and many other types of data described throughout this book but covered in detail in Chapter 4, "Design Elements." A major advantage to accessing the Domino server with a Web browser is that users are using generic Web browser clients. If the HTTP task is running on the Domino server, Domino provides the HTTP interface for Internet clients. Although some of the Notes client functions are not available, there is no need to install a Notes client on the user's system. Unlike traditional Web site design, where Web pages, images, data, and so forth are stored in hierarchical file structures, Domino stores information within the Notes database object store. Special Uniform Resource Locator (URL) commands are then used to access these design elements.

For users to access an HTML application in the Web browser, they simply enter the URL of the Domino server and the address of the Domino database as the Internet address. Unless a specific design element is passed in the URL address, the database opens to the design element specified in the Launch tab of the Database Properties dialog box.

If you are a Web developer or an experienced Notes developer beginning to develop applications for Web users, Domino 6 extends many of its most useful capabilities to the Web. More importantly, it also enables developers to use Web technologies within the Domino Designer IDE. Therefore, languages such as JavaScript and Java can be written directly to the properties and methods of the objects and compiled (if Java) from within Notes. Domino fully supports HTML 4, JavaScript, the Document Object Model (DOM, not to be confused with the Domino Object Model) as defined by the World Wide Web Consortium (W3C), XML, Cascading Style Sheets (CSS), Java, Java Servlets, Java Libraries, and JSP tag libraries. Domino Designer also supports CORBA/IIOP in the creation of distributed applications. *CORBA/IIOP* allows designers to write Java applications and Java applets that can remotely access Domino servers and data stored in Domino databases. Integrating these Web languages into the Designer IDE enables developers to more easily, quickly, and accurately build sophisticated applications.

You can preview the design of the design elements with either Internet Explorer 4.x or higher, or Netscape 3.x, 4.x, or higher. If the browsers are registered on the current system (in the Registry file), icons appear in the design toolbar (see Figure 13.1).

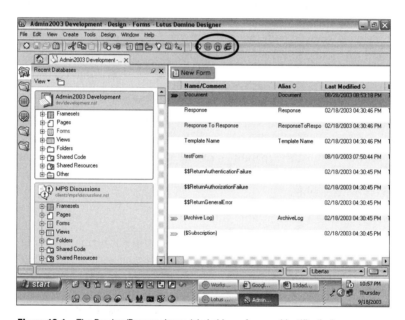

Figure 13.1   The Preview/Browser icons (circled here, for easy identification).

You can also preview the current design element by selecting Design, Preview in Web Browser, and then selecting Default Browser, Notes Browser, Internet Explorer, or Netscape Navigator.

Troubleshooting when developing and designing applications for the Web is covered in detail in Chapter 14 ("Design Elements"). Nevertheless, keep in mind that the most obvious way to troubleshoot Web applications is to preview the Web page during design. To test your Web design elements with a Web browser, select the Preview in Web Browser options from the Design pull-down menu. This automatically launches the browser specified in the current location document so that you can preview the current design element. When previewing local databases, Notes launches the Local Web Preview application.

 If you want to preview local databases, you must ensure that they are located in the Notes Data directory specified in the **notes.ini** file.

Because you may be designing applications to run on Internet Explorer as well as on Netscape, you can run the JavaScript debugger in JavaScript to help debug JavaScript code. If using Netscape (or Mozilla), simply type **JavaScript:** in the URL field within the browser. This launches a separate JavaScript window. Now, when the browser encounters JavaScript errors on the pages it loads, they are automatically written to the JavaScript debugger window, and the potential error is highlighted.

Java and JavaScript are both case sensitive, so check that errors are not a result of incorrect case. HTML and LotusScript are not case sensitive.

Many Domino design elements are supported for native Notes clients and Web clients. However, some of the design elements could not be simulated for Web clients within the capabilities of HTML. Therefore, some of the design elements are now available to Web clients as Java client-side applets. Four applets are available:

➤ *Embedded Outline*—Customizable site navigation.

➤ *View or Embedded View*—A view embedded on a page or form, providing a customizable interface for displaying and interacting with lists of documents and other objects. Supported by either Notes or Web clients.

 With embedded views on the Web, the view can be set to display a single category, and the number of lines to display can be controlled. Single-category views can be determined by hard-coding the category value or can be dynamically determined. Single-category views do not work in native Notes. When tested, it works in both clients.

➤ *Text Editor*—A fully functional, rich-text editor for creating and editing content.

➤ *Action Bar Applet*—Displays action on the Web (these buttons roll over and drop down menu options)

For more information on using these and other design elements, refer to Chapter 9, "Design Elements."

Another feature that is important when developing Web applications is the support of Common Object Request Broker Architecture (CORBA). Prior to R5, the back-end classes (previously referred to as the Notes Object Interface or NOI) were not available to the browser. Only the server could access these objects and then serve HTML to the browser, or accept the browser submission and process the user's request when saving. Now the back-end classes contained within the Domino Object Model (DOM) are available to the browser without requiring that you open or save the document with Java or JavaScript supporting W3C standards.

Since R5, you can import HTML files and/or cut and paste any elements from an existing Web page, and Domino preserves the full fidelity of the HTML page, including applets, animated GIFs, and so on. After these pages are imported or pasted, they can be displayed within the Designer or within Notes clients.

Text created on either forms or pages for Web applications can be entered by either of the following methods:

➤ Import text from an existing HTML file.

➤ Enter text directly onto the page or form (you can optionally use the new HTML pane when entering HTML directly on a page or form).

When importing text from an HTML file, the designer translates the imported HTML and renders the result on the Designer page or form. To import HTML, follow these steps:

1. Open a page or form in the Designer client.

2. Position the cursor in the desired location of the HTML.

3. Select File, Import from the pull-down menu

4. Select the HTML file (.HTM or .HTML).

5. Click Import.

Designing Web Applications That Read Non-Domino Data

In today's heterogeneous IT environments, capability to integrate applications with external, back-end systems is often necessary. Of course, Lotus Notes/Domino supports this requirement by offering several options. The benefits of building Web applications that integrate with external back-end data are numerous. Namely, this approach enables you to design applications that utilize core Domino features such as security, workflow, routing, and other automated business processes.

Domino Web applications can contain connectors to

> ➤ Relational databases (such as Oracle, DB2, SQL Server, MySQL, and so on)

> ➤ Enterprise Resource Planning systems (such as SAP/R3)

> ➤ Transactional Systems (such as CICS, IBM MQSeries, and IMS)

One option for connecting to non-Domino data is to use Domino Enterprise Connection Services (DECS). *DECS* provides a visual tool and a high-performance server environment used to create Web applications that provide live, native access to enterprise data and applications. DECS includes a wizard interface that enables users to define external data source connections to DB2, Oracle, Sybase, EDA/SQL, SAP/R3, ODBC, and text files. Users can define files within a Domino database that can be automatically updated with the external connector data.

In addition to using DECS, you can use the Domino driver of JDBC to access data. The JDBC driver provides standard JDBC access to data in Domino databases so that you can use Java applications in conjunction with the JDBC standard to access native Domino data.

Developers also can use the new Domino back-end classes—made available in LotusScript and Java—when accessing non-Domino data. The new LotusScript classes `NotesStream` and `NotesMIMEHeader`, as well as new Java classes `lotus.domino.Stream` and `lotus.domino.MIMEHeader`, enable designers to develop applications that programmatically access relational databases, transaction systems, and ERP systems.

Developers can use the forms-based development tools of DECS or the new Domino object Java and LotusScript classes to create Domino Connectors. *Domino connectors* are modules that provide native connectivity to external sources such as relational databases, transaction systems, and ERP systems.

A new feature available with Domino 6 is the Data Connection Resource. The *Data Connection Resource* enables you to utilize DECS functionality from within the Domino Designer client and link Notes fields to external database fields.

Data Connection Resources are shared resources and can be reused within an existing database and shared across multiple databases. You can expect to be required to define this on the exam.

An alternate option to connect to non-Domino data is to use Lotus Enterprise Integrator. *Lotus Enterprise Integrator* is a separate product that extends the DECS functionality by supporting high-volume data transfer and synchronization. LEI includes tools that enable users to manage integration, create event-driven data transfers, and schedule data transfers between Domino applications and relational databases and other enterprise applications without requiring anyone to perform any programming. Alternatively, LEI also allows for data transfers using LotusScript and Java.

Planning Applications That Work in Both Notes and Web Clients

Unique to designing applications for Lotus Notes and Domino 6 is the fundamental capability to "write once, run anywhere." The idea is simple enough: You can design an application that will work similarly for both native Notes clients and Web clients. Naturally, this reduces the amount of time required to develop applications that must support both clients. Although previous releases of Notes/Domino supported this feature for many of their design elements (sometimes with mixed capabilities), sophisticated applications often still required additional, specific development for each client supported. With the additional support for mobile clients added in Release 6, the idea of "write once, run anywhere" has become even more difficult to accomplish.

Nevertheless, when designing applications to be accessed by both Notes clients and Web browsers, there are some development standards and best practices (encouraged by Lotus, too, of course) to consider when building applications.

First, the database ACL is not the only way to control access to a database. Although the Basics section of the database ACL lists the access levels for users, groups, and servers; the Advanced section specifies the maximum level of access allowed from the Web. This is set in the Maximum Internet Name and Password field.

Other access control features are not available on the Web, nor are they available to mobile clients. For example, encryption is not supported on the

Web or for mobile users. This is not to be confused with implemented SSL, which encrypts the transmission of data to Web clients. The ability to actually encrypt Notes documents is specific to the Notes client. On the other hand, data that has been encrypted for the Notes client is safe from access by mobile clients or Web users.

When designing applications that will be accessed by Web users, graphics play an important role in building an intuitive and easy-to-use interface. However, unlike traditional Notes clients applications, where graphics are stored in the database design (running locally or on a Domino server), Web users must download the graphics in real time to their browsers before they are displayed. This introduces an issue of application performance if the graphics incorporated into the application are large. Nevertheless, you can use Web-specific features such as DHTML and Cascading Style Sheets (CSS) to reduce the file size for Web users and minimize page load times.

When using graphics for applications (specifically Web-enabled applications), you should use shared resources to insert graphic images and *not* paste them directly into the page or form. This can significantly improve performance because these images can then be cached by the Web client for subsequent HTML page requests. In addition, this saves space in the database and eases application maintenance because the image is stored in one central place but can be used throughout the application.

When designing applications for both Notes clients and Web clients, you must understand the fundamental principle that only back-end classes can be used when you use LotusScript in agents, servlets, and libraries. Therefore, when designing agents, servets, and libraries that can be referenced by both clients (and also mobile clients), avoid referencing front-end classes whenever possible. That way you can use the same code for multiple clients and minimize development time and effort.

One option when developing for multiple clients is to develop a separate, distinct design element (for example, a form or page) for each client type (for example, a Notes client, Web client, or mobile client). This initially gives the developer the most freedom to exploit the capabilities of each client without needing to consider the limitations inherent to each client. Unfortunately, developing separate design elements for each client type makes maintenance more difficult because a modification on one form (for example, changing the field type of graphic resource) requires the same change on another form. Consequently, another option is to design one design element (form or page) and use hide properties, subforms, and so on to make the same design element work for all required client types.

Notes/Domino has merged some of the capabilities previously limited to one client type to work better for multiple client types. JavaScript is now supported by Notes clients as well as Web clients. Therefore, features such as field validation can be implemented in JavaScript, and the same code base can be used to execute them for both clients.

Expect to see an exam question regarding the fact that JavaScript can be implemented in both Notes clients and Web clients for local input translation and field validation functions.

When using the Formula language to implement field validation for Web browsers, the form must be submitted so that the server can evaluate the formula. Then the results are served back to the Web client (a message is displayed to the user that the field validation failed and the user must navigate back to the prior form to correct the input field). This requires additional HTML requests to the server and degrades performance. Therefore, utilizing local JavaScript can improve performance and usability.

Keep in mind that although most fields work similarly for both Web clients and Notes clients, not all the field features are supported by both clients. For example, the Web clients cannot use dialog boxes, Calendar/Time controls, and so on. Therefore, if you attempt to design the fields for access by both client types, limit the field types to check boxes, dialog lists, radio buttons, and so on.

Another consideration when designing for Web clients is setting the database property for Web Access: Use JavaScript When Generating Pages. If this property has not been enabled, only the first button on the form is recognized and is automatically treated as a submit button. This result often isn't the one you want. When this button is enabled, all the buttons, actions, and hot spots are displayed, even if one of the buttons, actions, or hot spots uses @Commands that are not supported by Web clients.

When designing for Web clients, there are reserved fields and reserved form names that provide Web-specific functionality. The $$Return field allows you to return HTML to the user (typically a message or a URL to another Web page). Reserved forms make common Web functions easier to design and maintain. Table 13.1 outlines some of the reserved forms available for Web clients.

Table 13.1 Reserved Forms for Web Development	
Form Name	**Description**
$$ReturnAuthenticationFailure	Displays an error message to Web users when there is an authentication failure
$$ReturnAuthorizationFailure	Displays an error message to Web users when users attempt to perform an unauthorized command (for example, as determined by the ACL)
$$ReturnGeneralError	Displays a message to users when an error has occurred (rather than the default error message)
$$ReturnDocumentDeleted	Displays a message to users after a document has been deleted

Chapter 2 ("Database Management") covers database properties and their effects on Notes and Web clients. Nevertheless, you should be aware of a few of the properties that are specific only to Web applications and the effect they have on Web applications.

To examine the database properties, right-click on the database bookmark title and select Database, Properties from the drop-down menu. If the database is currently open, you can also click on the Properties Box icon from either the SmartIcon bar or the Properties Box button located by the Preview buttons in the top-right corner of the window.

The Database properties box has seven tabs (see Figure 13.2):

➤ Basics

➤ Information

➤ Print

➤ Design

➤ Launch

➤ Full-Text Indexing

➤ Advanced

Some of the properties available on the Basics tab involved in the creation of Web applications are located in the Web Access area of the tab; they are described as follows:

➤ *Use JavaScript when Generating Pages*—Allows the use of additional @Commands and multiple buttons on forms, and converts many @Commands to JavaScript (check box field type).

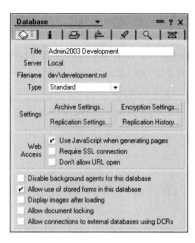

Figure 13.2   Domino Database properties dialog box.

➤ *Require SSL Connection*—Forces Web clients to use SSL (Secure Sockets Layer) to log in (check box field type).

➤ *Don't Allow URL Open*—Restricts Web users from entering URL commands such as `?openDatabase` to open the database and specific design elements.

On the Launch tab, the following setting affects the Web application:

➤ *When Opened in Browser*—Determines the default design elements to open when the database is opened by a Web client (dropdown field type).

The default launch options for Web clients are

➤ Use Notes Launch Option

➤ Open About Database Document

➤ Open Designated Frameset

➤ Open Designated Page

➤ Open Designated Navigator in Its Own Window

➤ Launch First doclink in About Database

➤ Launch Designated Doclink

➤ Launch First Document in View

In addition to database-specific Web features, several form design features are not applicable to Web applications and are, consequently, not available to Web clients. To gain access to these design elements, open an existing form (or create a new form) and open the Form properties box.

To examine the form properties, open the Form design element and click on the Properties box icon from either the SmartIcon bar or the Properties Box button located by the Preview buttons in the top-right corner of the window (see Figure 13.3).

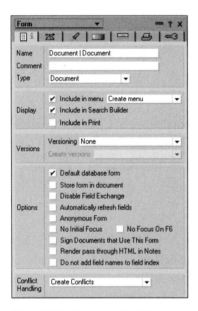

Figure 13.3   Form properties dialog box.

The Form properties box has seven tabs:

➤ Basics

➤ Defaults

➤ Launch

➤ Form Background

➤ Header

➤ Printing

➤ Security

Some of the form properties involved in the creation of Web and Notes applications are provided in the lists that follow.

Only one design feature specific to the Web is available on the Basics tab. That feature, Render Pass Through HTML In Notes, is in the Options area of the tab.

The design features specific to the Web available on the defaults tab are

➤ *Content Type*—Notes, HTML, or Other

➤ *On Web Access*—Character Set

➤ *On Web Access: Generate HTML for all fields*—This setting results in HTML being generated for hidden fields (whose type is still hidden). Otherwise, hidden fields are understood by the server but never served to the client as HTML; therefore, they are not accessible by the client.

➤ *On Web Access: Active Link*—Determines the color of font text to display for active links.

➤ *On Web Access: Unvisited Link*—Determines the color of font text to display for unvisited links.

➤ *On Web Access: Visited Link*—Determines the color of font text to display for visited links.

Many of the design elements now have an <HTML> tab on their respective properties boxes. This tab enables developers to specify attributes specific to those design elements (such as ID, Style, Title, Other, Access Name [for fields]), or that may be common across objects, such as Class with Cascading Style Sheets. Nevertheless, the properties specified here further assist developers who are using the HTML 4.0 standard to design applications that control the attributes of the Web objects. Using HTML with design elements is covered in more detail in Chapters 14 ("Design Elements") and Chapter 16 ("Programming").

Exploring Page Layout and Navigation

Notes/Domino provides the following navigational tools for your use when designing applications for the Notes client or Web client:

➤ *Outline*—Creates an organizing structure for an application and gives you control over how elements display in a navigation pane.

➤ *Navigator*—Objects and graphics that include programmed areas provide a graphical road map directing users to specific parts of a database.

➤ *Image Map*—A graphic you enhance with programmable hot spots that perform some action when a user clicks on the hot spots.

You can create a new outline by manually entering new entries or by generating a default outline. Of course, you can always add, edit, and delete entries in an outline you created with the Generate Default Outline option. Outline entries are excellent tools for site navigation because they link to practically any part of your application (pages, documents, views, folders, Web pages, and other Domino databases).

For the exam, remember that outline entries can also be clickable actions, links to design elements, links to a URL, or top-level categories used to organize other entries.

For more information on creating, troubleshooting, and modifying outlines, refer to Chapter 14, "Design Elements."

Navigators allow users to locate documents and take actions without having to open a view. Navigators usually include hot spots (text and/or graphics) that enable users to click and execute an action. To use a navigator in a Web application, select the Web Browser Compatible option on the Information tab of the Navigator properties dialog box (see Figure 13.4). This causes Domino to convert the navigator to an HTML image map when viewed by a Web browser. This image map will be displayed as a full-screen image map. However, you can control the size and display of the image map by embedding the navigator in a form.

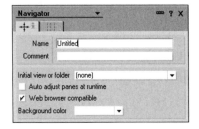

Figure 13.4   Navigator properties dialog box.

For more information about creating, troubleshooting, and modifying navigators, refer to Chapter 4.

Image maps are often used as navigational structures for Web applications. Because image maps are inserted into pages and forms, you can combine image maps with text and other page and form elements. In addition, you can manipulate the display of the image map by using hide-when formulas and computed-for-text formulas. A nice feature about image maps is that you can change the image used within an image map while leaving any previously created hotspots intact.

To create an image, follow these steps:

1. Paste, create, or import a graphic or an image resource into a page or form.

2. Select the image.

3. From the pull-down menu or by right-clicking on the image, select one of the options available:

   ➤ Add Hotspot Rectangle

   ➤ Add Hotspot Circle

   ➤ Add Hotspot Polygon—When drawing a polygon, click the points of the polygon and double-click to close the shape

   ➤ Add Default Hotspot—Draws a hot spot around the entire graphic

4. Click and drag the hot spot on the desired area of the graphic.

5. Select the picture. On the Content area of the Information tab, specify the content type as Link, Named Element, or URL (see Figure 13.5).

6. In the script pane of the designer IDE, enter a simple action, formula code, or LotusScript code to execute when the hot spot is clicked.

7. Select the target frame for the content action by entering the name of the frame in the Frame field of the Content area.

8. On the Advanced tab, you can set the Tab Key, which sets the hot spot position in the image map tab order (available for Notes clients only).

9. On the Advanced tab, you can enter alternate text for the hot spot.

10. On the HTML tab, you can enter optional HTML attributes for the hot spot, such as ID, Class, Style, Title, and Other HTML attributes.

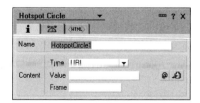

Figure 13.5 Hotspot Circle properties dialog box.

After you have created a hot spot, you can move the hot spot by clicking and dragging the hot spot with the mouse, or by selecting the hot spot and using the arrow keys to move the hot spot one pixel at a time. To delete a hot spot, you can select the hot spot and press the Delete button, or select one or more hot spots and select Picture, Delete Selected Hotspot(s) from the pull-down menu. To change the graphic for an image map, select the graphic, then select Picture, Replace Picture from the drop-down menu. This displays the Import dialog box, allowing you to select an alternate image.

When using graphics in your applications (as you most assuredly will), be sure to balance the visual benefits of using images with the additional time required for Web clients to download the images. You can either paste or import graphics in forms, pages, subforms, views, navigators, and documents. The Designer client stores the graphics in GIF (Graphical Interchange Format) or JPEG (Joint Photographic Experts Group) format. Therefore, it is best to use graphics as either JPEG or GIF in their native formats. Otherwise, if the images are not one of these formats, they are stored as a proprietary platform-independent 256-color format (similar to GIF89a format). You can implement the following types of graphics into your design:

➤ Standalone graphics to add to the design of the page or form

➤ Background graphics

➤ Image maps

Obviously, you want the images you integrate into your applications to look as much like the original image as possible. For Notes clients, the operating system and color mode (16-color, 256-color, High or True 24-bit color mode) makes a difference. For Web clients, however, you should use the Web color palette. Otherwise, image colors will be automatically matched to the color closest to the original, and that match may dramatically affect your image. Therefore, you can change from the Lotus color palette to the Web color by following these steps:

1. Select File, Preferences, User Preferences from the pull-down menu.

2. In the Additional Options section (located on the main Basics section), check the "Use Web Palette" option (see Figure 13.6).

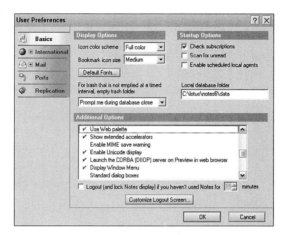

Figure 13.6   User Preferences, Additional Options section.

Summary

You should now have a good idea of the type of material and subject matter you will be expected to know for the exam. As you can see, designing for the Web is similar to designing for a Notes client, but there are many significant differences. The following chapters explore those differences in more granularity.

Exam Prep Questions

Question 1

> All of the following are design elements available to Web clients as Java client-side applets except for which one?
>
> ❑ A. Embedded Outline
> ❑ B. Embedded View
> ❑ C. Text Editor
> ❑ D. Scheduler Control

Answer D is correct. The Scheduler Control is available for Notes clients only and, therefore, is not available for Web clients. Answers B, C, and D are all incorrect because they can be used on the Web and all have the Web Access: Display Using Java Applet option.

Question 2

> Domino Web applications cannot contain connectors to which of the following?
>
> ❑ A. SQL Server
> ❑ B. SAP/R3
> ❑ C. CICS Transactional System
> ❑ D. Connectors can be created for all of the above

Answer D is correct. All the options are available for Domino to create connectors to. Specifically, connectors can be created for Relational databases (such as Oracle, DB2, SQL Server, MySQL, etc.), Enterprise Resource Planning systems (such as SAP/R3), and Transactional Systems (such as CICS, IBM MQSeries, and IMS). Therefore, answers A, B, and C are incorrect because they are incomplete.

Question 3

> The statement "Provides a visual tool and high performance server environment used to create Web applications that provide live, native access to enterprise data and applications" is the definition of what?
>
> ❏ A. Domino Connectors
>
> ❏ B. Domino Enterprise Connection Services (DECS)
>
> ❏ C. Data Connection Resource
>
> ❏ D. Lotus Enterprise Integrator

Answer B is the correct answer. The Domino Enterprise Connection Services provides a visual tool and high performance server environment used to create Web applications that provide live, native access to enterprise data and applications. DECS includes a wizard interface that enables users to define external data source connections to DB2, Oracle, Sybase, EDA/SQL, SAP/R3, ODBC, and text files. Users can define files within a Domino database that can be automatically updated with the external connector data. Answer A is incorrect because Domino Connectors are modules that provide native connectivity to external sources such as relational databases, transaction systems, and ERP systems. Answer C is incorrect because Data Connection Resources are shared resources and can be reused within an existing database and shared across multiple databases. Answer D is incorrect because the Lotus Enterprise Integrator is a separate product that extends the DECS functionality by supporting high-volume data transfer and synchronization.

Question 4

> When using the Domino Designer client to add a hot spot to an image located on a form or page, which of the following is not an option located by clicking on Picture from the drop-down menu?
>
> ❏ A. Add Hotspot Rectangle
>
> ❏ B. Add Hotspot Circle
>
> ❏ C. Add Hotspot Polygon
>
> ❏ D. Add Hotspot Square

Answer D is correct. The option to add a hotspot square is not an option from the menu. However, you could select the option to Add Hotspot Rectangle and shape the rectangle as a square. Answers A, B, and C are incorrect because they are all valid options when adding hotspots to images.

Question 5

> All of the following are navigational tools for your use when designing applications for the Notes client or Web client, except:
>
> ❑ A. Outline
> ❑ B. Navigator
> ❑ C. Navigation Applet
> ❑ D. Image Map

Answer C is correct. There is no such thing as a Navigation Applet included with Notes. Answer A is incorrect because an outline is included with Notes, which creates an organizing structure for an application and gives you control over how elements display in a navigation pane. Answer B is incorrect because a navigator is also included with Notes and is defined as objects and graphics that include programmed areas that provide a graphical road map directing users to specific parts of a database. Answer D is incorrect because an image map is also included with Notes that allows you to enhance your applications with programmable hot spots that perform some action when a user clicks on them.

Need to Know More?

Lotus Developer Domain. *Domino 6 Technical Overview*. Available in printed form or on the Web at http://www.lotus.com/ldd.

IBM International Technical Support Organization. *Domino Designer 6: A Developer's Handbook*. Available in printed form, PDF format, and HTML format from http://publib-b.boulder.ibm.com/Redbooks.nsf/RedbookAbstracts/sg246854.html?Open.

IBM Lotus. *Online Help Databases*: help6_admin.nsf, help6_client.nsf, help6_designer.nsf.

Design Elements

Terms you'll need to understand:

✓ Public Access
✓ Embedded Elements
✓ HTML
✓ HTML events
✓ HTML properties
✓ Shared Resources
✓ Shared Code
✓ Agents
✓ Libraries
✓ Java
✓ LotusScript
✓ JavaScript
✓ Applets
✓ View Templates
✓ Profile Documents

Concepts and techniques you'll need to master:

✓ Creating, modifying, troubleshooting design elements for Web clients
✓ Creating, modifying, troubleshooting libraries: Java, LotusScript, and JavaScript
✓ Creating Public access forms, views, and agents
✓ Using embedded elements
✓ Managing page layout
✓ Using JavaScript events
✓ Using and managing agents

When designing Domino applications, you need to consider a few important questions. First, who will be accessing this application—Notes clients, Web clients, or both? When designed for both clients, some elements function differently and may look different depending on the client. Second, can you control the browser accessing your application? If not, you may have to account for differences in how your application functions in the different browsers. Further, some functions just are not supported on the Web. This chapter looks not only at features that work on both clients, but features to avoid and some that just may need a little tweaking.

Creating Public Access Agents, Views, and Forms

Public Access grants users with limited or no access, read or write permissions to design elements set to allow public access. The Access Control List (ACL) manages the access to design elements within the database. Users granted No Access or Depositor accesses do not have the rights to access design elements in the database. In some circumstances you may want to allow certain users access to specific design elements only; you can do so by allowing Public access to those elements. A good example of the use of Public access is allowing others to read your calendar without giving them access to the rest of your mail file. Public access can be designated for forms (as seen in Figure 14.1), views, agents, subforms, pages, outlines, and style sheets. In this section we are going to look at allowing Public access for forms, views, and agents.

Follow these steps to assign Public access to a form:

1. Open the Form Properties and click the Security tab.

2. Select Available to Public Access Users.

3. On the form, create a Text, Computed When Composed field.

4. Name the field $PublicAccess.

5. In the Programmers Pane type "**1**".

6. Select the Paragraph Hide When tab in the Field Properties and select All Clients under Hide Paragraph From.

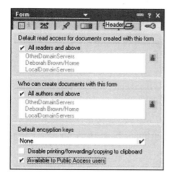

Figure 14.1   The Form Properties Security tab and *$PublicAccess* field.

Most $ fieldnames are built and used by Domino internally with predefined function-ality. Others, designers need to create for their specific functionality. It is important to know which functionalities are viable on the Web, such as the **$PublicAccess** field.

Now you must create a Public folder or view to display the Public Access documents. To designate Public access in a view, follow these steps:

1. Open the View Properties and click the Security tab.

2. Under Public Access select Available to Public Access Users.

Follow these steps to make manually run agents available to Public access users:

1. Open the Agent Properties and click the Security tab.

2. Under Public Access select Allow Public Access Users to View and Run This Agent.

After the design elements have been set to allow Public access there is one more step. As shown in Figure 14.2, you must allow Public access to the database through the ACL.

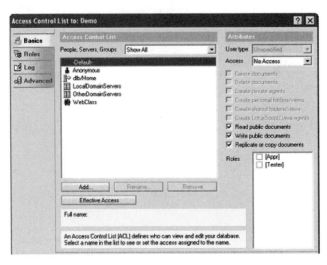

Figure 14.2 Access Control List.

Shared Resources

Shared resources can be used to hold one copy of an element (Files, Applets, Images, Style Sheets, or Data Connectors); using shared resources eliminates the need for multiple copies of the same resource scattered across your application. The resources can be used within their own database or included in multiple databases.

As well as storing resources in one location, shared resources provide an added maintenance benefit. If a resource needs to be updated or changed, it has to be done only in the resource—not in multiple locations.

 Web-based Distributed Authoring and Versioning (WebDav) is a Domino Web Server–supported technology. WebDav allows Designers access to the database without a Design client. Using Windows Explorer you can move an element out of the database, edit it, and then replace it. The Shared Resources available to WebDAV are File Resources, Images, and Style Sheets.

Creating, Troubleshooting, Modifying Style Sheets

Cascading Style Sheets (CSS) is the control of content presentation rather than control of the content itself. Style sheets can be embedded directly into a form; but for greater flexibility, they can be maintained separately. Shared

Resources allow style sheets to be maintained separately in one location, and each element that must apply its rules can insert a link to the resource in that location. To reference a CSS, follow these steps:

1. Place your cursor where you are inserting CSS.

2. Choose the Create Menu.

3. Click Resources, Insert Resources.

4. Select the Database, StyleSheets and the Available Resource (.css file).

5. Click OK.

You can apply separate style sheets to different clients on a single element by using the HideWhen properties. The Style Sheet properties dialog box does not have a Hide When tab, but you can use the Text properties to select the client to be hidden. Place each Style Sheet Anchor link icon on a separate line, open the Text properties, and select from the Paragraph Hide-When tab the client from which you want to hide that specific CSS.

Using Images in Applications

For ease of maintenance, shared image resources can be used throughout the database or across multiple databases maintained in one location. Any modification to the shared graphic image updates all the references to the image after it has been refreshed. GIF, BMP, or JPG–type graphics can be used to create the image.

One of the ways a shared image resource can be used is to create an image resource set. There are two types of sets: vertical and horizontal. A vertical set lets you add icons to the bookmark bar that can display in a small, medium, or large size. Using a horizontal set, you can create an image that appears to change depending on what state it is in, such as during a mouseover. To create a horizontal set, follow these steps:

1. Create a row of up to four images, depicting the different states you would like to represent (the image states are listed and described in Table 14.1). Images must be the same size, a GIF, BMP, or JPG, and separated with a one-pixel-wide space or line.

2. Create an image resource from this graphic and open its Properties.

3. Set the properties on the Basics tab, as shown in Figure 14.3.

4. Click OK.

Figure 14.3 Image resource properties.

Table 14.1	Horizontal Image Set States
Images Across	**State the Image Will Represent**
1	Normal
2	Mouse-over
3	Selected
4	Mouse-down

The image order is set by Domino and cannot be changed. This means that when you use two images, the first will always display in the normal state and the second image will always display in the mouse-over state. When the Images Across property is set to 2 or higher, the Web Browser Compatible option displays automatically in the Image resources properties and will be selected. If this Image Resource Set is not being used on the Web, deselect the Web Browser Compatible option to save space in your database.

Creating, Modifying, Troubleshooting File Resources

File Resources is a repository for non-.NSF files, such as HTML files, that will be shared within your application. File Resources Properties have a Web Properties tab that can be set when using the resource on the Web. There are two settings:

➤ Read Only sets the element to be only read on the Web.

➤ MIME type is set by Domino Designer if it recognizes the resource extensions and this is what the Content-Type header gets set to.

Employing Java Applets

Java Applets are self-contained programs that do not require a roundtrip back to the server when running on the Web. They also can be used in forms, documents, and pages on a Notes client.

Java applets can be stored

➤ As attached hidden files on forms, documents, or pages then imported.

➤ On the Web with a URL reference stored in the form, document, or page when you link to an applet.

➤ In the database when brought into Shared Resources.

All files associated with a Java applet must be available to your workstation, and Enable Java Applets must be checked in User Preferences before they are imported. File types associated with applets can be

➤ Class—.CLASS

➤ Source—.JAVA

➤ Archive—.JAR, .ZIP, .CAB

➤ Resource—.JPG, .JPEG, .GIF, .AU

When using Java applets on the Web, you must consider browser type. For Internet Explorer, include the CAB file; for Netscape include the ZIP and JAR files; if both may be used, include all three.

Creating, Modifying, Troubleshooting Fields for Web Clients

Currently 17 different data types can be assigned to a field in Notes. Not all are supported or work exactly the same on the Web. Comparisons of the HTML and Domino field types are listed in Table 14.2.

Table 14.2 Domino Field Types and HTML Equivalents	
Domino Field Type	**HTML Equivalent**
Text, Date/Time, Number, Authors, Names, Readers	Input (text)
Dialog list, Listbox, Combobox, Time zone	Select
Check box	Check box
Radio button	Radio

Table 14.2 Domino Field Types and HTML Equivalents *(continued)*	
Domino Field Type	**HTML Equivalent**
Rich Text, Rich Text Lite	Text area
Password	Password
None	Hidden
Formula, Color	None

Rich Text fields are translated as a multirow text box. If the functionality of Rich Text is needed, you can display Rich Text as a Java Applet. This option is set in the Field Properties, Basic tab under the Web Access section.

Dialog list, Combobox, and Listbox all display on the Web as a Combobox does in Notes.

Using the Allow Values Not in List setting on a Dialog list field works well in Notes, but on the Web it translates to an empty text box. If users need to add choices to a Dialog list field on the Web, the design requires two fields— one in which users can enter new values and a second to display the list. Also, if the page is being accessed from both clients, these field values must be synchronized with three fields—one for Notes and two for Web—and each version must be hidden from the other client. You can accomplish all of these requirements by using a computed subform or by using hidden fields.

If you choose the former method, you can create two subforms—one with the single field needed for Notes and the other with the two fields needed for the Web. Insert the subform with a formula, using @ClientType to ascertain which client is accessing the form. @ClientType returns Notes or Web, depending on the client.

Another option is to use the Hide paragraph from attribute on the Field Properties box, as shown in Figure 14.4.

Figure 14.4   Field property box.

The Paragraph Hide When property makes it very easy to hide design elements from one client or the other. Bear in mind, though, that hidden fields are handled differently in each client. Notes hides the field from the user, but the value is maintained in the document and can be used in formulas or views and seen through the Document Properties.

Hidden fields on the Web can be maintained in the document, used in formulas or views, and seen through View, Source. Hidden fields on the Web can also be ignored by Domino before they are rendered to the Web; these fields will be unavailable for use with JavaScript. These characteristics are determined by settings in the Form Properties shown in Figure 14.5.

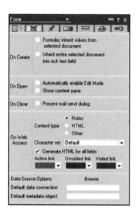

Figure 14.5 Form Property Box.

Selecting Generate HTML for All Fields on the Default tab in the On Web Access section makes this a Web-hidden datatype and maintains the value to be used by JavaScript. If this option is not selected, the Field and its value are not rendered to the Web.

Hidden fields generated by selecting the Generate HTML For All Fields Option in the Form property dialog box are not secure. Their names and values are translated to the Web and can be seen through View, Source with a <type=hidden> HTML tag.

Creating, Modifying, Troubleshooting Forms for Web Clients

Approximately 80% of a typical Domino application will work well on both the Notes and Web platform. Some tweaking may be required for elements that do not translate to the Web, are not suitable for both clients, or don't work well in Notes. This tweaking can be accomplished by using hide-when formulas or subforms. @BrowserInfo is a function that not only indicates a Notes client but can also differentiate between the different browsers. Using the BrowserType property, Notes clients return the value Notes and browsers return Microsoft, Netscape, Compatible (with Netscape, including Notes Navigator 5.0), or Unknown.

 Not all @Functions or @Commands work in Web clients. In preparing for the exam, be aware of which ones do (such as **@BrowserInfo**), and just as importantly, which ones don't (such as **@PickList**). @Functions and @Commands are discussed in detail in Chapter 16, "Exam 612—Programming."

Even though Domino is designed to work in a mixed-client environment, there may be times when it is more viable and/or just plain easier to create two separate forms, one for each client. Worrying about and coding for the different idiosyncrasies of each client is thus eliminated even though more maintenance may be required. Maintenance chores could also be lessened if you were to assign the same alias name to each form, then hide one from Notes and the other from the Web. In this way code would not have to question the type of client—just access the alias and the proper form will open to the correct client.

Creating, Modifying, Troubleshooting Layers

Layers are new with Domino 6. This design element gives the flexibility of positioning, placement, and layering on forms, subforms, or pages; layers work on both clients. Using layers can be as simple as overlapping two layers or placing a field on top of a graphic, or as complex as stacking multiple layers of graphics, text, and fields. Layers give greater control over how content is displayed.

Creating a layer on an element inserts the layer box itself and a Layer Anchor link similar to the Style Sheet Anchor link. As with the style sheet, you use Paragraph Hide When to control the display of layers to different clients. Also, as with the style sheet, you use the Text properties to hide a Layer Anchor link; each Anchor link needs to be placed on a separate line.

Creating Links for Web Clients

Links—text or graphic—can be used to navigate within an application or to another Web site. To create a link, follow these steps:

1. Highlight the text or graphic that will be the link.

2. Choose the Create Menu.

3. Click Hotspot, Link Hotspot.

4. Select the Type of hot spot on the Hotspot Info tab in the Hotspot Resources Link Properties box.

Three types of link hotspots can be created, as listed in Table 14.3.

Table 14.3 Types of Link Hotspots	
Type	**Description**
Named Element	Named elements are Pages, Forms, Framesets, Views, Folders, and Navigators. Named Element links are broken if the element's name is changed because this is how it is referenced. When an alias is used in the design element and in the Named Element the link will not be broken.
Link	Changing the elements when using Hotspot Links does not matter because the unique internal ID is what the link references. Documents, views, anchors, and databases are the design elements to which a hotspot link can be applied.
URL	URL links enable users to navigate to another Web site. The new URL value is hard-coded and would have to be manually changed if the URL changed.

Creating, Modifying, Troubleshooting Outlines for Web Clients

Outlines allow more creative control over the look, feel, and functionality of the navigational element. Outlines can be customized and programmed to control their functionality and accessibility. Created and stored within Shared Code, outlines can be embedded in a form, page, or rich text field, depending upon the application. When an outline is embedded in a form, that outline is then included in every document created from this form, giving users navigational access from every document they open.

Selecting Display formula in the programmer's pane gives you the ability to display different outlines depending on the client or users accessing them through formulas.

Creating, Modifying, Troubleshooting Pages for Web Clients

Though pages and forms are similar, forms allow the collection of data and pages are usually used to display information. Following are settings on the Page Info tab in the Page Properties (Figure 14.6) that affect how pages display:

➤ If the page contains in-line HTML and it is being used for Web and Notes clients, then selecting Render pass-through HTML in Notes allows it to appear correctly in the Notes client.

➤ In the Web Access area, select a type of content: Notes, HTML, or Other. Selecting Other opens a text box for you to enter your choice.

➤ Choose a character set to be used for Web clients.

➤ Choose the active, visited, and unvisited link colors that will appear on your page.

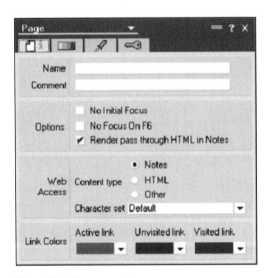

Figure 14.6   Page property box.

Creating, Modifying, Troubleshooting Libraries: Java, JavaScript, and LotusScript

Libraries are a place for maintaining and sharing programs within multiple design elements. Script libraries, LotusScript, and Java are not new to Domino, but JavaScript libraries are. All script libraries' scope is within the current database. They cannot be used outside the database in which they reside.

JavaScript libraries can be used in Page, Form, or Subform elements, and can be incorporated in-line or within the JSHeader.

To insert a JavaScript library, follow these steps:

1. Open the design element where you wish to insert JavaScript.

2. To insert a JavaScript library within the JSHeader, select the JSHeader event. To insert a JavaScript library in-line, click in the design element where you want to place the library.

3. Choose Create menu, Resource, Insert Resource to open the Internet Resource dialog box.

4. From the Insert Resource dialog box, select the JavaScript Library you want to insert.

5. Click OK.

Creating, Modifying, Troubleshooting Views for Web Clients

Views are a list of documents contained in the database and allow users access to those documents. Each database must have one view. Views do not have the same look or functionality on both Notes and Web clients. When a view is rendered to the Web, it is a full-screen display with default navigation buttons on the top and bottom of the screen. This is usually not an ideal look.

When designing for the Web you may want to consider displaying the view as a view applet, embedded view, or embedded view applet. Embedded views give you the added functionality of the element into which the view is embedded, such as a Form or Page. View applets display with more of the Notes view functionalities, such as selecting multiple documents and column resizing. These elements are discussed later in this chapter.

A few differences when displaying views on the Web include the following:

➤ Private views are not supported.

➤ View menu is not available on the Web; unchecking Show in View menu has no affect. To hide a view, use the Design Document property Hide design element from Web Browsers, or enclose the view name in parentheses (be aware this will also hide the view from Notes clients).

➤ The Show Selection property is not supported with view applets, but is for views rendered as HTML.

Creating, Modifying, Troubleshooting JavaScript for Notes and Web Clients

Design elements have events associated with them to which you can apply programming code; the code executes when the associated event happens. The types of events typically have been based on the client in which the events occur; onFocus is a JavaScript event that runs on a Web client, for example, and Entering is a LotusScript event that runs on a Notes client. New to Domino 6 are some dual client events that enable you to use different languages for coding two different clients in the same event. onFocus, for example, is the same type of event as Entering. Instead of coding in two separate events, the onFocus event allows coding LotusScript to run on Client (Notes) and JavaScript to run on Web. These dual client events are described in more detail in the next section.

Using JavaScript Events in Domino

The Dual Client Events table (Table 14.4) lists the dual events, the design elements in which they can be used, and the language that can be applied to each event.

Table 14.4 Dual Client Events		
Event and Elements	**Notes**	**Web**
JSHeader—form, page, subform	JavaScript	JavaScript
	Common JavaScript	Common JavaScript
onFocus—field	LotusScript	JavaScript
	JavaScript	Common JavaScript
	Common JavaScript	
onBlur—field	LotusScript	JavaScript
	JavaScript	Common JavaScript
	Common JavaScript	
onChange—field	LotusScript	JavaScript
	JavaScript	Common JavaScript
	Common JavaScript	
onLoad—form, page	Formula	JavaScript
	LotusScript	Common JavaScript
	JavaScript	
	Common JavaScript	
onUnload—form, page	Formula	JavaScript
	LotusScript	Common JavaScript
	JavaScript	
	Common JavaScript	
onSubmit—form, page	Formula	JavaScript
	LotusScript	Common JavaScript
	JavaScript	
	Common JavaScript	
onHelp—form, page	Formula	JavaScript
	LotusScript	Common JavaScript
	JavaScript	
	Common JavaScript	
Click event for Notes clients or **OnClick** event for Web clients— actions, hotspots, buttons	Formula	JavaScript
	Simple action(s)	Common JavaScript
	LotusScript	
	JavaScript	
	Common JavaScript	

In Table 14.4 there is a language listed as Common JavaScript, which is a new functionality in Domino 6. When JavaScript can be applied to the same event on both clients, select Common JavaScript. Common JavaScript executes in both clients and needs to be coded/maintained under only one client. Both clients are also synchronized; no matter in which client code changes occur, both clients are updated.

 For the exam, be prepared to answer questions regarding new functionalities, such as Common JavaScript or Coding for Dual Clients and the events in which these functionalities can be applied.

Creating, Modifying, Troubleshooting Web Agents

Automation can easily be added to an application through the use of agents. *Agents* are programs coded to do specific tasks. Agents can perform actions as simple as changing a value in multiple documents; agents also can perform complex operations, such as controlling workflow within a global application. Agents have to run on a Domino server; they do not run in a browser. Browsers can activate them, but not run them.

Running Agents on the Web

Agents are activated on the Web through @Commands or a URL command. The two @Commands you can use are

➤ @Command ([ToolsRunMacro]) is launched last in a formula.

➤ @Command ([RunAgent]) is new to Domino 6 and launches wherever it appears in a formula.

The OpenAgent URL command launches the agent and can be placed wherever URLs can be placed. URL commands are discussed in detail in Chapter 16.

WebQueryOpen and WebQuerySave are two form events that can use the @Command formula to trigger an agent from the Web. They are discussed in "Deploying and Utilizing LotusScript for Web Clients," later in this chapter.

Running Agents as Web Users

Normally agents run under the access rights of whoever signed the agent. New with Domino 6 are security settings that allow designers to override the signers' access rights. On the Security tab of the agent properties is one of the new security settings: Run as Web User. If you check this option, the agent runs with the rights of the user overriding the signers.

Setting Agent Properties

Scheduling agents is not supported on the Web. Web agents have to be triggered to run manually, which is done from the Action menu in a Notes client. The Web does not have an Action menu. To trigger Web agents to run manually you must—in the Agent properties—select On Event for the Trigger; then, from the On Event drop-down, select Agent List Selection.

Pasted documents and selected documents are foreign concepts to the Web. For the target, choose None if the agent is launched from WebQueryOpen or WebQueryClose. When the agent is launched from an OpenAgent URL, choose All documents in database.

Creating, Modifying, Troubleshooting Framesets

Framesets are collections of frames that are independent sections or windows. They enable designers to structure how an application is displayed and to manipulate multiple elements in one window. One way to control and manipulate these elements is through links. A frameset can have a navigation pane containing links that, when clicked, launch another element within a different frame within the frameset. Controlling where these links launch is important in displaying your application properly.

Controlling Document Target Frames

When a user clicks on a link in a frame, where does it launch? To control where a link launches, specify the target into which you want the link to launch.

One way to control where a link launches is to set the target in the Frame Properties. When you add frames to the frameset, assign a name to each frame. As shown in Figure 14.7, in the Frame Properties is a setting default target for links to frame, which is the field in which you can define where a link will launch when clicked.

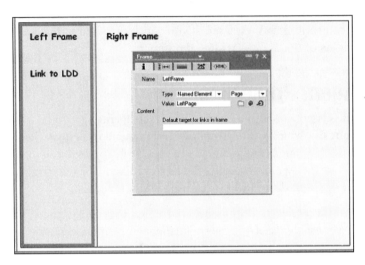

Figure 14.7 Frame Property box.

In Figure 14.7, the Left Frame property is where the target is set to launch Link to LDD. You have a number of options for the text you type in the Default target For Links In frame text field. Those target options are listed and their consequences described in Table 14.5. For clarity, the table uses frame names as specified in Figure 14.7.

Table 14.5 Text Options to Be Typed in Default Target for Links in Frame Field	
Typed Text	**Consequent Action**
None—field is left blank	Clicking the link launches the element into the same frame.
HTML predefined name _self	The element launches into the same frame.
Specific Frame name, as in example, RightFrame	Link loads the element into the frame that is named, such as RightFrame.
HTML predefined name _blank	Launches the link into a new window.
Non-existent name (could type aasdf as long as there is not a frame with that name)	Launches the link into a new window.
_parent	Loads the element over the frameset.
_top	Loads the element over all framesets (if multiple ones are open) in the window.

There are three other ways a target frame can be set. One is to use the link attribute `target=`. This method is used when you code the link in HTML:

```
<a href = "/database.nsf/ElementName?OpenElement" target="frameName">
```

Also the `@SetTargetFrame` function can set the target. This function needs to be placed before the command that opens the design element:

```
@SetTargetFrame("frameName");@Command([OpenElement];"ElementName")
```

In both examples, replace `element` with the design element you wish to launch, such as Page or Form.

Third, you can specify a target frame in the design element's properties on the Launch tab.

 If you want to set targets in both the design elements properties and in the Frame properties in which they will reside, make sure they specify the same target frame.

Embedded Elements: Using Embedded Views

An *embedded element* offers similar functionality to Web applications that Notes provides. When a view is rendered to the Web it doesn't have the same display as in a Notes client. Domino automatically adds navigation buttons to the top and bottom of the view's full screen display. Because the Web strips spaces, Column values and headings are crunched together (optionally, you can add pass-thru HTML into the column headings to remedy this). By embedding a view on a form or page you gain control over the overall display because you have full functionality of the design element—background colors, graphics, fields, and custom navigation buttons. Embedded views can be displayed with HTML, a View Applet, or the view's display properties. When displayed as a View Applet, features such as resizable columns, scrolling, selection margins, and multiple document selection are available.

Embedded Elements: Using File Upload Controls

A file upload control needs to be embedded if Web users are to be allowed to add attachments to documents. File Upload controls are for Web use only, but after a file is attached to a document, the attached file can be launched or detached from either client—Notes or Web.

To add a File Upload control to a form, place your cursor where you want the Upload to appear and select Create, Embedded element, File Upload control.

Understanding File Protection Documents

File protection documents are not unlike database ACLs. They are used to apply access control to non-database files being accessed through Web clients. File Protection documents are discussed in detail in Chapter 15, "Exam 612—Manage and Maintain."

Using Forms to Inherit Document Contents on Both Notes and Web Clients

There are two ways inheritance can be used: You can inherit field values from one document to another, or you can inherit the entire document contents into a Rich Text Field on another document. Setting up document content inheritance is identical no matter what client is using inheritance. Set up document content inheritence by following these steps:

1. In the response form, create a Rich Text field.

2. Select the Defaults tab on the Form Properties.

3. Select On Create: Inherit entire selected document into rich text field.

4. Select the Rich Text field name and select how to display the document: as a link (shown in Table 14.6), as a collapsible rich text field, or as a rich text field.

Table 14.6 Inheritance Types of Link Hot Spots	
Notes	**Web**
Select or open parent document prior to creating new document.	Open parent document prior to creating new document.
Can inherit with On Create options Link, Collapsible Rich text, or Rich Text.	Can inherit with On Create option Rich Text only. On Create options Collapsible Rich Text and Link are not supported on Web.
If new document is not included in the Create menu, a form or view action must be provided to create the new document.	A form action must be provided to create a new document from within the parent.
Holding the Ctrl key while choosing Create stops the inheritance.	No equivalent.

Using Native Domino Java Applets

Domino has built into four design elements the choice of rendering them to the Web as Java applets rather than HTML. This presents a more efficient element that is closer to the Notes client interface. Java applets are described as follows:

➤ Have an interactive interface

➤ Must run a Java-enabled Web browser

➤ Currently use Java Developer's Kit (JDK) Release 1.1.8

➤ Require more load time

➤ Easily enabled through the design elements' properties, as explained in Table 14.7

Table 14.7 Design Element Applets	
Design Element	**Description**
Outline	Allows the outline embedded in a page or form to be accessed from the Web. The Database property Use JavaScript when generating pages has to be selected.
View/Embedded View	Allows use of many view features without having to render the page.

Table 14.7 Design Element Applets *(continued)*	
Design Element	**Description**
Action Bar	Allows users to scroll and use subactions. The Database property Use JavaScript when generating pages has to be selected.
Editor	Gives Web users the capability to change text font, color, size, and style in a rich text field.

Using Tables to Manage Page Layouts

Tabs, extra spacing, indents, and outdents are not supported format styles on the Web. One way to incorporate this type of page layout functionality is by using tables in forms, pages, or subforms. Tables allow designers to position information, align elements such as graphics, text, and fields, and simulate effects not supported on the Web, such as picture text wrap.

Five types of tables are available: Basic, Tabbed, Animated, Caption, and Programmed. Animated is the only one that does not translate to the Web. Programmed tables display different rows of the table based on a formula that requires interaction with the server. Tabbed and Caption tables have two disadvantages when being used on the Web:

1. When a client switches between tabs or captions there may be a loss of data.

2. When a client switches between tabs or captions a roundtrip to the server is needed.

Fields, graphics, buttons, subforms, hotspots, objects, sections, attachments, Java Applets, embedded elements, and nested tables can be included within a table. Tables can be nested four levels deep. To display nested tables correctly on the Web, select the whole table, then choose Text, Pass-Thru HTML.

Because the Web strips extraneous spaces, designers must take into account blank cells. One way to work around this is to make sure there is data in all the cells. This could be white text on a white background, a pixel, or pass-thru HTML. Merging cells is supported on the Web and could be another solution for empty cells.

Many of the table attributes listed in the Table Properties translate to the Web; these are not supported:

➤ *Table Layout properties*—Column and row spacing, minimum height and table width.

➤ *Cell Borders properties*—Cell colors, ridge and groove border style, and border thickness (nothing other than 0 (none) or 1 (on)).

➤ *Table Cell Background properties*—Gradient color.

➤ *Table Borders properties*—Nothing on the tab has an effect on the Web.

➤ *Table Margins properties*—Nothing on the tab has an effect on the Web.

➤ *Table Rows properties*—Switch rows every *n* milliseconds, and Transition when row switching.

The last tab in the Tables properties dialog box, Table Programming, enables designers to add functionality to the table, such as applying style sheets, providing pop-up–type help boxes, and adding HTML code. This tab is similar to the HTML tab seen in other design elements; on the Table Programming tab, however, are two sections: one for the overall table and one for each cell selected. HTML tab properties are discussed in detail later in this chapter, under "Using HTML Properties on Views."

Creating View Templates

View templates make it possible to standardize the format and layout of views when they are rendered on the Web. By embedding a view onto a form, formatting the form to conform to standards, and using the Reserved Form name `$$ViewTemplateDefault`, a view template is created.

As the name implies, `$$ViewTemplateDefault` functions as a template for all views opened from this database on the Web. Graphics, background images, static text, tables, and other design elements will remain the same; the only thing to change is the display of the different views. With this capability, company logos, standard headings, or custom navigation buttons would be incorporated in all views and maintained on one form.

If some views should be displayed with a different layout, create a Form with that view embedded on it and with the necessary layout; name the form $$ViewTemplate for *ViewName*. All views will display with the `$$ViewTemplateDefault` form unless there is an explicitly named template for the view.

Hiding Design Elements from Different Clients

When working with a multi-client application, there are times when you need to hide design elements from one client or the other. Sometimes using different forms—one for Notes and one for Web—is more feasible than trying to create one form for both. In this case you would want to hide the form from the client who has no need of it. To hide a design element, follow these steps:

1. Click on the design category such as Forms or Views.

2. Select the element you want to hide.

3. Open the Design menu and select Design Properties.

4. On the Design tab select the client from which you want to hide the element under Hide design element from. Selecting multiple clients is allowed.

This procedure not only hides the element from the users but also from the server. Domino URL commands cannot access documents in hidden views and DBLookups cannot access hidden views. If this type of technique is needed, enclose the element name in parentheses.

Using HTML Events on Forms and Pages

Two HTML events are available to Forms and Pages. HTML Head Content passes information to the <Head> tag. HTML Body Attributes passes information to the <Body> tag. These HTML events are discussed in detail in Chapter 16, "Programming."

Using HTML Properties on Views

Many design element properties have an <html> tab included (tables have a <@> tab), which allows the addition of HTML attributes. Layers, Cascading Style Sheets, Applets, Pictures, Hotspots, and Fields all have <html> tabs (see Figure 14.8). These attributes are applied to the HTML that Domino generates at runtime. In Table 14.8 is a list of each HTML attribute and its description. Two things to bear in mind when working with these attributes: HTML must be ASCII characters and quotation marks are not used.

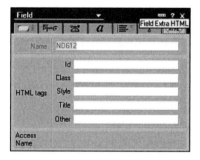

Figure 14.8   Field Properties HTML tab.

Table 14.8	HTML Tab Attributes
Attribute	**Description**
Name/ID	Used when referencing an object with JavaScript or CSS.
Class	If a CSS style is defined in the HTML Head Content, the class is listed here and applied.
Style	In-line CSS is used to apply a specific CSS style.
Title	Displays a prompt to the user.
Other	Add HTML tag attributes without quotes.

Views do not have an `<html>` tab to apply HTML attributes to, but through the View properties you can set how the view will display on the Web (see Figure 14.9). In Table 14.9 is a list of the Web Access settings in the View properties and their descriptions.

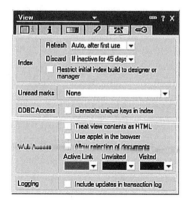

Figure 14.9   View Properties Advanced tab.

Table 14.9 Web Access Settings	
Web Access Setting	**Description**
Treat view contents as HTML	Allows you to change default settings by applying HTML attributes to a column. After you choose Treat View Contents as HTML, you can add HTML code to the column's Programmers Pane. This affects only how the view displays on the Web.
Use applet in browser	Notes type functionality is available, such as resizable columns, scrolling, F9 to refresh, expand/collapse without rendering the Web page again. The DEL key, selection margins, and multiple document selection are also available.
Allow selection of documents	Enables users to select more than one document. You could use this in conjunction with an Action, such as Delete or Move, where a user would want to select multiple documents.
Active Link, Unvisited, Visited color selection boxes	Select the color used to display the different link states.

Personalizing Web Site Experience Using Profile Documents

Profile documents enable designers to personalize an application. Personalization could be based on individual preferences or by associating a user to a group. Examples of individual personalization would be enabling each user to choose a background color on a page or allowing users to change a page's layout to match personal taste. An example of associating a user to a group might be in tracking user activity to personalize the user experience. If a user orders a Domino Exam Cram during a visit to your site, for example, you could associate that user to a Domino group. When that user next visits your site, he or she is shown a list of other Domino publications that may be of interest. Both types of personal information can be collected and stored in Profile documents.

Databases can contain one profile document for the database and multiple profile documents accessed by a unique key. This might be useful for designing personalized sites for users. These documents are cached when the database is opened, allowing for fast retrieval of the information as a person navigates through your site. Profile documents are created from a form designed in the database, but what makes them a little different is how they are accessed and maintained.

Profile documents do not appear in any view and are not included in the database's document count. Access to create and update profile documents is through code, so users create/update them through action buttons or agents. Table 14.9 describes the formulas and LotusScript that can be used to manipulate Profile Documents.

Table 14.10 Profile Document	
Code	**Description**
@GetProfileField	Retrieves field value from profile document.
@SetProfileField	Sets the value of a field in a profile field.
@Command([EditProfile])	Opens an existing document or, if one does not exist, creates a new Profile document. This is executed after all code.
@Command([EditProfileDocument])	Same as preceding, except this executes where it is coded.
GetProfileDocument method of the **NotesDatabase** class	Opens an existing document or, if one does not exist, creates a new Profile document.
GetItemValue method of the **NotesDocument** class	Retrieves field value from profile document.

Database ACL applies to Profile documents. Assign Author access if Web users are creating and updating their Profile documents.

Implementing Java Servlets

Servlets are Java programs that run on the Domino server in response to a request from a browser, and the result is then returned to the browser. They are loaded when the Web server starts and stay resident on the server. In contrast to applets, which are considered "client-side" programs because they are loaded and run in the browser, servlets are "server-side" programs, in that they are loaded and run within the Domino server.

Domino JSP tag libraries enable designers to create applications that can run on J2EE-compliant Web servers. Domino has two JSP tag libraries that comply with JSP 1.1 and Java Servlet 2.2 specs, and they are

➤ `domtags.tld` contains collaboration tags to access back-end objects.

➤ `domutil.tld` contains utility tags to perform tasks common to J2EE Web containers.

NOTE

The file extension .tld stands for Tag Library Descriptor.

Deploying and Utilizing LotusScript for Web Clients

LotusScript cannot be used directly on the Web, but can be used through shared agents that run manually or in URL commands (discussed in detail in Chapter 16). There are two events, WebQueryOpen and WebQuerySave, where the formula @Command([RunAgent]) (new with Domino6 and executes immediately) or @Command([ToolsRunMacro]) (runs last, after all other @Functions) would be coded. LotusScript classes NotesTimer, NotesUIDatabase, NotesUIDocument, NotesUIView, or NotesUIWorkspace are not valid within an agent activated from the Web.

WebQueryOpen is the last thing to run before Domino translates the element to HTML and renders it to the browser. Computed fields are not saved when set in this agent. They would have to be recalculated in the WebQuerySave agent; otherwise, you need to set the Generate HTML for All Fields attribute in the Forms property.

WebQuerySave is the last thing to run before the document is saved to disk. After the agent runs, the document is automatically saved, so coding a save within an agent is not required and could cause incorrect results. This agent can produce and return output back to the user. If the agent does return output, a $$Return field (discussed in detail in Chapter 16) on the form will be ignored.

Summary

We have just started to scratch the surface of design elements that can be used in designing Web applications. This chapter has discussed how to create public access agents, views, and forms. You have also learned techniques for working with shared resources, such as style sheets, images, Java applets, as well as techniques for creating, modifying, and troubleshooting forms, layers, outlines, framesets, and other elements. The chapter also discussed using Profile documents to personalize Web site experience, how to implement Java servlets, and how to deploy and utilize LotusScript for Web clients. As you have seen, knowing what will work on the different clients and how design elements render on the Web is important. Knowing what does *not* work on the Web is equally important.

Exam Prep Practice Questions

Question 1

Within Kirsten's database, she wants Web users to be able to read Schedule documents only and have no access to anything else. She has set the ACL to No Access with Read Public Documents rights, and she has created a form and special view made available to Public access users through their properties. What does Kirsten still need to do to complete her application?

❏ A. Create a computed field with a formula **PublicAccess = 1**.

❏ B. Create a computed field named **$Public** with a formula **1**.

❏ C. Create a computed field named **$PublicAccess** with **1** in the Programmers Pane.

❏ D. Create a computed field with **PublicAccess = "1"** in the Programmers Pane.

Answer C is the correct answer. To allow Public access, four things are required: ACL set to allow No Access with Public document rights in the database, a view set to allow public access so users can see the documents, the form set to allow public access and a $PublicAccess field with a value of one. Answers A, B, and D are not correct because there are no such parameters.

Question 2

Noah wants to hide a field from Web users, yet he wants to be able to access the field through JavaScript. He has used the field property Hide Paragraph From Web Users, yet when he tests the form the field value is not being rendered to the Web. What else needs to be done?

❏ A. When you hide a field, the field and its value are not rendered to the Web. What Noah is trying to do cannot be done.

❏ B. Select the Generate HTML for All Fields option on the Default tab of the Form property.

❏ C. Select the Generate HTML for All Fields option on the Default tab of the Field property.

❏ D. Use the reserved field name **$Hidden**.

Answer B is the correct answer. Using the Field Hide When in conjunction with the Form Generate HTML for All Fields will make this field a Web hidden datatype. Answer A, (though the first part by itself is correct) is incorrect as it can be done. Answer C is incorrect as this attribute is located on the Field Property. Answer D is incorrect as there is no such reserved name.

Question 3

What are the two Domino JSP tag libraries?

- ❑ A. **tags.tld** and **util.tld**.
- ❑ B. **domtags.tld** and **domtags.util**.
- ❑ C. **collab.nsf** and **utility.nsf**.
- ❑ D. **domtags.tld** and **domutil.tld**.

Answer D is the correct answer. Answers A, B, and C are incorrect as there are no such named files.

Question 4

Tiffany would like to use her existing Notes application on the Web. She has some LotusScript agents she would like to continue to use. How can Tiffany incorporate LotusScript agents into her Web apps?

- ❑ A. If they currently work for her Notes clients, there is nothing she has to do.
- ❑ B. LotusScript does not work on the Web and therefore cannot be utilized in her Web app.
- ❑ C. The **onSubmit** event allows use of LotusScript.
- ❑ D. Use the **WebQuerySave** and **WebQueryOpen** events.

Answer D is the correct answer. Though LotusScript cannot be used directly on the Web, manually run, shared agents can be accessed through the events WebQueryOpen and WebQuerySave. Answer A is incorrect because if one function works on a client it does not mean it automatically works on another. Answer B is incorrect because LotusScript can be utilized through specific events. Answer C is incorrect because the onSubmit event allows LotusScript for the only Notes client.

Question 5

Acme would like to standardize how views display on the Web and has asked Anthony to regulate all Web views. How can Anthony do this?

- ❏ A. Create a **$$ViewTemplateDefault** form.
- ❏ B. Create a **$$ViewTemplateDefault** view.
- ❏ C. Create a **$$ViewTemplateDefault** form for each view in the database.
- ❏ D. Create a **$$ViewTemplateDefault** view for each view in the database.

Answer A is the correct answer. A $$ViewTemplateDefault form will display all views in the database. Answers B and D are incorrect as there are no $$ViewTemplateDefault views. Answer C is incorrect as a $$ViewTemplateDefault form will be applied to all views and you do not need one for every view in the database.

Need to Know More?

IBM International Technical Support Organization. *Domino Designer 6: A Developer's Handbook*. Available in printed form, PDF format, and HTML format from `publib-b.boulder.ibm.com/Redbooks. nsf/RedbookAbstracts/sg246854.html?Open`.

LDD Today design articles are available in PDF format from `http:// www.lotus.com/ldd`.

IBM Lotus. *Release Notes and Product Documentation*. Available from the Design client, Help menu, Lotus Internet Resources, Domino & Notes Doc Library or from the Web site `http://www-10. lotus.com/ldd/notesua.nsf`.

IBM Lotus. *Online Help Databases*: `help6_admin.nsf`, `help6_client.nsf`, `help6_designer.nsf`.

Manage and Maintain

Terms you'll need to understand:

✓ Web site rules

✓ Incoming URL patterns

✓ Server tasks

✓ Global Web site settings

✓ Internet access

✓ Database properties

✓ Server documents

Concepts and techniques you'll need to master:

✓ Creating and setting Web site rules

✓ Understanding server tasks needed for Web browsing

✓ Understand and use server documents to manage Internet access

✓ How to set global Web site settings on the server

✓ Setting database properties for Web access

Designing applications and server administration are not mutually exclusive in Domino. Performance, security, client usage, and other application elements cross these boundaries. Domino has always maintained that Designers need to know some administration because it can have an impact on the functionality of their applications and vice-a-versa. This chapter discusses some administration areas such as Server documents, tasks, and Internet Site documents.

Domino Server documents have long been used to maintain and manage the Domino Server and Domino Web Server. Although you could continue using the Server document, setting up and using the Internet Site documents will make maintaining Internet protocols easier and more dynamic. For this reason, Internet Site documents are addressed seriously in the exam.

Understanding Server Tasks for Web Browsing

To enable your Domino server to act as a Web server, the HTTP task needs to be running. Administrators can enable the HTTP task when the server is first installed or anytime thereafter. After you enable the HTTP task, browser clients can access applications on your Domino server.

There is another task related to Web browsing called DIIOP (Domino Internet Inter-ORB protocol) . DIIOP enables Java applets/applications created with Notes Java classes to access Domino data.

 Security information—such as when server browsing is allowed and the DIIOP task is running, unwanted attempts to access or compromise data are possible with standalone Java applications that use CORBA/IIOP—is always useful to have when developing applications and should be studied in preparing for the exam.

Using Server Documents to Manage Internet Access to the Server

Internet Access controls Web users' rights to use information on your server. Although Internet Access can be controlled in many ways, this part of the exam concentrates on Internet Site documents and their associated Web Site Rule documents.

When using the Server document to change Web site configurations, the server or protocol needs to be restarted for the changes to take effect. When you use Internet Site documents to make changes, however, nothing needs to be restarted and these changes usually take effect within minutes.

Your server defaults to the use of the Server document for Internet configuration settings. If you enable, on the Server document, the use of Internet Site documents, the server uses these settings to acquire the configuration information for Internet protocols. Internet Site documents are created to configure Domino's supported protocols, which are HTTP (Hypertext Transfer Protocol), IMAP, POP3, SMTP Inbound, LDAP, and IIOP. An Internet Site document would need to be created for each protocol the administrator needs to set up. HTTP (Web site document) is the protocol discussed in this chapter.

Domino Server documents and Internet Site documents are mutually exclusive. In other words, you use one or the other, not the two together, when configuring Internet protocols. When administrators use an Internet Site document for HTTP, they have to continue to use them for the other protocols, not assume the Server document configurations for SMTP inbound are in effect.

Internet Site documents are required when

➤ Certificate Revocation Lists are used when SSL is enabled

➤ Setting up a service provider environment

➤ Designers want to use WebDAV (Web-based Distributed Authoring and Versioning)

As mentioned earlier, Domino Server documents and Internet Site documents are mutually exclusive. If Internet Site documents are enabled in the Server document, then the server obtains Internet configurations from the Internet Site document and ignores comparable settings in the Server document.

Administrators enable Internet Site documents through the Server document. To enable Internet Site documents, follow these steps:

1. Select the Server document you want to edit and Click the Edit Server button.

2. In the Basics section of the Basic tab, shown in Figure 15.1, enable the Load Internet Configurations from Server/Internet Sites Documents: field.

3. Close and Save the Server document.

4. Restart the server.

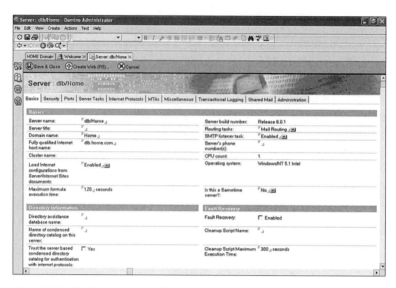

Figure 15.1 The Server document Basics tab.

Every time the server restarts, a console message indicates whether the HTTP task is using Internet Site documents or Server documents for Internet protocol configurations. Even though Internet Site documents have been enabled, a few settings are still configured in the Server document:

➤ Settings for the TCP/IP port on the Ports/Internet Ports tab

➤ Enabling the SSL port on the Ports/Internet Ports tab

➤ Server access on the Security tab

Along with Internet Site documents, administrators can create Global Web Settings documents to establish rules for multiple Web sites, as discussed in detail in the following section.

Understanding the Types of Global Web Site Settings You Can Define on the Server

Global Web Settings documents enable you to apply *Web Site Rules* documents to all the servers within a domain or a specific server. These documents differ from Internet Site documents in that you can apply only Web Site Rules globally, and with Internet Site documents you can define Web Site Rules, Web File Protection, and Web Site Authentication Realm documents. In addition, the Web Site rules apply to all the Web sites hosted by the servers specified in the Global Web Setting document.

Global Web Settings are usually associated with a Service Provider (hosted) environment, though they can be set in a standard enterprise environment also.

Defining Global Web Site Settings Using the Administration Client

Settings enabled within the Global Web Settings document apply to all the Web Site documents that are set up on the server. Creating a Global Web Settings document (as shown in Figure 15.2) is simple. To create one, follow these steps:

1. From the Configuration tab in the Administrator client, expand the Web section and click the Internet Sites view (this is available starting with Domino 6).

2. Click the Create Global Web Settings button.

3. Open the Basics tab, as shown in Figure 15.2.

4. In the Descriptive name for this site field, enter a descriptive name for the document that will display in the Internet Site view.

5. In the Domino Servers That Host This Site field, enter the names of all the servers within the domain that will host this site. You may use the wildcard (*) character.

6. Click the Save & Close button to close the document and save your changes.

Figure 15.2 The Global Web Settings document Basics tab.

Setting Up Web Site Rules

Before creating a Web Site Rule, you must first create a Web Site document. Rules are applied to Web Site documents and appear as their response documents in the Internet Sites view.

To create a Web Site document:

1. From the Configuration tab in the Administrator client, expand the Web section and click the Internet Sites view.

2. Click the Add Internet Site button.

3. From the Add Internet Site drop List (shown in Figure 15.3), select Web.

4. In the Web Site document, shown in Figure 15.4, complete the fields on the different tabs as described in Table 15.1.

5. Save and close the document.

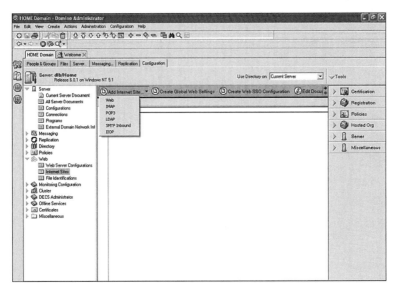

Figure 15.3 The Internet Site view.

Table 15.1	Tabs of the Web Site Document
Tab	**Description**
Basics	These fields are used to identify the Web site.
	➤ Descriptive name for this site—Displays in the Internet Site's view.
	➤ Organization—Optional in a nonhosted site; otherwise must be the name of the registered hosted organization.
	➤ Use this Web site…—Allows Administrators to set this document as the default Web site. As a new security feature of Domino 6, Domino refuses to process requests to a server that do not match to any Web Site documents, unless a default Web Site document has been created. Because Default Web Site documents do not map explicitly to any hostname or IP address, they can be a security risk from external probing. It is recommended not to use this setting on a public Internet, but on an internal test system or intranet.
	➤ Host names or address…—Enter one or more DNS hostnames or IP addresses that this site should handle. List DNS hostnames when you know the incoming requests have valid Host headers. There are two situations in which this may not occur and you would have to list the IP address:
	➤ When the Web site has SSL enabled.

Table 15.1	Tabs of the Web Site Document *(continued)*
Tab	**Description**
	➤ When there is a possibility that it will be accessed by HTTP 1.0 clients where the Host header is optional. It is mandatory for version 1.1. ➤ Domino servers that host this site—List of server names that share the Domino Directory set up to host this Web site. The names must be listed in Domino hierarchical format, such as dlb/Home, and not in DNS host name format, which looks like www.Home.com. You may also use the wildcard character *.
Configuration	Enter the Default Mapping Rules and the Allowed Methods.
Domino Web Engine	Specify the default settings such as Conversion/Display, Character Sets, and Languages.
Security	Define your allowable TCP and SSL Authentication.

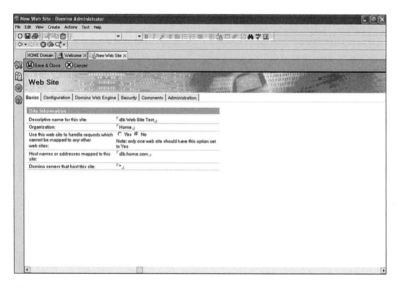

Figure 15.4   The Web Site document.

Be careful of the descriptive names you assign when using multiple Web Site documents.

Multiple Web Site documents may be created, each specifying a different hostname or IP address that maps to this site. Web Site documents are listed in the view sorted by the Descriptive name for this site: field. Domino 6 scans the Internet Sites view from top to bottom and uses the first Web Site document that matches the hostname or IP address. If the first match uses an IP address, the system will never reach the different hostname documents. In giving a descriptive name, make sure the IP address Web Site documents are named in such a way as to sort last in the view.

Web Site Rule Documents

Web Site Rule documents help administrators maintain their Web sites by providing a consistent navigation scheme and allowing relocation or reorganization without losing existing links.

After the Web Site document has been created, Web Site Rule documents can be added.

Creating Web Site Rule Documents

To create a Web Site Rule document, follow these steps:

1. From the Configuration tab in the Administrator client, expand the Web section and click the Internet Sites view.

2. Open the Web Site document to which you want to add a rule.

3. Click the Web Site button and select Create Rule.

4. Fill in the fields as described in the following sections and than click the Save & Close button.

Each Web Site Rule document has three constant fields: Description, Type of Rule, and Incoming URL Pattern. All other fields are based on the type of rule selected, as described in later sections.

Description is the first field on any rule, and is information designers may want to add for this specific rule. It does not appear in the view and is used for documentation purposes only.

Type of Rule is the next field, which is described in detail in later sections. First let's look at the third constant field.

Each Web Site Rule document has a field called *Incoming URL Pattern*. URL Pattern is a format or mask that is used to describe the URLs that will be affected by this rule. Before you continue creating Web Site Rule documents, you need to understand how the HTTP task manages URLs. As a security precaution, the Domino 6 HTTP task normalizes an incoming URL against an extensive, predefined set of URL filtering and validation procedures with the intent to reduce all URLs to a safe form before passing them to an application for processing. After a URL is normalized, the Web Site rules are applied.

The component parts of a URL are

```
http://<host>/<path>?<query>
```

Only the URL path component (the beginning slash is considered a part of the path) is used for pattern matching and the query is saved to be used by the application. The Incoming URL Pattern field should never include a hostname or query string, is not case-sensitive, and can contain the wildcard character *. Examples of Incoming URL pattern matching are shown in Table 15.2

Table 15.2 Incoming URL Pattern Matching Examples	
Incoming URL Pattern	**Matches**
/myplace/*.nsf	/myplace/personal.nsf
	/myplace/professional.nsf
/myplace/*professional	This will match any pattern that starts with **myplace** and ends in **professional**.
	/myplace/professional
	/myplace/documents/professional

The second constant field is Type of Rule and there are four types of Web Site Rule documents:

➤ Substitution

➤ Redirection

➤ Directory

➤ HTTP Response Header

When you create more than one type of Web Site Rule document per Web Site document, they are evaluated in the above listed order. Rules are a management function and not a security feature. When protecting resources, protect the resource itself—do not use rules.

Pay close attention to understanding Web Site Rule documents, especially the four different types, while preparing for the exam.

To select the type of rule, click on the drop-down in the Type of Rule field and select the type of rule you want to apply (shown in Figure 15.5) to this Web Site document.

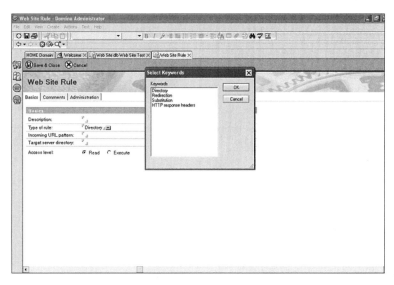

Figure 15.5   The Type of Rule field.

The following sections explain each of the Web Site Rule document types.

Substitution Web Site Rule Documents

Use Substitution Web Site Rule documents when you need to replace parts of an incoming path with new strings. For example, say that your company wants to move an application from the Products subdirectory to Catalog. There are many links referencing Products in the application and it would be too time-consuming to rewrite them. The solution is to write a Substitution rule with the Incoming URL pattern field set to /Products/* and the Replacement pattern set to /Catalog/*. These rules apply to the pattern fields:

➤ Replacement patterns may use the wildcard character *.

➤ Replacement patterns may contain the query string (even though they are not allowed in the incoming pattern), which overrides the query string in the original URL.

➤ If the wildcard character * is not specified in the Incoming URL pattern field and the Replacement pattern field, HTTP will automatically append /* to the pattern.

Redirection Web Site Rule Documents

Use this type of document when you want to redirect an incoming URL to another URL. There are two kinds of redirection rules:

> *External*—Used when the location has changed and you want the new URL to display in the browser. Also used when the Web site has moved and you want to allow existing links and bookmarks to keep working, yet new bookmarks will point to the new URL.

> *Internal*—Used when the location has changed and you do not want the new URL to display in the browser. These are similar to Substitution rules, except Redirection rules can be nested, and redirection does not require a wildcard, so exact matches can be forced on the URL path.

These rules define the kind of redirection pattern:

> External Redirect URL patterns must begin with the protocol.

> Internal Redirect URL patterns must begin with /.

> Redirect patterns may use the wildcard character *, but it is not required.

Directory Web Site Rule Documents

When a Domino 6 Web Server is initially created, three resource directories also are created. When the Web server first starts up, the following resource directories are mapped by internal directory rules and automatically defined on the Configuration tab in the Web Site document:

> *HTML*—Non-graphic files

> *Icon*—Graphic images

> *CGI*—CGI programs

If the preceding elements are not stored in the default directories, this Type of Rule redirects the incoming URL to the specified Target server directory. The URL pattern must match the incoming URL pattern and also have the proper Access Level as defined in this rule. Read is selected for HTML and Icon directories and Execute is selected for CGI directories. You cannot map other resources, Domino databases, or Java servlets with Directory rules.

HTTP Response Header Web Site Rule Documents

This rule differs from the others in that it is applied to outgoing responses just before HTTP transmits to the browser. By contrast, the first three rules apply to the incoming request before it is passed to the application.

One use of the Response Header rule is to improve performance of browser caching. Caching headers are

> *Last-Modified header*—Indicates when the resource used to generate a response was last changed.

> *Expires header*—Tells browser when the resource is expected to change.

> *Cache-Control header*—Has two options that Domino generates to provide instructions to the browser: "no-cache" and "private."

Response rules are also used to create your own headers. For example, if a 401 HTTP response code was returned for unauthorized access, you could create a custom error message that read "Sorry, you are not authorized to access this application. Please contact the Support team for help."

Response rules also differ from the other three in that they have to match the HTTP response status code as well as the URL pattern. As stated earlier, a 401 HTTP code is returned for unauthorized access; a 200 HTTP code is returned if the request has succeeded. These status codes are defined in RFC 2616.

Setting Database Properties for Web Access

Database Properties include settings that affect how a database displays and functions. Three parameters that you can set in *the Database Properties* that pertain to Web access are located on the Basics tab of the Database Properties box, as shown in Figure 15.6.

You can set three Database Properties parameters that apply to Web access:

> *Use JavaScript When Generating Pages*—Select this parameter if you need multiple buttons on your form or want to use certain @Commands. Using this parameter can affect the performance and functionality of your application, as discussed in Table 15.3.

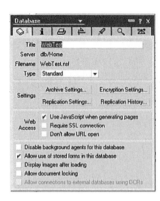

Figure 15.6 Basics tab of the Database Properties box.

Table 15.3 Consequences of the Use JavaScript When Generating Pages Parameter	
Use JavaScript When Generating Pages Is Selected	**Use JavaScript When Generating Pages Is Not Selected**
Hot spot formulas are calculated when clicked by user so documents display faster.	Hot spot formulas are all calculated before displaying the document so the display time is longer.
A Submit button is not automatically generated so you must create one.	A Submit button is automatically generated.
Multiple buttons can be applied to one form.	Multiple buttons are not supported. Only one button is created and that is the Submit button. If you have multiple buttons on the form, the first is converted to a Submit button and the rest are ignored.
@Command([FileSave]), **@Command([FileCloseWindow])**, and **@Command([ViewRefreshFields])** are supported on the Web.	**@Command([FileSave])**, **@Command([FileCloseWindow])**, and **@Command([ViewRefreshFields])** are not supported on the Web.
Domino does not check formulas before display.	Domino checks the formulas before displaying pages so @Commands and @Functions not supported are not displayed.

➤ *Require SSL Connection*—This parameter gives you an extra layer of security. SSL (Secure Sockets Layer) is a security protocol that encrypts data as it moves between your server and Web clients, as discussed in Chapter 17, "Exam 612—Security." If the administrator has enabled SSL, you can choose this setting to require that Web clients access this database through the SSL port only. If this is not checked, Web clients could access through SSL or TCP/IP.

➤ *Don't Allow URL Open*—This parameter prohibits browser users from manipulating an application that uses URL commands to open forms or views, such as a servlet. The restricted URLs include any command beginning with a ?, for example, `?OpenDataBase`. With this property set, users would receive an HTTP error 500. URL ? commands are discussed in detail in Chapter 16, "Exam 612—Programming."

Summary

Though most of this chapter pertains to understanding, creating, and setting documents usually controlled by Administrators, Domino considers them a vital part of Web development and the 612 exam tests your knowledge in this area. These documents and parameters control whether your Domino server is enabled as a Web server; they also determine how Web clients are directed after they enter your site. You may not have the authority to manipulate these settings, but you need to understand them to set up a Web application, possibly troubleshoot one—and to answer questions about these processes on the 612 exam.

Exam Prep Questions

Question 1

> Our administrator, Becca, has reorganized our Web site. She moved all databases pertaining to the Company Catalog from the Products subdirectory to the Catalog subdirectory. Our design team has started receiving reports that links referencing the Products subdirectory are no longer working. We do not have time currently to rewrite all the databases. How can this problem be resolved?
>
> ○ A. Take the application off the Web server until the links can be rewritten.
>
> ○ B. Create a Web site document for this application.
>
> ○ C. Display an error page that tells users the site is under construction and to please return later.
>
> ○ D. Create a Substitution Web Site Rule document that redirects /Products/* to /Catalog/*.

Answer D is the correct answer. Substitution rules enable you to replace parts of an incoming URL with new ones. Answer A and C are solutions that are not viable to the company. Answer B is incorrect because Rule documents are responses to Web Site documents.

Question 2

> If the Web Access: Use JavaScript When Generating Pages option on the Basics tab of the Database properties box is not checked, which @Commands are not supported?
>
> ○ A. **@Command([FileSave]), @Command([FileCloseWindow]),** and **@Command([FileExitWindow]).**
>
> ○ B. **@Command([FileSave]), @Command([FileCloseWindow])** and **@Command([ViewRefreshFields]).**
>
> ○ C. None. If this property is not checked, a Submit button is automatically created.
>
> ○ D. None. If this property is not checked, the first button found on the form is converted to a Submit button.

Answer B is the correct answer. Answer A is incorrect because the last @Command is not one of the three not supported. Answer C and D are true statements, but do not correctly answer the question given here.

Question 3

The Admin team needs to temporarily change the Web server. They would like to have Web clients automatically go to the new site without having to type in or even see the new address. What can be done to accomplish this?

- ○ A. Create an Internal Redirection Web Site Rule document.
- ○ B. Create an Internal Substitution Web Site Rule document.
- ○ C. Create an External Redirection Web Site Rule document.
- ○ D. Create an External Substitution Web Site Rule document.

Answer A is the correct answer. Internal Redirection rules allow you to redirect users to a new URL without displaying the address in the browser. Answer B and D are incorrect because Substitution rules do not have Internal or External types. Answer C is incorrect because an External Redirection rule shows the new address in the browser.

Question 4

Sandi would like to be able to use WebDev when developing Web applications. What changes must Paula, her Administrator, make to accomplish this.

- ○ A. Paula needs to enable Load Internet configurations from Server/Internet Sites documents in the Server document and then create an Internet Site document.
- ○ B. Paula needs to enable Load Internet configurations from Server/Internet Sites documents in the Configuration document and then create a WebDav document.
- ○ C. A WebDav application needs to be installed on the Web server.
- ○ D. Paula needs to enable WebDav and set its parameters on the WebDav tab in the Server document.

Answer A is the correct answer. Internet Site documents are required in order to use WebDav. Answer B is incorrect because there in not a WebDav document nor such a setting in the configuration document. Answer C is incorrect because WebDav is not an application. Answer D is incorrect because there is no WebDav tab.

Question 5

Stacy would like her server to be a Web server. What needs to be done to accomplish this?

- ○ A. Create the HTTP document and restart the server.
- ○ B. Load the Web Site task to start the Web server.
- ○ C. Load the HTTP task to start the Web server.
- ○ D. Create an Internet Site document to configure the Web server.

Answer C is the correct answer. The HTTP task needs to be running for Web access. Answer A and B are incorrect because there isn't an HTTP document or a Web Site task. Answer D is correct that an Internet Site document can be created to configure the Web server, but the Server needs to be a Web server first.

Need to Know More?

 IBM International Technical Support Organization. *Domino Designer 6: A Developer's Handbook*. Available in printed form, PDF format, HTML format from `publib-b.boulder.ibm.com/Redbooks.nsf/` 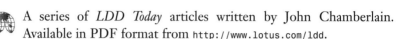 `RedbookAbstracts/sg246854.html?Open`.

 A series of *LDD Today* articles written by John Chamberlain. Available in PDF format from `http://www.lotus.com/ldd`.

 IBM Lotus. *Release Notes*.

 IBM Lotus. Online Help Databases: `help6_admin.nsf`, `help6_client.nsf`, `help6_designer.nsf`.

Programming

Terms you'll need to understand:

✓ Horizontal Rules
✓ IDE
✓ JavaScript
✓ URL
✓ HTML
✓ DHTML
✓ XML
✓ DXL
✓ @Commands
✓ @Functions
✓ $$Return
✓ LotusScript
✓ Applets
✓ Validation
✓ CGI variables
✓ Cookies

Concepts and techniques you'll need to master:

✓ Understanding, creating, and using HyperText Markup Language (HTML)
✓ Understanding, creating, and using JavaScript
✓ Using XML, DHTML, and CGI variables in applications
✓ Using @Commands and @Functions in Web applications
✓ Deploying and utilizing LotusScript agents
✓ Understanding and deploying Java Applets
✓ Understanding and using URL commands and URL syntax
✓ Understanding and working with $$Return fields

Domino incorporates these methods for programming your applications:

➤ Simple Actions

➤ Formula language

➤ Java

➤ LotusScript

➤ HTML

➤ JavaScript

When creating Web applications, designers must become familiar with the different programming methods available, which design elements translate to HTML, and what is the best way to program the application. This chapter looks at the different languages used to program Domino applications and how those languages apply to Web applications, Notes applications, or both. Understanding the programming methods available and how to apply them within your application is essential in developing good Web applications, and Exam 612 focuses on testing this knowledge.

Making Preferred Tools Readily Available to the IDE

New with Domino 6 is the capability to launch third-party design tools from within Domino's *Integrated Development Environment* (*IDE*). IDE is the programming interface where designers create, edit, and debug code. IDE enables designers to browse @Functions, @Commands, and script classes. When you need to use a graphics application or an editor, you no longer have to leave Designer to open them. After the tool is set up, these applications can be launched from the Tool menu within Designer. To add an application to the Tool Menu, follow these steps:

1. Select Tools menu.

2. Select Add Tool to open the Add Tool Property dialog box, as shown in Figure 16.1.

3. In the Tool Name field, type a name for this tool.

4. Select Run Program (enter path for executable) or Run Formula (use an @Command).

5. Select the Tool Context when you want the tool name to appear in the Tools menu. If you want a graphics tool to appear only in the Tools menu when the list of images is being displayed, select Image Resource List from the Tool Context list.

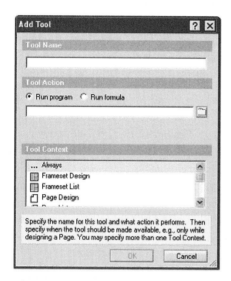

Figure 16.1 Add Tool properties.

Adding Horizontal Rules to Forms and Pages

Horizontal rules are design elements that add a graphic line to forms or pages to separate parts of the document. Gradient color is not supported on the Web.

JavaScript

JavaScript is an object-oriented scripting language that provides interactive components such as mouse effects or field validation. *Validation* checks the data users have entered against specific criteria designers have set. When using Domino formulas to validate, the validation request has to be processed on the server and the error message (if any) rendered back to the browser. This is called *roundtrip processing*. One of JavaScript's benefits is that processing is done at the workstation level and not on the server.

Processing at the workstation level improves performance because there does not have to be a roundtrip to the server, so network traffic is reduced.

Using JavaScript in Applications

JavaScript functions on different browsers, on Notes clients, and across platforms. JavaScript also does client-side processing. These two components of JavaScript give designers an easy, efficient way to code the client interface. JavaScript is best used for Web applications or if an application is being used on both clients.

JavaScript is coded in events listed in the Object tab, which vary depending on the design element being programmed. JavaScript can be used anywhere HTML is if the <SCRIPT LANGUAGE="JavaScript"> tag is used. By making it pass-thru HTML, Domino passes the code to browsers without interpreting the code. If designers want Notes clients to process HTML, they must make sure to check the Render pass through HTML in Notes in the Form Properties. Otherwise, designers must hide the HTML to prevent Notes from displaying it as text (you learn more about Hypertext Markup Language in "HTML," later in this chapter).

The locations of resources and files on the Internet are identified individually by a Uniform Resource Locator (URL); you use a URL to address a resource or file you want to access across the Internet. JavaScript can also be placed in a URL:

```
<a href="javascript:code here">link text</a>
```

JavaScript is not a language choice in agents. However, agents can run JavaScript by using print statements that send the code to the browser as HTML. In *LotusScript*, Domino's proprietary, object-oriented programming language, the statements look like this:

```
Print "<SCRIPT LANGUAGE=JavaScript>"
Print "JavaScript Code"
Print "</SCRIPT>"
```

By setting the href property of the location object to the URL to open an agent, designers can run an agent through JavaScript. Here is an example:

```
window.location.href="/databasename.nsf/agentname?OpenAgent"
```

Modifying Simple JavaScript

JavaScript events are listed on the Objects tab in the Programmers Pane, as shown in Figure 16.2. Events are object sensitive, onBlur is available for

Fields, and JS Header (which allows designers to enter JavaScript directly into the page header) is available on the Form. To program an object event, follow these steps:

1. Click the object event on the Objects tab.

2. Select the client in which JavaScript will run (choose Client for Notes and Web for Web browser).

3. JavaScript is selected by default in the second Run drop-down. This default setting codes for only one client. If you choose Common JavaScript, code is displayed and executes in both clients.

4. Type the JavaScript code in the Script area. Designers can also import JavaScript code from any file by clicking in the script area and choosing File, Import from the menu.

 Files with JS extensions appear by default in the Import dialog box. To display all file types, enter *.* in the File Name text box and press the Enter key.

5. Save or click the green check box. This compiles the current code.

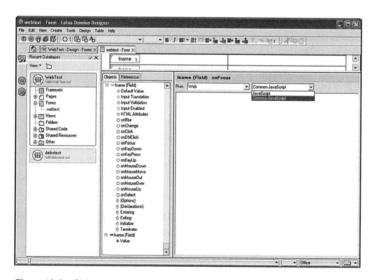

Figure 16.2 Object tab and Programmers Pane.

Using JavaScript to Access Field Contents

To reference a field in JavaScript, designers must first understand the Document Object Model, which is discussed in more detail later in this chapter. When you reference an object, you must reference its parent first. A field's parent is a form whose parent is a document whose parent is a window. JavaScript must drill down through the Document Object Model to access a field's content, as in the following example:

```
Var variableName = window.document.forms[0].fieldname;
```

Most Domino fields map to JavaScript objects and can be referenced by their field names. However, there are a few differences between JavaScript and Domino that designers have to bear in mind, including the following:

➤ JavaScript is case sensitive, and unlike Domino, JavaScript Field Name references are case sensitive.

➤ JavaScript can access fields in Web and Notes clients when in edit mode.

➤ In read mode, fields are never accessible to JavaScript in Notes clients. Fields are accessible in Web clients only if the Generate HTML for all fields option is selected in the Form Properties.

➤ Hidden fields are never accessible to JavaScript in Notes clients. Hidden fields are accessible in Web clients only if the Generate HTML for all fields option is selected in the Form Properties.

➤ FileUpload, an embedded object that allows Web clients to attach files, does not map to a Domino field type. FileUpload objects cannot be accessed in a Notes client.

Using JavaScript to Create a Redirect Page

Redirecting a page provides designers the ability to create dynamic user-friendly notifications that automatically return users to a set location. When a user submits a document, designers can program the $$Return field to display a "Thank You" message with a link to another page; or rather than display the link, designers can program the $$Return field to automatically redirect to another page after a few seconds. (You learn more about these fields in "Working with $$Return Fields," later in this chapter.)

In the JSHeader event of the form, you can use the location property of the window object to write a function that relocates to an alternate page. Location allows the manipulation of URLs.

```
function newPage()
{
window.location=/pat relative to data/databaseName.nsf/pageName?OpenPage;
}
```

Now a timer needs to be set in the `onLoad` event of the form.

```
setTimeout('newPage()',milliseconds)
```

The timing is set in milliseconds, so if you want to delay redirection for 5 seconds, enter **5000** in place of milliseconds; 10 seconds would be 10000.

Another good utilization of redirect pages is for security reasons. If users try to circumvent your access by typing a URL to access a hidden view, for example, you can redirect them. Using a `$$ViewTemplate for viewName` form, designers can display a deny access message and apply the above redirection code to the `$$ViewTemplate for viewName` form, which would redirect users to a safe area. `$$ViewTemplate` forms are discussed in detail in Chapter 14, "Design Elements."

Validating User Entered Data Using JavaScript

Input validation formulas, `@Success` and `@Failure`, work on the Web. Formulas are processed on the server, so the input validation formula makes a roundtrip to execute and render the information back to the Web. JavaScript validation's main benefit is client-side processing, which improves performance. JavaScript validation works for both Notes and Web clients. In JavaScript validation, only valid data makes the trip to the server; instant validation can be provided and the whole document doesn't have to be reloaded.

Validation can return an error message, return focus to the field, or change the value of the field. Validation can take place in the `onBlur` (exiting) or onFocus (entering) events. Users get instant per-field validations, one at a time, and designers can place focus back into the field that needs to be changed. Per-field validation can be bypassed and this is a major disadvantage to its use. If a cursor is not placed in the field, the event never happens.

Submit is another area where validation can take place. All fields are validated at one time and no validations will be missed. One disadvantage to validating at Submit is that, if multiple fields are being validated, users can be hit with multiple errors all at once.

Instead of returning focus to the field in question, a user-friendly way of validating is to offer a JavaScript prompt box for the users to enter missed information. The prompt box is executed before the submit is made and re-validates in case the client selects Cancel from the prompt. After doing the validation check on the field, set up the prompt as in this example:

```
promptMsg = "Please enter fieldName";
window.document.forms[0].fieldname.value = prompt(promptMsg,"");
```

Testing JavaScript

Unlike LotusScript, JavaScript does not have a built-in debugger. When you choose File, Save after writing JavaScript, or select the green check mark in the programmers' pane, JavaScript is compiled. If errors are detected, they are displayed, one at a time, in the status bar of the Programmer's Pane. JavaScript does not save as compiled code; it is recompiled every time it is run.

Understanding the JavaScript Document Object Model (DOM)

The Document Object Model (DOM) declares what objects are contained in the model and what objects can contain other objects. DOM also declares each object's list of methods, properties, and events.

 LiveConnect enables JavaScript to access components (such as a Java applet) and manipulate them. Without knowing in what language the component is written, designers who know the API for the component can use JavaScript to drive that component. Netscape Navigator, Internet Explore, and Notes have LiveConnect capability. Be prepared to answer exam questions on this topic.

When developing Web applications and implementing JavaScript, designers need to learn and understand the Document Object Model. JavaScript objects map to Domino design elements with some exceptions, as listed in Table 16.1.

Table 16.1 How JavaScript Objects Map to Domino Design Elements	
JavaScript Objects	**Domino Design Elements**
Window	Opened form, page, view, or frame that has focus.
Frame	Accessed by name as listed in the Frame Properties or as a frame array.
Document	Current opened Domino form, page, or view.

A JavaScript Document object can contain the following Domino form, page, or view elements:

➤ *Applets (self-contained programs) array*—Domino action bar, view, and Rich Text applets or applets you import.

➤ *Links array*—Domino actions, link hot spots, and action hotspots. Domino link hot spots do not have events associated with them, but designers can add JavaScript code in the Other field on the <html> tab of the HotSpot properties.

➤ *Images array*—Domino attachments, image resources, and pictures.

> The preceding objects can be referred to by name if they are specified on the **<html>** tab of the object's properties box.

➤ *Forms array* normally have only one element as Domino only renders one form at a time. Form arrays can be referenced two ways. One way is by their position in the array:

```
window.document.forms[0]
```

Another way is by the Domino form name preceded by an underscore:

```
window.document._formName
```

A forms array consists of an array of elements that can contain any of the following object types:

➤ *Button object*—Domino buttons.

> The button object can be referred to by name when specified on the **<html>** tab of the object's properties box.

➤ *Text object*—Domino field types Text, Date/Time, Number, Names, Authors, and Readers.

➤ *TextArea object*—Domino field type RichText.

➤ *Select object*—Domino field types Dialog list, Listbox, and Combobox.

➤ *Password object*—Domino field type Password

➤ *Radio object*—Domino field type Radio button.

➤ *Checkbox object*—Domino field type Checkbox.

➤ *Hidden object*—Domino hide-when is enabled and Generate HTML for all fields option is selected in the Form Properties.

 The objects in the preceding list can be referred to by their respective Domino field names.

➤ *FileUpload object*—Does not map to a Domino field type. FileUpload is an embedded object that allows Web clients to attach files and cannot be accessed in a Notes client.

Designers can display the JavaScript Document Object Model on the Design Client Welcome Screen by selecting it in the Show Me: drop-down box.

Working with Common JavaScript

Common JavaScript is new to Domino 6. Common JavaScript is applied to both Notes and Web users. Common JavaScript can be coded in seven events:

➤ onFocus

➤ onBlur

➤ onChange

➤ onLoad

➤ onUnload

➤ onSubmit

➤ onHelp

These events are discussed in detail in the "Using JavaScript events in Domino" section of Chapter 14, "Exam 612—Design Elements."

Deploying a Simple Java Applet on a Web Page

Applets are self-contained Java programs that can run in your Domino application. Java applets are mostly used for Web applications, as they are "client-side" programs, meaning the applet is downloaded and run by the browser. Browsers require Java support. Designers can include applets in the following Domino design elements:

> *Form*—Every document created from the form includes the applet.

> *Document*—The applet is available only on the document in which the applet was embedded.

> *Page*—The applet is available only in the page to which the applet was added.

An applet can be made up of one or more files; one of these files contains what is called the *main class*, which is where the applet starts. Image files, archive files, and Java source files can also be included. Java applets are stored in Domino when you

> *Import an applet*—Stores the applet file(s) as hidden file(s) attached to the element where the Java applet is included.

> *Link to an applet*—Stores the applet file(s) on the Web, and a URL reference to them is stored in an element where the Java applet is included.

> *Shared applet resource*—Stores the applet file(s) in the database where the applet is included.

HTML

Hypertext Markup Language (HTML) is a set of markup symbols or codes inserted in a file intended for display on a World Wide Web browser page. HTML tells browsers how to format or present the information they display. HTML markup symbols or codes are commonly referred to as tags, and usually are present in pairs that form a beginning tag and an ending tag.

Domino supplies an integrated Web server that renders Domino databases or HTML files to the Web. Domino databases are translated into HTML before they are rendered to the Web, and if the request is for an HTML file, Domino passes it directly, using the HTTP protocol.

Designers can include HTML on forms, subforms, form elements, pages, and views in many ways, including these:

> Code or paste HTML directly into the design element and set as pass-thru HTML.

➤ Select Domino elements, such as fields or tables, and use the new Convert to HTML function.

➤ Import an existing HTML file that is translated from HTML automatically.

Rendering HTML in Applications

Including HTML in an application is simple. Table 16.2 lists methods for coding, pasting, and importing HTML into a form, subform, or page.

Table 16.2 Rendering HTML	
Method	**Description**
Enter HTML directly	HTML can be entered directly into your application by following these steps:
	1. Open the design element (form, page, or subform).
	2. Enter the HTML code.
	3. Highlight the HTML code.
	4. Under the Text menu, Select Pass-Thru HTML or enclose the HTML code in square brackets [ ].
Paste HTML	HTML can be pasted into your application by following these steps:
	1. Highlight and copy the content from the source you want to copy. This can be from an existing Domino form or HTML file, or you can choose View, Source on a Web page.
	2. Open the Design element into which you want to paste the HTML code.
	3. Select Edit, Paste, or Ctrl+V.
	4. Highlight the HTML code.
	5. Under the Text menu, select Pass-Thru HTML.
Import HTML	HTML can be imported into your application by following these steps:
	1. Open the design element (form, page, or subform).
	2. From the menu choose File, Import.
	3. Select the HTML file you want to import and click OK.
	4. Domino translates the HTML into design elements onto your form, subform, or page.

Using HTML for Notes and Web Access

HTML code can be used with both Web and Notes clients. Designers need to set up HTML code differently for each client to render properly.

HTML code renders as plain text if not set correctly. For Web clients, HTML needs to be set as pass-thru; otherwise it is translated as static text. You can set HTML as pass-thru from the text menu or by using square brackets.

Rendering to Notes has the same problem; HTML is rendered as static text unless designated as pass-thru. To designate HTML as pass-thru, open the Info tab of the Form or Page properties; in the Options section, check Render pass through HTML in Notes. Designers may not want to render the HTML code on the Web; in this case, they can choose to hide the paragraph.

Rendering HTML to Notes does not work if designers use the square brackets to pass-thru the HTML code.

Using the HTML Editor

HTML editor is a new function with Domino 6. Designers can now convert their design elements into HTML and view them through the HTML editor. The HTML editor acts just like the Programmer's Pane with color-coding and auto-complete, as shown in Figure 16.3.

To convert your elements into HTML for viewing in the Editor, follow these steps:

1. Select the elements you want to convert.

2. Choose Edit, Convert to HTML from the menu.

Not every Notes element has an equivalent in HTML. The translation to HTML is an approximation and may not be exact. If something did not convert correctly, use Edit, Undo Delete to recover, not Edit, Convert to Notes.

3. Place your cursor anywhere in the HTML source code and from the View menu, choose HTML pane. This starts the HTML Editor. The screen splits with a Work pane on top and a Programmer's Pane on the bottom.

Figure 16.3 HTML Editor.

4. Using the bottom pane, edit the HTML source code and click the Refresh button to see the changes.

5. Press the Esc key to exit from the HTML Editor. You can convert back to Notes by choosing Edit, Convert to Notes Format but may get unexpected results (see the previous Note).

Creating HTML Fields on Pages Using Computed Text

You can prevent users from creating documents by giving them Reader access in the database ACL. You can allow users to create documents by giving them Author access with Create document privileges in the ACL. For security reasons, designers may want to allow only Reader access to the database, but still allow Web users to submit data.

An easy way to accomplish this task is to use pass-thru HTML on a page to create fields that allow users to submit data with only Reader access assigned in the ACL. Designers know that Domino fields can't be created on a page. HTML input fields, however, can be used.

Understanding an HTML Page and Its Format

The HTML page has two main parts—the Head and the Body. The Head is defined with a `<head>` tag and the Body is defined with a `<body>` tag. Some of the information contained in the Head area includes

➤ The scripting language that is being used, such as JavaScript. The scripting language is identified by a `<script>` tag.

➤ The browser's window title, defined with a `<title>` tag. Programming the Domino Window Title event will translate to an HTML `<title>` tag.

The body tag has many attributes to which most Domino elements translate directly. The body area of an HTML page contains information about elements such as text, graphics, or links, and these elements' format tags, which will display on the Web.

A sample of HTML code shows some of these tags:

```
<!DOCTYPE HTML PUBLIC "-//W3C//DTD HTML 4.01 Transitional//EN">
<html>
<head>
<title>HTML Test of Browser Window Title</title>
<script language="JavaScript" type="text/javascript">
<!—
```

Additional code goes here:

```
// —>
</script>
</head>
<body text="#000000" bgcolor="#FFFFFF">
<form method="post" action="/dlb/Home.nsf/htmltest?OpenForm➥
&amp;Seq=1" name="_htmltest">
<input type="hidden" name="__Click" value="0"><br>
<input name="myname" value="">
<br><br>
<input type="file" name="%%File.85256c4800698246.➥
be7b1f42a521085785256d9e001fb58c.$Body.0.118"><br>
<br>
<input type="button" value="submit" onclick="return➥
 _doClick('85256C4800698246.be7b1f42a521085785256d9e001fb58c/➥
$Body/0.156', this, null)">
<br>
</form>
</body>
</html>
```

Using HTML in Views

Designers can store HTML in view columns to change default column and row settings. To store HTML in view columns, check the Treat view contents as HTML option on the Advanced tab of the View Properties and add the code to the Programmer's Pane. The following example adds HTML code to display a graphic:

```
@If(Status="Past Due";"[<img src=/overdue.gif border=0>]";"")
```

Domino views do not always render to the Web in the expected format, for example, with the expected spacing between columns. By adding HTML to the view, you can add spacing between columns. The HTML code must be added to two places in the column—the Title text field in the Column properties dialog box and the Column Value in the Programmer's Pane, as shown in Figure 16.4.

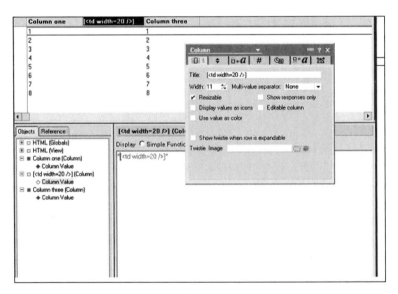

Figure 16.4   HTML code in View column.

Notice that the HTML code in the Programmer's Pane for the Column Value is enclosed in quotes and the HTML code in the Column Title is not enclosed in quotes. In addition, the Treat View Contents As HTML option still needs to be selected in the Advanced tab of the View properties box.

Using HTML in Tables

Tables can be created with pass-thru HTML, or enhanced if you add pass-thru HTML within an existing Domino table (such as when creating a nested table). In addition, as shown in Figure 16.5, HTML can be added to the Table Properties on the Table Programming (<@>) tab.

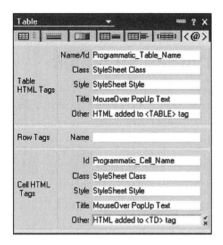

Figure 16.5 Table Properties **<@>** tab.

Increasing the thickness of a table border has no affect when the table is rendered on the Web. Table borders are translated to the Web simply as "on" or "off." Table border color doesn't translate to the Web, either. If these border attributes are required, you can add attributes of the <table> tag (Table HTML Tags section) or <td> tag (Cell HTML Tags section) to the Other field on the <@> tab of the Table Properties. Table 16.3 lists some of the attributes of the <table> or <td> tag.

Table 16.3	***table*** and ***td*** Tag Attributes
Attribute	**Description**
border	Changes the size of the table border. Add this to the Table tag.
bordercolor	Changes the color of the table border. Add this to the Table tag.
cellspacing	Changes spacing between cells in pixels. Add this to the Table tag.
cellpadding	Changes the spacing, in pixels, between the cell contents and its border. Add this to the Table tag.
colspan	Merges cells across multiple columns. Add this to the Cell tag.
rowspan	Merges cells across multiple rows. Add this to the Cell tag.

Table 16.3	*<table>* and *<td>* Tag Attributes *(continued)*
Attribute	**Description**
height	Changes the height of all cells in the table or row, depending on whether added to the Table or Cell tag.
width	Changes the width of all cells in the table or column, depending on whether added to the Table or Cell tag.

Working with HTML Attributes on Fields

Domino Designer enables you to add HTML attributes to fields in two places: on the Field Extra HTML (<html>) tab of the Field Properties dialog box or to the Field Objects HTML Attributes event. To add HTML to the <html> tab, follow these steps:

1. Open the Field properties and click on the <html> tab. (The <html> tag is discussed in detail in Chapter 14.)

2. Enter your HTML code in the HTML Tags: Other field. Do not enclose HTML code in quotes.

3. Save and close the form.

To add HTML to the Field Objects HTML Attributes event:

1. Click on the field.

2. Select the Field's HTML Attribute event.

3. In the Programmers Pane write your HTML code enclosed in quotes.

4. Save and close the form.

Rendering DHTML in Applications

Dynamic HTML (DHTML) is HTML, JavaScript, CSS, and the browser's Document Object Model presenting content dynamically. In Chapter 14, you read that tabbed tables must make a roundtrip to the server every time a tab is selected. DHTML can be used to bypass this limitation by simulating a tabbed table with no server interaction.

Using Domino URL Syntax

Domino URL commands enable designers to manipulate objects, such as forms or images, directly. Designers can provide navigational elements by adding URL commands as HTML on the form or button.

Domino URL syntax is as follows:

```
http://Host/Database/DominoObject?Action&Arguments
```

Table 16.4 explains URL syntax by listing its parameters and their descriptions.

Table 16.4 URL Syntax	
Parameter	**Description**
Host	Add DNS entry or IP address to identify the server. Do not use the server's name.
Database	Database in which **DominoObject** resides. If opening a database, the syntax would be **http://Host/Database.nsf?OpenDatabase** Database can be identified: By its filename or By its replica ID, preceded with a double underscore and appended with .nsf.
DominoObject	Object being accessed, such as a form, document, view, navigator, agent, image, and so on. **DominoObject** can be identified by the object's name, universal ID, or special identifier (**$defaultView** refers to the default view designated in database).
Action	Operation for specific **DominoObject**. Example: ?OpenDatabase, ?OpenView, **?OpenDocument**, **?EditDocument**. Explicit actions are **?OpenDocument** or **?EditDocument**. Implicit actions are **?Open** or **?Edit**. If an action is not specified, the default is **?Open**.
Arguments	Qualifier to the Action. **&count=5** with **?OpenView**, for example, limits rows displayed. **&Login** attached with **?OpenDatabase** forces authentication.
Special Identifiers	Identifies such things as default views and forms with **$defaultView** or **$defaultForm**. Some others are **$searchForm**, **$file**, **$icon**, **$help**, **$about**, and **$first**.

URLs cannot contain spaces, so designers need to replace spaces with a plus (+) symbol or the hex ASCII equivalent (%20). You must use the Hex ASCII equivalent if a symbol conflicts with the URL syntax. For example, imagine that a view named Sales&Commission is used in an URL. The Ampersand (&) symbol conflicts with the &Arguments and must be replaced with the HEX ASCII equivalent. Ampersands (&) use %26 and forward slashes use %2F.

To attach URLs to a button or a hotspot Click event, first select the Use JavaScript When Generating Pages option in the Database Properties. If this option isn't checked, the URL will be computed when rendered to the Web.

Table 16.5 shows some examples of DominoObjects and their URLs.

Table 16.5 URL Examples	
DominoObject	**URL**
Attachments	http://Host/Database/View/Document$File/ InternalFileName?OpenElement
Database	http://Host/__DatabaseReplicaID.nsf?OpenDatabase
View	http://Host/Database/ViewName?OpenView
DefaultView	http://Host/Database/$defaultview?OpenView
View data in XML form without attributes	This command returns only the documents a user is allowed to access. http://Host/Database/ViewName?
About This Database	http://Host/Database/$about?OpenAbout
Using This Database	http://Host/Database/$help?OpenHelp
Access Database Icon	http://Host/Database/$icon?OpenIcon
FrameSet	http://Host/Database/FramesetName?OpenFrameset
Agents	http://Host/Database/AgentName?OpenAgent
Form	http://Host/Database/FormName?OpenForm
Default Form	http://Host/Database/$defaultform?OpenForm
Read Form	http://Host/Database/FormName?ReadForm
Navigator	http://Host/Database/NavigatorName?OpenNavigator
Default Navigator	http://host/database.nsf/$DefaultNav?OpenNavigator The above displays all non-hidden views to the Web. Enclose View Names in parens to block this.
Pages	http://Host/Database/PageName?OpenPage

Table 16.5 URL Examples *(continued)*	
DominoObject	**URL**
Document	**http://Host/Database/FormName?CreateDocument**
	http://Host/Database/View/Document?OpenDocument
	http://Host/Database/View/Document?EditDocument
	http://Host/Database/View/Document?DeleteDocument
	http://Host/Database/View/Document?SaveDocument
SearchView	Limits search to one database view.
	http://Host/Database/ViewName/[$SearchForm]? SearchView[ArgumentList]
Image Resources	**http://Host/Database/ ImageResourceName?OpenImageResource**
File Resources	**http://Host/Database/ FileResourceName?OpenFileResource**
Web Preferences	**http://Host/$Preferences.nsf?OpenPreferences&Argument**
	Allows users to set time zone and regional settings such as date/time formats. These settings are stored in a cookie in the user's browser. Web preferences need to be enabled through Internet Site documents. **$Preferences.nsf** is a virtual database that resides at the root of the Domino 6 server.

Designers can also restrict users from opening forms or views with URL commands by setting the Don't Allow URL Open property in the Basics tab of the Database.

Passing Data from a Web Form to a Web Agent

As discussed in the "Deploying and Utilizing LotusScript Agents" section later in this chapter, when an agent is run from the WebQueryOpen and WebQuerySave events, the agent has access to all items in the document. Agents can access this data as they would any field value.

Agents called by a URL have access to a domino document, but only the document's CGI variables. (You learn more about these variables in "Using

CGI Variables," later in this chapter.) You can add parameters to the URL command ?OpenAgent to give the agent access to this data. An example:

```
http://Host/Database/AgentName?OpenAgent&Dept="Marketing"&Mgr="AnitaKnapp"
```

The URL can be dynamically created with JavaScript.

Using XML in Applications

eXtensible Markup Language (XML) uses markup tags to define or describe data, not display data (which is what HTML is for). XML is an industry standard that allows data to be exchanged between systems, whether the data is exchanged over the Internet or within an intranet. XML allows designers to define their document structure and create their own tags. Some terms associated with XML are listed and described in Table 16.6.

Table 16.6 XML Terms	
Term	**Description**
DTD	Document Type Defintion defines the data structure of the document, which guarantees consistency and proper interpretation of the data when exchanged with other systems. DTD includes element names and attributes, tree structure of the data, number of elements, and rules of the data structure.
Valid XML	XML that conforms to the specifications defined in a DTD. XML can be created without a DTD, but you can only determine that the XML is well formed syntactically, not that the XML is Valid XML.
XSL	Extensible Stylesheet Language formats the presentation of the data. XML delivers data in plain text without XSL.
XSLT	XSL Transformation is the engine that actually transforms the data.
DOM API	Document Object Model (DOM) API represents the XML data as a tree object model, making it easier to navigate through.
SAX API	Simple API for XML (SAX) is event driven. Elements in XML trigger events that are passed to event handlers.
NotesDXLExporter	LotusXSL processor to generate DXL.
NotesDXLImporter	LotusXSL processor to process DXL data.

Working with DXL Tools

Domino's architecture is similar to XML in that they both separate data from formatting. Domino presents a document, which is data, through a form that controls the formatting.

Domino XML Language (DXL) was developed to represent Domino data. It contains the tags and attributes needed to describe Notes elements stored in an .nsf file.

Designer ND6 includes some DXL Utilites that can be used as tools for handling XML. The three tools are

➤ *Exporter*—Converts design elements into DXL.

➤ *Viewer*—Displays the elements in the DXL format.

➤ *Transformer*—Applies a style sheet to design elements and outputs the elements to a display screen or creates an HTML file.

You can access these tools by selecting Tools, DXL Utilities from the Designer Client menu.

New with ND6 also, are LotusScript classes for working with DXL; most of the existing classes have been updated with methods to work with XML.

Writing Formulas to Support Different Clients

Domino formula language works quite well, in some instances, on the Web. Domino cannot translate its menu to the Web, but can translate menu commands attached to buttons, hot spots, or actions. Some formulas don't translate at all and others have restrictions. Design elements with formulas that work on the Web include these:

➤ Action

➤ Agent—started with the @Commands for `ToolsRunMacro` and `RunAgent` or a URL command

➤ Column

➤ Computed field value

➤ Computed text

➤ Default value

➤ Event—only the WebQueryOpen and WebQuerySave form events

➤ Form

➤ Hide properties—action, column, paragraph

➤ Hotspot

➤ Input translation

➤ Input validation

➤ Computed subform

➤ Keyword field

➤ Named element

➤ Sections—access and titles

➤ Selection

➤ Window titles

 In preparing for the exam, you need to know which formulas work on the Web and how they work. Pay special attention to the information in this chapter that discusses using @Commands and @Functions in Web applications.

Using @Commands in Web Applications

Standard menu commands, and some specialized commands, can be issued through @Commands. To add multiple buttons on a form or use certain @Commands, check the Use JavaScript when generating pages option in the Web Access section of the Database Property. Table 16.7 lists how selecting this option can affect your application.

Table 16.7 Effects of Use JavaScript when Generating Pages Property	
Selected	**Not Selected**
Documents display faster because hot spot formulas aren't evaluated until they are clicked.	Hotspot formulas are evaluated at display time, resulting in longer load time.
Submit button is not automatically generated. You must manually create and code a Submit button to allow users to save and close. Attach the following code to a Submit button: **@Command([FileSave]); @Command([CloseWindow])**	Submit button generated automatically and displays at bottom of form.
You can have multiple buttons on a form.	You can have only one button, a Submit button, on a form. If multiple buttons are added to the form, Domino converts the first button to a Submit button automatically and ignores all others.
The following commands are supported on the Web: **@Command([CloseWindow])** **@Command([FileSave])** **@Command([ViewRefreshFields])**	The following commands are not supported on the Web: **@Command([CloseWindow])** **@Command([FileSave])** **@Command([ViewRefreshFields])**
Domino does not check the formulas before displaying pages.	Domino checks the formulas before displaying pages. Actions that contain unsupported @Commands or @Functions are not displayed on the Web.

@Commands work in buttons, hot spots, and action formulas. @Commands do not work in column, selection, hide-when, section editor, window title, field, or form formulas, or in agents that run on a server.

Using @Functions in Web Applications

@Functions are predefined formulas that perform specific tasks and return a value. Some @Functions do not work at all on the Web, others are restricted, and still others are particularly useful. The following sections describe each of these types of @Functions.

@Functions That Work in Web Applications

In Table 16.8 is a list of @Functions that could prove to be quite useful in Web applications.

Table 16.8 @Functions	
@Function	**Description**
@ClientType	Retrieves client information to allow designers to make decisions based on client. Returns: ➤ **Web** from a browser client ➤ **Notes** from Notes client ➤ **None** from an agent Knowing which client is accessing your Web application would be useful when using hide-when formulas or computed subforms.
@BrowserInfo*(property)*	Retrieves browser information to allow designers to make decisions based on browser type. **@BrowserInfo** cannot be used in view selection and view column formulas. The syntax is **@BrowserInfo("***property***")** Properties associated with **@BrowserInfo** are described in Table 16.9, "**@BrowserInfo** Properties," following this table.
@URLOpen(urlstring)	Retrieves Web site specified in the URL. The following code opens LDD: **@URLOpen(http://www.lotus.com/ldd)**
@WebDbName	Retrieves the name of the current database in URL format. It replaces a backslash with a forward slash and a space with a **%20**(hexadecimal 20). **@WebDbName** is new to ND6 and replaces an equivalent formula that would need a combination of **@DbName**, **@Subset**, and **@ReplaceString**.
@GetHTTPHeader("requestHeader")	Returns the value of an HTTP request-header field, such as "From," "Host," or "User-Agent." **@GetHTTPHeader("Host")**

Table 16.8   @Functions *(continued)*

@Function	Description
@SetHTTPHeader ("responseHeader";value)	Sets the value of an HTTP response-header field, such as, "Content-Encoding", "Content-Length", "Set-Cookie". Value can be text, number, or date to which you want to set the field. Return value is True (1) or False (0) and the Notes client always returns False (0). **@SetHTTPHeader("Set-Cookie"; "COOKIE1=4646")**
@UrlQueryString(parameterName)	Returns the URL command and parameters, or just the value of one parameter. **http://www.your.com/dbname.nsf? OpenForm&ID=995764&FirstName= Deborah** **@UrlQueryString** The preceding URL returns the list: **OpenForm : ID=995764 : FirstName=Deborah** **@UrlQueryString(FirstName)** Returns the text: Deborah Notes clients always return null with this function.
@DbCommand("Domino";parameter)	When used with **"Domino"** as the first parameter, creates links to Previous or Next page. **@DbCommand("Domino";"ViewNextPage")** **@DbCommand("Domino";"ViewPreviousPage")** This is the only syntax where @DbCommand will work on the Web, and it is used for an embedded view when accessed from an action on a page or document.
@Command([Viewcommand])	Expands or collapses all categories in a view. **@Command([ViewExpandAll])** **@Command([ViewCollapseAll])** Works on the Web if Use Applet in the Browser is checked in the View properties

Table 16.8 @Functions *(continued)*	
@Function	**Description**
@UrlEncode(encodingFormat;token)	Translates into a URL-safe format. Two encoding formats are ➤ Domino—standard character set used by Domino Web server ND6. ➤ Platform—the current system's native character set. **@UrlEncode("Domino";"Manager/By Dept")** Above code would return **"Manager%2FBy%20Dept"**. Don't use this function to encode an entire URL because it wouldn't link successfully.
@UrlDecode(decodeType;token)	This function is the reverse of the preceding one: It decodes URL strings into regular text. Decode types are the same as the preceding function. **@URLDecode("Domino";** **"Manager%2FBy%20Dept")** Above code returns **"Manager/By Dept"**.
@Success and **@Failure**	Input validation formulas work on the Web. The message specified in the **@Failure** appears on a new page. HTML can be embedded in the message to provide a customized message and possibly a return link. These require a roundtrip to the server.

For the exam, remember that the code

```
@SetHTTPHeader("Set-Cookie";"COOKIE1=4646")
```

sets the response-header field **"Set-Cookie"** to **"COOKIE1=4646"** and appends it to the end of the standard HTTP response. This function registers a cookie for the server with this name and value with the Web client.

Table 16.9 @BrowserInfo Properties		
Property	**Browser Returns**	**Notes Returns**
BrowserType	➤ "Microsoft," ➤ "Netscape," ➤ "Compatible" (compatible with Netscape, including Notes Navigator 5.0), ➤ "Unknown"	"Notes"

Table 16.9 @BrowserInfo Properties *(continued)*

Property	Browser Returns	Notes Returns
Cookies	1 (True) supports cookies 0 (False) doesn't.	0 (False)
DHTML	1 (True) supports dynamic HTML; 0 (False) if not.	0 (False)
FileUpload	1 (True) supports file upload; 0 (False) if not.	0 (False)
Frames	1 (True) supports HTML <FRAME> tag; 0 (False) if not.	1 (True)
Java	1 (True) if the browser supports Java applets; otherwise 0 (False).	1 (True)
JavaScript	1 (True) if the browser supports JavaScript; otherwise 0 (False).	1 (True)
Iframe	1 (True) if supports the Microsoft HTML <IFRAME> tag; 0 (False) if not.	0 (False)
Platform	Operating System platform of the browser: "Win95," "Win98," "WinNT," "MacOS," "Unknown."	"Unknown"
Robot	1 (True) if browser is possibly a Web robot; 0 (False) if not.	0 (False)
SSL	1 (True) if supports SSL; 0 (False) if not.	
Tables	1 (True) if supports HTML <TABLE> tag; 0 (False) if not.	
VBScript	1 (True) if supports VBScript; 0 (False) if not.	
Version	The browser version number; -1 for unrecognized browsers.	Notes client build number

@BrowserInfo and all of its properties offer a lot of functionality to designers. Be prepared to answer questions regarding **@BrowserInfo** on the exam.

@Functions That Don't Work on the Web

Sometimes knowing what doesn't work on the Web is just as important as knowing what does work. Exam 612 will test your knowledge of both. Table 16.10 lists the @Functions that do not work (or work only with exceptions) on the Web.

Table 16.10 @Functions That Don't Work on the Web			
@Certificate	@Unique	@DDEExecute	@DDEInitiate@DDEPoke
@DDETerminate	@DocMark	@DeleteDocument	@DocChildren
@DocDescendants	@DocLevel	@DocNumber	@DocParentNumber
@DocSiblings	@IsCategory	@IsExpandable	@Responses
@DialogBox	@PickList	@Prompt	@IsModalHelp
@GetPortsList	@Environment; @SetEnvironment; ENVIRONMENT keyword (use CGI environment variables)	@IsDocBeingMailed	@MailEncryptSendPreference
@MailSend	@Domain	@MailDbName	@MailEncryptSavedPreference
@URLGetHeader	@MailSavePreference	@MailSignPreference	@Platform returns user's platform only
@URLHistory	@UserPrivileges	@IsAgentEnabled	

Using **Weekday** to Create Design Elements

The Weekday function returns a number value of 1 through 7 to represent the different days of the week. The value 1 represents Sunday. Weekday is a function of LotusScript and @Weekday is an @Function.

Working with **$$Return** Fields

When Web clients submit a document, Domino returns a generic confirmation message of "Form processed" by default. $$Return is a reserved field name that you can use to customize the generic Form Processed Confirmation message.

By adding a text—computed for display and field named $$Return—to a form, you can add HTML to the Value event of this field. Table 16.11 lists and explains some examples of $$Return.

Table 16.11 $$Return Code Examples	
Type of Custom Message	**Code to Be Placed in the Programmer's Pane of the Field's Value Event**
Thank You	*"Thank you for your suggestion."*
Personalized Thank You— with Users Name	If the site has forced authentication, then the users name is available and can be added to the formula to personalize it. *"Thank you " + @UserName + " for your suggestion."*
Thank You with Link to a New Page	HTML link code can be included in the **$$Return** field to give the user a way out of the Form Processed Confirmation document. *"Thank You" +" <a href \http://www.lotus.com\> Lotus Web Site</a>"*
Redirect to another Web site	If Designers want the Form Processed Confirmation to automatically redirect to another Web page or site, enclose the URL in brackets. *"[http://www.mycompany.com]"*

You may encounter other reserved $$Return names associated with forms rather than with fields. $$Return form names, like $$Return fields, allow you to display custom messages that include links or redirections instead of HTTP error messages. If an application requires authentication, a Web user would receive an Error 401 User not authenticated message if they failed.

Creating a $$ReturnAuthenticationFailure form is a method you can use to create a custom notification that the user could not validate; you also can use this method to provide a link to retry or redirect to a registration page. Table 16.12 lists and describes the four reserved form names that create custom error messages.

Table 16.12 Custom Error Message Forms	
Form Name	**Description**
$$ReturnAuthenticationFailure	Username and password could not authenticate with the server.
$$ReturnAuthorizationFailure	Database access is insufficient for what the user is trying to do.
$$ReturnDocumentDeleted	Validation that a document was successfully deleted.
$$ReturnGeneralError	All other error conditions.

To create a Custom Error Message Form to display non-generic messages if a user could not authenticate, follow these steps:

1. Create a form named $$ReturnAuthenticationFailure.

2. Create links, text messages, or computed redirection fields.

3. On the Security tab of the Form Properties, check Available to Public Access Users.

4. In the Database ACL, make sure Default and Anonymous access have Read Public Document privileges.

Optionally, you can choose to create a MessageString field option. MessageString is a reserved field name and displays the HTTP generated default error. This field could be used in conjunction with a Computed for display field, which contains a formula that creates the custom message based on the value in the MessageString field. MessageString can be referred to without adding the field to the form.

Other reserved field names are listed in Table 16.13.

Table 16.13	Reserved Field Names
Type	**Description**
HTML	HTML contained in this field is passed directly to the browser and Domino ignores all other fields.
$$HTMLHead	Information in this field is HTML code and will be passed to the browser as part of the **<HEAD>** tag for a document.

For the exam, familiarize yourself with the reserved fields used to create custom error messages (as listed in Table 16.12) and the reserved HTML fields (listed in Table 16.13).

Deploying and Utilizing LotusScript Agents

LotusScript and Java are usually used to write agents for the Web. Simple Actions are not supported and @Functions don't allow data to be returned.

LotusScript agents are executed from the WebQueryOpen and WebQuerySave events (as discussed in the "Deploying and Utilizing LotusScript" section in Chapter 14) and also from the OpenAgent URL command.

The `NotesSession.DocumentContext` property returns a `NotesDocument` when a LotusScript agent is executed from these events. The `NotesDocument` contains Web session information, CGI variables associated with the session, and access to all document items. The following code shows how to access these CGI variables:

```
Dim session As New NotesSession
Dim context As NotesDocument
Dim CGIValue As String
Set context = session.DocumentContext

CGIValue = context.HTTP_USER_AGENT(0)
Set webUserName = context.remote_user(0)
```

Domino design elements are easy and efficient, but you also can use agents to create Web pages. In LotusScript agents, the output is created with the Print statement. An agent can print three types of output:

➤ Data to be displayed on the Web (this could be an HTML page)

➤ URL to redirect, coded in square ([ ]) brackets

➤ URL to a new site, coded in double square ([[ ]]) brackets

Deploying and utilizing LotusScript is also discussed further in Chapter 14.

As an application designer, you also must think about basic security. A user may issue the Domino URL command ?OpenAgent repeatedly, tying up resources and causing a Denial of Service attack. To prevent users from issuing the URL command by themselves, check the HTTP_REFERRER CGI variable at the beginning of your LotusScript agent. This variable tracks the source of the Web request; a returned value of blank indicates the URL was entered directly. With this information, you can terminate agents before they do any harm to your system.

Using CGI Variables

Common Gateway Interface (CGI) is a standard interface used between external applications and HTTP servers. Domino uses CGI programs to parse data sent by the browser into *CGI variables* to collect data about the user. Most CGI variables available are listed and explained in Table 16.14. For a complete list of CGI variables, refer to Designer help. Domino enables you to access CGI variables in two ways:

➤ Create a field with the CGI variable as its name.

➤ Create an agent whose code contains a CGI variable as a DocumentContext property.

Table 16.14 CGI Variable Field Names Table	
Field name	**Returns**
Auth_Type	The type of authentication used when a user validates. For basic authentication on the Web, this CGI variable will return the value Basic.
Gateway_Interface	Returns the value of the CGI version.
HTTP_Accept	Returns a list of MIME types the client accepts.
HTTP_Accept_language	Returns the language the browser accepts.
HTTP_Referer	The URL the client used to obtain this element.
HTTPS	Indicates whether SSL mode is ON or OFF.
HTTPS_CLIENT_CERT_ COMMON_NAME	If SSL is ON, will return the common name listed on the x.509 certificate.
HTTPS_CLIENT_CERT_ ISSUER_COMMON_NAME	If SSL is ON, will return the who issued the x.509 certificate.
HTTP_User_Agent	The browser that the client is using to send the request.
Path_Info	Returns the path portion of the URL.
Path_Info_Decoded	If the URL was encoded, this CGI variable decodes the path portion of the URL string into regular text.
Query_String	Returns the URL from the action on or everything after the question mark (?). URLs are generated with an exclamation mark (!) rather than a question mark (?) if you allow search engines to search your Web site. Domino recognizes both.
Query_String_Decoded	If the URL was encoded, this CGI variable decodes the Query_String portion of the URL into regular text. This CGI variable is used in Domino applications only.
Remote_Addr	The IP address from which the request is coming.
Remote_User	Returns name of user if the user authenticated.
Request_Content	Holds the information sent with an HTTP POST request. This CGI variable is used for agents only.
Request_Method	Returns the method the request is using, such as GET or POST.
Server_Name	Returns the server's hostname, DNS alias, or IP address.
Server_Protocol	The name and revision of the protocol used in the URL such as HTTP/1.1.
Server_Port	The port the URL request uses. 80 is the default port for HTTP.
Server_Software	The software the server is using to run the CGI programs. An example return value would be Lotus-Domino.

Table 16.15 lists and explains an example of what a field named HTTP_USER_AGENT would return.

Table 16.15 Reserved Field Names	
Returned	**Browser**
MSIE	Microsoft Internet Explorer 4 or later
Mozilla 3.x	Netscape Navigator 3.x
Mozilla 4.x	Netscape Navigator 4.x
Mozilla 5.x	Netscape Navigator 6.x

Working with Cookies in Your Applications

Cookies are a mechanism a Web site uses to store information on the client (user's hard drive) to be used in the future. This information could be a user's color preferences or information about where the user has been in your application. Domino creates cookies in some instances, and when Domino uses these functions, Web browsers must support cookies. Two examples of when Domino uses cookies is to

➤ Track user sessions with session-based authentication.

➤ Set users' personal preferences. The OpenPreferences URL command sets a cookie to store users' time zones and regional language preferences.

Summary

By no means does this chapter encompass everything available in Domino ND6 Designer. It touched on only the basic factors in understanding the many and different programming features available. This chapter covered simple design elements such as horizontal rules, and more advanced elements such as agents and $$Return fields. The chapter also discussed programming languages such as LotusScript, @Functions, @Commands, JavaScript, HTML, DHTML, and XML, and how they relate to the Web. You learned ways to manipulate data through URL commands, CGI variables, Java applets, and cookies.

The information in this chapter has given you many options to consider when programming an application and valuable material to review when studying for this exam.

Exam Prep Questions

Question 1

> Kayla would like to use a Domino URL command to open the About This Database document. Which command is correct?
>
> ○ A. **http://Host/Database/About?OpenAbout**
>
> ○ B. **http://Host/Database/$aboutdocument?OpenAbout**
>
> ○ C. **http://Host/Database/AboutDocument?OpenAbout**
>
> ○ D. **http://Host/Database/$about?OpenAbout**

Answer D is the correct answer. $about is a special identifier for Domino-generated objects. Answers A, B, and C are syntactically incorrect.

Question 2

> While designing an application that will be used in both clients, Samatha would like to use Common JavaScript. Which event can she not use?
>
> ○ A. **onMouseOver**
>
> ○ B. **onFocus**
>
> ○ C. **onBlur**
>
> ○ D. **onLoad**

Answer A is the correct answer. OnMouseOver is not available to Notes clients. Answers B, C, and D are incorrect because they are available to both clients and to Common JavaScript.

Question 3

> Dawn has added HTML to her Domino form. She has made it Pass-Thru HTML
> through the Text menu, and the HTML works fine on the Web. When her Notes
> clients access it, though, the HTML code displays as static text. How can this be
> corrected?
>
> ○ A. HTML cannot be used on the Notes client.
>
> ○ B. She needs to use the Hide Paragraph from Notes R4.6 or later Text
> Property.
>
> ○ C. She needs to enable the Form property Render pass through HTML in
> Notes.
>
> ○ D. She needs to enable pass-thru HTML by placing her code within
> square ([]) brackets, not use the Text menu.

Answer C is the correct answer. Answer A is incorrect because HTML can translate on the Notes client if properly set. Answer B is incorrect; though this property would hide the HTML code from Notes clients, it still would not render it. Answer D is incorrect because setting the Render... Form property does not work with the square([]) brackets.

Question 4

> When adding a Java Applet to his application, Daniel was not sure how to best
> accomplish this task. Which of the following is an incorrect method for doing so?
>
> ○ A. Import the applet.
>
> ○ B. Code a URL link.
>
> ○ C. Use Share Code.
>
> ○ D. Use Shared Resources.

Answer C is the correct answer. Share Code stores elements such as Agents, Shared Actions, Subforms, Outlines, and Code Libraries. Answers A, B, and D all can be used to add a Java Applet.

Question 5

Sandra would like to prompt her Web users for correct input when validation fails rather than just place focus back into the field. How can Sandra do this?

- ○ A. Use the **@Prompt** function.
- ○ B. Use the JavaScript prompt.
- ○ C. Can't be done because prompts do not work on the Web.
- ○ D. Use the **@DialogBox** function.

Answer B is the correct answer. Not only do JavaScript prompts work on the Web, but they process on the client. Answers A and D are incorrect because these @Functions do not work on the Web. Answer C is incorrect because you can use a JavaScript prompt on the Web.

Need to Know More?

IBM International Technical Support Organization. *Domino Designer 6: A Developer's Handbook*. Available in printed form, PDF format, and HTML format from `publib-b.boulder.ibm.com/Redbooks.nsf/RedbookAbstracts/sg246854.html?Open`.

IBM Redbook. *XML Powered by Domino—How to Use XML with Lotus Domino*. Available in printed form, PDF format, and HTML format from `publib-b.boulder.ibm.com/Redbooks.nsf/RedbookAbstracts/sg246207.html?Open`.

LDD Today technical articles are available in PDF format from `http://www.lotus.com/ldd`.

IBM Lotus. *Release Notes*. Available as a zipped file, PDF format, and HTML format from `http://www-10.lotus.com/ldd/notesua.nsf`. Also available through Designer client Help menu by selecting Lotus Internet Resources which opens a sub menu and then selecting Domino & Notes Doc Library.

IBM Lotus *Help Databases*. `help6_admin.nsf`, `help6_client.nsf`, `help6_designer.nsf`. Also available in PDF format, HTML format, and .nsf format from `http://www-10.lotus.com/ldd/notesua.nsf`.

Security

Terms you'll need to understand:

✓ Access Control List (ACL)
✓ Anonymous access
✓ Web authentication
✓ Notes authentication
✓ Field Encryption
✓ Secure Socket Layers (SSL)
✓ Maximum Internet Access
✓ Roles
✓ File Protection Documents

Concepts/Techniques you'll need to master:

✓ Understanding security differences between Web and Notes clients
✓ How to plan application security based on Web Authentication
✓ Setting database access
✓ Setting field access
✓ Controlling access to CGI directories
✓ Setting File Protection documents
✓ Understanding and determining Secure Sockets Layer (SSL)

When developing an application, you need to know not only the purpose of the application but also what needs to be done to protect it. Understanding the Domino Security Model is a first step to securing your applications. Application developers use the Domino Security Model to guarantee data is accessible only to those users whom it was intended. This is especially true for Web browsers, where TCP/IP is an open protocol.

Security is a concern to both Administrators and Designers. This chapter discusses security issues related to accessing applications through both Notes and Web clients and addresses the security topics covered on the 612 exam.

Understanding Security Differences Between Web and Notes Client Access

Notes and Web clients use two different types of security procedures when accessing the server. *Notes authentication* uses what is called Validation and Authentication, which is actually two security procedures that interact with the users' Notes ID. Web clients do not use an ID file to authenticate; Web authentication uses what is called Basic Authentication. *Basic Authentication* is a simpler procedure that authenticates against the Name and Internet Password in a Person document.

First, let's explore Notes authentication using the Validation and Authentication procedures. Validation is the first step in this process, and it is used to establish trust with the user's public key. Validation checks the certificate(s) located in the user's Notes ID file, using the public key stored in that ID file. If the certificate(s) is valid, then the public key is trusted and authentication begins. If validation is successful, the second procedure, authentication, verifies identities by using what is called a challenge/response procedure.

During Authentication, the server sends the user a random number. The user's workstation encrypts this number, using the private key stored in the user's ID file, and returns the encrypted number back to the server. With the public key, the server decrypts this number and—if it matches the original—the user is authenticated. This is a two-way street and the same process is reversed to authenticate the server to the user. Web users do not use a Notes ID to access Domino; instead, they use a different security method called Basic Authentication. This is a simple procedure that authenticates a user's login name and password against the name and Internet Password stored in the user's Person document in the directory. (You learn more about this process in the next section of this chapter.)

Both Notes and Web clients can access a server as Anonymous. *Anonymous access* does not validate, authenticate, or record database activity. In other words, you do not know who is accessing the system. You may want to apply Anonymous access to a home page, a catalog, or company information. Settings to allow Anonymous access to the server are located in the Server document. For Notes users this is found on the Security tab, and for Web users it can be set for the different protocols (HTTP, Mail, Directories, and so on) on the Ports/Internet Ports tab under Authentication Options. After allowing Anonymous access has been set at the server level, Anonymous can be added to the ACL.

Planning Application Security Based on Web Authentication

As mentioned earlier, Web authentication is based on what is called Basic Authentication. When you are planning Web security you need to be aware that Basic Authentication does not happen automatically. Two actions force Basic Authentication:

➤ When a Server has been set to not allow Anonymous access (as mentioned above).

➤ When a Web user tries to do something he or she is not authorized to do.

Designers set the level of access that users or servers have to a specific database through the *ACL* (Access Control List). This access level determines what the user can do and what data servers can replicate. Every database has an Access Control List that needs to be set.

When users try to do more than they are allowed, they are prompted with a Name and Password login screen. Users who have a Person document with a matching Name and Internet Password are authenticated and get the individual or group access they are assigned in the database ACL.

An example of how the ACL could be set is if you have a designer who wants the general population to be able to open and read documents in your company's catalog. Just a select few should be able to create documents. If you set Anonymous to Reader access and the select few to Author access in the ACL, all users can open this database, read all the documents, and not be forced to authenticate. Any person who tries to create a new document (Anonymous is not authorized to do this) is forced to authenticate.

Determining Secure Sockets Layer Security

Secure Sockets Layer (SSL) is used to encrypt Internet transmissions and create a trusted relationship between servers and Web clients. SSL provides privacy through encryption and authentication between the server and the client. SSL also detects tampering. The following protocols can use SSL:

➤ Hypertext Transfer Protocol (HTTP)

➤ Internet Inter-ORB Protocol (IIOP)—Java applets that use this protocol must be set up to use SSL

➤ Lightweight Directory Access Protocol (LDAP)

➤ Mail Protocols—IMAP, POP3, and SMTP

Not all applications need to be secured. If you are building an application that requires users to supply personal or confidential information, such as credit cards or social security numbers, then using SSL is essential. SSL could be applied to just a single database or the whole Web site.

Your administrator can require users to use SSL through a Web site document when accessing the server, as discussed in Chapter 15, "Manage and Maintain." Designers can require users to use a secure SSL connection to access a single database, as discussed in section "Using SSL" later in this chapter.

For SSL type of authentication, Web users have been issued an X.509 client certificate and connect to the server over a SSL port; they are authenticated with this client certificate.

Setting Database Access

Each database needs to be secured individually. Many system databases do not need to be accessible through the Web. You may want to allow anonymous access to some system databases, or you may require authentication. Depending on the application, some databases you design may allow anonymous Web access, Web authentication access, and Notes access. The following sections discuss setting database access.

Controlling Web Authentication

Web authentication was discussed in the previous section "Planning Application Security Based on Web Authentication." When a person accesses a database from the Web, that person is unknown to the system and is regarded as Anonymous. Unless Anonymous is specifically designated in the Access Control List (ACL), he or she receives Default access.

When Web users enter a database, designers can force Web Authentication by adding Anonymous to the ACL, set to No Access. Another way to force Web authentication is to not allow TCP anonymous access through the server. You can set these configurations in the Server document or (if Web Site documents are enabled) on the Configuration tab of the Web Site document. When either of these configurations are set, Web users accessing the database are forced to authenticate. If they are not explicitly listed, they receive Default access.

Using SSL

As discussed earlier in this chapter, SSL is not always needed for every database on the server. Databases that contain information such as home pages, company information, and product catalogs may not need the added security of a SSL connection. On the other hand, an Order database requesting credit card information should have the added security of SSL. Domino enables you to set individual databases to require a SSL connection for access. To do so, you first must enable SSL on the Server; then you set the Require SSL Connections property for the individual database. To set the Database Properties, follow these steps:

1. Open the Database Properties box.

2. Select the Basics tab, as shown in Figure 17.1.

3. In the Web Access section, check Require SSL Connection.

4. Close the Properties dialog box to save your changes.

Using Anonymous Access

Controlling Anonymous access to your applications is a simple matter of adding the word Anonymous to the ACL (Access Control List) and assigning the desired access level. By doing this, Web users do not have to authenticate when accessing the database.

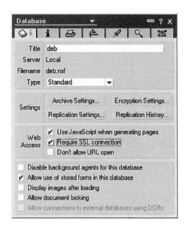

Figure 17.1 The Database properties Basics tab.

Using Maximum Internet Name and Password

On the Advanced tab of the ACL is a field called Maximum Internet name and password. You can use the Maximum Internet name and password access setting to limit Web users' access. If a Web user authenticates and is explicitly listed in the ACL with Designer access and Maximum Internet name and password is set to Author, that user will receive only Author access. At the same time, if users are listed with Author access but the Maximum field is set to Editor, they receive only Author access. The Maximum Internet name and password field does not increase user access; it can only restrict it.

By default the Maximum Internet name and password field is set to Editor. If your Administrator has enabled Web users to authenticate with SSL Client certificates, then the Maximum Internet name and password setting does not apply to them. These users are granted whatever access is applied to them in the ACL.

Using Roles

Roles are created and assigned in a database's ACL. *Roles* are used to refine or control access based on the role name instead of an individual user's name—not unlike groups. Roles can be assigned and used effectively with Notes clients as well as Web clients to control access to design elements or functions. One of two @Functions can be used to identify which roles a user has (and can be used on both clients). These @Functions are listed here:

➤ @UserRoles returns just the roles a user has been assigned in the ACL; for Web clients it also returns $$WebClient.

➤ @UserNamesList returns the user's common name, hierarchical name (including wildcards), all groups, and roles.

Setting Field Access: Using Encryption

Encryption is a means of protecting data from unauthorized access. Field encryption protects the information within a specific field and only users that have been given the key to decrypt the information can see the data stored in an encrypted field. Although field encryption is considered true security when used through a Notes client, through the Web it does not work. Field encryption is controlled through an Encryption Key that is created and stored in a Notes ID. Web users do not use a Notes ID to authenticate, so are not able to encrypt or decrypt a field.

When a document is created in a Notes client with an encrypted field, a Web user cannot see the value of that field. If the same document is created from a Web client, however, the field is not only seen and populated, it is not encrypted.

Readers and Authors type fields do work on the Web. If you created a document that contained a populated Readers field, a Web user would not be able to see that document. The only way a Web user would be able to access a document in this situation would be

➤ If the Readers field was populated with the word Anonymous.

➤ If the Web user authenticated and the Readers field was populated with that authenticated name.

Even though Reader and Author type fields are not listed in the TOC, they play an important part in security and are referenced in the exam.

Controlling CGI Directory Access

In Chapter 15, we looked at Web Site documents and how the cgi-bin directory is one of three directories created when the Web server is first started. Now it's time to look at how to secure the CGI directory. You can do this through *File Protection documents*, which you can set to control access from the Web to non-Domino databases. To create a File Protection document, follow these steps:

1. Select the Configuration tab in the Administrator client.

2. Click the twistie next to Web, which expands the list of Web views.

3. Click Internet Sites and open the Web Site document to which you want to apply the protection document. (File Protection documents are applied to specific Web Site documents, which are discussed in Chapter 15.)

4. Click on the Web Site... action button and choose Create File Protection to open the Web Site File Protection window shown in Figure 17.2.

5. Click the Basics tab and fill in the required fields, listed in Table 17.1.

6. When you're finished, click the Save and Close action button.

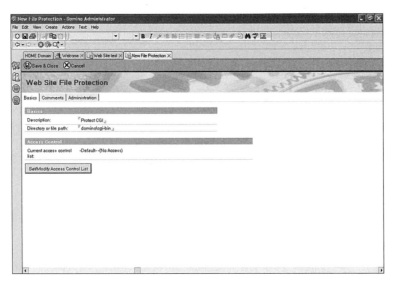

Figure 17.2 The Web Site File Protection document.

Do not create File Protection documents for **Domino\data\domino\java** and **Domino\data\domino\icons** directories. These contain default files used by the system and cannot be restricted.

Table 17.1 Basic File Protection Document Options	
Field Description	**Action**
Description	Optional—Enter a name that will identify this document in the Web/Internet Sites view.
Directory or File Path	List the directory or individual file that you wish to protect. This can be listed as a fully qualified path: **c:\lotus\domino\data\domino\cgi-bin** Or it can be listed relative to data: **domino\cgi-bin**
Current Access Control List	A list of access you have assigned when you click on the Set/Modify Access Control List button.
Set/Modify Access Control List Button	Clicking this button opens the Access Control List dialog box shown in Figure 17.3. You select users, servers, and groups, then specify the access allowed for this directory or file. The Access Control List dialog box is similar to database ACL, including a Default entry and an Anonymous entry. Your choices are: ➤ Read/Execute access (GET method) ➤ Write/Read/Execute access (POST and GET methods) ➤ No Access

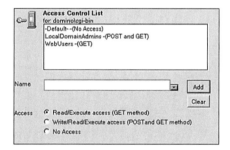

Figure 17.3   File Protection document's Access Control List dialog box.

When preparing for the exam, become familiar with the GET and POST methods referred to in the File Protection document's Access Control List. GET allows the opening of files and the starting of programs, whereas POST allows the sending of data to a CGI program.

Summary

Security is a priority for any application. This is especially true for applications that are accessed over the Web. Domino considers security an essential part of development and this knowledge is tested in Exam 612. Designers and administrators are responsible for system security, and should work together to ensure it.

Designers need to understand the whole Domino Security Model, not just design techniques. Designers may not have the authority to change all the security settings needed for an application, but they need to understand them. As a designer, you should know how these security settings affect your application and which ones you can set. Be prepared to answer questions pertaining to these methods on the 612 exam.

Exam Prep Questions

Question 1

Fumiko has Author access to her company's Web application. Maximum name and password is set to the default. What access will Fumiko have when she opens the database?

- ○ A. Fumiko will have Reader access, as that is the default setting in Maximum name and password.
- ○ B. Because the Maximum name and password default is Editor, Fumiko will have editor rights.
- ○ C. Fumiko will have Author access; even though Maximum name and password default is Editor, this setting will not increase the ACL.
- ○ D. Because the two contradict each other, Fumiko will be locked out of this database until the Manager corrects the discrepancy.

Answer C is correct. The default Maximum name and password field is Editor, but this will not increase ACL rights. A is incorrect as the default is Editor not Reader. B is incorrect, you cannot increase access listed in the ACL. Finally, D is incorrect because the ACL wins.

Question 2

Derek John has developed a database that will be used by Notes and Web clients. Web clients should be allowed to read and create documents, but not edit anyone else's. He wants Editor rights for the SelectGroup through Notes only. He has secured his site with SSL and has set Maximum Internet name and password to Author. Anonymous access is set to the Reader level, and he set SelectGroup as Editors. During testing, he finds SelectGroup has Editor access through Notes and the Web. Where did Derek John go wrong?

- ○ A. Maximum Internet name and password has been removed with Domino/Notes 6.
- ○ B. Setting Maximum Internet name and password cannot override the ACL, so SelectGroup has Editor access.
- ○ C. Maximum Internet name and password does not apply to Web users being authenticated with SSL client certificates.
- ○ D. SelectGroup is a reserved group name that has default rights.

Answer C is correct. Access defaults to what is listed in the ACL if SSL client authentication has been activated. Answers A and D are incorrect as there is no such thing. Answer B is incorrect; Maximum Internet name and password cannot increase access, but it does limit access.

Question 3

Shirley has two databases in her Web application. One, a discussion forum, requires basic authentication for access. For the second, a Product Catalog, she wants everyone to have only Read access from the Web and Author access from Notes. In the Product Catalog's ACL, Shirley has set Anonymous access to Reader and Default to Author. She later finds that some users are adding documents to the Product Catalog from the Web. How is this possible?

- ○ A. Users have an Internet password in their Person document.
- ○ B. The users able to add documents have a Notes ID. Anonymous applies to unknown users and Default applies to users with a Notes ID.
- ○ C. The Maximum name and password is Editor as default, which would allow this.
- ○ D. Database properties were set to allow Notes clients full access through the Web.

Answer A is correct. When a user has an Internet password, it applies to all databases on the server. When they create documents in the Catalog from the Web they are not denied; they are asked to authenticate. B is incorrect because Notes IDs do not apply on the Web. C is incorrect because the Maximum name and password field does not override the ACL. D is incorrect as there is no such property.

Question 4

Wenonah set up the following two File Protection documents for a file that is located in the html directory.

File Protection Document 1	File Protection Document 2
Path: **domino\html**	Path: **domino\html\home.html**
Access: -Default-(No Access)	Access: -Default-(No Access)
Access: WebUsers (GET)	Access: Joe User (GET)

What access does this give to Joe User and the WebUsers?

- ○ A. WebUsers have access to all files in the html directory and Joe User has access only to the **home.html** file.
- ○ B. WebUsers have access to all files in the html directory, but Joe User has no access. He cannot have access to a file if he does not have access to the directory in which it resides.
- ○ C. WebUsers have access to all files in the html directory but the **home.html** file, and Joe User has access only to **home.html**.
- ○ D. This cannot be done.

Answer C is correct. File protection documents work like database ACLs. If you are not explicitly listed, you get Default access. In both cases, Directory and File, Default is No Access, so you get access only if you are listed. A is incorrect because WebUsers are not explicitly listed in the home.html access list. B is incorrect because Joe User is listed for home.html and therefore has access, but WebUsers are not, so they have access to everything but. D is incorrect because this can be done.

Question 5

Which field-level security can be used for the Web?

- ○ A. Readers fields, Author fields, and Field encryption.
- ○ B. Field encryption only.
- ○ C. Author fields.
- ○ D. Reader fields and Author fields.

Answer D is correct. A and B are incorrect because Web users do not have access to a secret encryption key. C could technically be correct, but we are looking for the best answer.

Need to Know More?

IBM International Technical Support Organization. *Domino Designer 6: A Developer's Handbook.* Available in printed form, PDF format, HTML format from `publib-b.boulder.ibm.com/Redbooks.nsf/RedbookAbstracts/sg246854.html?Open`.

IBM Lotus White Paper. *A Guide to Developing a Secure Domino Application.* Available in PDF format from `http://www-10.lotus.com/ldd/notesua.nsf/White%20Papers?OpenView`.

IBM Lotus. *Release Notes.*

IBM Lotus. Online Help Databases: `help6_admin.nsf`, `help6_client.nsf`, `help6_designer.nsf`.

PART 4

Practice Exams

18

Practice Exam 610

Question 1

Sergey is listed in the Authors field of a document that has no Readers field. He also has Author access to the database where the document resides through the ACL. Stan has Editor access to the database and Martha has Reader access to the database. Who can read and/or edit the document?

○ A. Only Stan can read and edit the document.

○ B. Everyone can read and edit the document, but only Sergey can edit it.

○ C. No one can read the document because there is no Readers field.

○ D. Everyone can read the document but only Sergey and Stan can edit it.

Question 2

Greg wants to edit a form and he does not want other developers to work on it while he has it open. Does he need to explicitly lock the form?

○ A. Yes. Another developer with higher access could override Greg's access and work on the form.

○ B. No. The form is temporarily locked while it is being edited.

○ C. No. The form is automatically locked while it is being edited and will remain locked until Greg unlocks it.

○ D. Yes. Explicit locking prevents people from creating documents from the old form until the new one is finished and unlocked.

Question 3

Buddy is a developer with Manager access, and he has created a server agent that he wants to run with Manager access. How can he provide the agent with this access?

○ A. Have an administrator sign the database.

○ B. Sign the agent.

○ C. Edit and re-save the agent.

○ D. All of the above.

Question 4

Tedd has a view with three sortable columns: Name, Username, and ID #. He wants to make the background color of the Username column light blue so he can differentiate it from the Name and ID # columns at a glance. After saving this design change, Tedd looks at the view again and sees the light blue background in both the Username and ID # columns. What went wrong?

○ A. Tedd needs to add a hidden column before the Username column and set its background color to light blue.

○ B. Tedd must have accidentally set the background color of the ID # column and needs to restore the background property through the column's Text tab.

○ C. Tedd should add a hidden column before and after the Username column. The left column should be set to the light blue background and the right column should be set to the default white background.

○ D. Tedd has to change the background color to Transparent through the view's "Style" tab.

Question 5

Doris has just made a modification to a .gif file of a logo that is shared by seven databases. She decides to save the file into each database. Is this the most efficient way to update the logo on each database?

○ A. No. If the logo is a shared file resource, she can go to each database and refresh the file through the files work pane.

○ B. Yes. Although it is work-intensive, it is the best way to make sure the newly modified file is used by each database.

○ C. No. If the logo is on subforms, she can select all the subforms and change the logo on each of them at the same time.

○ D. No. She can select all design elements that contain the logo and change the logo on each of them at the same time.

Question 6

Paula has opened a document in **InsuranceForms.nsf**, a Notes database that resides on the INSHQ server. The picklists in the document are all set to perform lookups in another database, called **Keywords.nsf**, which also resides on the INSHQ server. After choosing a state from a picklist, Paula runs into trouble when she sees nothing but a blank list for the county picklist. Why has this happened?

- ○ A. The INSHQ server is down.
- ○ B. Paula does not have Reader access to the view used in the picklist lookup.
- ○ C. Instead of explicitly listing INSHQ as the server name in the **@DbLookup** function, double quotes ("") were used instead.
- ○ D. Paula's document was not in edit mode.

Question 7

Jeanmarie wants to show whether or not a document is locked. What @Function should she use?

- ○ A. **@IsDocLock([LOCK])**
- ○ B. **@DocLock([STATUS])**
- ○ C. **@DocLock([LOCKINGENABLED])**
- ○ D. **@IsDocLock([STATUS])**

Question 8

Lena has to change the name of a view that also has an alias. There is extensive code that refers to the old name of the view as well as its alias, and because the view is very important to its users, Lena must make the change as quickly as possible. What should she do?

- ○ A. Lena should copy the old view name to the left of the current alias in the view's alias box, using a vertical bar (|) as a separator.
- ○ B. Lena should change the code so that it refers to only the view's alias.
- ○ C. Lena should copy the old view name to the right of the new view name with a backslash (\ ) as a separator.
- ○ D. Lena can do nothing in the span of time she has to make a change in the view.

Question 9

To add a tool to Domino,

- ○ A. select Actions, Add Tool, then enter the name of the tool. Select the submenu under which it falls, then choose the tool action and tool location. Click OK.

- ○ B. select Tools, Add Tool, Tool submenu, then enter the name of the tool. Choose the tool action and tool location. Click OK.

- ○ C. select Tools, Add Tool, then enter the name of the tool. Select the tool action and tool location. Click OK.

- ○ D. select Tools, Submenu, Add Tool, then enter the name of the tool. Choose the tool action and tool location. Click OK.

Question 10

John has a database that has replicas on Server1, Server2, and Server3. Users have limited access to the database on Server1, which is the source server. However, some Depositor-Only users are able to see the documents on the replica located on Server2, although they can't see them on the replicas located on Server1 and Server3. What could be causing this?

- ○ A. The ACL of the replica on Server2 is different from those on Server1 and Server3.

- ○ B. Server2 and Server3 have different access to the database than Server1 has.

- ○ C. The users hacked into the database replica on Server2.

- ○ D. Nothing is wrong. Depositor-Only access allows users to see documents by default.

Question 11

How do you enable Auto-Complete?

- ○ A. Auto-Complete is enabled by default.

- ○ B. Select the Preferences, User Preference menu, then click on Basics to display the Auto-Complete options.

- ○ C. Select the options tab of the Programmer's pane, then enable the Auto-Complete options for LotusScript, HTML, and @Formulas.

- ○ D. Select the Options tab of the Programmer's pane, then enable the Auto-Complete options for LotusScript and @Formulas. HTML is not included because it is not a programming language.

Question 12

Buddy has an agent he wants to run with Manager access. How can he provide the agent with this access?

- ○ A. Have an administrator sign the database.
- ○ B. Sign the agent.
- ○ C. Edit and re-save the agent.
- ○ D. All of the above.

Question 13

Betty would like a set of "Contact Us" icons to appear in various events: a regular picture of a pencil if there is no event occurring, a larger picture of the pencil if the mouse moves over it, and a picture of the pencil writing if the mouse clicks it. What is the best way to create and store the images?

- ○ A. Name each image and store them individually in Image Resources.
- ○ B. Save each image with .ANI so that they will change depending on the mouse events.
- ○ C. Define an image well in the Basics tab of the Image Resource properties.
- ○ D. Embed the images in the form and use hide/when formulas to switch between images according to mouse events.

Question 14

Gary wants to provide expandable and collapsible rows in a table he has created. What should he do?

- ○ A. Select Show Only One Row at a Time in the Table Rows tab in the Tables property box and then check Expand/Collapse Rows.
- ○ B. Select Show Only One Row at a Time in the Table Rows tab in the Tables property box and then check Users Pick Row via Tab Buttons.
- ○ C. Select only Show Only One Row at a Time in the Table Rows tab in the Tables property box.
- ○ D. Select Show Only One Row at a Time in the Table Rows tab in the Tables property box, then check Users Pick Row via Captions.

Question 15

Jean wants to show indented response documents beneath their parent docu-ments. The first column is a Responses Only column that displays the name of the response document; the second column is sorted and is to display informa-tion about the parent document; and the third column is to display information about the response document. However, none of the response documents are displaying any information from the third column. Why?

- ○ A. Jean should make the third column a "Responses Only" column to make the data visible.

- ○ B. Jean should include the information on the response documents in the "Responses Only" column and delete the third column.

- ○ C. Jean does not have the Show Response Documents in a Hierarchy view property checked.

- ○ D. Jean does not have the Extend Last Column to Window Width view property checked, which is preventing the third column from being seen.

Question 16

To receive design changes from Server1, the database replica on Server2 must give Server1 at least

- ○ A. manager access, and the database replica on Server1 must give Server2 at least Reader access.

- ○ B. designer access, and the database replica on Server1 must give Server2 at least Editor access.

- ○ C. designer access, and the database replica on Server1 must give Server2 at least Reader access.

- ○ D. editor access, and the database replica on Server1 must give Server2 at least Editor access.

Question 17

Lynne has Author access to a database, but when she tries to create a document from a form that has no Authors field, she gets an error: **You are not authorized to perform this operation.** What is causing the error?

- ○ A. There are no Authors fields on the form to provide access.

- ○ B. Lynne needs Editor access to create the document.

- ○ C. Lynne is not included under Who Can Create Documents with This Form.

- ○ D. Lynne is not included under Default Read Access for Document Created with this Form.

Question 18

A traveling department manager wants to take a copy of **Saleries.nsf** on his laptop. Because this database contains sensitive information, Khalid needs to restrict access. What should he do?

- ○ A. Encrypt the database on the server with the server ID to restrict access.
- ○ B. Copy the database to the manager's laptop, then encrypt the database so that only the manager can access it.
- ○ C. Copy the database to the manager's laptop, then restrict the access through the ACL.
- ○ D. Nothing can be done because encryption cannot prevent access to API programs.

Question 19

Some users in Sanjay's company have been changing shared views on a database he maintains, and some have even changed the logo images on various forms. What steps should Sanjay take to prevent these users from changing the database design?

- ○ A. Hide the database design in both the production database and the template.
- ○ B. Hide the database design in the production database only.
- ○ C. Hide the database design in the production database and remove Designer or higher access from the users in the ACL.
- ○ D. Remove Designer or higher access from the users in the ACL.

Question 20

Terry wants to create a validation formula that is portable to any field. He should use

- ○ A. **@If(@GetField = ""; @Failure("Please enter a value for this field");@Success)**
- ○ B. **@If(@ThisName = "";@Failure("Please enter a value for this field");@Success)**
- ○ C. **@If(@Command([EditGotoField]) = "";@Failure("Please enter a value for this field");@Success)**
- ○ D. **@If(@ThisValue = "";@Failure("Please enter a value for this field");@Success)**

Question 21

What is true about document locking?

- ○ A. Document locking prevents replication of conflicts.
- ○ B. Users with Editor access or higher can lock documents.
- ○ C. Only the user who locks a document can unlock it.
- ○ D. A and C.

Question 22

Which of the following changes to a form requires updates to existing documents?

- ○ A. New fields, field names, graphics, and form types.
- ○ B. Computed field formulas, text properties, pop-ups, and deleted fields.
- ○ C. Field data types, computed field formulas, form names with a synonym, and static text.
- ○ D. Deleted fields, new fields, form types, and field data types.

Question 23

Chris has a field that is to be visible to anyone in the [Administration] and [Special Reader] roles. The field should not be visible to anyone if the document has never been saved. What should the hide/when formula look like?

- ○ A. (!@IsMember("[Administration]";@UserRoles) I
       !@IsMember("[Special Reader]";@UserRoles)) I !@IsNewDoc
- ○ B. (@IsMember("[Administration]";@UserRoles) &
       @IsMember("[Special Reader]";@UserRoles)) I @IsNewDoc
- ○ C. (!@IsMember("[Administration]";@UserRoles) &
       !@IsMember("[Special Reader]";@UserRoles)) I @IsNewDoc
- ○ D. (!@IsMember("[Administration]";@UserRoles) &
       !@IsMember("[Special Reader]";@UserRoles)) I !@IsNewDoc

Question 24

Ron opens a view on the Notes client and sees three columns. Sarah opens the same view on the Notes client and sees five columns. Why does Ron see fewer columns?

- ○ A. Ron is not in the Readers field of the documents.
- ○ B. Ron does not have the appropriate access to the view.
- ○ C. There is a hide/when formula that hides the columns when Ron opens the view.
- ○ D. Sarah has Reader access to the columns Ron cannot see.

Question 25

Which of the following is not a field type in Domino?

- ○ A. Date/Time.
- ○ B. Rich Text Lite.
- ○ C. OLE Object.
- ○ D. Time Zone.

Question 26

A Maintenance Request form has a **Call_Ranking** field, which contains the following values: Call Back, Routine, Urgent, Non-Routine. Jamal has a view that is to be sorted by the **Call_Ranking** field, but he does not want it sorted in alphabetical order. Rather, he wants it sorted in the order of Urgent, Call Back, Non-Routine, Routine. How should he do this?

- ○ A. Create two columns at the beginning of the view. The first column is visible and both columns are sorted. The first column should contain **@If(Call_Ranking="Urgent";"1";Call_Ranking="Call Back";"2";Call_Ranking="Non-Routine";"3";"4")**, and the second column should display the **Call_Ranking** field.
- ○ B. Create two columns at the beginning of the view. The first column should be one character wide and sorted. The first column should contain **@If(Call_Ranking="Urgent";"1";Call_Ranking="Call Back";"2";Call_Ranking="Non-Routine";"3";"4")**.
- ○ C. Create two columns at the beginning of the view. The first column should be hidden and sorted, whereas the second column is visible and not sorted. The first column should contain **@If(Call_Ranking="Urgent";"1";Call_Ranking="Call Back";"2";Call_Ranking="Non-Routine";"3";"4")**.

○ D.   Create two columns at the beginning of the view. The first column
should be hidden and sorted by the **Call_Ranking** field. The second
column should be visible and not sorted. The second column should
contain **@If(Call_Ranking="Urgent";"1";Call_Ranking="Call
Back";"2";Call_Ranking="Non-Routine";"3";"4")**.

Question 27

Which of these statements is true?

○ A.   To enter data, users have to type over any hints that appear in data
entry fields.

○ B.   Field hints disappear as soon as a user enters a field.

○ C.   Field hints disappear as soon as a user enters a field, but reappear in
the status bar.

○ D.   Field hint entries can be entered in the Info tab of the field properties.

Question 28

A keyword field displays various accountants' names from a view categorized by
department. The list is supposed to be non-repeating, but some accountants are
appearing more than once. Which formula is causing this error?

○ A.   **@DbColumn("Notes":"ReCache";"";"DeptView";2)**

○ B.   **@DbLookup("Notes":"ReCache";"";"DeptView";"Accounting";2)**

○ C.   **@Sort(@DbLookup("Notes":"ReCache";"";"DeptView";Accounting";2))**

○ E.   All of the above.

Question 29

A document expires in 30 days, but the owner of the document gets a 48-hour
grace period. What would be the correct way to set the **@Adjust** formula?

○ A.   **@Adjust(@Created;0;1;0;48;0;0)**

○ B.   **@Adjust(@Created;0;0;32;0;0;0)**

○ C.   **@Adjust(@Created;0;1;2;0;0;0)**

○ D.   **@Adjust(@Created;0;0;0;32;0;0)**

Question 30

Brenda created a new view called SalesCalendar. Upon opening SalesCalendar, users see rows showing icons for the various calendar entries, times, and the subject for each entry, but they do not see it in calendar format. What is wrong?

- ○ A. The view is missing a column displaying the dates.
- ○ B. The view needs to be refreshed.
- ○ C. The view is not in Standard Outline style.
- ○ D. The view is not in Calendar style.

Question 31

Aaron wants to print the code of a Java servlet he has imported through the Print Source dialog box. Which choice does he make to print the code?

- ○ A. Current section.
- ○ B. Current object.
- ○ C. All languages.
- ○ D. None of the above.

Question 32

Monika has an agent open in her designer panel, and wants to print all the agent's events. In the Print Source dialog box, she should choose:

- ○ A. Current section.
- ○ B. Current object.
- ○ C. All objects—all languages.
- ○ D. Current object—current language.

Question 33

Which of the following statement is false? Prevent replication or save conflicts by

- ○ A. selecting Merge Conflicts on the Form property.
- ○ B. giving users Author access or less in the database ACL to prevent them from editing other users' documents.
- ○ C. making as few design changes as possible.
- ○ D. using versioning so that documents can become new documents after editing.

Question 34

What is the editor applet?

- ○ A. It is an imported Java applet used to enable Web users to cut, paste, and copy text from outside the editor, as well as change the text's font, size, and color.
- ○ B. It is a native Domino applet that allows Web users to cut, paste, and copy text from outside the editor as well as change the text's font, size, and color.
- ○ C. It is an imported Java applet that allows Web users to bold, underline, and italicize text, create paragraphs and bulleted lists, and insert links.
- ○ D. It is a native Domino applet that allows Web users to bold, underline, and italicize text, create paragraphs and bulleted lists, and insert links.

Question 35

Is this code correct?

```
@Prompt([Ok]; "Acknowledgment";{You will receive a copy of
the "NotesNow" article within 3 weeks}
```

- ○ A. Yes. The curly brackets enable the message to include the double quotes around the magazine's name.
- ○ B. No. The curly brackets are used for commenting code only.
- ○ C. Yes. The curly brackets enable the message to show the magazine's title in bold type.
- ○ D. No. The prompt title must be in curly brackets as well.

Question 36

Tony has given users only Editor access to their own mail databases. Some users have reported problems setting their "out-of-office" program. What can Tony do to alleviate this problem?

○ A.   Give the users Manager access to their mail databases.

○ B.   Enable the **Allow user activation** property for the agent running the out-of-office program.

○ C.   Enable the **Run OnBehalf of** property for the agent running the out-of-office program.

○ D.   Enable the **Restricted operations** property for the agent running the out-of-office program.

Question 37

Which is not a document option for the Agent Menu Selection run option?

○ A.   All selected documents.

○ B.   All new and modified documents since last run.

○ C.   Run once.

○ D.   None.

Question 38

Mitchell wants a design element that shows the number of unread documents in a folder. What does he need to do?

○ A.   Select the unread rows of the folder Style properties.

○ B.   Select Show Folder Unread Information on the folder Info tab.

○ C.   Select Show Folder Unread Information on the folder Options tab.

○ D.   Select Show Folder Unread Information on the embedded outline Info tab.

Question 39

Lisa has a view that is updated constantly. What are some better ways to refresh this view?

○ A. Use the refresh time option of Auto, After First Use.

○ B. Use the refresh display option of the Display Indicator.

○ C. Use the refresh display option of Refresh Display from Top Row.

○ D. Use the refresh display option of Auto, At Most Over n Hours.

Question 40

Which set of commands is listed in the order they are executed?

○ A. **x:="";**
@Command([FileSave]);
@Command([ViewChange];"Main")

○ B. **duedate:=@Today;**
@Command([ToolsRunBackgroundMacros]);
@Prompt([OK];Macros";"All macros are running")

○ C. **@Command([FileCloseWindow]);**
@Command([ViewSwitchForm];"CDR");
@PostedCommand([EditGoToField];"Name")

○ D. B and C

Question 41

Steve is writing a view selection to contain the form OriginalThread and all its response documents. Which selection formula should he write?

○ A. **SELECT Form="OriginalThread" | @AllChildren**

○ B. **SELECT Form="OriginalThread" | @Responses**

○ C. **SELECT Form="OriginalThread" | @IsResponseDoc**

○ D. **SELECT Form="OriginalThread" | @AllDescendants**

Question 42

By default, a user with Author access can

- ○ A. create documents and write public documents.
- ○ B. create documents and create personal folders/views.
- ○ C. read public documents only.
- ○ D. create documents only.

Question 43

Where does a designer set customized twisties?

- ○ A. The View Info tab is where the designer must indicate where the image(s) is/are stored.
- ○ B. The Column Info tab is where the designer must indicate where the image(s) is/are stored.
- ○ C. The View Options tab is where the designer must indicate where the image(s) is/are stored.
- ○ D. Column Advanced tab is where the designer must indicate where the image(s) is/are stored.

Question 44

When a user is allowed to customize a view,

- ○ A. the user's resizing and resorting of columns is retained after the view is closed and reopened.
- ○ B. the user's resizing and resorting of columns is not retained after the view is closed and reopened.
- ○ C. if a user's ability to customize a view is removed, the user can still resize and sort columns through the menu option and the changes are retained after the view is closed and reopened.
- ○ D. A and C.

Question 45

Pages can contain…

- ○ A. Text, fields, and graphics.
- ○ B. Outlines, layers, and frames.
- ○ C. Links, computed text, and embedded objects.
- ○ D. Applets, frames, and text.

Question 46

Which of the following is not true about tables?

- ○ A. Collapsible sections within a table are called row captions.
- ○ B. Table tab lengths are pre-set and their captions must be brief in order to fit.
- ○ C. Animated tables are not good for data entry.
- ○ D. Table columns can be set to automatically adjust their width based on their content.

Question 47

Alvaro has several doclinks in the "About Database" document. When Notes users open the database, they are sent to the document associated with the first doclink only. What is happening?

- ○ A. The other doclinks were not enabled.
- ○ B. The "About" document has the doclinks in a controlled-access section.
- ○ C. The database Launch property was set this way.
- ○ D. The users do not have the access rights to the documents associated with the other doclinks.

Question 48

Garrett built a Notes database for his company's security department. Because of the sensitive information it will contain, the security head has asked Garrett to remove any access for himself to the database.

- ○ A. Garrett should not remove access for himself. He needs at least Designer access to make changes.
- ○ B. Garrett should not remove access for himself. He needs at least Manager access to push design changes to the database from a template.
- ○ C. Garrett should remove access for himself. He can give someone in the security department Designer rights.
- ○ D. Garrett should remove access for himself. He can make any design changes on a template, which can be inherited by the database.

Question 49

Which of the following is not true about displaying icons in a view column?

- ○ A. A column can display up to 10 icons.
- ○ B. Icons can be predefined or custom.
- ○ C. A column can display both predefined and custom icons together.
- ○ D. There is not predefined icons for the value of 0.

Question 50

Alicia had to change the name of her form and now she has to change it in all her agents. She selects Find/Replace in the Edit menu, types the old name of the form, the new name of the form, and chooses Case-Sensitive and Whole Words as her Find options. What should her scope be?

- ○ A. All Objects.
- ○ B. Current Section Only.
- ○ C. Current Object.
- ○ D. Find/Replace does not work in the designer pane.

Practice Exam Answer Key for Exam 610

1. D	18. B	35. A
2. B	19. C	36. B
3. D	20. D	37. C
4. C	21. A	38. D
5. A	22. D	39. C
6. C	23. C	40. A
7. B	24. C	41. D
8. A	25. C	42. C
9. C	26. C	43. B
10. A	27. B	44. A
11. A	28. E	45. C
12. D	29. B	46. B
13. D	30. D	47. C
14. D	31. D	48. D
15. B	32. B	49. C
16. C	33. C	50. A
17. C	34. D	

Question 1

The correct answer is D. Absence of a Readers field means anyone with at least Readers access in the database ACL can read the document, and this includes Martha. Sergey is in the Authors field, which allows him to edit the document. Unlike Stan, Sergey has only Author access in the ACL, and must be listed in an Authors field before he can edit a document. Stan, through his Editor access in the ACL, can edit any document. A is incorrect because in the absence of a Readers field, anyone who has access to the database can read the document. B is incorrect because Stan has Editor access through the database ACL. C is incorrect because in the absence of a Readers field, anyone who has access to the database can read the document.

Question 2

The correct answer is B. Locking prevents anyone, regardless of access, from editing a design element. The design element is automatically locked as soon as it is being edited; it is temporary because after the editing is finished, the lock is removed. It is important to remember that temporary locking does not require explicit unlocking. A is incorrect because locking prevents anyone, even users with Manager access, from editing that same design element. C is incorrect because temporary locking does not require explicit unlocking. D is incorrect because users will still be able to create documents using the old form until the new design changes to the form are saved.

Question 3

The correct answer is D. The designer is allowed to sign one or more agents at the same time by either clicking on the action button found in the agents list or through the menu that appears after right-clicking on the agent in the list. A designer can open and save an agent, thus signing it with his or her own access. The designer must have the same access rights as desired for the agent. Administrators can sign individual design elements or the entire database with an administrative ID file.

Question 4

The correct answer is C. Tedd should add a hidden column before and after the Username column. The left column should be set to the light blue background and the right column should be set to the default white background. A is incorrect because setting only the hidden column to the left of the Username column caused Tedd's problem in the first place—every column to the right of the hidden column is light blue. B is incorrect because for the background ID # column to be light blue, there must be a hidden column to its left set to light blue. D is incorrect because the Transparent setting refers to the rows of a view, not its columns.

Question 5

The correct answer is A. This method is the least labor intensive and is still accurate. The file's work pane shows a refresh icon if a file has been modified but has not been changed in the database. Also, the File Resources property box has the Needs Refresh check box checked if a file has been modified. B is incorrect because this method is more prone to human error—Doris may forget to save a form with the new logo change or even copy the wrong logo into a form. By using a shared file resource, Doris has the Needs Refresh check box to remind her to update the logo change. C is incorrect because a designer can select design elements of only one database at a time to modify. Also, modification is limited to setting design properties—such as preventing replication from changing a design element—and does not affect anything within the element—such as color, fields, or images. D is incorrect because the Transparent setting is used for background images.

Question 6

The correct answer is C. Even though both databases reside on the same server, the server name must be included in the @DbLookup. Double quotes ("") indicate that the lookup is to be used on a local database. A is incorrect because if the server was down, Paula would not have been able to use any other picklists, let alone open a document in the first place. B is incorrect because if Paula did not have Read access to a view, the picklist would display an error message to that effect. D is incorrect because the document would have to be in edit mode for Paula to use the picklist fields.

Question 7

The correct answer is B. @DocLock([STATUS]) provides a list of the users who have locked the document, or a null value if the document is unlocked. A is incorrect because there is no such function as @IsDocLock. C is incorrect because @DocLock([LOCKINGENABLED]) indicates whether or not the current database has document locking enabled. D is incorrect because there is no such function as @IsDocLock.

Question 8

The correct answer is A. Code referring to either the old view name or the current alias brings up the correct view: NewViewName | OldViewName | Alias. B is incorrect because Lena would have to spend time tracking down the code that refers to the old view name and she does not have that time to spare. C is incorrect because it would create cascading views of the new view name and the old view name. D is incorrect because it would take very little time to add the new view name at the head of the original view name, then separate the new and old view names with a |.

Question 9

The correct answer is C. Select Tools, Add Tool, then enter the name of the tool. Select the tool action and tool location. Click OK. A is incorrect because there is no submenu to select after choosing the name of the tool. B is incorrect because there is no submenu to select after the Add Tool step. D is incorrect because there is no submenu to select after the Select Tools step.

Question 10

The correct answer is A. John needs to select Enforce Consistent ACL in the Advanced section of the database ACL to keep the same ACL settings in all database replicas. He must also make sure Server1 has Manager access to all the replicas before selecting the enforcement, otherwise no change will be made. B is incorrect because user access is being affected. Even if a server had Reader access to the database, Depositor-Only users should not be able to see documents in the database. The only way these users could see documents is if they had Reader access or higher in the database ACL, although if they had at least Author access they would be able to read their own documents. C is incorrect because Lotus Notes' strong security (user roles, Authors and Readers fields, access control lists, and so on) deters unauthorized users. It is not impossible, but highly unlikely, that the users could have hacked into the database. D is incorrect because Depositor-Only access allows users to create and save a document, but these users cannot see their own or other users' documents.

Question 11

The correct answer is A. Auto-Complete is enabled by default. B is incorrect because Auto-Complete cannot be set through the Preferences, User Preference menu. C is incorrect because Auto-Complete is already enabled for LotusScript, HTML, and @Formulas, and Auto-Complete cannot be set through the Programmers pane. D is incorrect because Auto-Complete is already enabled for LotusScript and @Formulas, and includes HTML. Also, Auto-Complete cannot be set through the programmers pane.

Question 12

The correct answer is D. The subaction can be dragged in between subactions Level 1 and Level 3. A caveat to remember about subactions is that the parent action is not programmable; that button appears with a drop-down arrow. A is incorrect because a subaction can be replaced. B is incorrect because subactions can be sorted in order. C is incorrect because a subaction can be dragged into position without replacing the subaction already there. Instead, the original subaction moves down the action pane.

Question 13

The correct answer is D. The error can be caused by changing the subform name—the insert subform formula is still searching for SubformNew, even though that subform may have another name. This problem can be corrected by either correcting the insert subform formula to load the subform's new name, or changing the subform's name back to SubformNew. The error can also be caused by deleting the subform—the insert subform is still searching for SubformNew. This problem can be corrected by either correcting the insert subform forumla to load another subform, or creating a new subform with the name SubformNew. A is incorrect because B is also a cause of the error. B is incorrect because A is also a cause of the error. C is incorrect because the error message would report an access error, not a loading error.

Question 14

The correct answer is D. Rather than clicking on tabs, users can click on captions for each row to reveal data by expanding the row. Clicking on the caption or the open/close icon to the far right of the caption closes the row. Through the properties box, developers can also determine the label, wording, font, size, style, and color of the captions. A is incorrect because there is no Expand/Collapse Rows check box in the Table rows property. B is incorrect because enabling users to pick tab buttons in a table simply allows them to click on a tab in the table to bring the desired row forward. C is incorrect because enabling Show Only One Row at a Time is the first of the two steps needed to create expandable and collapsible rows.

Question 15

The correct answer is B. The Responses column should be created to the left of the column where the response documents are to be indented. This column must have Show Responses Only selected in its column properties. Jean has already accomplished this part. However, it must be noted that on the row where a response document appears, columns to the right of the Responses Only column do not appear; that is, data in these columns does not appear in the Response Document row. Any data concerning the response document must be placed in the first column. A is incorrect because with or without the third column being enabled to Responses Only, it will still not be visible because response data in columns to the right of the Responses Only column does not appear. Jean should place the information in the first column. C is incorrect because Notes views default to Show Response Documents in a Hierarchy. D is incorrect because response data in columns to the right of the Responses Only column does not appear.

Question 16

The correct answer is C. The source server, Server1, needs at least Designer access over all the design elements in the replicas. A is incorrect because Designer access is the least access needed for design changes. If Server1 were to control both ACL and designer changes, it would require Manager access. B is incorrect because the least access Server2 requires to pull design changes from Server1 is Reader. If Server2 were to add new documents and modify existing ones, it would require at least Editor access. D is incorrect because Editor access does not give Server1 control over the design elements.

Question 17

The correct answer is C. Either All Authors and Above has been deselected on the form's Security tab or Lynne has not been selected in the list of authors. A is incorrect because if a document has no Authors field, anyone with at least Editor access to the database can edit the document. If the user has at least Author access, he or she can edit his or her own documents. B is incorrect because Author access enables users to create documents. D is incorrect because Default Read Access for Document Created with this Form is used with Read access to the document, not Edit access.

Question 18

The correct answer is B. Copy the database to the manager's laptop, then encrypt the database so that only the manager can access it. A is incorrect because only administrators with the server ID will be able to read the database. C is incorrect because ACL settings do not restrict access to local databases. One example is that a local database could be copied without its ACL settings, thus allowing anyone to read the database. D is incorrect because if an encrypted database is copied, it remains encrypted, even from API programs.

Question 19

The correct answer is C. Hiding the database design and preventing users from replacing the design helps safeguard the database design. A is incorrect because hiding the template design would disable the design operations and hide all formulas and scripts. B is incorrect because although the design is hidden, users with designer access or above can still replace the database design. Higher access from users must be removed as well. D is incorrect because users could make a copy of the database to change the design; hiding the design prevents copying.

Question 20

The correct answer is D. @ThisValue returns the value of a field without requiring a field name. A is incorrect because @GetField requires a field name for its parameter. B is incorrect because @ThisName returns the name of the current field. C is incorrect because @Command([EditGotoField]) places the cursor in a predefined field of a document in edit mode.

Question 21

The correct answer is A. Other users with the same rights to a document cannot edit a locked document even on a different replica. B is incorrect because no one of any access can edit a locked document. C is incorrect because someone with Manager access can unlock a document. C and D are incorrect because A is the only correct answer.

Question 22

The correct answer is D. All of these changes require updates to existing documents.

Question 23

The correct answer is C. The field hides from users who are not in the [Administration] role and who are not in the [Special Reader] role, but it does not hide from users in these roles. The field will also hide if the document is new. A is incorrect because it is entirely a Boolean OR argument. In an OR argument, if any part of the argument is true, then all the argument is true. In this case, a user might be in the [Special Reader] role, but the field hides if the user is not in the [Administration] role; both roles need to see the field. B is incorrect because if the user is in both the [Administration] and [Special Reader] roles, the field hides. The field is supposed to hide from users not in these roles. D is incorrect because the field hides if the document is not new, that is, unsaved.

Question 24

The correct answer is C. The Advanced tab in the Column properties box allows the designer to check Hide Column If Formula Is True and then type in a formula. A is incorrect because if Ron did not have Reader access to the documents, he would not be able to see rows (documents), rather than columns (document values). B is incorrect because with view restriction, Ron would either see the view or not see the view at all. D is incorrect because columns are not restricted by Reader access, but through hide/when formulas.

Question 25

The correct answer is C. The Domino field types are text, date/time, number, dialog list, check box, radio button, listbox, combobox, rich text, Authors, Names, Readers, password, formula, color, rich text lite, and time zone. Developers can use an OLE object to incorporate other applications such as graphics tools or data sources into their own application. A is incorrect because date/time is a field type in Domino. B is incorrect because rich text lite is a field type in Domino. D is incorrect because time zone is a data type in Domino.

Question 26

The correct answer is C. The first sorted column, even though it is hidden, "drives" the second non-sorted column and places it in the desired order. A is incorrect because the first column should be hidden; otherwise the users may become confused or distracted by the numbers used to sort the call rankings. B is incorrect because even though the first column is one character wide, it is still visible and distracting. D is incorrect because the first column is sorting the column in alphabetical order: Call Back, Non-Routine, Routine, and Urgent.

Question 27

The correct answer is B. Field hints are added to the Advanced tab in the field properties. Although a user can see them in edit mode, field hints disappear after the user enters the field. Help Descriptions appear at the bottom of the screen in the status bar. A is incorrect because the field hints disappear as soon as a user begins typing in the field. C is incorrect because field hints do not reappear anywhere after a user begins typing in a field. D is incorrect because field hints are added to the Advanced tab of the field properties.

Question 28

The correct answer is E. DeptView is categorized by department. The keyword field should have the names of accountants only. @DbColumn brings in all the values of one specified column, and does not accept a specific key, whereas @DbLookup can use a specified key to do a lookup in a specific column. The @Unique function takes the returned textlist and removes duplicate values. @Sort would simply sort the names in ascending order. A is incorrect because using the @DbColumn function would simply bring in all the values in the second column, whether they were from the Accounting department or not. B is incorrect because the @DbLookup function would have brought in all the names in the Accounting department. C is incorrect because it would have sorted all the names @DbLookup found from accounting in ascending alphabetical order. D is incorrect because it wouldn't cause the error—the @Unique function would remove all duplicate names from the list @DbLookup found in the Accounting department.

Question 29

The correct answer is B. The @Adjust function contains these parameters: @Adjust(adjustment date; years; months; days; hours; minutes; seconds). Because days are always 24 hours long, it is correct to add 2 days (48 hours) to the 30-day limit, adjusting the date by 32 days. A and C are incorrect because not all months (January, February, March, May, July, August, October, and December) are 30 days long, as prescribed by the expiration requirement. D is incorrect because the parameter for hours was set to 32, rather than the parameter for days.

Question 30

The correct answer is D. Calendar must be chosen in the Style section on the View Info tab for the calendar format to appear and display the various entries correctly. A is incorrect because the users report that they are not seeing the entries in calendar format, not that they are missing data. B is incorrect because refreshing a view reflects changes in the documents it displays, not the view's format. C is incorrect because the standard outline view, the most common of Notes views that show documents, is not used for displaying calendar format.

Question 31

The correct answer is D. Although the source code for formulas, simple actions, LotusScript, HTML, JavaScript, and Java can be printed out, code belonging to imported Java programs cannot.

Question 32

The correct answer is B. Current objects print the source code of the current form, button, and so on being worked on. Current objects also allow the designer to select a language; if the object contains both formulas and LotusScript, the designer can choose to print out the formulas only, or print out all languages—both formulas and LotusScript in this example. A is incorrect because the Current section prints out what the designer sees in the Programmer's pane. C and D are incorrect because All Objects prints out the source code (current or all languages) of all programmable objects (forms, buttons, fields, and so on) in the design element currently being worked on.

Question 33

The correct answer is C. ACL and design changes do not result in replication or save conflicts because the most recent change always takes precedence. A is incorrect because merging replication conflicts combines documents if no fields are in conflict. B is incorrect because restricting users to editing their own documents greatly reduces the chances of any document being edited more than once at the same time. D is incorrect because versioning creates new documents after editing and saving. The newly edited document is a response to the older version, has the older version as a response, or is a sibling document to the older version.

Question 34

The correct answer is D. Although text that is located within the editor can be cut, copied, and pasted, JDK Release 1.0.2 restrictions do not allow pasting of text outside of the editor. Editor applets are enabled in rich text fields and allow bold, underline, and italicized text, changes in font, size, and color, creation and manipulation of paragraphs, use of bulleted and numbered lists, and addition of links. A is incorrect because it is a native Domino applet and JDK Release 1.0.2 restrictions do not allow pasting of text outside the editor. B is incorrect because although the editor is a native Domino applet, JDK Release 1.0.2 restrictions do not allow pasting of text outside the editor. C is incorrect because the editor is a native Domino applet.

Question 35

The correct answer is A. Curly brackets are used to delimit strings with quotation marks, replacing the old method of using a backslash. The curly brackets also make it easier to add REM statements to formula language. B is incorrect because not only can curly brackets be used to comment code, but they also allow strings to include quotation marks without requiring backslashes to indicate literal quotation marks. C is incorrect because curly brackets are used to delimit strings, not format them. D is incorrect because the prompt title is not using literal quotation marks. Curly brackets would be useful if the prompt title appeared in this manner: {Information About Your "Notes Now" subscription}.

Question 36

The correct answer is B. The Allow User Activation box is located on the Security tab of the agent. When it is checked, it allows users with Editor access in the database ACL to enable that particular agent. Enabling the agent does not re-sign it. A is incorrect because allowing users Manager access can enable them to change their mail forms, create their own agents, even delete their own mail database. Providing them with Editor access can prevent many accidents and mishaps. C is incorrect because Run On Behalf Of allows the designer only to specify on whose authority the agent can run.

D is incorrect because Restricted Operations lets users who have unrestricted rights determine whether or not the agent can run in unrestricted or restricted mode.

Question 37

The correct answer is C. Run Once is a document option for the Agent List Selection option, found in the Agent window. A and B are incorrect because the Document option can be set for either All Selected Documents or for All New and Modified Documents Since Last Run. D is incorrect because Run Once is not a document option.

Question 38

The correct answer is D. Unread counts for a folder can be shown only in an embedded outline, and Show Folder Unread Information is found only in the embedded outline Info properties. A is incorrect because Unread Rows in the Style tab of a folder control the color in which the unread documents appear, and Show Folder Unread Information is selected in the embedded outline Info tab. B is incorrect because Show Folder Unread Information is selected in the embedded outline Info tab. C is incorrect because Show Folder Unread Information is selected in the embedded outline Info tab.

Question 39

The correct answer is C. Because the view is updated constantly, users want to see the latest changes. Refresh Display from Top Row would show the latest document changes at the top of the view if a reverse chronological display is used. A is incorrect because Auto, After First Use shows changes only once. B is incorrect because Display Indicator does not show changes unless the user clicks on the refresh icon. D is incorrect because the view is constantly updated and users need to see the latest changes. Auto, At Most Over n Hours would allow users to see only the latest changes hourly. E is incorrect because since the view is updated constantly and the users want to see their latest changes, Refresh Display from Top Row would be the only correct answer of the four given.

Question 40

The correct answer is A. In formula language, assigned variables are executed first, then any and all @Formulas. Here are the @Command exceptions that run last of all: `EditClear`, `EditProfile`, `FileCloseWindow`, `FileDatabaseDelete`, `FileExit`, `Folder`, `NavigateNext`, `NavigateNextMain`, `NavigateNextSelection`, `NavigateNextUnread`, `NavigatePrev`, `NavigatePrevMain`, `NavigatePrevSelected`, `NavigatePrevUnread`, `ReloadWindow`, `ToolsRunBackgroundMacros`, `ToolsRunMacro`, `ViewChange`, `ViewSwitchForm`. B is incorrect because `@Command([ToolsRunBackgroundMacros])` executes last. C is incorrect because `@Command([ViewSwitchForm];"CDR")` is run last. D is incorrect because B and C are incorrect.

Question 41

The correct answer is D. `@AllDescendants` returns all response and response-to-response documents of the parent. A is incorrect because `@AllChildren` returns the first-level response documents. B is incorrect because `@Responses` returns the number of response documents. C is incorrect because `@IsResponseDoc` returns all response documents, whether or not they belong to the parent document selected in the view formula.

Question 42

The correct answer is C. The default privileges for Author access are Read Public Documents, Write Public Documents, and Replicate or Copy Documents; the latter two are privileges that can be removed by the database manager. A is incorrect because the privilege to create documents must be explicitly checked in the database ACL. B is incorrect because creating documents and personal folders/views must be explicitly checked in the database ACL. D is incorrect because Write Public Documents and Replicate or Copy documents are enabled for Author access as well.

Question 43

The correct answer is B. Column Info tab—is where the designer must indicate where the image(s) is/are stored. Show Twistie when Row Is Expandable must be checked, too. A is incorrect because the Column Info tab, not the View Info tab, indicates where the image(s) is/are stored. C is incorrect because the Column Info tab, not the View Options tab, indicates where the image(s) is/are stored. D is incorrect because the Column Info tab, not the Column Advanced tab, indicates where the image(s) is/are stored.

Question 44

The correct answer is A. The developer can select the Allow Customizations in a View option in the View Options tab; users can, among other things, make changes in sorting and resizing columns, and their customized changes remain in the view even after it has been closed and reopened. B is incorrect because the users' changes are retained in the view. C is incorrect because after the ability to customize has been removed, the changes a user has made to a view are also gone, with the exception of sorting. D is incorrect because B is incorrect.

Question 45

The correct answer is C. Pages can contain text, graphics, layers, tables, links, computed text, embedded objects, and applets. A is incorrect because pages cannot contain fields. B and D are incorrect because pages cannot contain frames.

Question 46

The correct answer is B. Selecting Size Tabs Equally, on the Table Rows tab of the Table properties, causes the table tabs to be the same length as the longest tab. A is incorrect because it is a true statement about tables. C is incorrect because it is a true statement about tables. Animated rows switch at various predetermined intervals, which would make it hard for a user to enter data. D is incorrect because it is a true statement about tables.

Question 47

The correct answer is C. The database Launch property has a selection called Launch First Doclink in "About Database." The users have been rerouted to the document as soon as they open the database. A, B, and D are incorrect because the users are immediately sent to the document associated with the first doclink, which prevents them from being able to click on any of the doclinks in the "About" document. It is a routing problem, rather than a problem with doclinks.

Question 48

The correct answer is D. As long as agents are signed by the server, and the database is enabled to inherit its design from the designated master template, Garrett does not need to have access to the database. A is incorrect because design changes can be made on a template to which Garrett has designer access; the database inherits these changes from the template later. B is incorrect because the database can inherit design changes from the template. C is incorrect because a user with designer access and little design experience may end up making changes to design elements that may compromise the database's security and/or ability to function correctly. It is also unnecessary because the database can inherit design changes from the template.

Question 49

The correct answer is C. Both predefined and custom icons cannot be displayed in the same view column. All multiple icons in the column must be predefined. A, B, and D are incorrect because they are all true statements about icons.

Question 50

The correct answer is A. This selection would have Find/Replace go through all the formula and scripts in the database. B is incorrect because Current Section Only would have Find/Replace go through the formula or script present in the designer pane. C is incorrect because Current Object would have Find/Replace go through all the formulas connected with a design element like an agent, or an action. D is incorrect because Find/Replace does work in the designer pane.

Practice Exam 611

Question 1

Betty would like a set of "Contact Us"–type icons to appear in various events: a picture of a quill pen, a picture of a quill pen with a bright background that appears during a mouse-over, and a dim picture of a quill pen that appears after a mouse-click. What is the best way to create these images?

- ○ A. Name each image and store them in Image Resources.
- ○ B. Save each image as an **.ANI** file so that the pictures will change depending on the mouse events.
- ○ C. Define an image resource set in the Basics tab of the Image Resource.
- ○ D. Use hide/when formulas to switch between images according to mouse events.

Question 2

Susan has a multi-database application and has stored the paths of various databases in a profile document called DatabaseProfile, which is included in each database. Using an @Function/@Command, how would Susan retrieve data from the profile document?

- ○ A. **@GetProfileField("DatabaseProfile")**
- ○ B. **@Command([EditProfile])**
- ○ C. **@GetProfileDocument("DatabaseProfile")**
- ○ D. **@GetProfileField("DatabaseProfile";"FieldName")**

Question 3

Eddy created an action agent that called certain documents by their NoteIDs and processed them; he placed the agent in the AcctsPayable database. A month later, Eddy replicated the AcctsPayable database to other servers. However, users on these replica databases reported that the action agent was not working, whereas users on the original AcctsPayable database reported no problems at all. Eddy checked the agent log of each database and the agents did run but no documents were processed. What happened?

- ○ A. The servers where the replica databases reside do not have Reader access in the database ACL, and were not able to replicate the documents used in the action agent.
- ○ B. The correct access to the documents was not replicated to the other databases along with the agent.
- ○ C. The documents' NoteIDs were not replicated to the replica databases.
- ○ D. The action agent was not replicated to the replica databases.

Question 4

Roland has a form with an embedded view. He wants users to be able to delete documents found in the embedded view. How would he do this?

- ○ A.   Documents in an embedded view cannot be deleted.
- ○ B.   Roland can add an action button to the form to delete the document.
- ○ C.   Roland can add an action to the embedded view that deletes documents and enable Show Action Bar in the embedded view.
- ○ D.   Roland can enable Show Embedded View Action Bar in the form.

Question 5

Which formula deletes selected documents in an embedded view on the Notes client?

- ○ A.   **@DocumentDelete**
- ○ B.   **@Command([EditClear])**
- ○ C.   **@ViewClear**
- ○ D.   None of the above

Question 6

Chris has a multiple value picklist and wants to display it on the Web. Which keyword selections would be his best choices for the Web?

- ○ A.   Listbox, radio button, and dialog list.
- ○ B.   Checkbox, dialog list, and radio button.
- ○ C.   Listbox, combobox, and radio button.
- ○ D.   Checkbox, combo box, and dialog list.

Question 7

Woody created a mail-in database, enabled Enforce a Consistent Access Control List Across All Replicas in the Advanced tab of the ACL, and replicated it out to four other servers. Three of the mail-in database replicas are receiving mail, but one is not. Why?

○ A. The fourth replica doesn't have the same ACL as the others, which prevents it from receiving mail.

○ B. The Mail-In Database document is missing from the Domino Directory.

○ C. The fourth replica's server is down.

○ D. The Enable Mail-In Database document is missing from the Domino Directory.

Question 8

James decides to embed a date picker for a calendar view in a Domino database accessed through the Web. What should he do?

○ A. Embed the date picker in a frameset and target the frame containing the calendar view.

○ B. Embed the date picker in the view and enable the Java applet.

○ C. Embed the date picker in a frameset, target the frame containing the calendar view, and enable the Java applet.

○ D. The date picker is not supported on the Web.

Question 9

Which of the following is not a reason an agent may be running too slowly?

○ A. Too many agents are running at the same time.

○ B. The agent code is too long.

○ C. The agent is working its way through one document at a time.

○ D. The database is not full-text indexed.

Question 10

The database **SalesInventory.nsf** is used on both the Notes and Domino client. Bill is explicitly listed in the database ACL with Editor access. When Bill logs onto the database through Domino, he finds he can only look at the documents, not edit them. Why?

- ○ A. Documents from a Lotus Notes database cannot be edited on the Web.
- ○ B. The Maximum Internet name and password access is Reader.
- ○ C. Bill is not listed in the Author fields of the documents.
- ○ D. Bill is a member of a group in the ACL that has only Reader access.

Question 11

Allen wants to display HTML on a form in the Lotus Notes client. What should he do?

- ○ A. Nothing. HTML does not appear on the Lotus Notes client.
- ○ B. Check the Render Pass Through HTML in Notes box on the Form Info tab.
- ○ C. Check the Render Pass Through HTML box on the Form HTML tab.
- ○ D. Type **<HTML>** on the form and any text following it will be rendered into HTML.

Question 12

What is the lowest number of times this formula will run?

```
@If(@Today > ReturnDate; FIELD Status := "Late"; "");
t := 1;
@DoWhile(
t := t +1;
t >= ((ReturnDate - @Today) / 86400)
```

- ○ A. Unable to tell.
- ○ B. 2.
- ○ C. 1.
- ○ D. Infinite.

Question 13

What will be the value of x when the @For loop runs for the final time?

```
@For(x := 1; x < 10; x := x + 1;
@Prompt([OK];"Count";"The count is now " + @Text(x)))
```

○ A. 10.

○ B. 1.

○ C. 9.

○ D. The loop will not run.

Question 14

A database contains documents and responses to documents. The parent documents have a field called Status, which is changeable from "New" to "Pending" to "Complete." The responses to these documents have a field called ParentStatus, which needs to reflect any changes made to the parent document. What formula can be used in the ParentStatus field to keep it current?

○ A. **@GetDocField($Ref;"ParentStatus")**

○ B. **@GetDocField(ParentStatus;$Ref)**

○ C. **Status**

○ D. **@GetDocField($Ref;"Status")**

Question 15

Kendra wants to allow users to create documents through a view without opening another window. She chose the appropriate settings in the view and the column where users will enter their data. However, the application does not work. What is missing?

○ A. **@Command([EditView])** must be placed in the PostQuery event of the view.

○ B. **@Command([EditView])** must be placed in the **InViewEdit** event of the view.

○ C. LotusScript code must be placed in the **InViewEdit** event of the view.

○ D. Either B or C.

Question 16

Which is a true statement about Effective Access?

- ○ A. Effective Access goes through the entire database to determine user access.
- ○ B. Effective Access means the highest level of access a user has in a database.
- ○ C. Effective Access means the lowest level of access a user can have to be effective.
- ○ D. Effective Access checks the access of all the users in the ACL and lists their memberships in groups and roles.

Question 17

Data Connection Resources (DCRs)

- ○ A. allow developers to bring in other applications for use as tools in the Designer client.
- ○ B. cannot be shared across applications.
- ○ C. require that the application to which you are connecting be installed on a Domino server.
- ○ D. are created before a data source server reference is designated.

Question 18

Which formula will result in the following value for the variable x?

```
"Erie Huron Michigan Ontario Superior"
```

- ○ A. @If(Lakes != ""; x := @Sort(Lakes); "")
- ○ B. @If(Lakes != ""; x:= @Sort([ASCENDING]; Lakes); "")
- ○ C. @If(Lakes != ""; x:= @Sort(Lakes; [ASCENDING]); "")
- ○ D. A and C

Question 19

The default Index Encrypted Fields option is selected when the index is created on a database. This means that

- ○ A. encrypted fields cannot be searched unless the user has an encryption key.
- ○ B. encrypted fields can be searched and their contents read.
- ○ C. the full text index file is unencrypted plain text and anyone with access to the server can read the file.
- ○ D. None of the above are true.

Question 20

Anne has just created a document that requires her approval before it can go on to Nicholas for his approval. Anne saves the document without approving it, and Nicholas receives an email message requesting his approval for the document. What has happened?

- ○ A. The form contains a **MailOptions** field set to 1.
- ○ B. The **SendTo** field was set to Nicholas' name.
- ○ C. The **SaveOptions** field was set to 1.
- ○ D. The **Sign** field value was enabled.

Question 21

@DialogBox requires two forms. The Host form has a button that uses **@DialogBox** to display the layout region in the Dialog form. The Dialog form contains text, graphics, and fields, and is set up to resemble a dialog box. Which of the following is not true about **@DialogBox**?

- ○ A. **@DialogBox** can be set so fields in the Host form do not get updated by fields in the Dialog form.
- ○ B. **@DialogBox** can pass values from fields on the Dialog form to the Host form without the Host form containing these fields.
- ○ C. **@DialogBox** works only in open documents.
- ○ D. A title parameter is required in **@DialogBox**.

Question 22

To find out whether a calendar view format is set for 7 days, the following @Function is needed:

- ○ A. **@GetViewFormat**
- ○ B. **@GetViewAttribute**
- ○ C. **@GetCalendarFormat**
- ○ D. **@GetViewInfo**

Question 23

Where is Extended ACL (xACL) used?

- ○ A. Domino Directory, Extended Directory Catalog, and Administration Requests database.
- ○ B. Domino Directory, Extended Directory Catalog, and **LOG.nsf**.
- ○ C. Domino Directory, Extended Directory Catalog, and **NAMES.nsf**.
- ○ D. Domino Directory, Extended Directory Catalog, and Execution Control List.

Question 24

Molly is running an agent that sends mail and creates documents; the agent has been set to run on her behalf. What can Molly expect from this agent?

- ○ A. The mail documents will list the server as the sender.
- ○ B. Molly will be listed as the author of any new documents the agent creates.
- ○ C. The agent will have access to any database from which it gathers data.
- ○ D. All of the above.

Question 25

There are three embedded views in a form. To how many embedded editors can they be linked?

○ A. Each embedded view is automatically linked to one embedded editor.

○ B. Each embedded view must have two embedded editors: one for edit mode, the other for read mode.

○ C. Each embedded view can be linked to one or more embedded editors.

○ D. A and C.

Question 26

Jeff assigns the value of a text field to a column in a view. To show whether or not an attachment file is present, he assigns the field where the attachment is stored to another column in the same view. When Jeff opens the view, which of the following events happens?

○ A. The column with the text field displays its contents and the other column displays a paperclip.

○ B. The column with the text field displays its contents and the other column displays **Unable to display rich text**.

○ C. Text from the file attachment spills its contents into the column on the right. Jeff cannot see the contents of that column.

○ D. The column with the text field displays its contents and the other column displays nothing.

Question 27

How are application bookmarks created?

○ A. Create Data Connection Resources (DCRs), then drag the application icon to the list of design elements.

○ B. Click on Import, located on the File menu, select the filename of the application, and click Import.

○ C. Locate an application icon shortcut and drag it to the bookmark bar.

○ D. Create the proper Data Connect Resource (DCR), then drag the application icon shortcut to the bookmark bar.

Question 28

Where is the private encryption key stored?

- ○ A. User ID file.
- ○ B. User's Person document.
- ○ C. The private key is always paired with the public key wherever the public key is stored.
- ○ D. A and B.

Question 29

Which of the following statements is true?

- ○ A. Any view can be included in view logging.
- ○ B. Only views such as **$All** should be in view logging.
- ○ C. Server restarts can perform faster if views are included in the transaction log.
- ○ D. All of the above.
- ○ E. A and C.

Question 30

This formula runs in a scheduled agent:

```
MsgBody := "This request was due on " + DueDate +
", and will be removed within 24 hours if the
document is not finalized." + @NewLine + @NewLine +
"Click on the document link to view the request ->";

@If(DocStatus="Pending" & DueDate=@Today;
@MailSend(Requester;RequesterMgr;"";"Request Past Due";
"";MsgBody;[INCLUDEDOCLINK]);"")
```

Although requests are due, emails are not being sent. Why?

- ○ A. The problem is in the **@If** statement. **DueDate** and **@Today** must be converted into the same data type.
- ○ B. The problem is in **MsgBody**. The sentences should be concatenated with "&" rather than "+".
- ○ C. The problem is in **MsgBody**. **DueDate** must be converted to the same data type.
- ○ D. The problem is in the **@If** statement. The **@MailSend** requires a Remark.

Question 31

Diane has an inventory view and would like various rows to display red text when quantities are 10 or less; otherwise regular text is displayed. What formula should she use?

- ○ A. **@If(Quantity<=10;255:0:0;0:0:0)**
- ○ B. **@If(Quantity<=10;255:0:0:0:0:0;"")**
- ○ C. **@If(Quantity<=10;255:0:0:;255:255:255)**
- ○ D. None of the above

Question 32

Jackie includes an **[Encrypt]** flag with her **@MailSend** command. How does the document get encrypted?

- ○ A. The document is encrypted with the recipient's private key, so that only the person with the matching public key can read the document.
- ○ B. The document is encrypted with the recipient's public key, so that only the person with the matching private key can read the document.
- ○ C. There is a **SecretEncryptionKeys** field in the document. Potential recipients have been sent an encryption key so that they can read the document.
- ○ D. The formula with the **@MailSend** command also includes **@MailEncryptSavedPreference** for encryption.

Question 33

The effective username is used for

- ○ A. Database access rights and directing actions an agent can perform; it also serves as a mail sender.
- ○ B. Document author and encryption rights, and is the authority under which an agent runs.
- ○ C. Ability to create databases on the server and locking and unlocking documents, and is the authority under which an agent runs.
- ○ D. Mail sender, encryption rights, and locking and unlocking documents.

Question 34

One type of application workflow is called the Individual Mail Databases method. This type of workflow is to be used when users do not go to a database to review and approve documents, but create, receive, respond, and route documents to other users all through email. One advantage to this application workflow is that these users can simply access their mail and do not need to access their mail and a remote database. What would be a disadvantage in this type of workflow?

- ○ A. Requires a lot of server disk space because forms must be stored with any documents sent to the user's mail database.
- ○ B. Requires remote access through a modem.
- ○ C. Workflow takes longer to complete because the work has to be done sequentially.
- ○ D. A and C.
- ○ E. A, B, and C.

Question 35

When Robert Bristow opens the "Regional" view, he sees his documents in blue text with a yellow background. He sees other documents in black text with a white background. Which row color formula makes this possible?

- ○ A. @If(@UserName="Robert
       Bristow";255:255:0:0:0:0;255:255:0:0:0:255)
- ○ B. @If(@Name([CN];@UserName)="Robert
       Bristow";255:255:0:0:0:255;255:255:255:0:0:0)
- ○ C. @If(@Name([CN];@UserName)="Robert Bristow" &
       DocCreator=@UserName;255:255:0:0:0:255;255:255:255:0:0:0)
- ○ D. @If(@Name([CN]="Robert
       Bristow";0:0:255:255:255:0;0:0:0:255:255:255)

Question 36

A document was deleted in one replica database and edited once in another. Which will take precedence during replication—the deletion or the edited document?

○ A. If the editing occurred after the deletion, the edited document takes precedence.

○ B. If the editing occurred before the deletion, the edited document takes precedence.

○ C. The deletion always takes precedence.

○ D. The edited document always takes precedence.

Question 37

If a scheduled agent misses its scheduled run because it was being enabled, disabled, modified, pasted, or saved, the following occurs:

○ A. The agent runs immediately if it was saved and scheduled monthly, weekly, or daily.

○ B. The agent runs immediately if it was enabled and scheduled monthly, weekly, or daily.

○ C. The agent runs immediately if it was modified and scheduled monthly, weekly, or daily.

○ D. All of the above.

○ E. A and C.

Question 38

Ian has a form that has the **Store Form in Documents** property enabled. Because the database containing this form is not a mail-in database and Ian wants to reduce the size of the database, he needs to create an agent that will remove this property from all the documents. Ian must

○ A. remove all internal fields connected with the form.

○ B. rename the form.

○ C. compact the database.

○ D. A and C.

○ E. All but D.

Question 39

What does the following formula return?

`@UserAccess(@DbName)`

- ○ A. A text list of default user access privileges in the current database.
- ○ B. A text list of the user's access privileges in the current database.
- ○ C. Nothing. A keyword is needed to determine particular access privileges.
- ○ D. Nothing will be returned if used on a local database.

Question 40

Keith's users want to be able to customize the color preference in the Main view. In response, Keith enables Use Value as Color and User Definable properties of the first column and sets some color choices, the default being black text. He also adds a color field to the database profile document to automatically open a color picker for the user to make his or her selection. Users are choosing colors, but they aren't seeing their choices in the view. Why?

- ○ A. The field containing the color picker has to be referenced in the first column.
- ○ B. Color pickers should be embedded in a **richtextlite** field.
- ○ C. The profile document has to be referenced by name on the column properties.
- ○ D. All but B.

Question 41

Which of the following does not convert a data type into a date-time value?

- ○ A. **@ToTime**
- ○ B. **@IsTime**
- ○ C. **@TextToTime**
- ○ D. All of the above

Question 42

What is the result of the following formula?

```
@Keywords("Lions lose season opener":
"prowling tigers win in extra innings":
"Endurance pushes the leoPards over the top":
"Cheetahs make burst of speed";
"lions":"tigers":"leopards":"cheetahs";";")
```

- ○ A. Lions;Tigers;Leopards;Cheetahs
- ○ B. lions;tigers;cheetahs
- ○ C. lions;tigers;leopards;cheetahs
- ○ D. tigers

Question 43

The VacationRequest form is created by users with at least Author access to the database. The form has a section that must be filled in and okayed by a departmental manager. Belinda is a departmental manager, but she cannot make changes in this section after she places the document in edit mode. What is causing the problem?

- ○ A. Belinda does not have Editor access in the database ACL.
- ○ B. Belinda does not have the proper role.
- ○ C. Belinda is not listed in the Authors field of the document.
- ○ D. Belinda does not have proper access to the VacationRequest form.

Question 44

Brandon wants to list a date range in a multi-value field. He creates a formula: **@Explode(01/01/2003 − 01/31/2003)**, but upon testing it, he sees: **ERROR: Incorrect data type for operator or @function: Text expected.** How can he correct the formula?

- ○ A. **@Explode(@Text(01/01/2003) - @Text(01/31/2003))**
- ○ B. **@Explode(@Date("01/01/2003") - @Date("01/31/2003"))**
- ○ C. **@Explode("01/01/2003" − "01/31/2003")**
- ○ D. **@Explode([01/01/2003] −01/31/2003])**

Question 45

What is not true about the Single Copy Template (SCT)?

- ○ A. Designers can enable SCT through the properties of the New Database Info tab.
- ○ B. Databases that use an SCT-enabled template do not need to store their design elements, but they must retrieve them from the template instead.
- ○ C. SCT reduces the drain on server resources, storage, and memory.
- ○ D. A database (**.nsf**) is smaller in size than its SCT-enabled template.

Question 46

Which database optimization properties require compaction of the database in order to take affect?

- ○ A. Don't Overwrite Freespace, Don't Support Specialized Response Hierarchy, and Limit Entries in **$UpdatedBy** Fields.
- ○ B. Allow Use of Stored Forms in This Database, Maintain LastAccessed Property, and Limit Entries in **$Revisions** Fields.
- ○ C. Display Images After Loading, Document Table Bitmap Optimization, and Don't Overwrite Freespace.
- ○ D. Don't Maintain Unread Marks, Document Table Bitmap Optimization, and Don't Support Response Hierarchy.

Question 47

Eric finds out that a user has created several profile documents. How should he get rid of the extra profile documents and what can he do to prevent this situation from occurring again?

- ○ A. Create a view showing the user's profile documents and delete them manually. Deselect Include in Menu from the profile document form properties.
- ○ B. Create a formula agent to remove the user's extra profile documents. Deselect Include in Menu from the profile document form properties.
- ○ C. Create a LotusScript agent to remove the user's extra profile documents. Deselect Include in Menu from the profile document form properties.
- ○ D. B and C.

Question 48

To get the name of a table, use

- ○ A. **@Command([TableName])**
- ○ B. **@GetTableFocus([TABLENAME])**
- ○ C. **@Table([TABLENAME])**
- ○ D. **@GetFocusTable([TABLENAME])**

Question 49

In order to mail documents automatically, the following field(s) are required to be in the form:

- ○ A. **MailOptions**
- ○ B. **SendTo**
- ○ C. **SaveOptions**
- ○ D. A and B

Question 50

Rachel wants to print only two particular frames in a frameset at one time. Which Print selection does she use?

- ○ A. Selected frames only.
- ○ B. As laid out on screen.
- ○ C. Each frame individually.
- ○ D. None of the above.

Practice Exam Answer Key for Exam 611

1. C	**18.** D	**35.** C
2. D	**19.** C	**36.** A
3. C	**20.** A	**37.** E
4. C	**21.** C	**38.** E
5. D	**22.** D	**39.** B
6. B	**23.** A	**40.** D
7. D	**24.** B	**41.** B
8. D	**25.** C	**42.** D
9. B	**26.** D	**43.** B
10. B	**27.** C	**44.** D
11. B	**28.** A	**45.** A
12. C	**29.** D	**46.** D
13. A	**30.** C	**47.** C
14. D	**31.** A	**48.** D
15. C	**32.** B	**49.** D
16. B	**33.** C	**50.** D
17. C	**34.** D	

Question 1

The correct answer is C. An image resource set, also known as an image well, contains more than one image. There are two types of image resource sets: horizontal, which creates an image that seems to change based on its state (for example, the image lights up during a mouseover and dims after it's clicked), and vertical, which includes an icon in three different sizes. Image resources can only use .bmp, .gif, and .jpg files. A is incorrect because image resource sets can contain more than one image. B is incorrect because .ani is the extension to an animation file and is not one of the three files used in the image resources. D is incorrect because hide-when formulas do not work with mouse events.

Question 2

The correct answer is D. @GetProfileField(*name of profile document;name of field in profile document; unique key [optional]*) allows formulas and scripts to retrieve data from a central source. This function is particularly useful for applications that must go between multiple databases to retrieve information, in that a profile document could contain the file paths of the databases, text to be used in picklists or email messages, and so on. A is incorrect because @GetProfileField requires both the name of the profile document and the name of the desired field. B is incorrect because @Command([EditProfile]; *form name [optional]; unique key [optional]*) allows users with the appropriate access rights to edit the profile document. C is incorrect because there is no such function as @GetProfileDocument.

Question 3

The correct answer is C. The NoteID of an object is unique only within the database in which it resides. It does not maintain its unique identity when it is replicated. To maintain this identity when replicating between databases, it is better to reference objects through their Notes UNIDs, which do not change during replication. A is incorrect because the users are not reporting that documents are missing, only that the action agent isn't working. If the documents had not been replicated, Eddy would have heard about missing documents before hearing about the malfunctioning action agent and he would have had to check the server access. B is incorrect because documents keep the same access across replicas; Authors and Readers fields do not change. D is incorrect because if the action agent had not been replicated, the users would have reported either being unable to see the action or they would not even know there was an action to use in the first place. Instead, they used the action and found it did not work.

Question 4

The correct answer is C. Roland can create an action that deletes a document and refreshes the view afterwards and places it within the view that's being embedded. Then he can enable Show Action Bar in the embedded view. A is incorrect because under R6, documents in an embedded view can be deleted. B is incorrect because documents are not affected by the action agents of the form in which their view is embedded. D is incorrect because there is no such property as Show Embedded View Action Bar in the form.

Question 5

The correct answer is D. `@Command([EditClear]);` `@PostedCommand([ViewRefreshFields])` is the correct formula. A is incorrect because there is no such function as `@DocumentDelete`. B is incorrect because there is no such function as `@ViewClear`. D is incorrect because `@Command([EditClear]);` `@PostedCommand([ViewRefreshFields])` deletes documents within an embedded view.

Question 6

The correct answer is B. Chris cannot control the width and height of the combobox or the listbox on the Web. They format themselves according to the width of the longest keyword string they contain. listbox, radio button, and dialog list automatically adjust width and height. A is incorrect because although listbox and radio button automatically adjust width and height, dialog list does not. C is incorrect because although listbox and radio button will automatically adjust width and height, combobox does not. D is incorrect because although checkbox automatically adjusts width and height, dialog list and combobox do not.

Question 7

The correct answer is D. This method is the least labor-intensive. Also the files workpane shows a refresh icon and the File Resources property box has the "Needs refresh" checkbox checked if a file has been modified.

Question 8

The correct answer is D. The date picker is not supported on the Web. A is incorrect in that although it is the correct procedure for embedding the date picker in Notes, James wanted the date picker to be used on the Web. B is incorrect because the date picker should be embedded in a frameset with a frame containing a calendar view as a target frame. C is incorrect because there is no need to enable a Java applet.

Question 9

The correct answer is B. The length of an agent's code has no bearing on its speed of execution. However, how a code is written matters. The more efficient the code, the quicker it executes. For instance, a GetAllDocumentsByKey or a FTSearch function is quicker than a db.Search when the code is searching for particular documents. GetAllDocumentsByKey searches for documents using a unique key and a view, which helps limit the number of documents through which it has to search. FTSearch uses the full-text index in its searches. However, db.Search searches the entire database, making it the least efficient of the three. A is incorrect because setting too many agents to run at the same time has a negative impact on server resources. C is incorrect because processing (editing, saving, creating, deleting, and so on) many documents one at a time slows the agent down. D is incorrect because full-text indexing creates an index, which allows faster retrieval of documents.

Question 10

The correct answer is B. Although Bill has Editor access in the Notes client, the Maximum Internet name-and-password access gives him only Reader access when he logs on to the database via the Web. Maximum Internet name-and-password access overrides even explicit access levels in the ACL if the user is accessing the database through the Web. A is incorrect because if the user has the proper access, documents can be edited on the Web. C is incorrect because the documents on Notes are the same documents seen on the Web. If Bill could edit the documents on Notes, then he should be able to edit them on the Web—unless Maximum Internet name-and-password access has been set to Reader on the database. That would prevent Bill from editing the documents. D is incorrect because in the database ACL, Bill is listed explicitly as having Editor access. Explicit access in a database for an individual always overrides group access. Although Bill may be in a group that has Reader access only, he has the Editor access explicitly assigned to him.

Question 11

The correct answer is B. Check the Render Pass-Through HTML in Notes box on the Form Info tab. A is incorrect because HTML can be used in the Notes client. C is incorrect because the Render Pass-Through HTML in Notes check box is found in the Form Info tab; there is no HTML tab in the Form properties. D is incorrect because although a developer can import, paste, or type HTML into form, or convert part of or the entire form into HTML, the result can only be seen through the Web. To use HTML in the Notes client, the Render Pass-Through HTML in Notes checkbox must be enabled.

Question 12

The correct answer is C. @DoWhile statements always execute at least once. A is incorrect because @DoWhile loops execute at least once to test the condition(s) under which they must run. B is incorrect because a @DoWhile loop runs at least once. D is incorrect because a @DoWhile loop runs at least once; also, the question called for the lowest number, and an infinite number of loops can never be least.

Question 13

The correct answer is A. The value of x must be 10 before it no longer meets the criteria of x < 10. B is incorrect because although the @For loop begins at 1 (x = 1), it must continue looping until x < 10. That means it will loop more than once. C is incorrect because the @For loop will continue until x is no longer less than 10: 1 < 10, 2 < 10, 3 < 10, 4 < 10, 5 < 10, 6 < 10, 7 < 10, 8 < 10, 9 < 10— nine loops—then after the tenth loop begins 10 < 10, then the condition x < 10 is no longer true and @For stops after the tenth loop. D is incorrect because the @For function continues looping until the condition x is no longer less than 10.

Question 14

The correct answer is D. @GetDocField requires the Unique ID of the parent document as well as the name of the field belonging to the parent document. The field name should be in quotation marks. A is incorrect because it is referencing the response document's field rather than that of the parent document. B is incorrect because not only are the parameters backwards (field, then Unique ID), but the field belongs to the response document and not its parent. C is incorrect because although the Status field could inherit the status value from the parent document, it can inherit only once. Because the parent document's status may change more than once, the status of the response documents must change with it, hence the need for @GetDocField.

Question 15

The correct answer is C. Only LotusScript can be used in the InViewEdit event of the view. A, B, and D are incorrect because the event accepts no other code.

Question 16

The correct answer is B. If a user is explicitly listed in the ACL with Editor access and is also a member of a group with Reader access, the user's Effective Access is Editor. A is incorrect because Effective Access has to do with access listed in the database ACL, not the contents of the database. C is incorrect because Effective Access is the highest level of access a user has through a database ACL. D is incorrect because Effective Access determines only the highest access of users. However, @UserNamesList provides the access of the current user, as well as the roles and groups to which the user belongs.

Question 17

The correct answer is C. Data Connection Resources (DCRs) require that the application to which you are connecting be installed on a Domino server. A is incorrect because the Tools menu allows designers to bring in other applications for use in creating applications. B is incorrect because one of the things that make DCRs so attractive to developers is that DCRs can be shared across applications, and are reusable as well. D is incorrect because a data source server reference to the external application must always be created before the DCR can be created and used. The data source server reference indicates the data source and what driver to use for the data exchange.

Question 18

The correct answer is D. The function `@Sort( list ; [ order ]; customSortExpression )` provides a variety of ways to sort a text, number, or date/time list. Among the keywords used in `@Sort` are `[ASCENDING]` and `[DESCENDING]`. Answer C has the keyword `[ASCENDING]` in its `@Sort` function and the list of lakes ascends in alphabetical order. Answer A shows that the keywords are optional, but `@Sort` sorts a list in ascending order with or without the `[ASCENDING]` designation. A is incorrect because it is not the only answer. B is incorrect because the parameters are out of order: the list is first, then the keyword. C is incorrect because it is not the only answer.

Question 19

The correct answer is C. The default Index Encrypted Fields option is selected when the index is created on a database. This means that the full text index file is unencrypted plain text and anyone with access to the server can read the file. A is incorrect because if the user has access to the server, then the user can locate the full-text index file, which is unencrypted plain text. Or the user could do a search for a particular word or phrase and get a list of documents containing them, even if the word or phrase is in an encrypted field. The user can't read the field, but knows the document contains the word or phrase. B is incorrect because although encrypted fields can be searched, their contents cannot be read. D is incorrect because leaving the Index Encrypted Fields option checked produces a full text index file that is in unencrypted text, which anyone who has access to the server can read.

Question 20

The correct answer is A. If the MailOptions field is set to 1, it forces the document to be mailed when it is saved. B is incorrect because although the SendTo field is a required field for a memo, it does not control when the document is sent. C is incorrect because a 1 in the SaveOptions field saves the document only when the document is submitted; the field does not determine when the document is mailed. D is incorrect because Sign is a field that is included if an electronic signature is to be included with a mailed document. Only one sign-enabled field is required and the Sign If Mailed or Saved in Section property must be selected.

Question 21

The correct answer is C. @DialogBox can work in the current document, which is an open document or one selected in a view. A, B, and D are all incorrect because they are in fact true statements about the @DialogBox function.

Question 22

The correct answer is D. @GetViewInfo([CalendarViewFormat]) returns 7. @GetViewInfo requires an attribute like [CalendarViewFormat] (returns the number of days displayed), [ColumnValue] (returns the value of a column on the current row and requires a second parameter of column number), or [IsCalViewTimeSlotOn] (returns @True if time slots are displayed, @False if not). A is incorrect because there is no such function as @GetViewFormat. B is incorrect because there is no such function as @GetViewAttribute. C is incorrect because there is no such function as @GetCalendarFormat.

Question 23

The correct answer is A. The Extended ACL (xACL) is used in the Domino Directory, Extended Directory Catalog, and Administration Requests database. Unlike Readers and Authors fields, which restrict user access on a form or document level, xACL can restrict user access at the field level. B is incorrect because LOG.nsf is used for monitoring databases and tracking replication events. C is incorrect because NAMES.nsf is the Name and Address Book. D is incorrect because the Execution Control List (ECL) is found on each user's workstation and allows the user to determine which formulas and scripts can be run on that workstation.

Question 24

The correct answer is B. Molly will be listed as the author of any new documents the agent creates. The agent Security property can now be set so that an agent is run on behalf of a specified person or on anyone's behalf. Any user who runs the agent must be in the ACL of any database being accessed by the agent. A is incorrect because Run on Behalf Of allows the designer to designate certain users or anyone. C is incorrect because if a user is not in the ACL of a database to which the agent must have access, the agent fails. D is incorrect because the agent has been set to run on Molly's behalf, which means that any documents the agent creates will list her name as the author.

Question 25

The correct answer is C. Each embedded view can be linked to one or more embedded editors. This method is called "targeting" and enables users to edit documents in a view without having to open another window. A is incorrect because an embedded view must have an embedded editor to target. Developers can enter the name of the editor through the Target Frame field in the Embedded View properties box. B is incorrect because embedded editors can be seen in either edit or read mode. D is incorrect because only C is the correct answer.

Question 26

The correct answer is D. A way to show the presence or absence of file attachments would be to use an @Function such as @Attachments (shows number of attachments) or @AttachmentNames (returns file names) in the column. A is incorrect because Jeff did not assign Display Values as Icons to that column, nor did he create a formula that would allow him to test for the existence of file attachments in the field. Had he done so, the paperclip would display. B is incorrect because no error message appears when a column displays the contents of a rich text field (which is the only kind of field that can contain attachments); the column appears empty even when the rich text field has something in it. Rich text fields cannot be displayed in views. C is incorrect because the contents of rich text fields are not displayed in columns, and even then only through formulas.

Question 27

The correct answer is C. No DCRs or import file commands are necessary to add an application as a bookmark to the Designer client. A, B, and D are all incorrect because they include either DCRs or import file commands.

Question 28

The correct answer is A. Users receive two encryption keys. A private key and a public key are stored in the User ID file, and a public key is stored in the user's Person document. B is incorrect because the user's Person document is where the public key is stored. C is incorrect because although the private and public keys are stored together in the User ID file, only the public key is in the user's Person document. D is incorrect because both the private key and the public key are stored in the User ID file, and only the public key is stored in the user's Person document.

Question 29

The correct answer is D. View logging can help avoid view rebuilds after a system crash, which in turn shortens recovery time. Although any view can be included in the transaction log, the view updates can slow the server's performance. Therefore, complex views such as $All or $Users would be the best candidates for view logging. A is incorrect because not only can any view be included in view logging, but the $All view in particular should be used in view logging (answer B) and server restarts can perform faster if views are included in the transaction log (answer C). B is incorrect because the $All view is not the only view that can be included in view logging (answer A), and server restarts can perform faster if views are included in the transaction log (answer C). C is incorrect because not only do server restarts perform faster if views are included in the transaction log, but any view, especially $All view (answers A and B), can be included in view logging. E is incorrect because not only can any view be included in view logging (answer A) and server restarts can perform faster if views are included in the transaction log (answer C), but the $All view in particular should be used in view logging (answer B).

Question 30

The correct answer is C. A date field is being used in a text statement and must be converted to text: `"This request was due on " + @Text(DueDate) +` `", and will be removed within 24 hours if the document is not finalized." +` `@NewLine + @NewLine + "Click on the document link to view the request ->"`. A is incorrect because in the @If statement, both `DueDate` and `@Today` are already the same data type: date/time. B is incorrect because an ampersand (&) is used for Boolean arguments, whereas a plus (+) is used to concatenate text strings. D is incorrect because `@MailSend` does not require a Remark parameter, although it does require a null value as a placeholder.

Question 31

The correct answer is A. A 3-number value determines the RGB value of the text in a row, leaving the background color unchanged, whereas a 6-number value determines first the RGB value of the background (the first 3-number value), then the RGB number of the text (the last 3-number value). B is incorrect because 255:0:0:0:0:0 shows black text on a red background. C is incorrect because 255:0:0:255:255:255 shows white text on a red background. D is incorrect because the first 3-number value determines the color of the text. In this case, 255:0:0:0:0:0 means red text on a white background.

Question 32

The correct answer is B. Upon receiving his Notes User ID, a user possesses special encryption keys: A public key is stored in his Person document in the Domino Directory, and a public key and a private key are stored in his User ID. If the sender sends an encrypted mail message, it is encrypted with the recipient's public key, obtained from the Domino Directory. The recipient needs the correct private key, obtained from the recipient's Notes User ID, which verifies his or her identity, to read the encrypted message. The private key prevents anyone other than the recipient from reading the encrypted email. A is incorrect because it is the private key that verifies the user's identity to allow decryption. C is incorrect because a `SecretEncryptionKeys` field stores special encryption keys with which users can encrypt documents. These keys are used instead of the users' own encryption keys to encrypt documents. These keys must be distributed to the proper users before they can decrypt the documents. D is incorrect because `@MailEncryptSavedPreference` is not a real function.

Question 33

The correct answer is C. Effective users are those under whose authority an agent runs—in many cases, this would be the current user. For instance, instead of a mail application sending an email in the name of the server or the name of the developer who signed the agent, the agent could be set to use the name of the person who invoked the agent. Effective usernames are used to grant database access; to grant the right to create databases, replicas, and templates on the server; to identify the mail sender; to identify the document author; and to lock and unlock documents. A is incorrect because effective usernames do not direct the actions an agent can perform. B is incorrect because effective usernames are not used for encryption rights. D is incorrect because effective usernames are not used for encryption rights.

Question 34

The correct answer is D. Disk space on the users' workstations, as well as the time it would take to complete the workflow, should be taken into account when considering this method. A is incorrect because C is also correct. B is incorrect because remote users still need a modem to reach their mail. However, time spent on the modem is reduced if they don't have to access both their mail and the remote database. C is incorrect because A is also correct.

Question 35

The correct answer is C. The @UserName function returns the username in canonical format and must be formatted to the common name, using the @Name function to match "Robert Bristow." Also, the name in the DocCreator field must match @UserName so that Robert Bristow sees only his own documents in blue text with yellow background, represented by the RGB value: 255:255:0:0:0:255. The first three values specify the background color, whereas the last three specify the text color. The value 255:255:255:0:0:0 represents the white background with black text. A is incorrect because the @Name function is needed to convert the username to the common name ([CN]) format. Also, the color formats are incorrect—255:255:0:0:0:0 is a yellow background with black text, whereas the color format for documents not belonging to Robert—255:255:0:0:0:255—is a yellow background with blue text. B is incorrect because the formula does not check the username against the DocCreate field value. D is incorrect because the @Name function is being used illegally and will cause the error Too many arguments for @Function: ')'.

Question 36

The correct answer is A. A document edited after its replica was deleted on another server is not removed by replication. B is incorrect because the edit must take place after the deletion. However, if the document had been edited more than once on one database and deleted on another, the document that was edited multiple times takes precedence over the deleted document, even if the document deletion was the most recent change. Multiple edits of a document always take precedence in replication. C is incorrect because deletions do not always take precedence when it comes to documents edited multiple times or documents edited at least once after the replica deletion. D is incorrect because if the document was edited only once, the deletion takes precedence.

Question 37

The correct answer is E. The scheduled agent runs immediately if it has been modified, pasted, or saved and scheduled monthly, weekly, or daily. A is incorrect because C is also true. B is incorrect because if the agent was scheduled daily and is enabled within a half hour of its scheduled run, it runs immediately. Otherwise, it runs at its next scheduled time. C is incorrect because A is also a true. D is incorrect because A and C are true and E is the only correct answer.

Question 38

The correct answer is E. The agent must remove the internal fields $TITLE, $INFO, $WINDOWTITLE, $BODY, and $ACTIONS. Also, the agent should remove the old form name and assign the name of the form that will display the documents. Compacting the database after running the agent reduces the database's size. A, B, and C are incorrect because all three should be done together. D is incorrect because A, B, and C should all be done together.

Question 39

The correct answer is B. `@UserAccess(server:file;[access privilege])` can be used without parameters. If used with parameters, `@UserAccess` can determine the current user's access to a specified database on a specified server. The parameter access privilege allows `@UserAccess` to test whether the current user has a particular access to the database. A is incorrect because `@UserAccess` returns only a list of access privileges for the current user. C is incorrect because no parameters are required in `@UserAccess`. D is incorrect because `@UserAccess` always returns 6;1;1 on local databases—which translates to `"Manager";"can create documents";"can delete documents"`.

Question 40

The correct answer is D. The color picker is contained by the field type color. A and C are incorrect because the color picker field must be referenced in the first column, along with the name of the profile document containing the color picker field so that users can successfully choose a color. B is incorrect because a rich text lite field can contain images, attachments, views, shared applets, OLE objects, text, calendar, DatePicker, or inbox, but not color.

Question 41

The correct answer is B. `@IsTime` tests a value and returns 1 (True) if it is a date-time or date-time list. A is incorrect because `@ToTime` can convert text or time to a time value. C is incorrect because `@TextToTime` converts a string into a date/time value. D is incorrect because because @IsTime tests a value to see if it is a date/time type, rather than converting it.

Question 42

The correct answer is D. `@Keywords(textlist1;textlist2;separator)` is case sensitive. The functions `@LowerCase`, `@UpperCase`, or `@ProperCase` should be used in conjunction with @Keywords so that the lists are of the same case before making a comparison. A is incorrect because the result is in proper case. Textlist2 is in lowercase (`"lions";"tigers";"leopards";"cheetahs"`) so no proper case matches could result. B is incorrect because although "tigers" matches the lowercase "tigers" in textlist2, "Lions" and "Cheetahs" do not match "lions" and "cheetahs." C is incorrect because although "tigers" matches the lowercase "tigers" in textlist2, "Lions," "leoPards" and "Cheetahs" do not match "lions," "leopards," and "cheetahs."

Question 43

The correct answer is B. Belinda was not given the proper role in the database ACL to allow her to edit the section. To edit a controlled-access section, the user must have at least Editor rights in the database ACL, as well as be listed as a section editor, whether by role, group, or individually. A, C, and D are incorrect because Belinda was able to place the document in edit mode and it is implied that she was able to edit other places in the document.

Question 44

The correct answer is D. When a date range is used in @Explode, it cannot be used as a string type. The brackets present the range as a date-time range. A is incorrect because the @Text function is being used to convert dates into text and the formula does not have the brackets to convert the range into a date-time range. B is incorrect because the @Date function is being used to convert text into dates and the formula does not have the brackets to convert the range into a date-time range. C is incorrect because the dates are rendered as text and there are no brackets to convert the range into a date-time range.

Question 45

The correct answer is A. The single copy template enables developers to store design information in one template rather than in each database that uses the template, which results in less disk space used by the database. For instance, using the single copy template with a mail template stores all the design information in one place, making users' mail databases smaller because the databases no longer have to store the design as well as the data. A is correct because the SCT must also be enabled through the Domino Administrator client. B, C, and D are incorrect because they are true statements about SCT.

Question 46

The correct answer is D. Domino tries to reuse unused space left behind when documents and attachments are deleted, rather than reducing the database's file size. Compaction can help in recovering space and reducing file size. Optimizing a database improves its access time on the server, and there are properties that can be set to help in that effort. Unread marks in a database takes up resources and slows down response time, especially if the view is a large one and users are reading only select documents rather than all of them. Selecting Don't Maintain Unread Marks can help increase the database's efficiency. Document Table Bitmap Optimization enables Domino to update views more efficiently by allowing it to search only the tables associated with the forms used by documents in the view being updated, rather than search each table during each view update. Selecting Don't Support Response Hierarchy means that data used by @AllChildren and @AllDescendants will no longer be stored. It must be noted that this option does not affect hierarchical views that do not use the @AllChildren and @AllDescendants functions. All these selections require database compaction to take effect. A is incorrect because Don't Overwrite Freespace and Limit Entries in $UpdatedBy Fields do not require database compaction. B is incorrect because Prevent the User of Stored Forms does not require database compaction. C is incorrect because Display Images After Loading and Don't Overwrite Freespace do not require database compaction.

Question 47

The correct answer is C. Profile documents, although their fields can be accessed through formulas and LotusScript, do not show up in views or database document counts. They cannot be deleted through formula language. A is incorrect because profile documents cannot be seen in views and therefore cannot be deleted manually. B is incorrect because profile documents cannot be deleted through formulas, but they can be deleted through LotusScript. D is incorrect because the only way to delete a profile document is to use LotusScript.

Question 48

The correct answer is D. `@GetFocusTable([TABLENAME])` returns the entry located in Name/ID of the Table Programming tab in Table Properties. If there is no name or the table isn't in focus, the return value is a null string. A is incorrect because there is no such formula as `@Command([TableName])`. B is incorrect because there is no such function as `@GetTableFocus`. C is incorrect because there is no such function as `@Table`.

Question 49

The correct answer is D. The `SendTo` and `MailOptions` fields are required to automatically mail documents. The `SendTo` field requires the name of the person, group, or mail-in database. `MailOptions` requires a 1 for automatic mailing. A is incorrect because B is required, too. B is incorrect because A is required, too. C is incorrect because it deals with saving the document when it is being mailed.

Question 50

The correct answer is D. To get printouts of only the two frames, Rachel would have to choose Selected Frame Only for each frame and run the printer twice. A is incorrect because only the selected frame is printed. B is incorrect because all the frames as seen by the user would be printed out. C is incorrect because all the frames would be printed out, one frame for each printed page.

Practice Exam 612

The questions and answers in this practice exam are for exam 612, Developing Web Applications. The questions cover the five core competencies required for this exam and are similar to the questions one will encounter when taking Domino exams.

Test-Taking Strategies

All Lotus Notes exams are difficult and require a broad working knowledge of the subject as indicated by the competencies for that exam. The exam questions are very rarely precise, and students should take note of the following considerations when choosing an answer from the four choices:

➤ All choices can be correct. Choose the most precise.

➤ All choices can be incorrect. Choose the least incorrect.

➤ After choosing an answer, apply the answer back to the question. The answer must answer the question. This may sound redundant, but quite often on applying what at first glance appears to be the correct answer back to the question, you realize that the answer is not correct for the question the way it is written.

➤ Questions and answers usually apply to the default behavior of Notes and not to workarounds or *very* advanced development, unless specified in the question and answer.

➤ Read all questions carefully, because a word such as *must* or *not* can make a huge difference in the correct answer.

Begin the Exam

Question 1

The three main rules for tags in HTML are

○ A. Tags are case sensitive.
Tags should have both a start and an end.
One set of tags should be wholly contained within another.

○ B. Tags are not case sensitive.
Tags should have both a start and an end.
One set of tags should be wholly contained within another.

○ C. Tags must be lowercase.
Tags should have both a start and an end.
One set of tags should be wholly contained within another.

○ D. Tags must be uppercase.
Tags should have both a start and an end.
One set of tags should be wholly contained within another.

Question 2

A user is viewing the source of a Web document that has been generated by Domino. How many sets of form tags will be seen?

○ A. One.
○ B. Two.
○ C. None.
○ D. As many as needed.

Question 3

John wants to display text and graphics with appropriate spacing and positioning in a browser. He needs to use which of the following to accomplish this?

○ A. A form.
○ B. A page.
○ C. A table.
○ D. A section.

Question 4

Mary has a computed field that shows the date 05/21/2003 in the browser. She writes some JavaScript code to subtract 2 months and 5 days from that date. When her code runs, which of the following occurs?

- ○ A. Her new date is 03/16/2003.
- ○ B. Her new date is 16/03/2003.
- ○ C. She gets an error message.
- ○ D. Her new date is 07/26/2003.

Question 5

Mary is hiding a field using Notes' Hide/When option. She wants to use the value in this field in calculations in a browser. To accomplish this she does which of the following?

- ○ A. Sets the field property Send to Browser.
- ○ B. Sets the field hide/when property Web browsers.
- ○ C. Sets the form property Generate HTML for all fields.
- ○ D. Sets the database property Use JavaScript when Generating Pages.

Question 6

Tom has a variable whose value is available to all scripts on a document and will hold the initial value of the Category field. He enabled this by doing which of the following?

- ○ A. Declaring and setting the value of the variable in the **onLoad** event of the Category field.
- ○ B. Declaring the variable in the **JS Header** event of the form and setting the value in the **onLoad** event of the form.
- ○ C. Declaring the variable in the **JS Header** event of the form and setting the value in the **onFocus** event of the Category field.
- ○ D. Declaring the variable in the **JS Header** event of the form and setting the value in the **onLoad** event of the Category field.

Question 7

John has created a field in one of his databases. He later realizes that he needs to create similar fields in other forms in his database and in another database. He wants to make the creation and maintaining of these fields as painless as possible, so he does which one of the following?

- ○ A. Copies and pastes the field into each form as needed.
- ○ B. Creates the field each time he needs it on each form.
- ○ C. Shares the field and creates a field with the same name when needed.
- ○ D. Shares the field and inserts the shared field on each form as needed.

Question 8

Bill has built a Web application that displays documents to users. However, when users look at the list of documents, the list is difficult to read because of poor column spacing. Bill implements which of the following solutions to solve this problem?

- ○ A. He creates new blank columns to act as spacers in his view design, and gives them a width of 10.
- ○ B. He creates new formula columns to act as spacers in his view design, and places the following HTML code in the column Titles"[**<td width = 10 />**] and [**<td width = 10 />**] for the formula.
- ○ C. He creates a new field containing blank spaces on the form that was used to create the documents, and then recalculates the documents. He then creates new columns to act as spacers in his view design, and uses the new field as the value for each of them.
- ○ D. He creates new formula columns to act as spacers in his view design, and places the following HTML code in the column Titles[**<td width = 10 />**] and "[**<td width = 10 />**]" for the formula.

Question 9

Users of a database complained that the display of documents was taking too long to download to their browsers, and that the display was not well organized because they were seeing lots of documents that were of no interest to them. Jenny did which of the following to solve the problem?

- ○ A. She created a single category view, with a default category, and allowed the users to choose the category that they wanted to see.
- ○ B. She created a single category view, with a default category.
- ○ C. She customized the interface to send fewer documents to the browser.
- ○ D. She used a table to organize the Web display, and sent fewer documents per request to the browser.

Question 10

A client has told Jeff that all of the 20 views in the database must display on the Web with the same look and feel. Jeff needs to choose which of the following options to accomplish this with the least amount of effort?

- ○ A. Create one view, copy it 19 times, and just change the selection formulas and column values.
- ○ B. Create a form named **$$ViewTemplate** for **<<view name>>**, copy it 19 times, and rename it appropriately for each view.
- ○ C. Create a form named **$$ViewTemplate** for **<<view name>>**, with a field named **$$ViewBody**, copy it 19 times, and rename it appropriately for each view.
- ○ D. Create a form named **$$ViewTemplateDefault** with a field named **$$ViewBody**.

Question 11

Faye wants to keep users focused on her Web site but needs to provide links to other sites. She decides to launch those links into a new window so that when users are finished and close the window, her site is still open. Which of the following options should she use in her code to accomplish this?

- ○ A. **_parent**.
- ○ B. **_blank**.
- ○ C. **_self**.
- ○ D. **_top**.

Question 12

When Mark previewed his page in a browser, a button he'd coded to perform an action disappeared. He investigated and found that one of the following was responsible:

○ A. The hide/when property **Notes R4.6 or later** was selected.

○ B. The button was coded in Common JavaScript to run on Client.

○ C. The button was coded in JavaScript to run on Client.

○ D. The button was coded in JavaScript to run on Web.

Question 13

When users of a Web site submitted documents, the designer wanted to display a specific acceptance page, but didn't want to display the URL of the page in the browser. Which one of the following will accomplish the task?

○ A. An agent to Absolutely Redirect the browser to the page.

○ B. An agent to Relatively Redirect the browser to the page.

○ C. A **$$Return** field with an Absolute URL formula.

○ D. A **$$Return** field with a Relative URL formula.

Question 14

When users submit registration information through a browser, Jill would like to check to see whether they've registered before, so that duplicate documents are not created. She has written code to perform this task and to inform users with a custom message that their registrations have been successful. Everything works as expected on the development server. When she moves the database to the testing server she gets a "Form Processed" message when users submit their documents; otherwise all is fine. Which of the following has most likely caused the problem?

○ A. The database is corrupt.

○ B. The database ACL does not allow the running of agents.

○ C. The database ACL does not allow anonymous access.

○ D. The server document does not allow Jill to run agents.

Question 15

Reggie has an agent that is triggered by an Action of a browser user. He wants to make sure that the agent cannot do more than the user could do if the user were doing it manually, so he sets which of the following options?

- ○ A. Agent property: Run as Web user.
- ○ B. Database property: Disable background agents for this database.
- ○ C. Agent Property: Run on behalf of.
- ○ D. Agent Property: Private.

Question 16

The database designer decided to use Profile documents to hold session information about users accessing the Web site. A decision is now needed as to which language to use to set and retrieve the values in each Profile document. Which one of the following languages would be more efficient to use?

- ○ A. Formula.
- ○ B. JavaScript.
- ○ C. LotusScript.
- ○ D. HTML.

Question 17

Xavier needs to move data among a wide variety of databases and sources. He is writing code to facilitate his data interchange electronically. He'll be creating his data elements using which of the following languages?

- ○ A. HTML.
- ○ B. XML.
- ○ C. SGML.
- ○ D. XSL.

Question 18

To create well-formed XML, which of the following has to be done?

○ A. Start and matching end tags must be same case.
Must have matching tags.
Tags must be properly nested.

○ B. Start and end tags need not be same case.
Must have matching tags.
Tags must be properly nested.

○ C. Tags must be lowercase.
Tags should have both a start and an end.
One set of tags should be wholly contained within another.

○ D. Tags must be uppercase.
Tags should have both a start and an end.
One set of tags should be wholly contained within another.

Question 19

Any organization that produces XML documents for data transfer must have standards for producing such XML. These standards are codified in which of the following?

○ A. XML.

○ B. XSL.

○ C. DXL.

○ D. DTD.

Question 20

When Web users submit their registration, Tom wants to ensure that all the mandatory fields are filled before the document is saved. He does his validations in which of the following languages?

○ A. Formula.

○ B. LotusScript.

○ C. JavaScript.

○ D. Java.

Question 21

To validate a Combobox field with JavaScript, what property must be examined?

- ○ A. **selected**.
- ○ B. **checked**.
- ○ C. **value**.
- ○ D. None of the above.

Question 22

Kayla is producing an application that will be browsed only by users using IE. She needs to validate a date entry. Which of the following options will she NOT need to check for?

- ○ A. **getDate()**.
- ○ B. **getMonth() + 1**.
- ○ C. **"Nan"**.
- ○ D. **"Invalid Date"**.

Question 23

Zainul imported some XML data from another organization. The data cannot be used in its current package because its DTD is different from Zainul's organization's DTD. Zainul needs to convert the imported data into an XML that his application can understand. He uses one of the following to do the conversion:

- ○ A. CSS.
- ○ B. DXL.
- ○ C. XSLT.
- ○ D. XSL.

Question 24

Dimitri's intranet application relies heavily on information stored in relational databases. Which of the following is NOT for accessing the information?

○ A. Formula.

○ B. Java.

○ C. LotusScript.

○ D. JavaScript.

Question 25

In using Java from a Web page to access data in backend sources, which of the following should be a choice of last resort?

○ A. Agents.

○ B. Enterprise Java Beans (EJBs).

○ C. JavaBeans.

○ D. Servlets.

Question 26

Sunitha is using legacy Java code in her application. She is accessing the Java code with LotusScript. To do this, she must do which one of the following?

○ A. Enter **Uselsx "*javacon"** in the Declarations event.

○ B. Enter **Uselsx "*javacon"** in the Options event.

○ C. Enter **%Include "lsconst.lss"** in the Declarations event.

○ D. Enter **%Include "lsconst.lss"** in the Options event.

Question 27

Paul is reading some HTML code. The following start and end tags appear in the code: **<% %>**. This part of the code is for which of the following?

○ A. A JSP.

○ B. JavaScript on a JSP.

○ C. A Java scriptlet on a JSP.

○ D. A space indicator in a URL.

Question 28

To ensure that only authorized Web users access her database, the database manager needs to set the database's ACL with which of the following settings?

- ○ A. **Anonymous: No Access; -Default-: Reader.**
- ○ B. **Anonymous: Reader; -Default-: No Access.**
- ○ C. **Anonymous: Reader; -Default-: Reader.**
- ○ D. **Anonymous: No access; -Default-: No Access.**

Question 29

Melanie has a series of buttons and Actions on a form that is to be used on an intranet. When she previews the form in the browser, all the buttons done with Formula are acting as submit buttons and the Actions coded with Formula are missing. Which one of the following is responsible for this behavior?

- ○ A. The Formula Actions were hidden from Web browsers.
- ○ B. The database property **Use JavaScript when generating pages** is not selected.
- ○ C. The form property **Use JavaScript when generating pages** is not selected.
- ○ D. The browser property **Use JavaScript when generating pages** is not selected.

Question 30

The database administrator is worried about Web users gaining access to documents via the 0 view, so he asks a developer to prevent anyone from accessing the 0 view. The designer should do which of the following?

- ○ A. Create a view named 0 with a Form Formula of **"Blank Form"** and create a fieldless form named Blank Form.
- ○ B. Create a view named 0 with a Selection Formula of **"Blank Form"** and create a fieldless form named Blank Form.
- ○ C. Create a view named 0 with the Read Access List set to LocaDomainAdmins.
- ○ D. Delete the 0 view.

Question 31

Jerome has numerous views in his Web database. He wants to ensure that only those views that he wants the users to see are available through the browser, so he does which of the following?

- ○ A. Encloses each nonauthorized view's name in parentheses ().
- ○ B. Creates a form named **$$ViewTemplateDefault** with a field named **$$ViewBody**.
- ○ C. For each authorized view he creates a form named **$$ViewTemplate** for the view's name with a field named **$$ViewBody**.
- ○ D. Creates a form named **$$ViewTemplateDefault**, and for each authorized view a form named **$$ViewTemplate** for the view's name with a field named **$$ViewBody**.

Question 32

Kamila would like her Web users to have basic access to read and update data stored in a non-Notes data source. She doesn't want to involve a database designer to implement this. Which one of the choices should she implement?

- ○ A. Data Connection Resource (DCRs).
- ○ B. Domino Enterprise Connection Services (DECS).
- ○ C. Open Database Connectivity (ODBC).
- ○ D. It can't be done without involving a database designer.

Question 33

Blaine is trying to secure his Web database. He wants to limit his Web users to Read access only, but unfortunately they sometimes want to submit search requests, which requires that he provide fields where users can input the search criteria. Can he overcome his dilemma? If so, how?

- ○ A. He can't overcome his dilemma. He has to grant Author access.
- ○ B. He can't overcome his dilemma, but grants Read access anyhow. His users will just have to do without searching.
- ○ C. He creates a Notes page, uses Pass-Thru HTML to generate an input object (field) in the browser, and places a button to submit the search. When clicked, the button is coded to generate a URL based on the information in the input object.

○ D.   He creates a Notes Form, uses Pass-Thru HTML to generate an input
object (field) in the browser, and places a button to submit the search.
When clicked, the button is coded to generate a URL based on the
information in the input object.

Question 34

Jade is ready to set up her DCR to a DB2 database. She creates the DCR data
connection, and it's working fine. She now attempts to create the fields to
access the data in the DB2 database, but she doesn't see any Data Source
Options in the field properties. What is she missing?

○ A.   She forgot to select the External data source option on the first tab of
the Field properties box.

○ B.   She forgot to select the External data source option on the second tab
of the Form properties box.

○ C.   She forgot to select the Show field delimiters option on the second tab
of the Field properties box.

○ D.   She forgot to select the Allow connections to external databases using
DCRs option on the first tab of the Database properties box.

Question 35

Jade finally got her Field properties box to show her Data Source Options, but
she has to enter the DCR's name for every link field that she creates. This is very
frustrating and she wonders whether there's a way to automatically have it generated every time she creates a new link field. Choose the option that solves her
problem.

○ A.   Select the External data source option on the first tab of the Field properties box.

○ B.   Use the Browse button to select the default data connection and the
Default metadata object on the second tab of the Form properties box.

○ C.   Use the Browse button to select the Metadata object name and the
Data connection resource on the first tab of the Field properties box.

○ D.   Select the Allow connections to external databases using DCRs option
on the first tab of the Database properties box.

Question 36

Sandra is building an application for Web users to submit their resumes. She wants them to be able to attach their resumes to the submission form. She needs to add which one of the following to provide the users with the appropriate functionality?

○ A. Rich Text field.

○ B. Rich Text Lite field, with input limited to attachments.

○ C. File Upload field.

○ D. File Upload Control.

Question 37

Jazmine is creating a form for use on an intranet and in Notes. The client for whom she is creating the form has made her rearrange her form design over and over in the past, because although the client knows what needs to be on the form, the client is not sure about the layout. Jazmine is determined to have an easier time this time. She should attempt to facilitate this by implementing which of the following?

○ A. She creates separate forms, one for each possible configuration that the client could possibly want.

○ B. She uses tables to arrange the contents of the form.

○ C. She uses sections to arrange the contents of the form.

○ D. She uses layers on the form. She places each complementary set of information on a different layer. For example, each graphic is on its own layer, each grouping of text is on its own layer, and so on.

Question 38

Kevin is creating style sheets. Every time he needs to work on a style sheet he has to navigate to his style sheet editing application. He works on his style sheets when he is working in his Shared Resources Style Sheets list. Choose an option that will give Kevin easy access to his style sheet editor.

○ A. Add the editor to the Tools menu.

○ B. Add the editor to the Tools menu, and set it to show when the Style Sheet Resource list is accessed.

○ C. Create a shortcut to the editor and place the shortcut on the Designer Client desktop's bookmark bar.

○ D. Add the editor to the Tools menu, and set it to show when the Database Resource List is accessed.

Question 39

Zainool is moving his Web application to another server. He does not want to notify his users that the database is being moved. This means that unless he implements the correct option from the following list, his users will not be able to access the application. Which of the options will Zainool implement to allow his users to continue to access the application, without his notifying them of the move?

○ A. Create a Web Site Redirection Rule document.

○ B. Create a Web Site Substitution Rule document.

○ C. Create a Web Site Directory Rule document.

○ D. Create a Web Site Document.

Question 40

Robyn has a form that is to be used in both Notes' clients and browsers. Validations need to be done. Choose the best validation option for Robyn.

○ A. Write all validations in the **Input Validation** event of each appropriate field.

○ B. Write all validations in the **QuerySave** event.

○ C. Write all validations in JavaScript in the **OnSubmit** event of the form.

○ D. Write all validations in Common JavaScript in the **OnSubmit** event of the form.

Question 41

Yuri wants to record each access to a particular page in his Web application, but does not want to grant any access other than Reader to anyone using a browser. How can Yuri accomplish this?

○ A. He writes an agent that will run on the Web users' behalf.

○ B. He writes an agent and signs it with an ID that has edit access to the document that will record the hits.

○ C. He writes an agent and signs it with the server's ID.

○ D. He grants Create LotusScript/Java Agents privileges to the WebUsers group in the ACL of the application.

Question 42

As Web users navigate through the Web site, they are asked to authenticate several times. This is annoying, so the Web site designer has been asked to fix the problem so that users authenticate only when they first access the site, but authentication must still occur as per usual. She should do which of the following to accomplish this?

- ○ A. Enable Session authentication for **Multiple Servers(SSO)** in the Domino Web Engine tab of the Internet Site document.
- ○ B. Enable Session authentication for Single Server in the Domino Web Engine tab of the Internet Site document.
- ○ C. Write code to create cookies for depositing in Web users browsers.
- ○ D. Assign Reader access to Anonymous for all the databases used in the Web site.

Question 43

Gordon is developing pages in Pass-Thru HTML. He sees his HTML code translated into output display as soon as he refreshes his screen. He enabled this by which of the following?

- ○ A. Deselecting Pass-Thru HTML in the Text menu, then deselecting HTML Pane in the View menu.
- ○ B. Deselecting Pass-Thru HTML in the Text menu, then selecting HTML Pane in the View menu.
- ○ C. Selecting Pass-Thru HTML in the Text menu, then deselecting HTML Pane in the View menu.
- ○ D. Selecting Pass-Thru HTML in the Text menu, then selecting HTML Pane in the View menu.

Question 44

As Pascale is developing her Web application, she needs to use the graphics being created by several graphic designers. Unfortunately, these designers are not part of her Notes Domain and are not using Notes. Which of the following will allow her to access the designers' graphics?

○ A. She has them email her the files as attachments.

○ B. She has them upload the files to an Internet site to which she has access and downloads them from there.

○ C. She enables WebDAV, creates a database to store the graphic files, and makes the graphic designers set up WebDAV access on their machines.

○ D. She makes her unfinished application available over the Web to the designers, so that they can upload their files on a special form that she has designed for this purpose.

Question 45

Stavros is a member of a Web design team that is working on a Web application. He doesn't want anyone to accidentally work on any of his design elements until he's finished designing them. How does he prevent them from doing so?

○ A. He makes sure that the Allow design locking option in the Database properties is selected, then selects the element in the element list and chooses Design -> Lock Design Element.

○ B. He makes sure that a Master Lock Server is assigned to the database, then makes sure that the Allow Design Locking option in the Database properties is selected, then selects the element in the element list and chooses Design -> Lock Design Element.

○ C. He makes sure that a Master Lock Server is assigned to the database, then makes sure that the Allow Document Locking option in the Database properties is selected, then selects the element in the element list and chooses Design -> Lock Design Element.

○ D. He doesn't need to do anything. Each design element is automatically locked as soon as it is being edited.

Question 46

Colleen has some files to which her Web users need Read access. She wants to make sure that all they can do is read. What does she need to do to ensure the security of her files?

- ○ A. Create a Web Site Rule document that gives her Web users Read/Execute access (GET Method).
- ○ B. Create a Web Site File Protection document that gives her Web users No Access.
- ○ C. Create a Web Site File Protection document that gives her Web users Read/Execute access (GET method).
- ○ D. Create a Web Site File Protection document that gives her Web users Write/Read/Execute access (POST and GET method).

Question 47

Ziggy placed a series of transparent sibling layers on his form. He numbered them in the order in which he placed them as siblings; Layer_1, Layer_2, Layer_3. He then stacked them and changed their Z-Indexes to reflect the stack order with Layer_1 being on top and Layer 3 being on the bottom. When he tested the form, he realized that he needed Layer_2 to be calculated before the others. Which one of the following options must he choose to make this happen?

- ○ A. Give Layer_2 a Z-Index of 1.
- ○ B. Change the Z-Indexes to reflect a stack order of Layer_2 on the bottom and the others above.
- ○ C. Place the Layer Anchors in the following order: Layer_2, Layer_1, Layer_3.
- ○ D. Change the Z-Indexes to reflect a stack order of Layer_2 on top and the others below.

Question 48

Anmarie's client wants all the company's Web pages to have the same look and feel for the text content. Anmarie will not be responsible for the text content of most of the pages. How can she best fulfill her client's wishes?

- ○ A. Manually format all the Web pages to the client's specifications.
- ○ B. Use Extensible Stylesheet Language Transformers (XSLT) to format the text.
- ○ C. Use Extensible Stylesheet Language (XSL) to format the text.
- ○ D. Create Cascading Style Sheets (CSS) that contain the client's specifications and apply them to all the Web pages.

Question 49

Thelma is creating an application for the company's intranet. The users will be creating and submitting documents based on other documents to which they have access. Thelma wants to have some of the fields filled in automatically with information from the parent document. What's the best way for her to do this?

○ A. She creates forms that have inheritance enabled and writes formulas in the appropriate fields to inherit the information from the parent document.

○ B. She creates forms that have inheritance enabled and writes JavaScript in the appropriate fields to inherit the information from the parent document.

○ C. She creates Response forms and writes formulas in the appropriate fields to inherit the information from the parent document.

○ D. She creates forms that have inheritance enabled and writes JavaScript in the onLoad event to inherit the information from the parent document.

Question 50

Marva's intranet workflow application needs to send mail when users submit certain documents via the browser. The mail will contain excerpts from the submitted document. She implements this by doing which one of the following?

○ A. She writes a Simple Action(s) agent to send mail and calls the agent in the **WebQuerySave** event of the form.

○ B. She writes a JavaScript agent to send mail and calls the agent in the **WebQuerySave** event of the form.

○ C. She writes a Formula agent to send mail and calls the agent in the **WebQuerySave** event of the form.

○ D. She writes a LotusScript agent to send mail and calls the agent in the **WebQuerySave** event of the form.

Practice Exam Answer Key for Exam 612

1. B	**18.** A	**35.** B
2. A	**19.** D	**36.** D
3. C	**20.** C	**37.** D
4. C	**21.** A	**38.** B
5. C	**22.** D	**39.** A
6. B	**23.** C	**40.** D
7. D	**24.** D	**41.** B
8. D	**25.** B	**42.** B
9. A	**26.** B	**43.** D
10. D	**27.** C	**44.** C
11. B	**28.** D	**45.** B
12. C	**29.** B	**46.** C
13. A	**30.** A	**47.** C
14. D	**31.** D	**48.** D
15. A	**32.** B	**49.** A
16. C	**33.** C	**50.** D
17. B	**34.** A	

Question 1

The correct answer is B. Tags are not case sensitive, they should have both a start and an end, and one set of tags should be wholly contained within another. A is incorrect because tags are not case sensitive. C is incorrect because even though tags are in lowercase in HTML 4 and above, this is by convention and not by a language rule. D is incorrect because neither convention nor rule requires that tags be uppercase.

Question 2

The correct answer is A. By default, Domino generates only one set of form tags. It is possible to have more than one set of form tags, but such tags will have to be generated by writing Pass-Thru HTML.

Question 3

The correct answer is C. Forms, pages, and sections can have text and graphics, but the only way to appropriately position text and graphics for display in a browser—whether on a form or page or in a section—is to use tables (either Notes-created or Pass-Thru HTML–created). Forms are used to collect and display information, pages to display information, sections to display information in an expanded state and hide it in a collapsed state, and tables to position information appropriately on the form or page or in a section.

Question 4

The correct answer is C. Computed fields cannot be accessed by JavaScript code in a browser.

Question 5

The correct answer is C. This form property causes fields hidden with Notes' Hide/When to be sent to the browser with values accessible to JavaScript code, but not visible to the viewer unless View Source is used.

There is no Send to Browser option in the Field Properties. The field's Hide/When Property Web Browsers is for hiding the field from browsers. The Use JavaScript When generating pages database property is for generating JavaScript along with the HTML when the database is accessed with a browser. If this property is not set, only HTML is generated.

Question 6

The correct answer is B. There is no onLoad event for a field. If the variable is declared in the JS Header and set in the onFocus event of the Category field, then the value becomes available only after the Category field has achieved focus. The value is not available before then and therefore cannot fulfill the requirement of being available to all scripts. Any variable that has to be available to all scripts on the form (thus a global variable), has to be declared in the JS Header event of the form. Any variable whose value has to be available to all scripts on the form should have that value set in the onLoad event of the form.

Question 7

The correct answer is D. Although Copy and Paste distributes the field, each has to be maintained individually. Creating a field with the same name as a shared field does not link that field to the field. A shared field can be inserted and used in any form in any database. Any change made to the shared field is propagated to all forms where the shared field has been inserted. This makes maintaining the fields very easy. If one of the inserted fields needs a change different from all the others, it can be converted to single use so that it no longer is linked to the shared field. B is incorrect because maintaining multiple single fields is not cost effective.

Question 8

The correct answer is D. The 10 is the number of pixels that the space will occupy. A blank column with no title is ignored in a browser, thus answers A and C do not work. Unless used in an @Function or @Command, unquoted square brackets in a formula are treated as a Date/Time constant, so answer B does not work and the quotes in the title will also show as quotes in the view.

Question 9

The correct answer is A. All the other answers speed up the displaying of documents but do nothing about the users seeing documents that are of no interest to them. Single category views speed up the loading of displays because they load only a specific set of documents per request. If users are allowed to choose which category to load, they see only documents that they want to see and thus the display is more organized.

Question 10

Answer D is correct. Only one form need be created and formatted, and all views will display with this form, thus retaining the same look and feel while requiring the least effort. When a browser requests a view, the server checks to see whether that view is explicitly linked to a $$ViewTemplate for <<view name>> form. If it's not linked, the server then checks for a form named $$ViewTemplateDefault, containing a field named $$ViewBody. If such a form exists, it is used to display the view; otherwise the view is displayed as per the view properties settings for the browser. Answer B is incorrect because the template form must contain the field $$ViewBody. Answer C is incorrect because it produces one of the required results—look and feel—but requires a lot of work to copy and rename, so doesn't fulfill the requirement for least effort. Answer A is incorrect because it somewhat fulfills the look-and-feel requirement, but the result is not very attractive in the browser, and requires quite a bit of work to customize selection formulas and column values.

Question 11

The correct answer is B. The reserved target value _blank launches the page into a new window in the browser. _parent launches the page over the current frameset. _self launches the page into the current frame. _top loads the page over all framesets in the window.

Question 12

The correct answer is C. Buttons coded in JavaScript to run on Client do not show in a browser. Answer A is incorrect because to hide something in the browser, the hide/when property Web browsers has to be selected. Answer B is incorrect because buttons coded in Common JavaScript to run either on Web or Client will show in a browser. D is incorrect because buttons coded in JavaScript to run on Web will show in a browser.

Question 13

The correct answer is A. An absolute redirect done by an agent shows the URL of the agent in the browser, but not the URL of the loaded page. B is incorrect because an agent that relatively redirects causes the URL of the loaded page to show in the browser. C and D are incorrect because the $$Return field displays the URL of the page whether it's an absolute URL or a relative URL.

Question 14

The correct answer is D. By default, an agent triggered from a browser runs with the permissions of the creator (signer) of the agent. If the server document does not permit the signer to run that type of agent, then the agent does not run, and a message is generated to the server console indicating such. The only indication in the browser that this particular agent did not run is that the user is informed with the default message of Form Processed rather than the custom message as the save completes. Answer A is incorrect because if the database were corrupted, this would not be the only problem. B and C are incorrect because if it were an ACL problem, the users would have encountered it on the developing server.

Question 15

Correct answer is A. The Run As Web User option in the agent property allows the agent to run with the permissions of the browser user. B is incorrect because disabling background agents has nothing to do with permissions. C is incorrect because although the Run On Behalf option in the agent properties can work if the Web user was always the same name, it is not the best of the options here. Answer D is incorrect because making an agent private means that only one name can use it. If the Web user is always the same name, it can work, but it's not the best option.

Question 16

The correct answer is C. LotusScript and Java can access Profile documents in any database and require only one document load for all reads and writes. A is incorrect because Formula can access only Profile documents that are in the same database as the Formula, and requires a document reload for each read/write so is not as efficient as LotusScript (answer C). B is incorrect because JavaScript cannot access Profile documents. D is incorrect because HTML cannot access Profile documents.

Question 17

The correct answer is B. XML is the language used to package the data into elements that can be moved. These data elements are then transformed into other data elements that can be understood by the database or application that needs to use them. A is incorrect because HTML is used for formatting text so that it can be searched or displayed in the browser. C is incorrect because SGML is the root language of HTML and XML and can be used to create the data elements; however it is very complex and difficult to use, and so is not the most correct choice. D is incorrect because XSL is used to format XML for display.

Question 18

The correct answer is A. XML is case sensitive so that each start tag must be the same case as its end tag or the two tags will be regarded as two different tags. There must be an end tag for each start tag. Tags must be ended in the reverse order of that in which they were started, so the first tag started on the document must be the last ended on the document, and so on. B is incorrect because XML is case sensitive. C and D are incorrect because there is no convention or rule that start and end tags must be lowercase or uppercase, only that they be same case. There is also nothing that says that all tags have to be same case, just that each start and its matching end must be same.

Question 19

Answer D is correct. XML (Extensible Markup Language) is the language used to package the data. XSL (Extensible Stylesheet Language) is the language used to produce the stylesheet to format the data packaged by XML, and to convert one XML schema to another XML schema (XSLT). DXL (Domino XML) is Domino's version of XML. DTD (Document Type Definition) is the codified rules that an organization has to follow to produce standardized XML. To produce Valid XML, the DTD's rules are imposed on the XML document. Answer D is thus the correct answer. A is incorrect because XML (Extensible Markup Language) is the language used to package the data. B is incorrect because XSL (Extensible Stylesheet Language) is the language used to produce the stylesheet to format the data packaged by XML, and to convert one XML schema to another XML schema (XSLT). C is incorrect because DXL (Domino XML) is Domino's version of XML.

Question 20

The correct answer is C. Because Tom is only checking to see whether the mandatory fields are filled, JavaScript can be used to check before the document is passed for saving to the server. This results in a user-friendly response to unvalidated entries. The cursor can be returned to the problem field and a trip to the server is avoided. If the validations have to be done against values stored in the database or other source, then JavaScript cannot be used and one of the other languages (Formula, LotusScript, or Java) needs to be used. A is not as correct because if Formula is used, the document has to go to the server before being validated, and the response is not user friendly, causing the user to have to use the Back buttons and look for the problem field. B is incorrect because to use LotusScript, an agent has to be created and the document submitted to the server. The same is true for Java.

Question 21

The correct answer is A. Because a Combobox is a list field, each member of the list must be examined to determine whether it is selected. The selected property of each member in the list is examined to determine whether the option is selected. The value property of the list member is the alias (if one exists) of that list member. Although it might be argued that one can check the value property as part of the validation, checking such would be useless until it is determined that the list member has been selected. So A is a more correct answer than C. The checked property is examined to determine whether the field is a radio button or check box.

Question 22

The correct answer is D. IE treats a blank value that has been designated as a Date value as "NaN" (Not a Number), so Kayla needs to test for "NaN". getDate() gets the day, and getMonth() + 1 gets the correct month number; (months are in an array from 0 to 11), so she needs to test for these also. Netscape treats a blank value that has been designated as a Date value as "Invalid Date". Kayla does not need to test for "Invalid Date" because her users are using IE.

Question 23

The correct answer is C. XSLT (Extensible Stylesheet Language Transformations) is used for transforming one form of XML into a different XML, or usually to transform XML data to HTML for rendering on a client. A is incorrect because CSS (Cascading Style Sheets) is used for formatting HTML or XML for display in a browser. B is incorrect because DXL (Domino XML) is an end result (like XML). D is incorrect because XSL (Extensible Stylesheet Language) is for formatting XML for display.

Question 24

The correct answer is D. JavaScript cannot be used for accessing anything not in the UI or in the source HTML. A is incorrect because Formula can access information in relational databases via ODBC. B is incorrect because Java is probably the most useful for accessing such information. C is incorrect because LotusScript can also access relational databases.

Question 25

The correct answer is B. EJBs require a significant amount of overhead when they are invoked and are not a good choice for requests from individual Web pages. C is incorrect because JavaBeans are code components or building blocks and have to be included in another Java program. These are very useful when writing Java programs, as they are reusable. D is incorrect because a servlet is a special type of Java program that runs on the server. They are great for responding to requests for access to backend data sources. A is incorrect because agents are usually one of the first choices to use to access backend data sources. TIP: Agents can invoke EJBs and also use JavaBeans. If given the choice between using an agent or a servlet for repetitive access, servlets would be the way to go because after they are loaded, they remain in memory. Agents use a lot of resources to activate, and are removed from memory as soon as they are finished running, only to incur the same costs to run again.

Question 26

The correct answer is B. The proper place to enter the Uselsx "*javacon" code is the `Options` event. C and D are incorrect because `%Include "lsconst.lss"` has nothing to do with accessing Java libraries (legacy Java code); instead it is for using a pre-defined constants file named `LSCONST.LSS`. A is incorrect because entering Uselsx "*javacon" in the Declarations event will result in the code being transferred to the Options event, so entering it here, even though it will go to the right place, is improper.

Question 27

The correct answer is C. The start tag `<%` and end tag `%>` are tags used to indicate the start and end of a Java scriptlet in a JSP. A is incorrect because it is a JSP that Paul is reading, but that is not as correct as C. D is incorrect because the space indicator in a URL is either the + sign or `%20 not %`. B is incorrect because it's not JavaScript on a JSP.

Question 28

Answer D is correct. Anonymous is any person who accesses the database but does not have to supply a name and password. –Default- is for any user who is not listed individually or in a listed group in the ACL. If Anonymous is set to No Access and –Default- is set to No Access, then only authorized users (listed individually or in a listed group in the ACL) can access the database after supplying a name and password. A is not correct because A is not as secure as D as it allows all Web users Read access after they authenticate.

Question 29

The correct answer is B. If buttons and Actions are coded in formula and the database property Use JavaScript When Generating Pages is not selected, then all Formula buttons on the form act as Submit buttons and no Formula Actions will be displayed. If there are no Formula buttons and only Formula Actions, then only one button is displayed on the form, which acts as a Submit button and is named Submit regardless of the name of the Action. In an R5 Database on an R5 server, the results of this database property not being selected would be somewhat different, so C and D are incorrect because there is no `form` or `browser` property. A is incorrect because it is possible that the Formula Actions are hidden from Web browsers, but this does not account for the Formula buttons acting as Submit buttons.

Question 30

A is the correct answer. If a Form Formula based on an existing fieldless (blank) form is used with the new 0 view, access is denied because a blank document is sent to the browser. This form that is sent to the browser should contain information informing the user that the area is restricted, should provide navigation aids to authorized areas, and should redirect automatically to an authorized area after a few seconds. D is incorrect because the 0 view cannot be deleted. It is used internally by Domino for accessing documents via their unique ID and cannot be seen. C is incorrect because if a view named 0 is created and someone tries to access the 0 view, that user will access the newly created view rather than the one inherent in Domino. However, if the Read Access List of the newly created 0 view is set to deny access to anyone, the inherent 0 view now becomes accessible. Note that if you are not on the Read Access list of the new 0 view, it disappears from your designer client and you have to access the database locally to see it. B is incorrect because creating a new 0 view and using a Selection Formula based on an existing fieldless (blank) form does not deny access to the 0 view and subsequently allows access to all documents by their unique IDs in the database.

Question 31

The correct answer is D. If you create a `$$ViewTemplateDefault` form without a `$$ViewBody` field, any view not using a `$$ViewTemplate` for *view's name* displays the `$$ViewTemplateDefault` form when requested by a browser. Because there is no $ViewBody field or embedded view, the view cannot be seen. This means that if there's *x* numbers of non-authorized views, none are accessible to a browser request. When you create for each authorized view a $ViewTemplate for *view's name* form with a $ViewBody field, all authorized views are accessible from the browser. Tip: The same results can be had if for each view a $ViewTemplate for *view's name* form is created. The forms for authorized views would also have the $ViewBody field and the forms for non-authorized views would not have the $ViewBody field. However this is much more work than the solution in D.

A is incorrect because enclosing the name of a view in parenthesis usually hides it from Notes clients but not from explicit URL requests. B is incorrect because a form named $ViewTemplateDefault with a field named $ViewBody displays any view not assigned a $ViewTemplate for *view's name* form. C is incorrect because creating the $View template for *view's* name with the $ViewBody field enables each authorized view to be displayed appropriately, but does not stop the non-authorized ones from being displayed when requested.

Question 32

The correct answer is B. A database designer is not needed to implement DECS. However, it requires the use of a Domino server administrator to make sure that the DECS task is running on the server and the DECS Administration Database administrator to create the necessary Connection and Activity documents. A is incorrect because DCRs require that a database designer implement design features to retrieve and update data from a non-Notes data source. C is incorrect because ODBC requires the use of a database designer to write the code to use ODBC. D is also incorrect because Kamila's problem can be resolved without using a database designer.

In question 32, it might be argued that the database designer has to be involved because there would be no database without the use of the designer. However, the question is only about implementing a data source connection—not about the existence of a database. The database already exists, and even if it didn't, Kamila wouldn't need the designer to implement DECS. She'd need the designer only to create the database. This kind of question is quite often found in Notes exams, so read the questions carefully.

Question 33

Answer C is correct. Creating an input object with Pass-Thru HTML on a Notes page generates a field when the page is viewed in a browser. Any data entered in such an object is accessible for use in generating a URL to access documents. The minimum access required to read a Notes page is Reader. Answers A and B are incorrect because the dilemma can be overcome. Answer D is incorrect because the minimum access required to enter data in a Notes form is Author.

Question 34

The correct answer is A. If the External data source option on the first tab of the Field properties box is selected, the Data Source Options section appears at the bottom of the first tab of the properties box. B is incorrect because there is no External Data Source option on the second tab of the Form properties box. However, there is a Data Source Options section there for browsing to select the default data connection and the default metadata object. C is incorrect because the Show field delimiter option on the second tab of the Field properties box is for showing the borders of a field. D is incorrect because the Allow Connections to External Databases Using DCRs option is for allowing any DCRs to actually connect to the specified data source. If this option hadn't been set, Jade's DCR connection would not have been working fine as stated in the question.

Question 35

The correct answer is B. After the default data connection and the default metadata object on the second tab of the Form properties box has been populated, all fields linked to external data sources will have the information that Jade requires filled in by default. A is incorrect because selecting the External data source option on the first tab of the Field properties box just displays the section to enter the information that Jade would like to see there by default. C is incorrect because using the Browse button to select the Metadata object name and the Data connection resource on the first tab of the Field properties box is just another way of entering the information that she'd like to see there by default. D is incorrect because selecting the Allow connections to external databases using DCRs option on the first tab of the Database properties box just enables the DCRs to connect to their respective data sources.

Question 36

The correct answer is D. File Upload Control exists and it allows Web users to browse for files to create attachments in the browser. C is incorrect because a File Upload field does not exist. A is incorrect because a Rich Text field is for anything in Notes, but only for Rich Text in a browser. B is incorrect because while Rich Text Lite fields are for limiting the types of entries in a Rich Text type field and can be set to accept attachments only, they work only in Notes because there are no equivalent input tags in HTML. A Rich Text Lite field is converted to an input text area in a browser.

Question 37

The correct answer is D. Layers make arranging form content layout easy. Place the different blocks of content on individual layers and then drag and drop each layer to its appropriate spot on the form. There is no need to cut and paste to an area where the cursor is placed. Answer A is incorrect because creating a form for each possible configuration is very time consuming. B and C are incorrect because although sections and tables are great for arranging content, the content still needs to be copied and pasted to other areas if a move is necessary.

Question 38

The correct answer is B because it's the most precise option available. If the editor is added to the tools menu, and set to display when the Style Sheet Resource List is accessed, Kevin will have access to the application via the tools menu when he opens Shared Resources, Style Sheets. The editor is not available when he is in any other area of the Designer client. A is incorrect because adding the editor to the Tools menu makes it available throughout the Designer client, so it is not as precise a response to the question as B. C is incorrect because creating a shortcut to the application and placing it on the Bookmark bar of the Designer client makes it available throughout the Designer client, so it is not as precise a response to the question as B. D is incorrect because adding the editor to the Tools menu and setting it to show when the Database Resource list is accessed will make the editor not visible when he is working in his Shared Resources Style Sheets List.

Question 39

The correct answer is A. Creating a Web Site Redirection Rule enables the server to redirect an incoming URL request to a new URL. This means that a database can be moved to a new location and that location's URL be used as the redirect target when a request with the old location's URL is presented. B is incorrect because a Web Site Substitution Rule usually is for when a Web site is being redesigned and the links need to remain unchanged. C is incorrect because a Web Site Directory Rule is for access to certain files in the file system and not for databases. D is incorrect because a Web Site document is any Web Site Rule Document.

Question 40

The correct answer is D. Common JavaScript works in either the Client or Web UI, so it needs to be written only once. The validations are done without submission to the server and cursor positioning can occur. This makes for a very user friendly UI. A is incorrect because if the validations are written in the Input Validation event of each appropriate field, then browser users will not be well served. The validations occur on the server, so error messages are returned to the browser and cursor positioning cannot occur. The users have to use the Back button to return to the form and data loss can occur. B is incorrect because the QuerySave event is available only for backward compatibility and its use is discouraged; more importantly the QuerySave event does not run when documents are submitted from browsers. C is incorrect because if JavaScript is used, the validations run only when the UI (Web or Client) for which the script was written is used. It does not run for both UIs unless it's written twice (once for Web and once for Client).

Question 41

The correct answer is B. Agents activated from the Web run with the signer's permissions unless otherwise designed. Signing such an agent with an ID that has permission to edit the document that will record the hits is perfect for this purpose. A is incorrect because Web users are granted only Reader access, so any agent run with their permissions cannot write in the application. C is incorrect because signing the agent with the server's ID works if the server has permission to edit the document, but this is not as precise as answer B. D is incorrect because granting Create LotusScript/Java agents privileges to the WebUsers group in the ACL of the application is of no benefit to anyone because the agent needs to have edit access, which the Web Users group does not have.

Question 42

Answer B is correct. Only the Session authentication for Single Server needs to be enabled if the Web site is hosted on one server. This is the best answer with the information provided. For authentication to occur as usual, but have the user prompted to authenticate once only, the server creates a cookie to store the user's information and places it in the user's browser. The information in the cookie is accessed every time authentication is required rather than the user being prompted for it. Answer A is incorrect because if the Web site encompasses more than one Domino server, SSO must also be enabled by an administrator who is using a Web SSO document. Enabling Session authentication either in the Server document or in an Internet Site document generates the cookie when required. Answer A enables the site for Multiple Servers (SSO) Session authentication, which requires SSO be configured, but makes no mention of the Web SSO document being created. Answer C is incorrect because writing code to generate cookies to be placed in a user's browser is not for authentication but usually for shopping carts. Answer D is incorrect because although giving Anonymous access to all the Web site databases stops the prompting for authentication after the initial prompt; it also stops authentication from occurring as per usual.

Question 43

Answer D is correct. Only by selecting Pass-Thru HTML in the Text menu, then selecting the HTML Pane in the View menu, will Gordon be able to see the HTML code he writes in the bottom pane on the screen, translated into output displayed in the top pane when he refreshes his screen. If he has this option turned on and then deselects the HTML pane in the View menu, his screen reverts to normal with all his code now showing as Pass-Thru HTML on the page. This is useful for placing images on the page without having to code it. A and B are incorrect because if Pass-Thru HTML is not selected in Text menu, the HTML Pane option in the View menu is not available.

Question 44

The correct answer is C. Web Distributed Authoring and Versioning (WebDAV) is Lotus's way of acting like a file server. After WebDAV is enabled via a Web site document on the server, a database designer just needs to designate a database to accept the files deposited by WebDAV-compliant applications (such as Word/Excel 2000+, Macromedia Dreamweaver 4.01+, IE5, and so on). The user who will be depositing the files sets up a connection to the database via My Network Places and the system is now ready for use. The deposited files are transferred over the network via HTTP and assigned to Shared Resources in the database. The database designer now has access to them. Other graphic designers with WebDAV access to the database can also work on any stored file if necessary. Although some of the other methods may work, WebDAV is the better solution.

Question 45

The correct answer is B. To lock a design element so that others cannot work on it, a Master Lock Server must be assigned in the ACL Advanced tab. After this has been done, Design locking can be enabled in the Database properties box Design tab. Any design element in the database can now be locked by selecting the element from the list of elements and choosing Design, Lock Design Element from the menu or Lock from the right-click menu. Only the user who locked the element or someone with Manager Access can unlock the element. Answer A is incorrect because it made no mention of the Master Lock Server. C is incorrect because selecting the database property Allow document locking is for documents and not design elements. D is incorrect because all design elements and documents are locked while they are being edited, however they become accessible after they are closed or in Read mode.

Question 46

The correct answer is C. A File protection document that gives Colleen's Web users Read/Execute access (GET method) will allow them to read but not write. A is incorrect because a Web Site Rule document that gives users Read/Execute access (GET Method) cannot exist. Rule documents are usually for dealing with URL strings. A Directory rule allows either Read access or Execute access to the directory, but not necessarily to the files in the directory. B is incorrect because if her File Protection document gives her users no access, they cannot read. D is incorrect because Write/Read/Execute access (POST and GET method) allow her Web users Write access to her files.

Question 47

The correct answer is C. The calculation order of forms and layers is left to right, top to bottom. So the order in which the Layer Anchors are placed on a form or layer impacts the order in which they are calculated. To have Layer_2 calculated before the others, Layer_2's anchor must be positioned before the anchors of the other layers. A, B, and D are incorrect because the Z-Index of a layer has no impact on when the layer is calculated. The Z-Index is strictly for the stack order of the layers.

Question 48

Answer D is correct. Cascading Style Sheets are usually used for imposing text-formatting rules on Web pages. If Anmarie creates Cascading Style Sheets with formatting rules according to the client's specifications, and applies them appropriately to the Web pages, all present and future text content will be affected. It does not matter who creates the text content; it will be formatted according to the rules imposed by the CSS. B and C are incorrect because XSL and XSLT are for use with XML data and are not appropriate for this scenario. A is incorrect because although manually formatting all the pages to meet the client's needs is possible, it represents a significant amount of effort, and because Anmarie will not be responsible for the text content, it is not feasible.

Question 49

The correct answer is A. For document-to-document inheritance to occur, the inheriting document must have inheritance enabled in the Form properties, and it must have fields on the form coded with formula to access the information in the parent document. Answer A is more correct than answer C because a form does not have to be a Response form for inheritance to occur. Designating a document as a Response type or Response-to-Response type is for view display and not for inheritance, so answer A is correct and C is incorrect. B and D are incorrect because JavaScript plays no part in inheritance.

Question 50

The correct answer is D. LotusScript is the only option presented that can fulfill the scenario. B is incorrect because JavaScript cannot be used in agents. A and C are incorrect because although it might be possible to use Formula and Simple Action(s) to send mail on a WebQuerySave event, such mail cannot contain excerpts from the submitted document.

PART 5
Appendixes

A Resources

B What's on the CD-ROM

C Using the PrepLogic Practice Tests, Preview Edition Software

Glossary

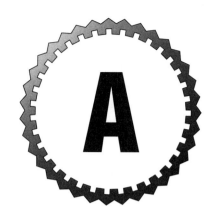

Resources

This appendix includes several resources that you will find helpful in your preparation for the Domino exams. Many of these resources were used in the preparation and writing of this book. Although you may not have time to read all these resources as you prepare for the exam, you may find them helpful in your studies and in your application development.

Lotus Developer Domain. *Notes 6 Technical Overview*. Available in printed form or on the Web at http://www-10.lotus.com/ldd.

Lotus Developer Domain. *Domino 6 Technical Overview*. Available in printed form or on the Web at http://www-10.lotus.com/ldd.

IBM International Technical Support Organization. *IBM Redbook—Upgrading to Lotus Notes and Domino 6*. Available in printed form, PDF format, and HTML format from www.redbooks.ibm.com/pubs/pdfs/redbooks/sg246889.pdf.

IBM Redbook. *XML Powered by Domino—How to Use XML with Lotus Domino*. Available in printed form, PDF format, and HTML format from 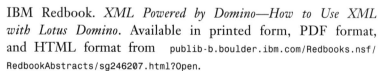 publib-b.boulder.ibm.com/Redbooks.nsf/RedbookAbstracts/sg246207.html?Open.

IBM International Technical Support Organization. *Domino Designer 6: A Developer's Handbook*. Available in printed form, PDF format, and HTML format from `http://publib-b.boulder.ibm.com/Redbooks.nsf/RedbookAbstracts/sg246854.html?Open`.

IBM International Technical Support Organization. *New Features of Lotus Domino 6.0.1: Single Copy Template*. Available in printed form, PDF format, and HTML format from `http://publib-b.boulder.ibm.com/Redbooks.nsf/RedbookAbstracts/redp3681.html?Open`.

IBM Lotus. *Release Notes*. `http://www-10.lotus.com/ldd/notesua.nsf/RN?OpenView`.

IBM Lotus. *Release Notes and Product Documentation*. Available from the Design client, Help menu, Lotus Internet Resources, Domino & Notes Doc Library or from the Web site. `http://www-10.lotus.com/ldd/notesua.nsf`.

LDD Today. Design articles are available in PDF format from `http://www.lotus.com/ldd`.

IBM Lotus White Paper. "A Guide to Developing a Secure Domino Application." Available in PDF format from `http://www-10.lotus.com/ldd/notesua.nsf/White%20Papers?OpenView`.

A series of *LDD Today* articles written by John Chamberlain. Available in PDF format from `http://www.lotus.com/ldd`.

IBM Lotus. *Online Help Databases*: `help6_admin.nsf`, `help6_client.nsf`, `help6_designer.nsf`.

IBM Certification Site. `http://www.lotus.com/services/education.nsf/wdocs/certificationhomepage`.

What's on the CD-ROM

This appendix is a brief rundown of what you'll find on the CD-ROM that comes with this book. For a more detailed description of the PrepLogic Practice Tests, Preview Edition exam simulation software, see Appendix C, "Using the PrepLogic Practice Tests, Preview Edition, Software." In addition to the PrepLogic Practice Exams, Preview Edition, software, the CD-ROM includes an electronic version of the book, in Portable Document Format (PDF), and the source code used in the book.

PrepLogic Practice Tests, Preview Edition, Software

PrepLogic is a leading provider of certification training tools. Trusted by certification students worldwide, PrepLogic is, we believe, the best practice exam software available. In addition to providing a means of evaluating your knowledge of the Training Guide material, PrepLogic Practice Tests, Preview Edition features several innovations that help you to improve your mastery of the subject matter.

For example, the practice tests allow you to check your score by exam area or domain to determine which topics you need to study more. Another feature allows you to obtain immediate feedback on your responses in the form of explanations for the correct and incorrect answers.

PrepLogic Practice Tests, Preview Edition exhibits most of the full functionality of the Premium Edition but offers only a fraction of the total questions. To get the complete set of practice questions and exam functionality, visit www.PrepLogic.com and order the Premium Edition for this and other challenging exam titles.

Again for a more detailed description of the PrepLogic Practice Tests, Preview Edition features, see Appendix C.

Using the PrepLogic Practice Tests, Preview Edition Software

This Training Guide includes a special version of PrepLogic Practice Tests—a revolutionary test engine designed to give you the best in certification exam preparation. PrepLogic offers sample and practice exams for many of today's most in-demand and challenging technical certifications. This special Preview Edition is included with this book as a tool to use in assessing your knowledge of the Training Guide material, while also providing you with the experience of taking an electronic exam.

This appendix describes in detail what PrepLogic Practice Tests, Preview Edition is, how it works, and what it can do to help you prepare for the exam. Note that although the Preview Edition includes all the test simulation functions of the complete, retail version, it contains only a single practice test. The Premium Edition, available at www.PrepLogic.com, contains the complete set of challenging practice exams designed to optimize your learning experience.

Exam Simulation

One of the main functions of PrepLogic Practice Tests, Preview Edition is exam simulation. To prepare you to take the actual vendor certification exam, PrepLogic is designed to offer the most effective exam simulation available.

Question Quality

The questions provided in the PrepLogic Practice Tests, Preview Edition are written to highest standards of technical accuracy. The questions tap the content of the Training Guide chapters and help you review and assess your knowledge before you take the actual exam.

Interface Design

The PrepLogic Practice Tests, Preview Edition exam simulation interface provides you with the experience of taking an electronic exam. This enables you to effectively prepare for taking the actual exam by making the test experience a familiar one. Using this test simulation can help eliminate the sense of surprise or anxiety you might experience in the testing center because you will already be acquainted with computerized testing.

Effective Learning Environment

The PrepLogic Practice Tests, Preview Edition interface provides a learning environment that not only tests you through the computer, but also teaches the material you need to know to pass the certification exam. Each question comes with a detailed explanation of the correct answer and often provides reasons the other options are incorrect. This information helps to reinforce the knowledge you already have and also provides practical information you can use on the job.

Software Requirements

PrepLogic Practice Tests requires a computer with the following:

➤ Microsoft Windows 98, Windows Me, Windows NT 4.0, Windows 2000, or Windows XP

➤ A 166MHz or faster processor is recommended

➤ A minimum of 32MB of RAM

➤ As with any Windows application, the more memory, the better your performance

➤ 10MB of hard drive space

Installing PrepLogic Practice Tests, Preview Edition

Install PrepLogic Practice Tests, Preview Edition by running the setup program on the PrepLogic Practice Tests, Preview Edition CD. Follow these instructions to install the software on your computer:

1. Insert the CD into your CD-ROM drive. The Autorun feature of Windows should launch the software. If you have Autorun disabled, click Start and select Run. Go to the CD's root directory and select setup.exe. Click Open, then click OK.

2. The Installation Wizard copies the PrepLogic Practice Tests, Preview Edition files to your hard drive; adds PrepLogic Practice Tests, Preview Edition to your Desktop and Program menu; and installs test engine components to the appropriate system folders.

Removing PrepLogic Practice Tests, Preview Edition from Your Computer

If you elect to remove the PrepLogic Practice Tests, Preview Edition product from your computer, an uninstall process has been included to ensure that it is removed from your system safely and completely. Follow these instructions to remove PrepLogic Practice Tests, Preview Edition from your computer:

1. Select Start, Settings, Control Panel.

2. Double-click the Add/Remove Programs icon.

3. You are presented with a list of software installed on your computer. Select the appropriate PrepLogic Practice Tests, Preview Edition title you want to remove. Click the Add/Remove button. The software is then removed from your computer.

Using PrepLogic Practice Tests, Preview Edition

PrepLogic is designed to be user friendly and intuitive. Because the software has a smooth learning curve, your time is maximized because you start practicing almost immediately. PrepLogic Practice Tests, Preview Edition has two major modes of study: Practice Test and Flash Review.

Using Practice Test mode, you can develop your test-taking abilities as well as your knowledge through the use of the Show Answer option. While you are taking the test, you can expose the answers along with a detailed explanation of why the given answers are right or wrong. This enables you to better understand the material presented.

Flash Review is designed to reinforce exam topics rather than quiz you. In this mode, you are shown a series of questions but no answer choices. Instead, you are given a button that reveals the correct answer to the question and a full explanation for that answer.

Starting a Practice Test Mode Session

Practice Test mode enables you to control the exam experience in ways that actual certification exams do not allow:

➤ *Enable Show Answer button*—Activates the Show Answer button, allowing you to view the correct answer(s) and full explanation(s) for each question during the exam. When not enabled, you must wait until after your exam has been graded to view the correct answer(s) and explanation.

➤ *Enable Item Review button*—Activates the Item Review button, allowing you to view your answer choices and marked questions, and to facilitate navigation between questions.

➤ *Randomize Choices button*—Randomize answer choices from one exam session to the next. Makes memorizing question choices more difficult, therefore keeping questions fresh and challenging longer.

To begin studying in Practice Test mode, click the Practice Test radio button from the main exam customization screen. This enables the options detailed in the preceding list.

To your left, you are presented with the option of selecting the preconfigured Practice Test or creating your own Custom Test. The preconfigured test has a fixed time limit and number of questions. Custom Tests allow you to configure the time limit and the number of questions in your exam.

The Preview Edition included with this book includes a single preconfigured Practice Test. Get the compete set of challenging PrepLogic Practice Tests at PrepLogic.com and make certain you're ready for the big exam.

Click the Begin Exam button to begin your exam.

Starting a Flash Review Mode Session

Flash Review mode provides you with an easy way to reinforce topics covered in the practice questions. To begin studying in Flash Review mode, click the Flash Review radio button from the main exam customization screen. Select either the preconfigured Practice Test or create your own Custom Test.

Click the Best Exam button to begin your Flash Review of the exam questions.

Standard PrepLogic Practice Tests, Preview Edition Options

The following list describes the function of each of the buttons you see. Depending on the options, some of the buttons are greyed out and inaccessible or missing completely. Buttons that are appropriate are active. The buttons are as follows:

➤ *Exhibit*—This button is visible if an exhibit is provided to support the question. An exhibit is an image that provides supplemental information necessary to answer the question.

➤ *Item Review*—This button takes you out of the question window and opens the Item Review screen. From this screen you can see all questions, your answers, and your marked items. You also see correct answers listed here when appropriate.

➤ *Show Answer*—This option displays the correct answer with an explanation of why it is correct. If you select this option, the current question is not scored.

➤ *Mark Item*—Check this box to tag a question you need to review further. You can view and navigate your Marked Items by clicking the Item Review button (if enabled). When grading your exam, you are notified if you have marked items remaining.

➤ *Previous Item*—Click this button to view the previous question.

➤ *Next Item*—Click this button to view the next question.

➤ *Grade Exam*—When you have completed your exam, click to end your exam and view your detailed score report. If you have unanswered or marked items remaining, you are asked whether you would like to continue taking your exam or view your exam report.

Time Remaining

If the test is timed, the time remaining is displayed on the upper-right corner of the application screen. It counts down minutes and seconds remaining to complete the test. If you run out of time, you are asked whether you want to continue taking the test or end your exam.

Your Examination Score Report

The Examination Score Report screen appears when the Practice Test mode ends—as the result of time expiration, completion of all questions, or your decision to terminate early.

This screen provides you with a graphical display of your test score with a breakdown of scores by topic domain. The graphical display at the top of the screen compares your overall score with the PrepLogic Exam Competency Score.

The PrepLogic Exam Competency Score reflects the level of subject competency required to pass this vendor's exam. Although this score does not directly translate to a passing score, consistently matching or exceeding this score does suggest you possess the knowledge to pass the actual vendor exam.

Review Your Exam

From the Your Score Report screen, you can review the exam that you just completed by clicking on the View Items button. Navigate through the items, viewing the questions, your answers, the correct answers, and the explanations for those questions. You can return to your score report by clicking the View Items button.

Get More Exams

The PrepLogic Practice Tests, Preview Edition that accompanies your training guide contains a single PrepLogic Practice Test. Certification students worldwide trust PrepLogic Practice Tests to help them pass their IT certification exams the first time. Purchase the Premium Edition of PrepLogic Practice Tests and get the entire set of all new challenging Practice Tests for this exam. PrepLogic Practice Tests—Because You Want to Pass the First Time.

Contacting PrepLogic

If you would like to contact PrepLogic for any reason including information about our extensive line of certification practice tests, we invite you to do so. Please contact us online at www.preplogic.com.

Customer Service

If you have a damaged product and need a replacement or refund, please call the following phone number:

800-858-7674

Product Suggestions and Comments

We value your input! Please email your suggestions and comments to the following address:

feedback@preplogic.com

License Agreement

YOU MUST AGREE TO THE TERMS AND CONDITIONS OUT-LINED IN THE END USER LICENSE AGREEMENT ("EULA") PRESENTED TO YOU DURING THE INSTALLATION PROCESS. IF YOU DO NOT AGREE TO THESE TERMS, DO NOT INSTALL THE SOFTWARE.

Glossary

@Command

@Commands are a special type of @Function that provide a mechanism for developers to programmatically execute a Lotus Notes/Domino command.

@Function

An @Function is a native function that can perform a calculation or task and return a value.

$$Return

$$Return is a reserved field name that you can use to customize the generic Form Processed Confirmation message.

access-controlled section

An access-controlled section is a section that restricts the ability to edit fields within the section to named users.

action

An action is a programmable button that can be used to automate tasks.

Administration Server

The Administration Server is the server whose Admin process is used to update the ACL and to determine whether the Admin process should update Names fields in the database.

agent

An agent is a self-contained program that can perform tasks on one or more databases.

Anonymous access

Anonymous access does not validate, authenticate, or record database activity. In other words, you do not know who is accessing the system.

applets

An applet is a self-contained program considered to be client-side because applets are loaded and run in the browser.

Authors field

An Authors field is a special type of text field that interacts with the database ACL to restrict who can edit a document. Any user with Author access not named in an Authors field cannot edit the document.

Auto-complete

Auto-compete is a new Domino 6 Designer feature that uses type-ahead functionality to select and paste certain syntax elements directly into the Programmer's Pane as you are coding.

automation controller

As an automation controller, Lotus Notes/Domino can use LotusScript to access OLE objects.

automation server

As an automation server, Lotus Notes/Domino registers itself in your Registry as an automation server so that other applications can access both front-end and back-end Notes objects.

bookmark

Bookmarks are graphical links to help you quickly access and organize your databases.

CGI variables

Common Gateway Interface (CGI) is a standard interface used between external applications and HTTP servers. Domino uses CGI programs to parse data sent by the browser into CGI variables to collect data about the user

column

A column is an object in a view that provides the developer with a mechanism with which to display one of four possible values: the contents of an item stored in a document, a value computed by a formula, a total, or a category.

Consistent Access Control List

The Consistent Access Control List feature of a database enables you to ensure that all replica copies of a database, whether on a server or workstation, maintain the same ACL.

cookies

Cookies are a mechanism a Web site uses to store information on the client (user's hard drive) to be used in the future. This information could be a user's color preferences or information about where the user has been in your application.

data connection (Data Connection Resource)

Design elements that enable you to establish a data exchange between a Domino application and an external data source.

data type

The data type of a field specifies the type of data that can be stored in a field.

database Access Control List (ACL)

The database Access Control List (ACL) restricts access that specific users and servers have to an application. It is a highly integrated component of the Domino kernel architecture that describes seven levels of access (Manager, Designer, Editor, Author, Reader, Depositor, and No Access).

Database Properties

Database Properties include settings that affect how a database displays and functions.

date picker

The embedded date picker is a design element that works with calendar views. When placed in a page or form, it enables users to choose a date that is then displayed in a calendar view.

design locking

Design locking is a new and long-awaited Domino capability that allows you to lock a design element so that other designers cannot modify it while you are working on it. After you have completed your work on an element, you can unlock it so that other designers can access it.

Design Pane

The Design Pane is one of the panes of the Domino Designer IDE that maintains a list of databases that have recently been opened in the Designer as well as the design elements they contain.

Design Synopsis

The Design Synopsis feature of Domino allows you to generate very detailed reports about the design of a database, which can then be written to the screen or to a database.

Designer Reference Panel

The Designer Reference Panel is a pane in the Domino Designer IDE that provides reference information about the current programming context.

DHTML

Dynamic HTML (DHTML) combines HTML, JavaScript, CSS, and the browser's Document Object Model to present content dynamically.

document hierarchy

The parent-child relationship between documents is known as the document hierarchy.

document locking

Document locking enables users with Author access or higher to lock documents within a database. Locking a document gives exclusive rights to the person who has locked the document to modify it. Other users with the same rights cannot modify the document even if they are working on another replica on the same local area network. Therefore, document locking prevents editing of documents and replication conflicts.

design template

Design templates are databases that contain the structure for the databases (design elements such as pages, forms, and views) but do not contain documents.

Domino Designer

The Domino Designer is the Domino IDE.

DXL

Domino XML Language (DXL) was developed to represent Domino data. It contains the tags and attributes needed to describe Notes elements stored in an .nsf file.

editor

A design element that enables you to embed one or more forms into an existing form.

effective access

A user's effective access is the actual access he or she has been granted to the database.

electronic signature

Electronic signatures provide the capability to verify that particular messages and documents have been modified by particular individuals. Electronic signatures ensure that the ID of the user that created or modified the specified document is genuine and that the document and information contained within it have not been modified since the user saved and/or mailed the document.

embedded element

Embedded elements are design elements which can be inserted into the design of either forms or pages. Embedded elements include Outline, View, Navigator, Date Picker, Scheduler, Editor, Folder Pane, File Upload Control design elements.

encryption

Encryption is a type of digital lock used to protect data from unauthorized access.

Execution Control List

The ECL is responsible for two basic things. First, it determines whether the signer of code being executed is allowed to run the code from a particular workstation. Second, if the signer can run the code, the ECL defines the level of access that the code has to various workstation functions.

Extended ACL

An Extended Access Control List is an optional access control feature that can be used with a Domino Directory created from the PUBNAMES.NTF template.

field

Fields are used to enter, modify, and display data stored in items.

field encryption

Encryption is a means of protecting data from unauthorized access. Field encryption protects the information within a specific field and only users that have been given the key to decrypt the information can see the data stored in an encrypted field.

File Protection documents

File Protection documents are set to control access from the Web to non-Domino databases.

file upload control

A design element that creates a file upload control (INPUT type="file">) that allows a user to upload file attachments in Web applications.

folder

Folders are design elements that present a sorted and/or categorized list of documents that are either manually or programmatically added.

Folder pane

A design element that displays folder objects.

form

Forms provide the structure for creating and displaying documents.

Form Create List

Form Create Access Lists provide control over who can create documents with a form

form formula

A form formula is used within views or folders to determine which form is to be used to create or display documents opened from within the view or folder.

Form Read Access List

Form Read Access Lists provide control over how individuals can use forms to read the contents of documents.

formula

A formula, according to Lotus, is "an expression that has program-like attributes."

frameset

A frameset is a design element that enables you to add structure to your applications (whether Notes or Web) by dividing the main window into subwindows.

full-text index

Creating a full-text index of a database will speed searches performed within a database and, optionally, allow for searching attachments and encrypted fields.

Global Web Site settings

Global Web Setting documents enable you to apply Web Site Rules documents to all the servers within a domain or a specific server. These documents differ from Internet Site documents in that you can apply only Web Site Rules globally. The Web Site rules apply to all the Web sites hosted by the servers specified in the Global Web Setting document.

group

A group is a list of users, servers, and other groups that have something in common.

group scheduling control

A design element that displays schedules of multiple people at the same time.

horizontal rules

Horizontal rules are design elements that add a graphic line to forms or pages to separate parts of the document.

hot spot

Hot spots provide a simple mechanism for users to initiate an action when clicked.

HTML

Hypertext Markup Language is markup code used to describe how to display data on a Web browser. The markup code is also known as tags.

HTML events

HTML events passes information to HTML tags. There are two HTML tags available to Forms and Pages; HTML Head Content passes information to the `<Head>` tag, and HTML Body Attributes passes information to the `<Body>` tag.

HTML properties

Layers, Cascading Style Sheets, Applets, Pictures, Hotspots, and Field properties have an `<html>` tab (tables have an `<@>`) which allows the addition of HTML attributes. These attributes are applied to the HTML that Domino generates at runtime.

image resource

An image resource is a shared graphic file that can be displayed throughout an application from a central location within the database. The image resource can be stored in its native image type (JPEG, GIF, or BMP).

Incoming URL Pattern

Each Web Site Rule document has a field called Incoming URL Pattern. URL Pattern is a format or mask that is used to describe the URLs that will be affected by this rule.

inheritance

Inheritance is the process of distributing design changes (automatically or manually) to one or more databases set up to inherit some or all design elements from the template database.

integrated development environment

The Domino Designer is an integrated development environment (IDE) enabling Notes developers and Web designers to create, manage, and deploy secure interactive Notes client/server and Web applications.

Internet access

Internet Access controls Web users' rights to use information on your server through Server documents, Internet Site documents, and their associated Web Site Rule documents.

Java

Java is an object-orientated programming language created to use on the Internet. Java is the language used to create applets.

JavaScript

JavaScript is a script language that is a set of instructions executed on the Web.

keyword field

Keyword fields are computed or editable (which are more common) fields that present the user with a list of choices. The list can be pre-determined by the application designer, generated by formula, or entered manually by the application's users.

layer

Layers are a new tool introduced in Domino 6, enabling you to position blocks of content over each other on a form, subform, or page.

libraries

Libraries are places for maintaining and sharing programs within multiple design elements. Script libraries contain LotusScript, Java, and JavaScript libraries. All script libraries' scopes are within the current database.

link

Links provide a simple but powerful way to quickly and easily open a Web site or Notes object such as a database, view, or document.

LotusScript

LotusScript is Domino's proprietary, object-orientated programming language.

LZ1 compression

The new enhanced compression method available with Domino 6 that increases performance for downloading, uploading, or opening attachments.

mail-in database

A mail-in database enables users to send mail to a database, in much the same manner as they would send mail to another user.

Master Lock Administration Server

The Domino server designated as the administration server that is required for design locking. A Master Lock Administration Server must be specified in the Advanced panel of the database Access Control dialog.

Maximum Internet Access

Maximum Internet name and password access setting is used to limit Web users' access. The Maximum Internet name and password field does not increase a user's access set in the ACL; it only restricts it.

navigator

Navigators enable you to build a graphical image of folders, views, and other design elements so that users can easily find information.

non-summary data

Non-summary data is a type of Notes item (typically rich-text data) that is very long text, binary data, images, and so on, and cannot appear in views and folders.

NoteID

The NoteID of a document is an 8-character combination of hexadecimal values (0–9, A–F) that uniquely identifies the document within a given database.

Notes authentication

Notes authentication uses what is called Validation and Authentication, which is actually two security procedures that interact with the user's Notes ID. Validation checks the certificate(s) located in the user's Notes ID file, using the public key stored in that ID file. If the certificate(s) is valid, then the public key is trusted and authentication begins. Authentication verifies identities by using what is called a challenge/response procedure.

Object Linking and Embedding (OLE)

Object Linking and Embedding (OLE) enables you to extend and enhance the capabilities and functionality of your applications by integrating data from other applications, such as spreadsheets, databases, and other data sources.

On Disk Structure

The On Disk Structure (ODS) is the actual physical file format of a Notes database.

outline

A design element that displays a skeleton of an application containing outline entries representing individual elements within the application.

page

Pages are similar to Notes forms, with one key difference: They can only display information.

profile document

A profile document is a special type of document that is similar in most ways to standard documents, but there are a few key differences. First, profile documents do not display in views, nor are they included in a document count of a database. Additionally, they are cached in memory while the database that contains them is open, meaning that they can be accessed very quickly, making them handy for temporary storage.

Programmer's Pane

The Programmer's Pane is the pane in the Domino Designer where programming logic is coded for Domino elements.

Public Access

Public Access grants users with Depositor or No Access accesses, read or write permissions to design elements that are set to allow public access.

Readers Field

A Readers field is a special type of text field that interacts with the database ACL to restrict who can read a document.

reserved word field

Reserved word fields are intended to provide an easy mechanism for incorporating some of the more common features of Domino.

Using these reserved field names enables developers to easily add functionality rather than program it from scratch. Developers need only use the reserved word names and appropriate values to create fields, and Domino automatically enables the respective functionalities.

role

Roles contain a subset of the database users, groups, or servers to provide or restrict access to particular database design elements, functions, or document contents.

routing

Routing is the start, intermediate, and end points of the workflow process.

rule

Rules are conditions that affect the workflow object. Rules help determine various formulas that apply to workflow and security issues within an application.

section

Sections provide a collapsible area within forms and subforms.

Server Access List

The Server Access List determines who can access a Domino server.

Server documents

Domino Server documents are used to maintain and manage the Domino Server and Domino Web Server.

server task

Server tasks are pre-defined programs that are available when the server software is installed and only run when the specific server task is loaded. HTTP is a Domino server task.

shared action

A shared action is a programmable button that can be used to automate tasks and can be shared across multiple design elements.

shared code

Shared code enables you to create agents, outlines, subforms, fields, actions, and script libraries in one location to be used throughout an application.

shared field

A shared field is a field the can be defined once and shared across multiple design elements.

shared resource

Shared resources enable you to create certain types of design elements that can be reused throughout an application and maintained in a single location.

signing

Signing a document causes Domino to combine the user's private key and the value of the signed field to create a unique electronic signature.

soft delete

Soft deletions allow for deleted documents to be held in the database for the specified amount of time before they are permanently deleted.

SSL

Secure Sockets Layer is used to encrypt Internet transmissions and create a trusted relationship between servers and Web clients. SSL provides privacy through encryption and authentication between the server and the client. SSL also detects tampering.

style sheet

Cascading Style Sheets provide the capability to control page layout, headers, links, text, fonts, styles, color, margins, and so on.

subform

A subform is a design element that can contain the same elements as regular forms and can be included in a form so that you can make your applications more modular.

summary data

Summary data is a type of Notes Item that can appear in views and folders.

Universal ID

The Universal ID of a document is a 32-character combination of hexadecimal values (0–9, A–F) that uniquely identifies a document across all replicas of a database.

URL

The locations of resources and files on the Internet are identified individually by a Uniform Resource Locator (URL); you use a URL to address a resource or file you want to access across the Internet.

Validation

Validation is the checking of data users have entered against specific criteria designers have set.

view

Views are design elements that present a sorted and/or categorized list of documents and serve as the primary way to access data in a Notes database.

View Access List

A View Access List determines who can use a view to read documents.

view icon

View icons are small images that can be displayed in the column of a view.

view logging

View logging is a new feature made available with Domino/Lotus 6 that tracks all view updates and changes in the transaction log. All logged transactions are written to disk sequentially to be committed to the database at a later time. The transaction logs can be used for backups and backup recoveries (such as if the system crashes or a hard drive fails). Another advantage to using view logging is that many view rebuilds can be avoided.

View template

View templates make it possible to standardize the format and layout of views when they are rendered on the Web.

Web authentication

Web users do not use a Notes ID to access Domino; instead, they use a different security method called Basic Authentication. This is a simple procedure that authenticates a user's login name and password against the name and Internet Password stored in the user's Person document in the directory.

Web Site Rule

Web Site Rule documents help administrators maintain their Web sites by providing a consistent navigation scheme and allowing relocation or reorganization without losing existing links.

WebDav (Web Distributed Authoring and Versioning)

WebDav (Web Distributed Authoring and Versioning) is a standard incorporated into Domino Designer 6 that enables developers to integrate third-party tools into the developer IDE. In addition, when working within Domino Designer, developers can launch alternate applications (for example, an image editor, and XML parser, and so on).

window title

A window's title is the text in the title bar of a window.

Work Pane

The Work Pane is a pane of the Domino Designer that displays a list of particular design elements of a given type such as forms, views, or agents, within the selected database.

XML

eXtensible Markup Language uses markup tags to define or describe data, not display data (which is what HTML is for). XML is an industry standard that allows data to be exchanged between systems, whether the data is exchanged over the Internet or within an intranet. XML allows designers to define their document structure and create their own tags.

Index

X-Y-Z